Democracy in the Arab World
Explaining the deficit

Despite notable socio-economic development in the Arab region, a deficit in democracy and political rights has continued to prevail. This book examines the major reasons underlying the persistence of this democracy deficit over the past decades and touches on the prospect for deepening the process of democratization in the Arab world.

Contributions from major scholars of the region give a cross-country analysis of economic development, political institutions and social factors, and the impact of oil wealth and regional wars, and present a model for democracy in the Arab world. Case studies are drawn from Algeria, Egypt, Iraq, Jordan, Lebanon, Syria, Sudan and the Gulf region; they build on these cross-country analyses and look beyond the influence of oil and conflicts as the major reason behind this democracy deficit. The chapters illustrate how specific socio-political history of the country concerned, fear of fundamentalist groups, collusion with foreign powers and foreign interventions, and the co-option of the elites by the state also contribute to these problems of democratization facing the region.

Situating the democratic position of the Arab world in a global context, this book is an important contribution to the field of Middle Eastern politics, development studies and studies on conflict and democracy.

Ibrahim Elbadawi, formerly Lead Economist at the Development Research Group of the World Bank, he is currently Director of the Macroeconomics Research and Forecasting Department at the Dubai Economic Council and has published widely on macroeconomic and development policy and the economics of civil war. His regional specialization covers Africa and the Middle East, where he is widely networked with academic research and policy forums in the two regions. He is also a visiting research fellow with the Center for Global Development and an Associate Editor of the *Middle East Development Journal*.

Samir Makdisi is Professor Emeritus of Economics, Founder of the Institute of Financial Economics, and Distinguished Senior Fellow, Issam Fares Institute for Public Policy and International Affairs at the American University of Beirut. He has served as Deputy President of AUB; as chair of the Board of Trustees at the Economic Research Forum for the Arab Countries, Iran and Turkey; on the Board of the Global Development Network; and as Minister of Economy and Trade for the Republic of Lebanon. He has published widely on macroeconomic, financial and developmental issues in the Arab World.

Routledge Studies in Middle Eastern Politics

1. Algeria in Transition
Reforms and development prospects
Ahmed Aghrout with Redha M. Bougherira

2. Palestinian Refugee Repatriation
Global perspectives
Edited by Michael Dumper

3. The International Politics of the Persian Gulf
A cultural genealogy
Arshin Adib-Moghaddam

4. Israeli Politics and the First Palestinian Intifada
Political opportunities, framing processes and contentious politics
Eitan Y. Alimi

5. Democratization in Morocco
The political elite and struggles for power in the post-independence state
Lise Storm

6. Secular and Islamic Politics in Turkey
The making of the justice and development party
Ümit Cizre

7. The United States and Iran
Sanctions, wars and the policy of dual containment
Sasan Fayazmanesh

8. Civil Society in Algeria
The political functions of associational life
Andrea Liverani

9. Jordanian–Israeli Relations
The peacebuilding experience
Mutayyam al O'ran

10. Kemalism in Turkish Politics
The Republican People's Party, secularism and nationalism
Sinan Ciddi

11. Islamism, Democracy and Liberalism in Turkey
The case of the AKP
William Hale and Ergun Özbudun

12. Politics and Violence in Israel/Palestine
Democracy versus military rule
Lev Luis Grinberg

13. Intra-Jewish Conflict in Israel
White Jews, black Jews
Sami Shalom Chetrit

14. Holy Places in the Israeli–Palestinian Conflict
Confrontation and co-existence
Edited by Marshall J. Breger, Yitzhak Reiter and Leonard Hammer

15. Plurality and Citizenship in Israel
Moving beyond the Jewish/Palestinian civil divide
Edited by Dan Avnon and Yotam Benziman

16. Ethnic Politics in Israel
The margins and the Ashkenasi Center
As'ad Ghanem

17. Islamists and Secularists in Egypt
Opposition, conflict and cooperation
Dina Shehata

18. Political Succession in the Arab World
Constitutions, family loyalties and Islam
Anthony Billingsley

19. Turkey's Entente with Israel and Azerbaijan
State identity and security in the Middle East and Caucasus
Alexander Murinson

20. Europe and Tunisia
Democratization via association
Brieg Powel and Larbi Sadiki

21. Turkish Politics and the Rise of the AKP
Dilemmas of institutionalization and leadership strategy
Arda Can Kumbaracibasi

22. Civil Society and Democratization in the Arab World
The dynamics of activism
Francesco Cavatorta and Vincent Durac

23. Politics in Morocco
Executive monarchy and enlightened authoritarianism
Anouar Boukhars

24. The Second Palestinian Intifada
Civil resistance
Julie M. Norman

25. Democracy in Turkey
The impact of EU political conditionality
Ali Resul Usul

26. Nationalism and Politics in Turkey
Political Islam, Kemalism and the Turkish issue
Edited by Marlies Casier and Joost Jongerden

27. Democracy in the Arab World
Explaining the deficit
Edited by Samir Makdisi and Ibrahim Elbadawi

"*Democracy in the Arab World* is a welcome contribution to the literature examining the democracy deficit in the region. Unlike other studies that deal with democratization, the book zeroes in on the major drivers behind the democracy deficit in various Arab countries and offers a complex set of analytical explanations. Eschewing simplistic dichotomies and culturalist dogma, *Democracy in the Arab World* diagnoses the critical role of conflicts and oil, but also reveals the influence of political leadership, foreign interventions and the cooption of elites, in inhibiting the democratic process in the region despite its notable socio-economic development. Another major strength of the book is that it bridges the gap between theory and history. An impressive list of researchers and scholars of the region!"

Fawaz A. Gerges, *London School of Economics*

Democracy in the Arab World

Explaining the deficit

Edited by Ibrahim Elbadawi
and Samir Makdisi

LONDON AND NEW YORK

International Development Research Centre
Ottawa • Cairo • Dakar • Montevideo • Nairobi • New Delhi • Singapore

First published 2011
by Routledge
2 Park Square, Milton Park, Abingdon, Oxon OX14 4RN

Simultaneously published in the USA and Canada
by Routledge
270 Madison Avenue, New York, NY 10016

A copublication of the
   International Development Research Centre
   PO Box 8500, Ottawa, ON K1G 3H9, Canada
   www.idrc.ca / info@idrc.ca
   ISBN 978–1–55250–491–8 (ebook)

Routledge is an imprint of the Taylor & Francis Group, an informa business

© 2011 editorial selection and matter, Samir Makdisi and Ibrahim Elbadawi; individual chapters, the contributors

Typeset in Baskerville by
Book Now Ltd, London
Printed and bound in Great Britain by
CPI Antony Rowe, Chippenham, Wiltshire

All rights reserved. No part of this book may be reprinted or reproduced or utilised in any form or by any electronic, mechanical, or other means, now known or hereafter invented, including photocopying and recording, or in any information storage or retrieval system, without permission in writing from the publishers.

British Library Cataloguing in Publication Data
A catalogue record for this book is available from the British Library

Library of Congress Cataloging in Publication Data
Democracy in the Arab world: explaining the deficit/edited by Samir Makdisi and Ibrahim Elbadawi.
   p. cm.—(Routledge studies in Middle Eastern politics; 27)
Includes bibliographical references and index.
1. Despotism—Arab Countries. 2. Arab Countries—Politics and government. 3. Political culture—Arab Countries. I. Makdisi, Samir A., II. Elbadawi, Ibrahim.

JQ1850.A58D46 2010
320.17'4927—dc22   2010004661

ISBN 978–0–415–77999–9 (hbk)
ISBN 978–0–203–85286–6 (ebk)

This book is dedicated to all Arab intellectuals who have striven towards a restoration of national dignity and revival of the Arab World that goes beyond material achievements, in the hope that their aspirations for democracy, freedom and justice will eventually be accomplished.

Contents

List of figures	xi
List of tables	xiii
List of contributors	xv
Acknowledgements	xix

Introduction IBRAHIM ELBADAWI AND SAMIR MAKDISI	1

PART I
Democracy and development: conceptual and cross-country perspectives — 9

1 **Political culture and the crisis of democracy in the Arab world** ABDELWAHAB EL-AFFENDI	11
2 **Explaining the Arab democracy deficit: the role of oil and conflicts** IBRAHIM ELBADAWI, SAMIR MAKDISI AND GARY MILANTE	41

PART II
Case studies: oil, conflict and beyond — 83

Mashreq countries

3 **Jordan: propellers of autocracy – the Arab–Israeli conflict and foreign power interventions** TAHER KANAAN AND JOSEPH MASSAD	86
4 **Lebanon: the constrained democracy and its national impact** SAMIR MAKDISI, FADIA KIWAN AND MARCUS MARKTANNER	115

5 **Syria: the underpinnings of autocracy – conflict, oil and the curtailment of economic freedom** 142
RAED SAFADI, LAURA MUNRO AND RADWAN ZIADEH

Oil-dependent countries

6 **The Gulf region: beyond oil and wars – the role of history and geopolitics in explaining autocracy** 166
SAMI ATALLAH

7 **Algeria: democracy and development under the aegis of the 'authoritarian bargain'** 196
BELKACEM LAABAS AND AMMAR BOUHOUCHE

8 **Iraq: understanding autocracy – oil and conflict in a historical and socio-political context** 227
BASSAM YOUSIF AND ERIC DAVIS

Nile Valley countries

9 **Egypt: development, liberalization and the persistence of autocracy** 256
GOUDA ABDEL-KHALEK AND MUSTAPHA K. AL SAYYID

10 **Sudan: colonial heritage, social polarization and the democracy deficit** 282
ALI ABDEL GADIR ALI AND ATTA EL-BATTAHANI

PART III
Summing up 311

11 **The democracy deficit in the Arab world: an interpretive synthesis** 313
IBRAHIM ELBADAWI AND SAMIR MAKDISI

Index 328

Figures

2.1	Average polity score by region/type, 1960 to 2003	43
2.2	Average and median polity for the world and the Arab world, 1960 to 2003	44
2.3	Country years of freedom, 1972 to 2002	46
2.4	Mean change in polity: Arab and non-Arab world	49
2.5	Limited democratic progress in the best Arab reformers, 1974 to 2004	50
2.6	Average growth profile in 10 years following democratization	72
2.7	Average and median annual growth rates for Arab and East Asian countries	76
3.1	Actual polity scores, from yearly data	88
3.2	Jordan: actual and predicted polity scores in five-year averages, in the EMM Model	89
3.3	GDP annual real growth, 1977–2007	101
3.4	GDP per capita at 1994 factor cost, 1976–2007	102
3.5	GDP, population, and student enrolment trends, 1976–2007	102
4.1	Major determinants of Lebanon's polity	123
4.2	Determinants of national polity	127
4.3	Determinants of regional polity	128
5.1	Ease of doing business in Syria – global rank	146
5.2	Democratization in Syria, or lack thereof	154
5.3	Polity residual and index of economic freedom	156
5.4	Observed and estimated polity in Syria	157
6.1	Polity score for Gulf and Arab non-Gulf countries, 1960–2003	170
6.2	Polity scores for the Gulf countries, 1960–2003	175
6.3	The Gulf states	180
7.1	Democracy and development in Algeria, 1962–2006	197
8.1	Actual and predicted levels of democratization in Iraq	234
9.1	Democratization in Egypt	260
9.2	Annex: polity score for Egypt, 1960–2003	276
9.3	Annex: alternative measures of democracy for Egypt, 1960–2003	277
9.4	Annex: GDP per capita, 1960–2003	277

Tables

2.1	Two regime classifications, 1960 to 2003	47
2.2	Correlation of an education index and measures of education	53
2.3	Descriptive statistics	56
2.4	Explaining the Arab democracy deficit (dependent variable: polity)	58
2.5	Robustness checks with interaction effects	63
2.6	Alternative specifications for Arab war (dependent variable: polity)	64
2.7	The effect of the Cold War and international intervention	66
2.8	Alternative measures of democratization	67
2.9	Comparison of mean growth rates by democratization attempt	70
2.10	Comparison of variance in growth rates for three types of country	71
2.11	Impact of growth on the success rate of democratization	73
2.12	Impact of democratization on growth	74
2.13	Predicted probability of successful democratization per annum	75
3.1	Jordan polity scores, 1951–2003	88
4.1	Data and sources	125
4.2	Summary regression results, dependent variable: polity	128
4.3	Summary regression results, dependent variable: regional polity	129
5.1	Syria, selected economic indicators, 1997–2006	144
5.2	Annex: parameter estimates using EM parsimonious model	162
6.1	Dependent variable polity scores 1960–2003, with robust standard error	171
6.2	Dependent variable polity score 1960–2003: robust standard error in a parsimonious model with alternative war measure	173
6.3	Dependent variable polity score 1960–2003, with robust standard error for Kuwait	176
6.4	Dependent variable polity score 1960–2003: robust standard error in a parsimonious model with alternative war measures for Kuwait	178
7.1	Gastil Index, 2006	207
7.2	Institutions and polity, Algeria 1988–2007	208

7.3	Polity simulation, EMM Model	213
7.4	Causality test between polity and modernity variables	215
7.5	Estimation results of the modernity model, 1962–2004	217
8.1	Per capita GDP, oil output and value added in the oil sector	230
8.2	Indicators of income inequality	232
8.3	Select human development indicators	233
8.4	Results of the application to Iraq of the Humana Index	236
8.5	Score for questions omitted for lack of information	237
8.6	Proposed modifications to the Humana Index	239
8.7	Results of the modifications made to the Humana Index	239
9.1	Periods of economic and political liberalization	260
9.2	Econometric results	263
9.3	Annex: alternative democracy measures for Egypt	278
10.1	Polity score, modernization and other variables for Sudan: averages 1960–2003	286
10.2	Democracy deficit in Sudan	287
10.3	Regional basis of political parties in 1953: parliamentary seats from geographic constituencies	296
10.4	Social groups of the members of the first elected parliament	297
10.5	Economic growth under political regimes in Sudan, 1960–1989	303
10.6	Structural transformation in Sudan, share of sectors	305

Contributors

Gouda Abdel-Khalek: Professor of Economics at Cairo University. Formerly, he was Visiting Professor at Johns Hopkins University, University of California at Los Angeles, and the University of Southern California. He is the author of *Stabilization and Adjustment in Egypt* (2001). He has a PhD from McMaster University.

Abdelwahab El-Affendi: Reader in Politics at the Centre for the Study of Democracy, University of Westminster, and Co-ordinator of the Centre's Democracy and Islam Programme. He is the author of *The Conquest of Muslim Hearts and Minds: Perspectives on U.S. Reform and Public Diplomacy Strategies* (2005). He holds a PhD from the University of Reading.

Ali Abdel Gadir Ali: Deputy Director General, Arab Planning Institute, Kuwait. Formerly Chief, Economic and Social Policy Analysis Division, UNECA. He has also taught at the Universities of Khartoum and Gezira, Sudan. He is the author of *The Challenges of Poverty Reduction in Post Conflict Sudan* (2006). His PhD is from the University of Essex.

Sami Atallah: Economist and currently a PhD candidate in politics at New York University. He has consulted for government ministries and international organizations in the Middle East, and holds graduate degrees in economics and quantitative methods from Yale and Columbia Universities.

Atta El-Battahani: Associate Professor of Political Science and Political Economy at Khartoum University, and Senior Adviser for the International Institute for Democracy and Electoral Assistance in Sudan. He is the author of *Nationalism and Peasant Politics in the Nuba Mountains Region of Sudan* (2009). He received his PhD from the University of Sussex.

Ammar Bouhouche: Professor of Political Science at the University of Algiers. Formerly, he was Chair of the Department of Public Administration at Al Albeyt University (Jordan). He is the author of *Modern Theories in Public Administration* (2006). He holds a PhD from the University of Missouri at Columbia.

Eric Davis: Professor of Political Science at Rutgers University and former Director of the University's Center for Middle Eastern Studies. He is the author of *Memories of State: Politics, History and Collective Identity in Modern Iraq* (2005). He has a PhD from the University of Chicago.

Ibrahim Elbadawi: Director, Macroeconomics Research Department, Dubai Economic Council. Previously he served as Lead Economist at the Development Research Group of the World Bank and Professor of Economics at the University of Gezira in Sudan. He is co-editor of *Can Africa Claim the 21st Century?* (2000). He received his PhD from North Carolina State and Northwestern Universities.

Taher Kanaan: CEO, Jordan Centre for Policy Research. He also serves as Board Member for the Institute of Palestine Studies, Economic Research Forum, and Arab Anti-Corruption Organization. Formerly he was Programs Director, Arab Fund for Economic and Social Development, and Deputy Prime Minister for Development (Jordan). He is the author of *Higher Education in Jordan, Access and Equity* (2009). He has a PhD from Cambridge University.

Fadia Kiwan: Professor of Political Science and Director of the Institute of Political Science at Saint Joseph University, Beirut, and member of the UNU Council. She has also taught at the Lebanese University. She is the editor of *Social Role of Working Women in a Comparative Perspective* (2008). She received her PhD from Université Paris I-Sorbonne.

Belkacem Laabas: Economic Expert at the Arab Planning Institute, Kuwait. Previously he was Senior Lecturer at the Institute of Economics, Algiers University. He is the editor of *Arab Development Challenges of the New Millennium* (2002). He has a PhD from the Bradford University.

Samir Makdisi: Professor Emeritus of Economics; Senior Fellow, Institute of Financial Economics; and Distinguished Senior Fellow, Issam Fares Institute for Public Policy and International Relations, at the American University of Beirut (AUB). He has served as Minister of National Economy (Lebanon) and as Deputy President of AUB. He is the author of *The Lessons of Lebanon: The Economics of War and Development* (2004). He has a PhD from Columbia University.

Marcus Marktanner: Assistant Professor of Economics and Fellow at the Institute of Financial Economics, the American University of Beirut. He holds a PhD from the Technical University of Ilmenau, Germany.

Joseph Massad: Associate Professor of Modern Arab Politics and Intellectual History at Columbia University. He is author of *Desiring Arabs* (2007). He received his PhD from Columbia University.

Gary Milante: Research Economist at the World Bank. He has a PhD from the University of California at Irvine.

Laura Munro: Formerly an Economic Researcher at the Organisation for Economic Co-operation and Development (OECD). She has been pursuing graduate work at Columbia University since September 2009.

Raed Safadi: Deputy Director of the Trade and Agriculture Department at the Organisation for Economic Co-operation and Development (OECD). Previously he worked at the World Bank, taught at the University of Antwerp, and served as Chief Economist at the Department of Economic Development, Government of Dubai. He is the Editor of *Globalization and Emerging Economies* (2008). He received a PhD from Georgetown University.

Mustapha K. Al Sayyid: Professor of Political Science at Cairo University. He has also taught at the American University in Cairo, as well as Harvard and Colgate Universities. He is Lead Expert for the *Arab Human Development Report, 2009*. He has a PhD from the University of Geneva.

Bassam Yousif: Assistant Professor of Economics at Indiana State University. Previously he taught at California State University, Fullerton. He is the author of a forthcoming book, *The Development History of Iraq*. He received his PhD from the University of California, Riverside.

Radwan Ziadeh: Founder and Director of the Damascus Center for Human Rights Studies. Since October 2008 he has been a visiting scholar at the Carr Center for Human Rights at Harvard University. He is the author of *Political Islam in Syria* (2008). He has an MA degree from Damascus University.

Acknowledgements

This book is the outcome of a collaborative research project on the determinants of the democracy deficit in the Arab world. Our deep gratitude goes to a number of institutions and individuals who have supported, advised and encouraged this project.

A generous grant from the International Development Research Centre (IDRC, Canada) made it possible to assemble a first-class research team to undertake the often arduous research work this project has entailed. Emma Naughton of IDRC has been greatly supportive of the research project from its inception and to her we extend our sincere appreciation.

The Institute of Financial Economics (IFE) at the American University Beirut (AUB) where the project was housed was an ideal place from which to direct the project. We owe special gratitude to the IFE, which provided excellent secretarial and research assistance in an intellectually congenial environment. We also would like to acknowledge the support of the AUB administration and in particular Khalil Bitar, the Dean of the Faculty of Arts and Sciences, who always stood ready to facilitate the administrative requirements of the project. Our thanks also go to the Office of Grants and Contracts, which provided very helpful administrative support. The Development Research Group of the World Bank has provided generous support, including the time of Ibrahim Elbadawi. In particular, we would like to thank Luis Serven, Manager of the Macroeconomic and Growth Division for his support, and Gary Milante for his substantive and technical contributions to the project.

We would like to express our great appreciation to several institutions that hosted meetings on the project's research work. AUB hosted a workshop pertaining to the preliminary findings of the research team as well as a dissemination conference to present the project's final results. The Economic Research Forum for the Arab Countries, Iran and Turkey (Cairo) organized a panel on the preliminary findings of the cross-country work; the Dubai School of Government hosted a workshop on the research methodologies of the various papers; and the Center for the Study of Democracy at the University of Westminster in London organized a session to present the findings of the project. Furthermore, both the IFE and the Center for Public Policy Research and Dialogue in Amman organized workshops on the Lebanon and Jordan case studies, respectively. All these meetings provided valuable feedback and insights that helped improve the ongoing research.

It was gratifying to work with our colleagues on the research team. Their unflinching collaboration and engagement in the research work for a period of over two years greatly facilitated our task as co-managers and editors. We hope that as a team our joint aspirations to fulfil the objectives of the research project have been realized. Our sincere thanks go to Kristine Stroad Moore for her capable technical editing of the manuscript.

Samir Makdisi would like to acknowledge his great debt to his wife Jean for her support and patience in putting up with the various demands that the work on the project entailed. Equally importantly, he benefited greatly from her penetrating intellect and, whenever called upon, her enriching of the written text. His three scholar sons, Saree, Ussama and Karim, often provided critical intellectual engagements that helped him focus more sharply on particular issues being addressed. He would also like to extend special thanks to Rima Shaar, secretary of the IFE, for first-rate secretarial support, and to acknowledge the research help of graduate research assistants at the IFE who have efficiently carried out the tasks assigned to them: Moon Baz, Sandra Chaoul, Hanan al Fakih and especially Layal Wehbeh who, for two years, assisted in the research project.

Ibrahim Elbadawi would like to acknowledge the support and patience of his wife Enayat and the stimulating discussions with his daughter Lina. He would also like to thank his assistant Tourya Tourougui for her superb secretarial support.

Introduction

Ibrahim Elbadawi and Samir Makdisi

When the Arab countries were still under colonial tutelage, the burning question for them was how and when to gain independence. Most of them in fact became independent only after the Second World War,[1] and democracy did not arise as a political issue except as a potential post-independence question. However, with the exception of Lebanon and early isolated cases of democratic engagement that did not last long, Arab political regimes since independence have generally been characterized by varying forms of authoritarian rule, despite notable growth in the levels of real per capita income and levels of education.

Intermittent attempts at political reform might over time have permitted limited political liberalization, but the essential nature of authoritarian rule has not changed materially. Indeed, throughout this period Arab intellectuals and groups advocating substantive political reform have condemned authoritarianism and the absence of democracy in the Arab world. Denial of full political rights of citizens and restrictions on civil liberties and, hence, lack of representative and accountable governments, are also blamed for the failure of Arab regimes to achieve sustainable and equitable economic and social development, or to address the major issues presently faced by the Arab world, including, among others, the Palestinian question.

The primary objective of this book is to address the following important questions: why has the Arab region generally experienced what has been termed a 'democracy deficit' (however democracy is defined, a matter we take up below), and what explains the general persistence of this deficit over the decades since independence? A secondary objective is to discern the growth and development consequences of autocracy.

To identify the factors that explain the continuation of the Arab democracy deficit, a two-tier research approach was adopted that combines both quantitative and qualitative analyses: cross-country work followed by intensive country case studies. The cross-country work is an extended modernity regression model of democracy (measured by the widely used Polity IV index) for a global sample covering most Arab countries. It is preceded by an analysis of the crisis of Arab democracy, which draws a political framework for the penchant of Arab autocratic regimes to hold on to their rule.

The model finds that after controlling for a host of economic, social and historical variables, as well as for religion, a negative and highly significant Arab region-specific effect remains, that we refer to as the Arab dummy. This finding suggests that, given the level of economic development of the Arab world, as well as other historical and social characteristics, even an extended theory of modernization (in the sense of the Lipset hypothesis of 1959) fails to explain the persistent nature of the Arab democracy/freedom deficit, and stands in contrast to the experience of countries in other regions of the world where economic development has been positively correlated with the democratization process. What we do find is that oil and, more importantly, regional conflicts (notably the Arab–Israeli conflict, but also other civil and international wars) seem to be the major factors that account for this negative Arab dummy.

The most striking result of the analysis of cross-country work is that once it is interacted with the conflict variable, the direct Arab dummy effect not only disappears, but its interaction effect is negative and highly significant, while the same effect is positive and significant for other developing regions. This finding does not carry over to other determinants of democracy (e.g. oil or female labour force participation), where interactions with the Arab and other dummies were neither significant nor do they influence the direct region-specific effect. These results remain robust against a variety of diagnostic tests.

The above findings suggest two important conclusions. First, unlike conflict, both oil and gender[2] – like other determinants of democracy – had an impact that does not vary across regions. Second, however, the Arab world *is* different with regard to the impact of conflicts on democracy; while conflicts have led, for whatever reasons, to a subsequent democratization process in other regions, in the Arab world they have not. Thus, drawing from the robust and persistent findings of the econometric analysis, the central premise of this work is that oil and conflicts are the two major overarching factors behind the persistence of the gaping democracy deficit in the Arab world. At the same time, it probes beyond the generality of cross-country work by focusing on selected Arab countries in an attempt to identify country-specific factors that could provide supplementary explanations for the survival of their autocracies.

Thus, with the cross-country model as a starting point, the following eight case studies, carried out by teams of economists and political scientists, were selected for in-depth analyses of the factors that account for their persistent, though varying, democracy deficits: Algeria, Egypt, Iraq, Jordan, Lebanon, Sudan, Syria and the Gulf region. Their choice was governed by one or a combination of the following three criteria: that they be: (1) major countries in the region and/or important oil producers, (2) countries involved in the Arab–Israeli conflict and/or have experienced civil wars, and (3) be highly polarized or fractionalized countries.

The case studies critically assess how oil and conflict have influenced, directly and/or indirectly, the evolution of democracy in the countries concerned. Equally importantly they analyse country-specific factors (historical, political, economic and institutional) that further explain the persistence of the democracy deficit – factors that are not necessarily captured by the global model, thereby shedding additional light on why autocracy has tended to survive in the Arab world. These idiosyncratic country-specific factors were found to be critical in shaping the dynamics of the influence of oil and conflict in blunting and pre-empting democracy in these countries and thus help explain the observed diversity across these countries in terms of the extent and stability of autocracy. What is noteworthy is that religion as such (Islam, of course, being the major religion of the Arab world) does not appear to play a significant role.

There have been a number of studies, both inside and outside the Arab world, on the characteristics of contemporary Arab societies and how they relate to the nature of prevailing undemocratic Arab regimes. Gender inequality (whose multifaceted aspects have been addressed by a vast and growing feminist literature), familial, patron–client or tribal relationships, and, in some cases, religion, have been put forward as explaining the intrinsically non-democratic nature of Arab societies. In this vein, culturalist approaches in particular, have been advanced as alternative explanations of the persisting Arab autocracy.[3]

However, as Chapter 1 argues, major scholarly work has put aside social preconditions or the region's cultural aversion for democracy as being responsible for the turbulent and undemocratic politics of the region. Culturalist approaches that make too many assumptions about the universal acceptance, uniform exposure and internalization of particular views are not supported by historical evidence. This conceptual analytical perspective strongly coheres with our own cross-country empirical work in Chapter 2. We find that while the ratio of female labour force participation is positively and significantly associated with democracy, unlike oil and conflict, it does not, however, explain the direct Arab dummy effect. Moreover, unlike conflicts, the gender effect is uniform across all regions, suggesting that the Arab world is not different from other regions with regard to the potential impact of the empowerment of women on democracy. Similar findings have also been found in the empirical literature, with an even more robust set of gender indicators. For example, based on their extensive empirical cross-country analysis, Donno and Russett (2004: 601) conclude that, 'Overall, it does not seem either that Islam or Arab countries are autocratic because they oppress women's rights or that Islamic or Arab countries oppress women simply because their governments are autocratic.'

Indeed, other societies in the developing world have similar social characteristics to those attributed to the Arab region, yet they still made the transition to democracy. Thus, whatever the explanation for this transition in some societies, and for its absence in the Arab world, the persistence of the Arab democracy deficit has remained a question that we felt needed to be critically addressed, and was at the heart of this research, while the causes and nature of the transition from autocracy to democracy lay outside its purview.[4]

In undertaking the task of explaining why the democratic process has failed to take root, we have been cognizant not only that notions and meaning of democracy have been explained in various ways, but that its empirical measurement suffers from certain limitations. There is perhaps broad agreement (as noted in Chapter 1) that the concept of democracy encompasses a political system in which members regard themselves as political equals, collectively sovereign and possessing all the capacities, resources and institutions they need to govern themselves. Democratic regimes become consolidated (i.e. no significant political group attempts to overthrow them) when, among other things, the state becomes authoritative, civil society is active and the political and economic institutions that guard democratic values are well established.

Whereas liberalism and democracy are distinct concepts, they have tended to converge. Contemporary democratic regimes are generally liberal ones, though in a few cases non-liberal fundamentalist or other parties have come to power via free elections. This phenomenon poses an interesting challenge to the prospects of the continued congruence between liberalism and democracy, mainly (but not solely) in developing countries, where fundamentalist movements are potentially strong and could assume the reins of power democratically. Whatever these prospects, fear of such movements is not an argument at all, though some writers have propagated it to promote the perpetuation of autocratic regimes. Instead, greater civic and political rights across the board should be promoted, and, in the Arab region, it is imperative that outstanding regional conflicts, primarily the Palestinian question, be justly resolved.

In our view the root causes for the growth of fundamentalism in the region may be traced to three interacting factors: the unwillingness of the Arab governing classes to democratize, fearing loss of domestic control and privileges; the persistently strong Western support of Israel's position not to recognize legitimate Palestinian rights; and Western support of Arab autocracies in the belief that this support would protect the West's oil and other regional interests. Meeting the challenges posed by these interlocking factors would, among other things, greatly help in promoting the cause of democracy in the Arab world.

It is particularly important to distinguish between formal/procedural and consolidated/substantive democracy. In the former case a polity may demonstrate the trappings of democracy – including elections, ideologically diverse political parties and the appearance of political participation, to name a few indicators – but may not possess a political culture in which citizens evince loyalty to a set of democratic rules of the game, to the idea of an autonomous civil society and to notions of individual social and political rights, including gender equality, as would be the case in a substantive or mature democracy. In the Arab region this distinction is important. A number of Arab political regimes have the trappings of a democratic system, i.e. they create nominally democratic institutions with the objective of stabilizing their regimes, but remain essentially autocratic (for empirical analysis of this question see Gandhi and Przeworski, 2007).

The gap between a theoretical understanding of a democracy and its actual implementation is often wide, especially in developing countries. But even among the so-called mature democracies there are distinct differences in this regard. For example, the influence of corporate capital on the democratic process, including control of the media, is much stronger in certain Western countries than in others; or the degree of social equity and the quality of social coverage (pertaining to the social rights of citizens), as well as of civil liberties and political participation, may differ markedly from one country to another. Such differences, it might be argued, render some of these countries more democratic than others (see Economist Intelligence Unit, 2007). In other words, empirical measurements of democracy that attempt to capture its basic features – such as political competition, participation, and civil liberties – do not necessarily succeed in fully reflecting the true democratic status in any given country; this is debatably more true in developing than in developed countries. In part this may be attributable to methodological flaws of the measurements, but could also be attributed to their coding rules, which do not always capture accurately the abuses of the governing classes and/or of special interest groups.

Equally importantly, any measure of democracy must fully recognize the universal right to political participation as reflected, for example, in universal suffrage. The Polity IV index (and other indices, with one or two exceptions) does not account explicitly for female suffrage. To that extent it suffers from an inadequate assessment of the democracy status of any given country in the period prior to the enactment of the right of women to participate in national or even municipal elections. This problem is of greater relevance for measures that attempt to identify transitions to democracy than measures concerned with the level of democracy at any particular point in time, as in the case of Polity IV, especially as they focus on recent periods that witnessed a growing extension of female suffrage across countries.[5]

Suffrage is, of course, part of the wider issue of gender equality that Polity IV and other indices of democracy do not explicitly recognize. In many countries the struggle for women's rights has led to a higher level of gender equality accompanied by wider female participation in various domains, including the political and economic domains. Such gains reflect the recognition that a real democracy implies gender equality as well as equal opportunities for all segments of society.[6]

Important as they are, the above limitations of Polity IV do not bear significantly on the polity analysis of the case studies included in this volume, particularly as the analysis focuses on explaining the persistence of their autocratic regimes and not on any transition from a state of autocracy to a state of democracy. Lebanon is an exception in that from the beginning of independence it has had its own special form of (constrained) democracy.

Regarding universal suffrage, in six of the case studies (Algeria, Egypt, Iraq, Lebanon, Syria and Sudan) women's suffrage was introduced prior to the period of the study that begins in 1960 or shortly afterwards. Jordan introduced the right of women to vote in 1974. The Gulf region, with the exception of Bahrain and Kuwait, has yet to introduce female suffrage. The former introduced it in 2002 and the latter in 2005. The remaining Arab countries, not included in this volume, introduced female suffrage before 1965.

As for the wider question of gender equality, the pace of its implementation in the Arab world, under the influence of women's movements and international pressure including international agreements such as the Convention on the Elimination of All Forms of Discrimination Against Women (CEDAW), has varied from one Arab country to another. In all of them however, various forms and degrees of gender discrimination continue to exist, giving an additional signal of the non-democratic nature of political regimes in place.

What matters for our purposes is that for all the countries in this volume the persistence of autocracies goes beyond the question of universal suffrage or gender equality in general. Those states that introduced female suffrage early on have remained non-democratic despite subsequent limited political reforms. And for the few that followed suit later on, the granting of women's right to participate in the political process, a positive step on its own, did not change the basic nature of the political regime in place. This assessment remains valid even after we account for other measures that might have been introduced to reduce gender inequality. With or without greater gender equality, as we note below, the Arab countries (with the exception of Lebanon) remain autocratic and the question of explaining the persistent Arab democracy deficit remains to be addressed.

Thus, while we have relied on a widely used empirical measure of democracy, i.e. the Polity IV index, in both the cross-country work and the individual case studies, we have, with the above in mind, been fully cognizant of some of its limitations both on methodological and definitional grounds. Perhaps, as pointed out by some researchers, one main empirical limitation of this index (along with alternative indices of measurement) is the applied aggregation rule: no justification is provided for the weighting schemes of the index attributes, which may lead to potential double counting.[7]

On the other hand, Polity IV possesses a number of positive attributes (e.g. clear and detailed coding rules), and whatever its flaws its wide use by researches renders it useful for comparative empirical assessments of the democracy status of different countries and regions. Furthermore, it appears to cohere with other indices of democracy (e.g. Van Hannen's and the more subjective Freedom House) in terms of the cross-regional comparisons and the dynamic behaviour over time. Indeed, the fundamental results regarding the role of oil and conflicts as the two major factors behind the Arab democracy deficit were robustly corroborated when the democracy model was tested using the Freedom House and Van Hannen's indices as dependent variables (Chapter 2). This enhances its validity though it does not necessarily establish its total reliability.[8] In any case, measures of democracy can and should be supplemented by additional investigations and, where necessary, their assessment should be modified accordingly.

Now, while the Polity IV rankings of Arab countries may not always have accurately reflected their evolving political situation, in general they have not been far off the mark in assessing the status of democracy in the Arab region.[9] In Chapter 2 we note that Arab autocracies have persisted in relying on various forms of oppression, including legitimacy by default, the engineering of crisis politics, and, more recently, the pretext of containing fundamentalist movements. There is plenty of evidence that the political and civic rights record in Arab countries has been marred by serious violations, attested to by various reports of Arab and international human rights organizations. All this lends support to the empirical assessment that, excepting one case (Lebanon), various shades of autocracy have prevailed in these countries since independence. The limited political liberalization that some of them undertook at various times does not materially change this picture. Indeed, the case studies clearly point out how political regimes and practices reflect various forms of autocratic behaviour, the intensity of which could change from one period to another depending upon circumstances. The obstacles to the strengthening of democratization in the Arab region are yet to be overcome.

Over the course of the project, three workshops were held during which the research teams discussed the progress of their work and critiqued the methodologies employed. These proved to be extremely beneficial. They allowed for a constructive and enriching exchange of views among the participants in the project. Mutual feedback helped shape the final drafts of the studies. Toward the end of the project a dissemination conference was organized to present the findings of the cross-country and case studies to academics and civil society organizations, among others. Their feedback provided many helpful insights. In addition, a few separate individual country workshops were also organized to engage experts in the research findings of the case studies concerned. All these engagements were greatly advantageous to the progress of the research being undertaken. They allowed for a critical discourse of research methodologies and findings that could only serve to improve the ultimate outcome of the research project.

The volume is divided into three parts. Part I, on conceptual and cross-country work, sets the framework of the analysis. Part II, the main part, includes the case studies, which are divided into three groups: the Mashreq countries, the oil-dependent countries and the Nile Valley countries. Part III is an interpretive synthesis summing up the question of democracy in the Arab world.

Notes

1. They had been governed by the Ottomans since 1516/17, and by the British and French following the First World War and the collapse of the Ottoman Empire. Indeed, Egypt and the rest of North Africa had effectively been lost to Ottoman rule many decades before the First World War.
2. Admittedly, due to data limitation, we could only account for the gender question through the share of females in the labour force, which is only one aspect of women's empowerment.
3. See e.g. Al-Naqib (1996a, 1996b); Kedourie (1994); Sharabi (1988). According to Sharabi, patriarchy is a deep-seated characteristic of Arab societies that has survived through the ages and managed to adapt itself to modernity by transposing the acquired dependency relations vis-à-vis imperialist powers into the enduring features of the old patriarchy, hence becoming 'neopatriarchy'.
4. The extent to which current theories of transition to democracy that are based on the historical experience of the Western countries are useful in identifying the path from autocracy to democracy in the Arab world is an issue that will need to be carefully examined.
5. For a critical evaluation of this question see Paxton, 2000.
6. For whatever it might imply, the regression model of Ch. 2 indicates the positive impact on democratization of the growing share of the female labour force.
7. For a critical evaluation of alternative empirical measures of democracy, see Munck and Verkuilen, 2002.

8 Furthermore, some researchers have referred to data-induced measurement errors (Bowman *et al.*, 2005) which could reduce the validity of the long-term cross-national scales of democracy, and other researchers to the non-interchangeability of the various indices of democracy (Liu, 2003–4; Casper and Tufis, 2003) which reduce their reliability.
9 For some of the case studies, their authors judged that the assigned Polity IV country scores did not always reflect appropriately the evolving political situation and relied instead on their own modified polity scores.

References

Al-Naqib, K. (1996a) *The Struggle between Tribe and Democracy* (in Arabic), London: Dar al-Saqi.
—— (1996b) *The Imperious State in the Arab East* (in Arabic), Beirut: Centre for Arab Unity Studies.
Bowman, Kirk, Lehoucq, F. and Mahoney, J. (2005) 'Measuring Political Democracy: Case Expertise, Data Adequacy, and Central America', *Comparative Political Studies*, 38: 8.
Casper, G. and Tufis, C. (2003) 'Cooperating across Crises: Patterns of Elite Behavior in Least Likely and Most Likely Cases of Democracy', paper presented at the annual meeting of the American Political Science Association, Philadelphia.
Donno, D. and Russett, B. (2004) 'Islam, Authoritarianism, and Female Empowerment: What are the Linkages?', *World Politics* 56: 582–607.
Economist Intelligence Unit (2007) *Index of Democracy*. Online at: www.economist.com/media/pdf/Democracy_Index_2007_v3.pdf
Gandhi, J. and Przeworski, A. (2007) 'Authoritarian Institutions and the Survival of Autocrats', *Comparative Political Studies* 40/1, Nov.
Kedourie, E. (1994) *Democracy and Arab Political Culture*, Washington, DC: Washington Institute for Near East Policy.
Liu, A. (2003–4). *Index Correlation, Measurement Reliability and Biased Estimation: Measuring Democracy as a Latent Variable*, The RM Institute Reports. Online at: www.researchmethods.org/democracy-indicators.pdf.
Munck, G. and Verkuilen, J. (2002) 'Conceptualizing and Measuring Democracy Evaluating Alternative Indices', *Comparative Political Studies* 35/1: 5–34.
Paxton, P. (2000) 'Women's Suffrage in the Measurement of Democracy: Problems of Operationalization', *Studies in Comparative International Development* 35/3.
Sharabi, H. (1988) *Neopatriarchy: A Theory of Distorted Change in Arab Society*, New York: Oxford University Press.

Part I
Democracy and development
Conceptual and cross-country perspectives

1 Political culture and the crisis of democracy in the Arab world

Abdelwahab El-Affendi

When the scandal over the abuse of Iraqi prisoners in the Abu Ghraib prison broke out in early 2004, Seymour Hersh, one of the key figures behind the revelations, pointed to the irony that Abu Ghraib had been a notorious torture centre under the Saddam Hussein regime that was thoroughly looted and stripped even of windows and doors after the fall of the regime. The United States military took over the deserted building, gave it a thorough face lift, with 'the floors tiled, cells cleaned and repaired, and toilets, showers, and a new medical center added' (Hersh, 2004a). Then they proceeded to do exactly what the Saddam regime had done there before, only this time they took pictures to amuse themselves.

In the heated controversy that followed, the US authorities and mainstream media argued that the torture at Abu Ghraib was an aberration, the responsibility of only a 'handful of rogue elements' in the US military. However, many analysts argued that the abuses reflected the erosion of democratic and human rights standards in the post-9/11 era, and were linked to the overall US policies in Iraq, Afghanistan and Guantanamo, involving the widespread use of torture on terror suspects (Hersh, 2004b). Some even compared the process to the creeping Nazification of Germany in the 1930s (Rajiva, 2005).

Other observers compared this latest Western incursion into the Arab world to the first: that of Napoleon Bonaparte in 1898. That one also used the pretext of bringing 'liberty' to the Arabs, and ended equally disastrously. Two prominent US historians (Richard Bulliet of Columbia University and Juan Cole of the Global Americana Institute) made the comparison almost simultaneously in August 2007. Napoleon had 'proclaimed his intention of liberating the Egyptians from their Mamluk oppressors. And he brought an army of scholars and advisers with him to make the occupation of Egypt a model of European benevolence' (Bulliet, 2007). Both leaders displayed a 'tendency to believe their own propaganda (or at least to keep repeating it long after it became completely implausible).

> Both leaders invaded and occupied a major Arabic-speaking Muslim country; both harbored dreams of a 'Greater Middle East'; both were surprised to find themselves enmeshed in long, bitter, debilitating guerrilla wars. Neither genuinely cared about grassroots democracy, but both found its symbols easy to

invoke for gullible domestic publics. Substantial numbers of their new subjects quickly saw, however, that they faced occupations, not liberations.

(Cole, 2007)

Napoleon's promise of liberation soon confronted the locals as 'an avalanche of bothersome regulations' and predatory practices aimed at raising revenue for the invaders (Flower, 1972: 48). When the people could take it no more and revolted, the advocates of liberty used the most brutal of tactics, including resorting to indiscriminate shelling of Cairo and even the mosque. Every rule in the book was broken, and all pretence of promoting liberty or respecting Islam was dropped. Al-Azhar was occupied and desecrated.

> Horses were tethered to the Kiblah, furniture was hurled around and the Koran kicked about the floor. El Djabarty, aghast, saw soldiers spit on the carpets, urinate on the walls, and litter the mosque with broken wine bottles... Heavy fines were imposed all round, and ten Sheikhs believed to have been implicated were stripped naked and shot in the Citadel.

(Flower, 1972: 50)

Sound familiar? It could be Fallujah 2004, Hebron 1986, Hama 1982, or Halabja 1987.

1. Democracy, liberalism, occupation

This convergence of regime conduct across times and cultures should cast a sharp light on some of the unspoken assumptions that underpin much of the current discussions on democracy and democratization. One could cite numerous other examples, from the way the British conducted themselves in the face of the 1857 rebellion in India, through the French atrocities in Algeria, to Israel's behaviour today, to highlight aspects of this phenomenon, which I would like to call the 'Napoleon–Saddam Syndrome'. It is a condition that seems to infect rulers and other political actors in the region, regardless of their cultural background or origin, and suck them into a spiral of abuses, oppression, mounting resistance and more repression, leading to eventual collapse.

An inkling of the nature of this pathology can be found in remarks made by Israeli leaders who, in their attempt to defend Israeli's aggressive and often brutal behaviour towards the Palestinians by claiming that the Middle East is a brutal area where only the language of violence is understood, betray a sense of siege and isolation (Barak, 1999). The resulting paranoia is self-reinforcing; the actor who feels threatened by everyone around him acts in a manner that further alienates people and confirms his fears. Ironically, this paranoia is also shared by entrenched and increasingly beleaguered Arab regimes, and the excuses are comparable. When challenged about the horrendous abuses they engage in, Israeli officials often use the refrain: 'This is not Switzerland, you know.' Arab despots respond to mild suggestions that they moderate their abuses of human rights by quipping: 'If I were to do what you ask, the fundamentalists would take over... Is that what you want?' This invariably silences the interlocutor, who quickly changes the subject (Zakaria, 2001).

Many theoreticians tend to follow the autocrats in emphasizing the role of the 'environment,' usually delineated in cultural terms. For example, Flower argues that Napoleon's problem was that his slogans about the 'rights of man' had little resonance with 'the inward-looking Egyptians' (Flower, 1972: 47), before giving a catalogue of the endless oppressive measures introduced by Napoleon under these slogans. This blaming of the victims suggests that it is not just Napoleon and Bush who tend to believe their own propaganda, but that many analysts do so as well. For the Egyptians did not rebel against the 'rights of man', but against unbearable oppression by an alien and insensitive power which ruled by force of arms.

To start, we can draw one logical conclusion from the encounters just mentioned: that the amount of repression needed to sustain a regime is proportional to the depth and breadth of rejection it faces from the people. That the US occupation forces in Iraq are having to use similar techniques of repression to the Ba'athist regime they displaced is a sign that they are facing comparable resistance from Iraqis. By definition, democracy should not face popular resistance, since democracy is rule by the people, which cannot be in revolt against itself. So if a certain order provokes a fierce resistance, that order is, by definition, not a democracy.

While there are many disagreements about defining democracy, David Beetham is right to argue that:

> Disputes about the meaning of democracy which purport to be conceptual disagreements are really disputes about how much democracy is either desirable or practicable; that is, about where the trade-off should come between democratic and other values.
> (Beetham, 1993: 55)

For Beetham, democracy can be defined as:

> A mode of decision-making about collectively binding rules and policies over which the people exercise control, and the most democratic arrangement to be where all members of the collectivity enjoy effective equal rights to take part in such decision-making directly – one, that is to say, which realizes to the greatest conceivable degree the principle of popular control and equality in its exercise. Democracy should properly be conceptualized as lying at one end of a spectrum, the other end of which is a system of rule where the people are totally excluded from the decision-making process and any control over it.
> (Beetham, 1993: 55)

There is a broad agreement on this conception of democracy as a political system 'in which the members regard themselves as political equals, as collectively sovereign, and possess all capacities, resources and institutions they need in order to govern themselves' (Dahl, 1989: 1). The theoretical disputes, as Beetham points out, revolve around rival and contestable claims as to how much democracy can be realized in a sustainable form. This is an important consideration since democracy has been 'a remarkably difficult form of government to create and sustain' (Held, 1993: 13).

Sustainability, or 'consolidation', is a key concern for theoreticians of democratic transitions, and is said to occur when democracy becomes 'the only game in town', i.e. 'when no significant political group seriously attempts to overthrow the democratic regime or to promote domestic or international violence in order to secede from the state' (Linz and Stepan, 1998: 49). One could argue that this requirement is too stringent, since it could imply that today's Spain or Britain during the IRA insurgency are not consolidated democracies. However, the general idea is that a democracy can be considered consolidated when such activities do not pose a serious threat to its stability. Linz and Stepan stipulate six conditions needed for a democracy to be consolidated: an authoritative state, a lively civil society, an autonomous political society, the prevalence of the rule of law, an effective state bureaucracy and an institutionalized economic society (Linz and Stepan, 1998: 51–8).

However, modern democracy has another dimension to it. As Bernard Crick puts it, what is usually meant by democracy today is 'a fusion (but quite often a confusion) of the idea of power of the people and the idea of legally guaranteed individual rights' (Crick, 1998: 257). More often described as 'liberal representative democracy' (Held, 1993: 18–20), to distinguish it from ancient direct democracies (like those of Athens) or from other forms that do not respect individual liberties, modern democracies are also referred to as 'constitutional democracies'. Liberal constitutionalism seeks to limit the powers of the state through guarantees of individual rights and private property. Liberalism ('a doctrine devoted to protecting the rights of the individual to life, liberty, property, and the pursuit of happiness': Plattner, 1999: 121) could and did exist without democracy, while constitutionalism could be, and has been, used to curb democracy. The designers of the American constitution in particular had used complex constitutional curbs on democratic rights (indirect elections of the president and senate, special role for the Supreme Court, etc.) in order to guard against the 'tyranny of the majority' as much as to guard against the tyranny of the few (Blondel, 1998: 74).

Given that liberalism contains principles that 'have been profoundly hostile to democracy', the evolution of modern democracy has been the 'history of successive struggles between liberals and various types of democrat over the extent and form of democratization' (Beetham, 1993: 58). In spite of this, the convergence was seen as inevitable, since liberalism's values of liberty and rights cannot long survive the denial of equal rights for all (Plattner, 1999: 122). In fact, attempts made to abolish some of the liberal features of modern democracies 'in the name of a more perfect democracy have only succeeded in undermining the democracy in whose name [these rights] were attacked' (Beetham, 1993: 57). To a large extent then, modern democracy can be seen as having been 'conceptualized and structured within the limits of liberalism' (Parekh, 1995: 165).

However, and of central relevance to our current investigation, the consciousness of the distinction and tension between liberalism and democracy has led to another startling conclusion. Taking as its premise the same point made above (that democracy and liberalism have become inseparable), some analysts have argued that in cases where democracy could lead to illiberal regimes (as was the case in the former Yugoslavia or some Arab and Muslim countries where Islamists could come to power), it might not be wise to promote democracy. Instead, some form of authoritarian liberalism should be championed (Miller, 1993; Zakaria, 1997; Plattner, 1999). From this perspective, it could be seen that what Napoleon and George W. Bush were trying to promote in the Arab world was not really democracy, but some form of authoritarian liberalism (cf. Cole, 2007). The claim that Arab culture is hostile to democracy has thus been reinterpreted to argue that Arabs are in fact hostile to liberalism.

2. The basics of 'culture talk'

The appeal to culture as an explanatory variable determinant of social and political change, most recently publicized by Huntington's 'Clash of Civilizations' thesis, has a long pedigree, stretching back to Max Weber's famous citing of the 'Protestant Ethic' as the driving force behind modern capitalism (Wedeen, 2002: 713). Other theorists trace the genealogy back to de Tocqueville and even to Aristotle (Diamond, 1994: 10). The political culture approach has in recent years been eclipsed by rival approaches, after a brief ascendancy in the first half of the last century (Almond, 1994: pp. x–xi; Diamond, 1994: 1). Proponents of this approach stake the claim 'that we can identify distinctive and relatively stable distributions of political values, beliefs and understandings among populations' that can act as independent explanatory variables for political behaviour (Diamond, 1994: 1). In this regard, certain cultural attributes can cause democracy to flourish, including a level of individualism, moderation, pragmatism and mutual trust among the elite, coupled with an 'intelligent mistrust of leadership' (Diamond, 1994: 12). Central also is a solid commitment to the democratic process by all actors as stipulated above.

> This overriding commitment to democratic proceduralism is a critical political cultural condition for democracy. In combination with policy pragmatism and political tolerance, it promotes moderate partisanship, and these qualities together are most likely to limit the politicization of social life and the rancor of political intercourse.
> (Diamond, 1994: 11)

It is of course a truism to say that the culture of a society determines how individuals and groups conduct themselves publicly, especially if political culture is defined as 'a people's predominant beliefs, attitudes, values, ideals, sentiments, and evaluations about the political system of its country, and the role of the self in that system' (Diamond, 1994: 7). For if one includes evaluation of the political system in the definition of political culture, then the assertion about the influence of culture becomes a tautology. Nevertheless, attempts to identify causal links between political development and existing identifiable cultural traits in given societies face a number of problems. This is especially so when we add the assumptions that the components of this culture are widely shared, at least within the elite, and 'represent coherent patterns which fit together and are mutually reinforcing', and must also be constant over time and fairly resistant to change (Diamond, 1994: 8–9).

In view of numerous challenges to these assumptions, the recent revival of the political culture approach thus stakes only modest claims, rejecting outright the determinist version on theoretical and empirical grounds, since masses of evidence from field research and surveys continue to reveal that the causal relationship between culture and political behaviour is a two-way process, and political culture is seen as 'fairly plastic'. Determinism is rejected also on normative grounds, because belief in the rigidity of culture and a one-way causal relationship would condemn whole societies to perpetual lack of democracy (Diamond, 1994: 9–10). In addition, proponents of this modified political culture approach want to look at culture in terms of 'geological strata of history', where competing layers of cultural tradition coexist, and where the latest dominant traits have not completely eclipsed or supplanted earlier legacies (Diamond, 1994: 230–1). Put differently, this approach calls for a further dilution of the initial thesis by advising analysts to 'disaggregate political culture: look at subcultures (vertical and horizontal); look at elite cultures and mass culture' (Hudson, 1995: 73). Also, to understand political culture 'as a multi-layered phenomenon, amenable therefore to "geological" study: look at formal ideologies (on the "surface"), then at opinions (easily changeable), then at attitudes (less so), and finally try to plumb the deep structure of enduring collective values and orientations' (Hudson, 1995: 73).

These multiple qualifications look like the prudent preparation of multiple escape routes. But critics continue to reject these claims as 'either fundamentally tautological or empirically invalid' (Wedeen, 2002: 713). In any case, recent empirical studies on democratic transition 'explicitly dismiss the importance for transition of the prior consensus on democratic values', emphasizing instead splits within authoritarian regimes and the subsequent calculation by one faction 'that its interests are best served (or risks best minimized) by liberalization' (Diamond, 1994: 4–5). Acceptance of democratic norms evolves at a later stage, as a consequence of the compromises reached and the deals struck between former enemies. In a sense, it can be said that, apart from the elite commitment to democratic procedures (which may be initially instrumental and expedient) there may not be any specific preconditions for democracy. Moreover, many of the requirements postulated as preconditions for democracy may, in fact, be outcomes of democracy (Diamond, 1994: 15).

Any viable appeal to cultural explanations must take account of this interactive aspect of culture. While cultural norms and identities of necessity condition reactions to political challenges, political realities also condition culture. Culture as a process of meaning construction 'implies a social process through which people reproduce together the conditions of intelligibility that enable them to make sense of their worlds' (Wedeen, 2002: 717). The way, for example, ethnic identification evolves and shifts (even within similar groups) depends on many contextual factors as well as conscious choices (Wedeen, 2002: 724–5).

3. On arab political culture and the 'missing bourgeoisie'

The political culture approach has been at its most problematic when applied in the Arab-Muslim context of 'Culture Talk', a discourse which 'assumes that every culture has a tangible essence that defines it, and . . . then explains politics as a consequence of that essence' (Mamdani, 2005). This discourse comes in two main versions.

> One thinks of premodern peoples as those who are not yet modern, who are either lagging behind or have yet to embark on the road to modernity. The other depicts the premodern as also the antimodern. Whereas the former conception encourages relations based on philanthropy, the latter notion is productive of fear and preemptive police or military action.
> (Mamdani, 2005: 18)

Both versions, however, look at culture, especially Muslim culture, as having 'no history, no politics, and no debates'. In both, 'history seems to have petrified into a lifeless custom of an antique people who inhabit antique lands' (Mamdani, 2005). This position has a political purpose. The message it seeks to send when it argues that the clash of Western powers with Arabs and Muslims is a clash of civilizations rather than a genuine political conflict (Lewis, 1990; Huntington, 1993), is that these people are not worthy of political engagement. Even if the alleged grievances are addressed (and here is a long list that starts with Palestine and does not end there) then these 'barbarians' would still remain hostile to the West. These arguments are additionally suspicious when they are promoted by experts known for their right-wing views and sympathies for Israel.

In some of its more recent recastings, the slightly more sophisticated thesis defines the problem in terms of a fundamental contrast between the world of jihad and the McWorld. The anti-modern world of 'jihad' ('the ancient forces of culture, geography, tradition, and community': Farazmand and Pinkowski, 2006: 70) and the commercialized 'McWorld' of high-tech consumerism and globalized pursuit of profit, may be antagonistic, but they are also interconnected. McWorld represents 'the natural culmination of a modernization process–some would call it Westernization – that has gone on since the Renaissance birth of modern science and its dominant paradigm of knowledge construed as power' (Barber, 2003: 156). It embodies the Enlightenment's 'trust in reason, its passion for liberty, and (not unrelated to that passion) its fascination with control' (Barber, 2003: 156). Jihad, by contrast, stands for forces of 'dogmatic and violent particularism' which seek to 'defend and deny, reject and repel modernity wherever they find it' (Barber,

2003: 7, 11). Needless to say, McWorld predominates in the modernized West, symbolized by America. 'Its template is American, its form style ... It is about culture as a commodity, apparel as ideology' (Barber, 2003: 17). Jihad, by contrast, is found predominantly outside the West, or on its periphery and in small pockets within it.

Apart from the interesting (Freudian?) inversion which uses 'jihad' (a term that signifies the struggle in defense of universal truth) to symbolize parochialism, and a term derived from a Scottish clan name to symbolize universalism, this restatement of the old 'Orientalist' tautology (East is East and West is West) does not say very much. It does not explain why parochialism persists among some groups and not others. More important, it does not tell us why adopting certain lifestyles, such as eating certain types of food or wearing certain types of clothes, should have magical powers to transform people's perceptions and conduct in very radical ways.

In the end, we are finally referring to the Orientalist thesis proper, but in an even more simplistic form. In the Muslim world, where 'the struggle between Jihad and McWorld has been much more than a metaphor for tribalism or a worried antimodernism', empirical data appear to point to 'a certain lack of affinity between Islam and democracy' (Barber, 2003: 156). While fundamentalism is a phenomenon that has emerged in most religious traditions, 'only in Islam do fundamentalist tendencies appear to play a central role' (Barber, 2003: 206–7; cf. Manji, 2004).[1] In the end, it appears the long detour of jihad versus McWorld, to paraphrase Anderson (1995) on royal marriages and war in dynastic successions, leads back to the short route of Orientalist Culture Talk.

Hudson attempts to tackle the issue by dividing studies that apply the political culture approach to Arab politics into two categories: the reductionist (of which the Orientalists are the oldest and most influential) and the empiricist. The reductionists are given to 'grand generalizations' and plenty of stereotyping, tending to descend into absurd caricatures (Hudson, 1995: 65–7). While the empiricists have improved somewhat on the theses of '*ex cathedra* Orientalism and armchair psychology', they remain 'better at questions than answers' (Hudson, 1995: 70, 68). But in spite of all these misgivings, Hudson argues that to understand 'conditions such as legitimacy, liberalism or democracy it is hard to ignore culture ... even if it is a residual variable after structural, economic and exogenous factors' (Hudson, 1995: 71–2). One has to tread carefully, however, observing the demands outlined earlier and avoiding reductionism and being 'methodologically multifaceted' (Hudson, 1995: 73).

Lisa Anderson is less charitable to the political culture crowd, accusing them of residual racism and extremely negative attitudes to their subject of study (Anderson, 1995: 79, 88–9). They either characterize Arabs as 'aliens' who are radically different from everyone else, blame Islam and the transcendental notions of divine sovereignty (and the failure to render unto Caesar what is rightly his), or dwell on tribal culture, patriarchy, patrimonialism, the informality of patterns of authority, etc. Their work is riddled with logical and epistemological flaws, reflecting 'an inability to think critically about change' (Anderson, 1995: 89).

Most of these writers fail to notice that the attitudes and behaviour patterns they refer to (when they are not mere projections or misreadings of the facts) are neither uncaused nor unchanging. To say with Hudson that 'it is infinitely difficult to govern in the face of a hostile, recalcitrant, skeptical populace' is to overlook the point that 'most of the people of the Arab world are quite right to be angry, reluctant and suspicious participants in politics' (Hudson, 1995: 86). As a consequence, to examine political change 'through the lens of political culture rather than structure may not be the most parsimonious vehicle' (Anderson, 1995: 86). In the end, 'the nature of political regimes in the Arab world, like those elsewhere in the world, can best be understood as reflections of the political economy of the countries in question, particularly the character of their integration into the world economy' (Anderson, 1995: 78).

A position which tries to link political economy and culture argues that the parochialism of the 'jihad world' and its resistance to democracy and modernization is a function of an underdeveloped bourgeoisie, or its lack of autonomy from state control (Waterbury, 1994; Salamé, 1994; Ayubi, 1995). This is also the reason why Arab and Muslim countries remain averse to liberalism, since liberalism has been historically associated with the rise of the bourgeoisie (Binder, 1988: 336–58). The rise of an indigenous bourgeoisie and a 'bourgeois revolution' is needed for liberalism and democracy to evolve in Muslim lands (Binder, 1988: 66–8). In the absence of such a revolution, democracy in the areas dominated by the parochial forces of 'jihad' tends to evolve into an 'illiberal democracy', making it perhaps imperative to experiment with spreading liberalism without democracy (Zakaria, 1997; Barber, 2003: 207–11).

To postpone democratization until liberalism evolves first, some form of 'guardianship' scheme (one could even call it *wilayat al-librali*, guardianship of the liberal, in contrast to *wilayat al-Faqih*, guardianship of the jurist) would be needed to guide the communities in question towards liberalism and democracy. A 'liberal autocracy', like the one the British ran in Hong Kong during most of the last century, could be the sort of guardianship scheme needed for this job (Zakaria, 1997). This also appears to be what the G8's 'Broader Middle East Initiative', launched in June 2004 to promote democracy in the Arab region, has boiled down to. The project envisages what amounts to a loose international guardianship which could help mould the region's despotic regimes into quasi-liberal autocracies (El-Affendi, 2005). After the debacles in Iraq and the success of Islamists in elections in Egypt and Palestine in late 2005 and early 2006, even this limited goal appears to have been abandoned.

However, like the argument about the rise of civil society as a precondition for democratization (Norton, 1995), this pinning of the hopes on an emerging bourgeoisie seems to beg the question where the 'Black Hole State' (AHDR, 2005) does not permit a space for civil society to function, and where 'the emerging private sectors in most Arab countries are still largely "clientalized" by the state, or else remain "informal" or underground' (Ayubi, 1995: 405).

4. The perspectives of Arab intellectuals

In spite of Said's demolition of Orientalism (and a plethora of other critiques[2]), a significant number of Arab intellectuals did not shy away from indulging in their own forms of 'Culture Talk'. This approach was given its most coherent (and, one could add, blatant) formulation in Hisham Sharabi's *Neopatriarchy* (1988), where he ascribed the longevity of Arab authoritarianism to the enduring patriarchical tendencies in Arab societies. According to Sharabi, patriarchy has been a feature of Arab culture since before Islam, which failed to modify it significantly. It has survived through the ages and managed to adapt itself to modernity, becoming 'neopatriarchy', combining both the enduring features of the old patriarchy with the relation of dependency vis-à-vis imperialist powers (Sharabi, 1992: 15–16, 45–66). Similar views are expressed by Khaldoun Al-Naqib, who uses the concept of tribalism to illustrate the same point. He defines tribalism as a hierarchical 'mode of organization' based on alliances as well as kin relationships, but also on an 'ethos', derived from 'primordial associations and loyalties existing deep within the consciousness of the group' (Al-Naqib, 1996: 9). However, Al-Naqib admits that 'tribalism', which he regards as the dominant organizing principle in many countries in the Arab East, is extremely adaptable to changing circumstances (Al-Naqib, 1996: 10–11, 20). This qualification squarely contradicts the central claim that Al-Naqib (following Sharabi) also makes about tribalism being so powerful that 'Islam has been unable to displace political tirbalism . . . to achieve the cohesion of the *umma* along moral principles' (Al-Naqib, 1996: 19).

Other writers such as Hasan Hanafi similarly argue that the problems we face in attempting to build free societies can be traced back to deep roots in our shared heritage, transmitted across generations through texts or direct oral inculcation (Hanafi, 1998: 176–9). These trends include literalism, authoritarianism (distilled through *Ash'arism*), rejection of the other, and the rejection of rationality (under the influence of thinkers such as Abu-Hamid al-Gazali, d. 1111) (Hanafi, 1998: 179–89).

This 'archaeological' digging in the past to explain the present makes too many assumptions about the universal acceptance, uniform exposure and internalization of particular views, which is not supported by historical evidence. The criticism of Sharabi's approach can also apply to Hanafi and similar schools. Like Hanafi, Sharabi, it has been correctly pointed out, indulges in sweeping generalizations for which he provides only sketchy and anecdotal evidence (Hamoudi, 2000: 18). He also neglects important facts regarding the role of mothers and the exposure of children to influences outside the home, such as schools or the media (Hamoudi, 2000: 18–21). Moreover, he fails to demonstrate any causal link or coherent interdependence between the traits he ascribes to neopatriarchy (for example, why should a society that embraces patriarchy – supposing that this was the case – tend to be irrational or lacking in initiative?).

Needless to say, this 'culturalist' conception does not induce its proponents to be enthusiastic supporters of democracy. For if the basic problem inheres in the culture, and therefore in the people, it would be useless to advocate democracy.

The Orientalists are frank about this, as we see in Kedourie, who cites the fact that democracy has been tried and tested in the Arab world before and was a dismal failure, and who hence argues that the Arabs cannot understand, let alone embrace, democracy (Kedourie, 1994: 1–2).

The slightly more sophisticated stance expressed by Farid Zakaria (1997) and others entails demands for the setting up of a 'benevolent dictatorship' in each Arab country, to see it through to liberal maturity, a point made bluntly by an Arab intellectual (Elhadj, 2007).

Another Arab intellectual, speaking in 1979, reminded his audience that democracy had taken over 200 years to mature in the West, concluding that what is needed is not only to create the social and economic conditions for democracy first, but also to 'educate the people in a democratic way, and to train them to practice democracy until democracy becomes a value deeply ingrained in their souls' (Abdalla, 1998: 119). Another intellectual, El-Tahir Labib (in CAUS, 1998: 327) puts it thus: 'a backward society cannot but produce a backward socialism and cannot but produce a backward democracy'. Therefore, priority must be given to the revolutionary transformation of that society.

It has been noted that a significant section of Arab intellectuals made a (very reluctant) conversion to democratic ideals in the late 1970s and early 1980s (Ismael, 1995: 95). A deep sense of crisis that engulfed Arab thought in the aftermath of the 1967 defeat by Israel was made more acute by the slide of most Arab regimes into an intolerably repressive mode. Cataclysmic events such as the Israeli invasion of Lebanon in 1982 and the Gulf War of 1990–1, which saw direct American hegemony imposed on the region, further enhanced this sense of crisis (Ismael, 1995: 93–6; Abu-Rabi, 2004: 50–2). An intellectual writing during that period (in 1983) tried to explain the sudden 'insistence on the issue of democracy in this period of our history by all political and intellectual trends in our homeland' by offering three reasons. First, the lesson of the previous decades was that the social and political gains sought by revolutionaries needed the masses to protect them; second, the regimes that promised economic development and Arab unity in exchange for suspension of human rights have achieved neither, and had become so gratuitously and brutally repressive that it had become impossible to tolerate the levels of violence they deploy against opponents; and, finally, the situation in the Arab world had deteriorated dramatically in the face of US-backed Israeli hegemony, leading to a marked increase in Arab dependency in all spheres (CAUS, 1998: 11–12).

How reluctant and incomplete this conversion to democracy was can be clearly seen from the very debates announcing it. In one such debate organized by the Centre for Arab Unity Studies in Beirut in 1979, one leading Algerian intellectual and diplomat (Lakhdar Ibrahimi) argued point blank that 'the democratic model operating in the West will not help us to achieve our goals in building a modern progressive society', mainly due to the general condition of dependency surrounding Arab societies (CAUS, 1998: 95–7). Also, the social conditions of Arab societies, plagued as they were by tribalism, sectarianism and ignorance, make it imperative to prioritize social transformation and social justice rather than formal democracy (CAUS, 1998: 81–3). Another intellectual speaking in the same debate (George Corm) argued that the admiration for democracy in Arab opinion clashes with the antipathy to all things Western and the attachment to values hostile to the individualism that is central to Western democratic norms (CAUS, 1998: 83). A number of intellectuals engaged in that debate accepted that the call for democracy has arisen in Arab thought and practice, not for its intrinsic qualities, but as a tool to achieve independence and development (CAUS, 1998: 97). Another added that the issue of democracy did not arise in the 1950s (during the Nasserist period in Egypt) due to the 'full confidence that power was in the hands of a resolute and able nationalist leadership' (Adil Hussein, in CAUS, 1998: 102). In answer to a point made earlier about managing the revolutionary transformation democratically, this same intellectual rejected the idea, arguing that revolutionary change is a protracted affair, occupying an extended period characterized by a fierce struggle, not only with the former ruling classes, but also 'against the consumerist norms among broad social groups, and against mentalities based traditionally on concepts that do not accord with the needs of development or independence, and so on' (CAUS, 1998: 102–3).

Similar ideas were repeated in other writings and debates during the years that followed. It is to be noted that discussions of democracy by Arab intellectuals, including that in the much celebrated *Arab Human Development Report*, rely heavily on Western concepts and sources in their definitions and explications (Al-Naqib, 1996; CAUS, 1998; Ayubi, 1995; Sadiki, 2004). Often there are differences between those who adopt radical leftist views and those who would like to follow the more traditional liberal line, even though the recent shift referred to above points to a convergence between the two positions. This has led to a criticism that this convergence is another problematic adoption of democracy as an ideology of salvation that is espoused equally irrationally (Tarabishi, 2006: 918). Like many other Arab intellectuals, Tarabishi adopts the Culture Talk stance, arguing that the problem is a social-intellectual, rather than a political, one. Giving freedom to the people could lead to the tyranny of the majority, given the multiple 'pathologies of Arab civil society' (Tarabishi, 2006: 16–18).

In a supreme irony, speakers in the above debates tended to heap tons of blame on the intellectuals who, it was alleged, 'failed dismally in performing any democratic role', or to maintain their independence vis-à-vis the ruling regimes (Corm, in CAUS, 1998: 84). Others were even more scathing, accusing intellectuals of becoming too pro-Western and alienated from the masses, or concerned merely with their individual interests. The intellectuals were generally socially and politically apathetic and/or (more seriously) preferred to act as agents of authoritarian regimes. Some intellectuals not only serve despotic regimes as propagandists and apologists, but even 'rationalize [repression] and push for it. [One has only to] survey the huge number of intellectuals dispersed throughout newspapers, magazines, media channels, publishing houses and research centers to become aware of this shameful reality' (Abdalla, 1998: 50–1).

These criticisms notwithstanding, a number of the intellectuals participating in those debates were already officials or sympathizers of regimes that were undemocratic. Many more went on to become ministers in cabinets that could not be described as democratic except by an extreme stretch of the imagination and terminology.

This probably provides the key understanding as to the nature of the democratic crisis in the Arab world. From the beginning, the concern in Arab and Muslim circles has not been with democracy as an intrinsic value, but as a means to something else. The fact that the early generation of Arab reformers like Rufa'a al-Tahtawi, Khayr al-Din al-Tunisi and Abd al-Rahman al-Kawakibi (and including Abduh) advocated *Islah* (reform) rather than democracy (Sadiki, 2004: 218–28) was due mainly to the sense of a need to give priority to communal survival over individual freedoms. It was the same with the revolutionaries of the post-war era. For that early generation and their latter day – more radical – successors, some key objectives were too important to be left at the mercy of democratic process. Both groups did not concentrate on empowering the people as an urgent necessity, for the priority was to empower communities or states.

The fact that the elite remained at best reluctant democrats is not a problem in itself, since studies of democratic transformation have consistently revealed that political actors more often than not opt for democracy as a last resort, or as the 'lesser evil' from their perspective. Only later does commitment to democracy evolve and solidify, receiving an unequivocal and enduring commitment from main actors. However, the problem in the Arab world is that rival political groups continue to entertain the view that many things are too important to entrust to the vagaries of a democratic process and the whims of the populace.

5. The religious dimension

The reluctant conversion to democracy among many former radicals coincided with the 'Islamic revival', which further complicated the renewed quest for democracy, and ensured that it would 'further divide rather than unite secular and religious visionaries and polarize their polities and societies' (Sadiki, 2004: 251). The debate on governance in the Arab world on the threshold of modernity became entangled from early on with the debate on what form of government is required by Islam. In its early form, the debate centred on the caliphate and whether it could be saved or restored (El-Affendi, 2008: 81–100). Additionally, this debate was also influenced by developments such as the Constitutional Revolution of 1905–6 in Iran, the first experiment of its kind in the Muslim world. Iran's brief success in establishing a constitutional monarchy modelled on the Belgian constitution, with an elected parliament incorporating a five-man council of *ulama* to vet all legislation for conformity with Shari'a, became an inspiration for modern Islamic thinkers since Rashid Rida (El-Affendi, 2004a: 172–94; El-Affendi, 2008: 83–96). The combination of a popular uprising demanding participation in decision-making, with a call for incorporation of Shari'a as a basis of legislation, was seen as proof that democracy and Islam are compatible (and it explains the phenomenon that baffled die-hard Culture Talk adepts such as Elie Kedourie, who argued that polls showing the majority of Egyptians demanding democracy and Shari'a are an indication that the Arabs do not understand what democracy is about: Kedourie, 1994: 1–2).

Out of that debate, a myriad of proposals emerged for forms of an 'Islamic' system of rule that usually combined an elected government with presumed safeguards to ensure that elected bodies would not transgress Shari'a. Many of the proponents of these models were reluctant to describe them as democratic. In fact, many were adamant that democracy and Islam were incompatible (El-Affendi, 2006). Maududi made the partial concession of calling his proposed system a 'theo-democracy', a partial democracy restricted by Islamic law (Adam, 1983: 117–26). This model was perfected in Khomeini's *wilayat al-faqih* (jurisdiction of the learned man) system currently being implemented in Iran. According to this formula, elected bodies should be constantly under the supervision of a *faqih*, a man of profound religious learning and integrity who has the power to overrule any decision deemed in contravention of Islamic law.

The emergence of Islamist visions of the state has become a hindrance to democratization on two counts. First, the Islamist–secularist divide has become the primary divide in Arab politics, hindering a democratic consensus and also giving autocratic regimes and their foreign backers excuses to avoid a commitment to democracy. The association of Islamism with violent resistance to Israel (Hamas, Hizbullah, etc.) and pro-Western regimes, not to mention terrorism, has been used as a pretext by Western powers not to support Arab democracy and, indeed, to endorse autocratic regimes.

Secondly, Islamist ideas and practices have themselves tended to be anti-democratic. Islamic rule in Iran and Sudan, and the anti-democratic models mentioned earlier, have tended both to build anti-democratic constituencies and to make democrats sceptical about the democratic commitments of Islamists, notwithstanding the fact that moderate Islamist groups have generally made these commitments.

As explained in some detail elsewhere,[3] the Islamist 'guardianship formulas' remain problematic because of a number of untenable assumptions underpinning them. For one thing, these formulas appear to assume that governance is essentially a judicial process, with the ruler assuming the role of a chief justice issuing rulings about conformity to law. That characterization of governance is too narrow. Governance is about much more than law enforcement, involving as it does the constant negotiation of rival demands, interests and perceptions. The skills required here are not merely those relevant to the task of determining conformity to law.

But even if we accept this characterization, it becomes difficult to reconcile the basic contradiction between two central presuppositions inherent in these models. At one level, treating the ruler as chief justice assumes that that Shari'a law has already been clarified and laid down sufficiently for a judge to implement. But in this case, the demand for a supremely pious and learned leader to help determine the law (and the wide area of discretion granted to him) becomes superfluous. That such an expert is called for seems to suggest that the law is not that clear, needing a special guide through its mazes. But if the law is not already laid down, a question arises as to whether one individual (or a small group of experts) is better placed to determine and expound on it than a larger pool of people, which is the essence of the anti-democratic prescriptions of the proponents of the model.

The anti-democratic ethos of these 'Islamic' models is underpinned by a further set of interconnected assumptions, starting with the common claim about Islamic teachings encompassing every facet of life, coupled with the claim that these teachings have already been clearly laid down in such a manner that the specific recommended 'Islamic' option in every case cannot be missed. In addition, it is assumed that all Islamic teachings could be subsumed under Shari'a, which must in turn be enforced by a public authority, or by the state. Finally, it is held that public opinion is not a reliable arbiter when seeking to determine what Islamic law dictates, and only specialized experts can tell us what the law is.

The problem with these assumptions is not only that Islamic teachings cannot be all subsumed under the law, but also that these teachings cannot be regarded as a long catalogue of 'off-the-shelf' rules that could be consulted on every occasion. In fact, Islamic teachings are not all legal injunctions, since the bulk are ethical norms requiring and offering a wide area of discretion and initiative. Also the myth that Islamic teachings cover every facet of life and offer ready guidance is contradicted by unequivocal Quranic verses demanding that believers should not ask too many questions of the Prophet (Quran 5: 101). This is, in turn, related to an incident when the Prophet became upset because one individual kept demanding unnecessary clarifications about a command he gave to perform a pilgrimage, prompting the Prophet to advise his audience not to risk burdening themselves with additional duties by asking for details.[4] This makes it clear that not only did Islam not have a rule for every conceivable situation, but that it is moreover a fundamental rule of Islam not to have such rules. This leaves the widest possible margin for initiative and fresh thinking on the most appropriate ethical conduct in all areas, including the area of governance, on which the texts say very little anyway.

The argument that an individual or a class of individuals is better placed to resolve matters of dispute than the community as a whole contradicts another fundamental Islamic tenet: that no priesthood is permitted or acceptable. The Quran condemns earlier religious communities for trusting too much in their 'priests and monks', to the extent that they have practically treated them as deities beside God (Quran 9: 31). It makes it clear time and time again that going astray by following the authority of 'our masters and nobles' is not an acceptable excuse in the eyes of God. Every individual is responsible for his/her own action, and only they are responsible (Quran 37: 28–35).

The Quranic injunctions against accepting authority (even presumed 'religious' authority) unquestioningly shift moral responsibility squarely onto the shoulders of the individual on the one hand, and the community as a whole on the other. This also rules out the prescription of the models generally offered as 'Islamic alternatives' to democracy. Ascribing 'religious authority' to an individual or a class contravenes the most fundamental Islamic tenet of all: the injunction against polytheism. A *khalifah* or a *faqih* who puts himself up as an absolute authority in fact claims divine powers for himself, an unacceptable situation that can only be negated if the individual in question becomes accountable to the community as a whole.

It would appear from the above that Islamic teachings are not only compatible with democracy, but demand it. For the assumption that the state, controlled by self-styled men of religion, is needed to guide the Muslim community to virtue, both robs the community of its autonomy without which it cannot perform its religious function and, more seriously, usurps God's own authority.

The challenge posed for Arab democracy by Islamist thought and practice is probably the most important one at the moment, and it needs to be tackled at several levels. The Islamists themselves need to revise their models in order to reflect Islam's true spirit, which is not only favourable to democracy, but is also, as we have shown above, one which finds democracy indispensable. Further, all political forces in the Arab world, including Islamists, need to build democratic coalitions constructed around mutual reassurances and understandings, with a commitment to peaceful coexistence and mutual recognition. This is necessary in order to deprive the despotic regimes of their divide-and-conquer advantage. Finally, a clear international stance in favour of democracy must be developed on the basis of the rejection of all excuses that maintain Arabs are not worthy of freedom for one reason or other. Nothing ever justifies the deprivation of whole peoples of their non-negotiable rights of self-determination and a life of freedom and security.

In particular, international support must be withdrawn from the militantly authoritarian 'secular fundamentalist' regimes which use opposition to Islamism as a pretext to deny fundamental rights. As Waines aptly put it,

> What is seldom acknowledged is that the strident authoritarian voices of contemporary religious fundamentalists have confronted for decades the powerful forces of secular fundamentalism, which have striven to eliminate them. One consequence of this has been the muting through co-optation by secular fundamentalists of the religiously authoritative voices of modernists.
>
> (Waines, 2003: 27)

While the Islamists certainly need to clean up their act in order to make a positive contribution to democratization, key obstacles to Arab democratization are the so-called 'eradicationists' (*Isti'saliyyin*), entrenched elites in countries like Algeria, Tunisia, Syria and Egypt who believe in the 'eradication' of Islamists by force, and in the process close all avenues of civil action in the name of combating fundamentalism.

6. The search for Arab democracy

The account above highlights some key issues impinging on the stubborn democracy deficit in the Arab world. The glaring absence of democracy in the Arab world is not in dispute. Between 1976 and 2006, not a single Arab country has been classified as free in the Freedom House annual survey. Polity IV scores tell a similar story. But it is not just the persistence of autocracy in the Arab world, but its depth. As Elbadawi and Makdisi (2007: 819) pointed out, 'even if we consider only authoritarian regimes, Arab dictatorships are the most oppressive, with a mean polity score of –7.8 compared to –5.2 for non-Arab regimes'.

> A similar story also emerges from comparing annual mean changes of Polity IV in and outside the Arab world . . . Out of 600 observations of change in the polity score for Arab states, only 31 of them are positive (i.e. associated with political liberalization or improved status of democracy).
> (Elbadawi and Makdisi, 2007: 819)

There are, of course, problems with both indexes, as they do not necessarily reflect accurately the existing conditions due to their reliance on subjective measures. Thus, unrealistically, the Polity IV index gives Libya a higher score than Qatar and UAE and equal to Bahrain, while Tunisia scores higher than Morocco.

More recently, Saliba Sarsar tried to develop a composite index that

> quantifies democratization through consideration of multiple variables: four variables address governance and representative government. These mark how heads of state and members of the legislature are selected, as well as political party development, suffrage, and the maturity of political rights and civil liberties. The annual Freedom House survey provides a fifth variable measuring media freedom. Measurements of religious liberty can be derived from US Department of State reports. A seventh addresses the observance of human rights with the information from Amnesty International, Human Rights Watch, and the US Department of State. The United Nations Development Program's human development index provides a measurement of human development. The Heritage Foundation's index of economic freedom quantifies economic freedom. The status of democracy index assigns each of these nine variables 2 points for a total of 18 points. Each score ranges from 0 to 2, with 0 being nonexistent and 2 being the highest measurement.
> (Sarsar, 2006)

On this basis, Arab states were ranked according to performance, with Morocco at the top, with 11 points, and Saudi Arabia at the bottom, with 2.5 in 1999. In the 2005 rankings, Saudi Arabia was given 4, but still remained at the bottom, while Morocco was downgraded to 8, leaving Jordan and Lebanon at the top spot with 10.5 each (the same ratings they had in 1999). Again, many of the rankings display anomalies, ranking Libya, Bahrain, Oman and Qatar on the same level (5 points; Qatar was raised to 6 in 2005), while Tunisia is given a score of 10 (9 in 2005), well above UAE (6) and one point above Kuwait (9, downgraded to 8.5 in 2005). At 8.5 points (downgraded to 7 in 2005), Syria also towers above most of these countries, and was level with Yemen (raised to 9 in 2005). Clearly, there is also something fundamentally wrong with this classification (Sarsar, 2006).[5]

However, the overall picture cannot be mistaken. The 2004 *Arab Human Development Report* (AHDR, 2005), confirms this reading, further noting the convergence of Arab regimes into an authoritarian model it dubs 'the Black Hole State', a polity that collapses on itself by concentrating power at the centre, normally in the hands of one person or a small clique, assisted by draconian measures and an overpowering repressive apparatus (AHDR, 2005: ch. 5).

In the 2003 report, the AHDR cited empirical evidence from the World Values Survey (WVS) that directly contradicts the Culture Talk explanation of the Arab situation. The survey has shown that the population of Arab countries values democracy as 'the best form of government', higher than any other region in the world. Its score in rejecting authoritarianism is also the highest, significantly higher, in fact, than the population of Western Europe in both scores (AHDR, 2003: 19). The 2004 report conducted surveys of its own that confirmed this inclination (AHDR, 2005: 89–98).

Other empirical analyses based on the WVS and other data further revealed that 'Islamic orientations and attachments have, at most, a very limited impact on views about democracy' (Tessler, 2002: 240). This was further confirmed by empirical research conducted specifically to test Francis Fukuyama's assertion that 'Islam has stood as a major barrier to democratization', using data from several Arab and Muslim countries (Al-Braizat, 2002). Again, the overwhelming evidence suggests that Arabs value democracy highly, and have no particular tolerance (as measured by attitude surveys) for authoritarianism, even among the religious, thus squarely disproving Fukuyama's claims (Al-Braizat, 2002: 280–6).

> The correlation between support for [democracy] as a very good way of governance and religiosity is insignificant although slightly positive. Predominantly Islamic societies show very high levels of support for [democracy] as a very good way of governing their countries, while simultaneously showing high levels of religiosity.
>
> (Al-Braizat, 2002: 281)

Al-Braizat goes further, finding a strong correlation between the Human Development Index (HDI) and the actual progress to democratization. While support for democracy in most Muslim countries remains high, actual democratization (as measured in years of uninterrupted democracy) correlates positively with HDI and negatively with religiosity (Al-Braizat, 2002: 288–90). Al-Braizat takes this to reflect a correlation between actual democratization and modernization, since he assumes a correlation between modernization and decline of religious observance, in line with classical modernization theory.

A similar stance in support of modernization theory is taken by Epstein *et al.* (2006), who take issue with the influential challenge by Przeworski *et al.* (2000) to the theory's central assumption regarding the correlation between modernization (as measured in terms of per capita GDP growth) and democratization. Przeworski and his associates tried to show that the positive association between high GDP and democracy only 'results from the reduced likelihood of modern countries sliding back, as it were, into undemocratic forms of government once having (randomly) become democratic' (Epstein *et al.*, 2006: 551).

Using polity scores, Epstein *et al.* (2006) try to disprove the Przeworski thesis by introducing a third category of partial democracies (Przeworski *et al.* use only two categories of democratic and authoritarian regimes). After correcting for some 'errors' in the Przeworski *et al.* models, they claim to have reestablished the finding that 'high incomes per capita significantly increased the likelihood of democratic regimes, both by enhancing the consolidation of existing democracies and by promoting transitions from authoritarian to democratic systems' (Epstein *et al.*, 2006: 566).

However, another study using the same polity scores has concluded that, regardless of its merits, the modernization hypothesis does not work in the Arab world (Elbadawi and Makdisi, 2007). In fact, the richer oil-producing Arab countries, whose per capita GDP is topped only by the OECD income levels, have consistently obtained the lowest polity scores, with some scoring –10 for prolonged periods. Ironically, while income levels in most Arab countries were higher than the median income in developing countries worldwide, Arab countries lagged behind developing countries in democracy as reflected in polity scores, while the sporadic spells of democratization occurred mainly in the poorer Arab countries (Elbadawi and Makdisi, 2007: 820–2).

The research by Elbadawi and Makdisi uncovers another interesting anomaly pertaining to the Arab world: that 'while regional military conflicts are positively associated with democracy . . . [with] conflicts usually lead[ing] to democratic transformation, the Arab region has been an exception' (Elbadawi and Makdisi, 2007: 828). The authors attribute this anomaly, represented by the tenacious hold on power by regimes after being defeated in war, to the fact that 'the highly polarized and emotional discourse created by the Arab–Israeli conflict and the perceived adversarial global power interventions in the region have provided potent arguments for authoritarian Arab regimes to escape accountability for disastrous failures, including major military defeats' (Elbadawi and Makdisi, 2007: 829).

7. Exceptionalism and the 'missing bourgeoisie'

This important insight takes us back to the Napoleon–Saddam Syndrome, the persistent pathology specific to the Arab region in particular and the Middle East in general. As noted, the remarks attributed to former Israeli Prime Minister Barak show that 'the highly polarized and emotional discourse' is not restricted to the Arab arena, while the sense of siege and isolation reflected in Barak's remarks also animates the discourse of entrenched and increasingly beleaguered Arab regimes to justify their brutality, by citing both foreign threats and the internal threat of chaos and mayhem. If we observe democratic norms and human rights, their argument goes, all will be lost. Enemies of the people (or civilization or religion or freedom) will take over (Zakaria, 2001).

The convergence in attitudes between the alien invaders and occupiers (Israelis, Americans in Iraq) and the local despots in advancing the claims that the Arab region is a brutal jungle where violence and repression are needed to keep order, betrays deeper structural similarities between the forces of alien occupation, and the indigenous post-colonial state which has inherited the colonial legacy and sought to perpetuate it. Rather than reflecting the cultural traits of the region, both structures betray their alien nature vis-à-vis the region and its peoples. As the Tunisian activist Moncef Marzouki (see below) and others argue, the current despotic Arab state has come to resemble an alien occupation.

While there is clearly a difference in the degree of alienation between foreign colonial forces (in particular, Israeli settler colonialism) and home-grown despotism, there are also some significant parallels. If Israel believes itself to be an alien entity facing rejection, the state in the Arab world is equally alien and at war with society (Ayubi, 1995: 442–4). The 'Black Hole State' is one that is engaged in trench warfare with the population under it, seeing in every move within civil society a threat, every independent economic development a mortal danger (AHDR, 2005).

Again, it is not the fact that the Arabs 'were rather slow in internalizing the concept of the state itself, or the "ethics" of public service and the attitudes of collective action' (Ayubi, 1995: 22). Rather, it is the fact that the state, 'an "imported commodity," partly under colonial pressure and partly under the influence of imitation and mimicry' (Ayubi, 1995: 21), continued to arrogate to itself the privileges and powers of the colonial state it had inherited. It jealously safeguarded its autonomy from society and has sought to rely more and more on foreign support.

This character of the state has made it precarious and vulnerable. In this regard, 'the violence of this state is in reality an indication of its weakness and fragility' rather than its strength (Ayubi, 1995: 23). In fact, violence and constant war against societies ensures that the result will be 'both a weak state and a weak society, with the forces of coercion and repression taking charge and acting largely on their own behalf' (Sluglett, 2007: 100).

The fact that a number of Arab states have come to resemble occupation powers is dialectically related to the tendency of some opposition groups to seek foreign support and even court foreign occupation (or presence) in their counties.[6] In Iraq, first the Kurds and later other Iraqis sought foreign protection against the brutalities of the former regime. In Libya and later in Sudan, the opposition sought foreign support to topple the regime and, in the case of Sudan, supported the presence of foreign troops to protect civilians. It thus appears that for at least certain opposition groups the regimes they oppose are seen as worse than foreign occupation.

The Arab situation is further complicated by a precarious and conflictual regional system, which had its local 'cold war' between radicals and conservatives between the 1950s and 1970s, and structural dependency on the outside world (Kerr, 1971; Al-Naqib, 1996: 45–56; Ayubi, 1995: 172). This combination of regional volatility and 'imperialist penetration' has coalesced to bring about the practical disintegration of the system following the Iraqi invasion of Kuwait in 1990, and the arrival of US-led foreign troops into the region. At the very moment when Soviet troops were leaving Eastern Europe to pave the way for independence and democratization, foreign troops were pouring into the region to back authoritarian regimes. More troops have since arrived and vast funds have also been deployed to support favoured regimes.

The aftermath of September 11 reinforced these trends. The USA and its allies became even more involved in the region's affairs; Israel under Sharon became even more repressive and nihilistic; regimes grew even more repressive, incompetent and devoid of legitimacy; and the region's people continued to feel even more resentment and frustration. The impression created by American leaders that the US intervention in the region would herald a new era of democratic reform, and their promises which inspired a few, including members of the 'liberal' opposition in Saudi Arabia, Kuwait and other Gulf states, and some opposition activists in Iraq, Syria, Egypt and elsewhere at the end of 1990,[7] lay in ruins, buried, together with many other hopes and promises, under the rubble of destroyed Palestinian homes and devastated Iraqi cities. Everything pointed to system meltdown.

In view of all this, it can be argued that the reason why the Middle East remains inhospitable to democracy is the same reason why it also remains inhospitable to the rise of an autonomous and influential bourgeoisie. The indigenous bourgeoisie bears the stamp of this war environment. Where the state acts as a 'protection racket', and manages the economy as if it was at war with important sections of society, the bourgeoisie will have to adapt and join the racketeers, despots or warlords. Otherwise, it stands no chance. In most Arab countries the state manipulates economic measures for political ends.

In any case, the region's ruling elite have sought to pre-empt the anticipated bourgeois revolution by engineering a 'bourgeois' revolution of their own. Emulating the model that evolved in the Gulf, the elites in other countries embarked on their own ingenious schemes of privatization: the state itself was now privatized, becoming the preserve of the ruling families and their allies in the ruling 'political parties', which are no more than coalitions of self-interest.

This trend has led to a convergence between monarchies and republics in the Arab Middle East, leading to the term *jumlukiyya* (coined by Saad Eddin Ibrahim), or monarchic-republic, to refer to the new privatized polity, where rule is 'all in the family', passing from father to son and shared within the family during the life of the founder of the ruling family. The old and new monarchies not only foster divisions by sect, class or ethnicity, but also work to create a new 'aristocracy', made up of a favoured class, segregated physically and emotionally from the masses of poor who are relegated to shanty towns, inner cities and rural areas. The phenomenon is akin to internal colonialism, with the privileged rich acting like a settler community. This has led one commentator to liken the new class to the Janissaries, or Memlukes, the professional 'mercenary' class of slave soldiers used by the ruling elites since the late Abbasid period as a tool of subjugating the populace (Umaymur, 2006). Another commentator who despaired of reform in his country was led to argue that this 'internal colonialism' made the function of political opposition redundant, calling instead for a culture and approach of (peaceful) resistance to this virtual colonialism (Marzouki, 2006).

More significantly, the new regimes appear to have in fact almost abolished the public–private distinction, leaving the state elite to treat both as a legitimate domain. In this regard, it is 'only the traditional artisan-commercial sector in some countries and the emerging so-called "Islamic business" sector in other countries that can claim a relative (but by no means absolute) degree of autonomy from the state' (Ayubi, 1995: 404). In any case, the rentier state has less need of the bourgeoisie than the latter has of the state.

Against this background, we need to be reminded that the appearance of an *independent* bourgeoisie signals the end result, and not the starting point, of the 'bourgeois revolution'. The bourgeoisie (and the mythical 'McWorld' of globalization) begin to have the magical powers ascribed to them only after many of the transformations ascribed to the bourgeoisie have already taken place. Political structures and cultural orientations which could oversee and underpin the atomization of society, the dissolution of feudal or traditional bonds, a massive urbanization, relative indifference to religious strictures, the pauperization and uprooting of farm labourers, etc., had to be already in place for capitalism to grow. In particular, a relatively impartial state which is not also a private business enterprise is absolutely essential.

This requires not only a 'disenchanted' world where 'rationality' rules, but also a trivialized world where actions and events are stripped of momentous significance. Secularization does not bring about indifference to religious issues; it is widespread indifference to religious issues that enables secularization. An 'enchanted' world is not only populated by spirits and spiritual individuals and communities, it is also haunted by taboos and horrors of 'unspeakable' acts: sacrilege, sexual deviance, threats to cultural identity and cohesion, etc. A disenchanted world, by contrast, is a bland universe of acts which are indifferently alike. The area of what is considered 'private', what is regarded by the state and society as a matter of indifference, expands to cover almost every aspect of personal and social conduct.

In the case of the Middle East, the trend has been moving in the other direction. It is true that in some countries economic liberalism has made some progress. In places like the United Arab Emirates, and in particular its thriving emirate of Dubai, the system has witnessed some reform and streamlining. While the 'family business' is still the largest one there is, the thriving economy is currently the most open in the Arab world. However, Dubai has been criticized for having achieved its success by becoming a site of runaway globalization where the creation of wealth is deliberately de-linked from citizenship rights (Devji, 2005). The nearby state of Qatar is also moving in the same direction of the liberalized bourgeois state, but has additionally institutionalized the distinction between the private wealth of the rulers and state revenues. It has also taken tentative steps towards institutionalizing democratic citizenship. However, in all these countries, some very important taboos remain, most significantly with regard to political action. Governments regard any unsanctioned attempts at political or civil society organization as a very serious matter.

In recent decades, the region has also witnessed twin processes of Islamization and traditionalization. The first phenomenon is now well known and has been extensively studied. It has been reflected both in increased personal religious observance and also in membership of Islamic activist groups. Such groups tend to endow more and more social activities with religious meaning, and either encourage or oppose them on this basis. Most of these activities relate to sexual mores and the public conduct of women (Islamic dress, mixed dancing, etc.). Simultaneously with this, and even prior to it, some governments adopted a reverse attitude of investing personal and social acts (such as the wearing of headscarves by women) with utmost political significance, and treating them as a most serious threat. This contagion has now moved to Europe and beyond with the headscarves and *niqab* controversies.

At the same time, regimes in the area began to deliberately revive and exploit traditionalist social structures, such as tribes, clans, sects and rural dignitaries and heads of families, in their bid to strengthen their hold on power and to further marginalize the rebellious intelligentsia from which came most of the opposition to their rule. Opposition groups also resorted to the mobilization of sectarian, ethnic and tribal identities in order to fight back, while ordinary citizens sought protection from the threat of the expanding authoritarian state in these traditional bonds, a process made more imperative by the deliberate weakening of any viable civil society mechanisms of defence or solidarity.

To top it off, the 'distorted' and 'dysfunctional' (from the perspective of free-market theorists) systems have been sustained and subsidized by a 'pyramid scheme' of complex local, regional and international alliances, which kept them going at an ever rising cost. We point here to the huge rents emanating from oil, aid, strategic assets, etc., as well as alliances with tribal or religious elites, the secular intelligentsia, sections of the military, Islamist groups, and sectarian or regional interests. The regimes that participated in the 1990–1 war on Iraq, for example, received massive foreign funding vital for their longevity at a time when dictatorships in Eastern Europe and elsewhere were unravelling.

The overall picture illustrates how the 'pyramid scheme' of distorting factors, which includes the input of major Western powers, operates to nullify any presumed impact of class polarization. While these factors apply mainly to the Arab political arena, they also apply to Israel, a heavily subsidized entity which is founded on very 'unbourgeois', if not anti-bourgeois, principles. The aspirations to build an exclusive religious-ethnic state in a hostile environment, and the paranoid sentiments inherited from memory of the Holocaust and the perceived threat of annihilation, cause Israel to embody the ethos of Barber's 'jihad'. Ironically, however, this 'jihad' is unsustainable without the heavy external subsidies and the complex networks of economic and political support which keep Israel plugged into McWorld. The resulting strong and modernized economy helps to subsidize a host of unproductive or counterproductive activities and make it financially attractive enough for bourgeois families to abandon the bastions of McWorld in Europe and the USA for a life on the frontline settlements on the hills of Judea. The generous flow of external resources has helped this extraordinary juxtaposition of jihad and McWorld. In the subsidized settlements, the profit motive and religious activism are satisfied in one move, and the salvation ideology meshes beautifully with the bourgeois economy.

The USA, which has had its own contingent of militias, Armageddonites and other jihadists since the 1970s (Barber, 2003; El-Affendi, 2004b), has been a long-term contributor to jihadism in the region. It funds and backs extremist settler groups in Israel as it had earlier backed jihadists in Afghanistan. Recently, Washington itself has begun to look and sound more like Jerusalem and Baghdad than Jefferson's capital. The Napoleon–Saddam Syndrome is catching up not only in Gaza, South Lebanon, Abu Ghraib and Baghdad's Green Zone, but also in Guantanamo and the Beltway. Dealing with the 'Middle Eastern Question' has thus become essential not only to bring peace and stability to the region, but also for the health of the world's major democracies.

As this author has explained in detail elsewhere, contrary to its declared announcements about promoting democracy in the Middle East, the real problem with US policy in the region has been its contravention of every democratic norm when dealing with the region's peoples (El-Affendi, 2005, 2004b). American jihadism in the region has triggered a powerful defensive reaction in the Muslim world, further undermining the prospects for democracy.

One can thus argue that the central issue relating to democratization in the Arab world pertains to the robustness of authoritarian regimes and their sources of power, given the nature of the alien state and the widespread opposition to despotism and alien control. As Eva Bellin perceptively put it:

> Thus, the solution to the puzzle of Middle Eastern and North African exceptionalism lies less in the absent prerequisites of democratization and more in present conditions that foster robust authoritarianism, specifically a robust coercive apparatus in these states. The will and capacity of the state's coercive apparatus to suppress democratic initiatives have extinguished the possibility of transition. Herein lies the region's true exceptionalism.
> (Bellin, 2004: 143)

The robustness of the coercive apparatus of the Arab state is derived from ample resources put at its disposal by the states (and their foreign backers); the reassurance and legitimacy provided by international networks of support; the patrimonial nature of the state; and its security apparatus, where private links of kin and patronage reinforce loyalty and demobilize the opposition. The beleaguered opposition is, in turn, weakened and discouraged from mounting campaigns due to the harsh measures deployed against it (Bellin, 2004: 144–7).

8. Conclusion

It can thus be concluded that neither a presumed cultural aversion to democracy nor an underdeveloped class structure can be said to be responsible for the turbulent politics of the Middle East. The structural causes of the region's dysfunctional politics stem from its 'haunted' (as opposed to 'disenchanted') character. Nothing here is permitted to be trivial or mundane. Every stone, every barren desert strip, is 'strategically important' or 'holy'. Every actor, including the USA and Israel, has a messianic project, a sacred cause, a vital interest. Nothing is treated as trivial or neutral. On the contrary, everything here, from food to dress, from language to cities, is invested with an irreplaceable value. As Reza Aslan points out, in this region, 'the personal is political, and religion is always both' (Aslan, 2005).

This has little to do with ingrained cultural traits and a lot to do with conscious political choices. The entrenched despotic regimes have deliberately (and sometimes inadvertently) engineered modes of polarization that would make their despotic ways look as if they are the last bulwark against the total disintegration of their countries. In their desperation to remain in power, even 'progressive' regimes (including the Ba'ath regimes in Iraq and Syria, and even the former Communist regime in Yemen) cultivated tribal or sectarian loyalties, and played group against group. By posing as arbiters between these polarized groups, they have engineered a latent civil war that continues by 'peaceful' means, refereed by a despot who continues to blackmail society with this threat. Like a terrorist with an explosive belt, the despot makes sure that, if he goes, the whole house will go up in flames.

The USA, Israel and other intruders have acted in the same way. These intruders brought over their own messianic projects to rival the region's resident messianism. A British minister recently argued that Afghanistan is now the 'new Cliffs of Dover', implying that ending the occupation there would be like abandoning Britain's southern coast! This echoes the rhetoric of Israeli officials about Jerusalem being the 'eternal and undivided capital of Israel', thus ruling out any compromise or negotiations. These foreign actors also emulate local despots in creating and fostering, in their desperation, polarized identities that end up holding them and everyone else hostage. This can be seen in the way sectarianism has been fostered in Iraq and encouraged in Lebanon.

This goes to support our point that the infectious 'Napoleon–Saddam Syndrome' is linked closely to the Machiavellian short-sightedness of political actors, including foreign actors. The frequent flare-ups that have raised the region's political temperatures to volcanic levels have a little to do with the region's history and a lot to do with its present. It is not only that we are faced here with a durable coalition of opportunist and messianic actors who believe that too much is at stake for one to bother about such mundane concerns as majority opinion, the rate of profit, budget deficit, bourgeois pleasures or even life itself. What is more alarming is that, in the shadow of these coalitions, extremely dangerous and disturbing structures of domination and disenfranchisement are becoming so entrenched and so alien that the amount of violence required to dislodge them will be phenomenal. Instead of progressing towards the open spaces of the bourgeois revolution, the systems here are recreating the Ancien Régime. The guillotine is sure to follow.

The despotic order in the Arab world is not a reflection of the region's cultural preferences. Had it been so, then there would have been no need for the extreme violence being deployed by regimes to maintain their grip on power. As Bellin rightly pointed out, the issue here is not the preferences of the locals, but the ability of the regimes to defy these preferences. This happens due to the patrimonial nature of the repressive apparatus, which combines sectarian and clannish links to isolate itself from the polarized society, and the ample resources and international support it enjoys. It is this extreme situation, and the mounting resistance to it, that fosters the polarization and extremism infecting the region.

From Napoleon to Bush, and the numerous local despots in between, the modern state in the Arab world (and its allies and adversaries, including Israel) is at war with the people. As the resistance to it mounted, it also worked to increase its repressive capacity, culminating in the 'Black Hole State' which tolerates no opposition and no independent civil society or economic sphere. As Ayubi and others rightly pointed out, this has also shaped opposition to these regimes. The Islamist or tribalist/ethnic character of the opposition reflects in part the nature of the enclaves the repressive state has failed to subjugate. The polarization and rising tension has become self-reinforcing. The regimes use the uncompromising stance of the radical opposition to convince the elite that it is the lesser of two evils, and to secure foreign support against the perceived threats of 'fundamentalism' and chaos.

There are nevertheless, positive signs. Arab intellectuals, politicians and civil society actors are realizing more and more that this situation is no longer tenable. Nascent coalitions of democrats, including moderate Islamists, are emerging to challenge authoritarian regimes. In spite of brutal crackdowns and deliberate attempts to sow divisions, the movements persist, and others are emulating their action. That is where the future of the Arab world lies.

Notes

1 For the record, we should note here that Barber tried to revise this thesis in a lecture delivered at the University of Westminster in May 2005 under the title: 'Islam and Democracy: Compatibility or Clash of Civilisations?'
2 See Said 1978, 1985, 2003.
3 See El-Affendi 2006.
4 According to a report in the authoritative compendiums of Bukhari and Muslim, 'the Prophet (peace be upon him) said in a sermon: "O people! Allah has prescribed Hajj for you, so you must perform it.' A man asked: 'Every year, O Prophet of Allah?" The Prophet (peace be upon him) remained silent. When the man repeated it thrice, the Prophet (peace be upon him) said: "Had I said 'yes', it would have become a yearly obligation, and this would have been beyond your power." Then he added: "Leave me alone so long as I leave you alone (i.e. do not pester me with questions about things which I omit and do not mention). Some people who lived before you were destroyed because they asked too many questions and disagreed with their Prophets. So when I command you to do something, do it to the best of your power, and if I forbid you from something, then just avoid it" (Bukhari and Muslim, quoted in Nasir al-Din al-Albani, 1995: 505).
5 The author does not indicate at what point a country would be considered democratic, but appears to suggest that no Arab country is fully democratic.
6 Related to this is the observation that, in some Arab countries, 'the rudimentary parliamentary regimes of the mandate period... should continue to arouse a degree of nostalgia among those old enough to remember them' (Sluglett, 2007: 97).

7 Encouraged by promises given by US officials, a group of women demonstrated in Riyadh in late 1990 to demand the right to drive cars, while a group of forty 'liberal' personalities submitted a memorandum to the King in early 1991 asking for political reforms and more freedoms.

References

Abdalla, I. S. (1998) 'al-Muqawwimat al-Iqtisadiyya wa'l-Ijtima'iyya li'l-Dimuqratiyya fi'l-Watan al-'Arabi', in Hilal *et al.*, 1998: 105–21.

Abu-Rabi, I. M. (2004) *Contemporary Arab Thought: Studies in Post-1967 Arab Intellectual History*, London: Pluto Press.

Adam, C. J. (1983) 'Maududi and the Islamic State', in John Esposito (ed.), *Voices of Resurgent Islam*, Oxford: Oxford University Press: 99–123.

AHDR (Arab Human Development Report) (2002) *Arab Human Development Report 2002: Creating Opportunities for Future Generations*, New York: UNDP.

—— (2003) *Arab Human Development Report: Building a Knowledge Society*, New York: UNDP.

—— (2005) *Arab Human Development Report 2004: Towards Freedom in the Arab World*, New York: UNDP.

Al-Braizat, F. (2002) 'Muslims and Democracy, an Empirical Critique of Fukuyama's Culturalist Approach', *International Journal of Comparative Sociology* 43/3–5: 269–99.

Al-Din al-Albani, N. (1995) *Silsilat al-Ahadith al-Sahiha*, vol. 2, Riyadh: Maktabat al-Ma'arif.

Almond, G. A. (1994) 'Foreword', in Diamond, 1994: pp. ix–xii.

Al-Naqib, K. (1996) *Sira' alqbilah wa'l-Dimuqratiyyah: Halat al-Kuwait*, London: Dar al-Saqi.

Anderson, L. (1995) 'Democracy in the Arab World: A Critique of the Arab Culture Approach', in Brynen *et al.*, 1995: 77–92.

Aslan, R. (2005) 'Aunt Kobra's Islamic Democracy', *The Boston Globe* (17 April). Online at: www.boston.com/news/globe/ideas/articles/2005/04/17/aunt_kobras_islamic_democracy?pg=full

Ayubi, N. (1995) *Overstating the Arab State*, London: I. B. Tauris.

Barak, E. (1999) 'Speech to the National Defense College', 12 Aug. Online at: www.israel-mfa.gov.il/mfa/go.asp?MFAH0fh80 (Israel Foreign Ministry website).

Barber, B. R. (2003) *Jihad versus McWorld*, London: Corgi Books.

Beetham, D. (1993) 'Liberal Democracy and the Limits of Democratization', in Held, 1993: 55–73.

Bellin, E. (2004) 'The Robustness of Authoritarianism in the Middle East: Exceptionalism in Comparative Perspective', *Comparative Politics* 36/2 (Jan.):139–57.

Binder, L. (1988) *Islamic Liberalism: A Critique of Development Ideologies*, Chicago: University of Chicago Press.

Blondel, J. (1998) 'Democracy and Constitutionalism', in Inoguchi *et al.*, 1998: 71–86.

Brynen, R. *et al.*, eds (1995) *Political Liberalization and Democratization in the Arab World*, vol. 1, *Theoretical Perspectives*, Boulder, CO: Lynne Rienner.

Bulliet, R. (2007) 'Bush and Napoleon', *International Herald Tribune* (2 Aug.). Online at: www.nytimes.com/2007/08/02/opinion/02iht-edbulliet.1.6957129.html?r=1

CAUS (Centre for Arab Unity Studies) (1998) Centre for Arab Unity Studies 1998: *al. Dimuqratiyya wa Huquq al.Insan fi%Watan a;'Arabi*, Beirut.

Cole, J. (2007) 'Bush's Napoleonic Folly', *The Nation* (24 Aug). Online at: www.globalpolicy.org/component/content/article/168/36520.html

Crick, B. (1998) 'A Meditation on Democracy', in Inoguchi *et al.*, 1998: 255–65.

Dahl, R. (1989) *Democracy and its Critics*, New Haven, CT: Yale University Press.
Devji, F. (2005) *Landscapes of the Jihad: Militancy, Morality, Modernity*, Ithaca, NY: Cornell University Press.
Diamond, L., ed. (1994) *Political Culture and Democracy in Developing Countries*, Boulder, CO: Lynne Rienner.
El-Affendi, A. (2004a) 'On the State, Democracy and Pluralism', in Taji-Farouki and B. M. Nafi (eds), *Islamic Thought in the Twentieth Century*, London: I. B. Tauris: 172–94.
—— (2004b) 'Armageddon: The "Mother of All Empires" and its Middle Eastern Quagmire', in D. Held and M. Koenig-Archibugi (eds), *American Power in the 21st Century*, Queensland: Polity Press.
—— (2005) 'The Conquest of Muslim Hearts and Minds? Perspectives on U.S. Reform and Public Diplomacy Strategies', Brookings Project on US Policy towards the Islamic World, Working Paper, Sept.
—— (2006) 'Democracy and its (Muslim) Critics: An Islamic Alternative to Democracy?', in M. Khan (ed.), *Islamic Democratic Discourse*, Lanham, MD: Lexington Books: 227–56.
—— (2008) *Who Needs an Islamic State?* (2nd edn), London: Malaysian Think Tank London.
Elbadawi, I. and Makdisi, S. (2007) 'Explaining the Democracy Deficit in the Arab World', *Quarterly Review of Economics and Finance* 46/5 (Feb.).
Elhadj, E. (2007) *The Islamic Shield: Arab Resistance to Democratic and Religious Reforms*, Boca Raton, FL: Brown Walker Press.
Epstein, D. L., Bates, R., Goldstone, J., Kristensen, I., and O'Halloran, S. (2006) 'Democratic Transitions', *American Journal of Political Science* 50/3: 551–69.
Farazmand, A. and Pinkowski, J., eds (2006) *Handbook of Globalization, Governance, and Public Administration*, London: CRC Press.
Flower, R. (1972) *Napoleon to Nasser: The Story of Modern Egypt*, London: Tom Stacey.
Hamoudi, A. (2000) *al-Shaykh wa'l-murid: al-nasaq al-thaqafi li'l-sultah fi'l-mujtama at al-Arabiyah al-hadīthah*, tr. Abd al-Majīd Jahfah, Casablanca: Dar Tubqal.
Hanafi, H. 'Al-Judhur al-Tairikhiyya li-azmat al-Hurriyya wa'l-Dimuqratiyya fi Wujdanina al-Mu'asir', in Hilal *et al.*, 1998: 175–89.
Held, D. (ed.) (1993) *Prospects for Democracy*, Cambridge: Polity.
Hersh, S. (2004a) 'Annals of National Security: Torture at Abu Ghraib', *The New Yorker* (10 May). Online at: www.newyorker.com/archive/2004/05/10/040510fa_fact
—— (2004b) *Chain of Command: The Road from 9/11 to Abu Ghraib*, New York: HarperCollins.
Hilal, A.(1998) 'Muqaddima: al-Dimuqratiyya wa Humum al-Insan al-'Arabi al-Mu'asir', in CAUS, 1998: 7–21.
Hudson, M. (1995) 'The Political Culture Approach to Arab Democratization: The Case for Bringing it Back in, Carefully', in Brynen *et al.*, 1995: 61–76.
Huntington, S. P. (1993) 'The Clash of Civilizations', *Foreign Affairs* (Summer): 22–49.
Inoguchi, T., Neman, E. and Keane, J., eds (1998) *The Changing Nature of Democracy*, Tokyo: United Nations University Press.
Ismael, S. (1995) 'Democracy in Contemporary Arab Intellectual Discourse', in Brynen *et al.*, 1995: 93–112.
Kedourie, E. (1994) *Democracy and Arab Political Culture*, Washington, DC: Washington Institute for Near East Policy.
Kerr, M. (1971) *The Arab Cold War: Gamal 'Abd Al-Nasir and his Rivals, 1958–1970*, London: Oxford University Press for the Royal Institute of International Affairs.

Lewis, B. (1990) 'The Roots of Muslim Rage', *Atlantic Monthly* (Sept.). Online at: www.theatlantic.com/doc/199009/muslim-rage

Linz, J. and Stepan, A. (1998) 'Towards Consolidated Democracy', in Inoguchi *et al.*, 1998: 48–67.

Mamdani, M. (2005) *Good Muslim, Bad Muslim: America, the Cold War, and the Roots of Terror*, New York: Three Leaves.

Manji, I. (2004) *The Trouble with Islam: A Muslim's Call for Reform in her Faith*, Edinburgh: Mainstream.

Marzouki, M. (2006) 'al-Muqawama: al-Hal wa'l-Wajib al-Akhir', *al-Ma'rifa* (10 Oct.). Online at: www.libya.alhora.com/forum/showthread.php?t=9218

Miller, J. (1993) 'The Challenge of Radical Islam', *Foreign Affairs* (Spring).

Norton, R. (1995) *Civil Society in the Middle East*, vols 1 and 2, Leiden: E. J. Brill.

Parekh, B. (1995) 'The Cultural Particularity of Liberal Democracy', in Held, 1993: 156–75.

Plattner, M. (1998) 'Liberalism and Democracy: Can't Have One without the Other', *Foreign Affairs* (March/April). Online at: www.foreignaffairs.org/19980301faresponse1382/marc-f-plattner/liberalism-and-democracy-can-t-have-one-without-the-other.html

—— (1999) 'From Liberalism to Liberal Democracy', *Journal of Democracy*, 10/3 (July): 121–34.

Przeworski, A., Alvarez, M., Cheibub, J. and Limongi, F. (2000) *Democracy and Development*, New York: Cambridge University Press.

Rajiva, L. (2005) *The Language of Empire: Abu Ghraib and the American Media*, New York: Monthly Review Press.

Sadiki, L. (2004) *The Search for Arab Democracy: Discourses and Counter-Discourses*, London: C. Hurst.

Said, E. (1978) *Orientalism*, New York: Pantheon.

—— (1985) 'Orientalism Reconsidered', *Race Class* 27.

—— (2003) 'Orientalism 25 Years Later', *Counter Punch* (4 Aug.).

Salamé, G. (ed.) (1994) *Democracy without Democrats? The Renewal of Politics in the Muslim World*, London: I. B. Tauris.

Sarsar, S. (2006) 'Quantifying Arab Democracy: Democracy in the Middle East', *Middle East Quarterly* (Summer): 21–8. Online at: www.meforum.org/article/970

Sharabi, H. (1988) *Neopatriarchy: A Theory of Distorted Change in Arab Society*, New York: Oxford University Press.

—— (1992) *Al-Nizam al-Abawi*, Beirut: Centre for Arab Unity Studies.

Sluglett, P. (2007) 'The Ozymandias Syndrome: Questioning the Stability of Middle Eastern Regimes', in O. Schlumberger (ed.), *Debating Arab Authoritarianism: Dynamics and Durability in Nondemocratic Regimes*, Palo Alto, CA: Stanford University Press.

Tarabishi, G. (2006) *Hartaqat*, London: Dar al-Saqi.

Tessler, M. (2002) 'Do Islamic Orientations Influence Attitudes toward Democracy in the Arab World? Evidence from Egypt, Jordan Morocco, and Algeria', *International Journal of Comparative Sociology* 43/3–5: 229–49.

Umaymur, M. (2006) 'al-Inkishariyyun al-Judud wa Dhayl al-Asad', *Al-Quds al-Arabi* (20 Nov.): 18.

Waines, D. (2003) 'Religion and Modernity: Reflections on a Modern Debate', *ISIM Newsletter* (12 June): 27.

Waterbury, J. (1994) 'Democracy without Democrats? The Potential for Political Liberalization in the Middle East', in Salamé, 1994: 23–47.

Wedeen, L. (2002) 'Conceputalizing Culture: Possibilities for Political Science', *American Political Science Review* 96/4 (Dec.): 713–28.
Zakaria, F. (1997) 'The Rise of Illiberal Democracy', *Foreign Affairs* (Nov./Dec.).
—— (2001) 'How to Save the Arab World', *Newsweek* (24 Dec., US edn). Online at: www.fareedzakaria.com/articles/newsweek/122401_how.html

2 Explaining the Arab democracy deficit

The role of oil and conflicts[1]

Ibrahim Elbadawi, Samir Makdisi and Gary Milante

1. Introduction

The Arab world initiated a short-lived move toward democratic practices in the 1950s that was reversed in the 1960s. While there was some limited progress on democratization in a few Arab states during the 1970s, the Arab world has generally failed to catch up with the rest of the world, falling further behind in the period following the breakup of the Soviet Union and the ushering in of the current era of globalization. Since the early 1990s, the distance between world and Arab median polity scores has widened dramatically, and authoritarian regimes have thrived in the Arab region, prompting the *Arab Human Development Report* (UNDP and Arab Fund for Economic and Social Development, 2002) to note that 'There is a substantial lag between the Arab countries and other regions in terms of participatory governance.' Despite predictions of democratization following economic development, this gap is widening, even with the extreme wealth in many of these countries. Arab autocracies have tended to survive much longer than the median length of regime of their type in the world, suggesting that there is something unique about the process of democratization in the Arab world.

Beyond the untold human suffering due to the denial of political rights and restrictions on civil liberties associated with authoritarian governance, there are also questions of whether lasting economic growth and equitable, sustainable development are possible in autocratic regimes. The dire consequences of the lack of participatory governance for protection of property rights, investment, growth and, hence, for the overall development agenda of the region, have been emphasized by several Arab writers.[2] The failures of Arab authoritarian regimes to sustain earlier gains, or to at least contain mounting economic and social crises of the Arab world, have been directly linked to the non-democratic and non-participatory nature of the regimes. In particular, the apparent difficulty of managing the consequences of frequent oil shocks – which affect all Arab countries, oil and non oil-producing alike – has been linked to the lack of political institutions for mediating the conflicting interests of various social groups in a way that ensures sustainability of growth-promoting policies and maintenance of a basic social development agenda.[3]

This chapter brings together results from two previous papers (Elbadawi and

Makdisi, 2007 and Elbadawi, Makdisi and Milante, 2006) and the most current research on democratization to explore these questions.[4] In the following section we discuss the past five decades of democratization in the Arab world. Then we consider three different measures of democracy (section 3) and introduce the variables associated with measuring democracy (section 4). In section 5 we present some tests to assess the impact of these variables and discuss the results of the tests. In a departure from the main analysis of the longer term determinants of the level of democracy, section 6 discusses the symbiotic relationship between past growth spells and the relatively short-run process of 'successful' democratization, as well as between successful democratization and subsequent growth.

2. Democratization in the Arab world

The Lipset hypothesis and modernization theory in general suggest that standard of living is the most robust determinant of a country's propensity to experience democracy.[5] While countries in the Arab world enjoyed substantial economic growth between the 1960s and the 1980s, it is puzzling that these gains have not been associated with increased political rights, much less full-scale democratization. This phenomenon suggests that, while economic progress may be necessary for political liberalization, it has not been a sufficient condition in the Arab world. In the Arab environment, history, conflicts and ideology appear to be more important in determining political progress. For example, it can be argued that during the 1960s and 1970s legitimacy was not necessarily derived from political liberalization but instead from ideologies associated with Arab nationalism, socialism and the declared struggle to liberate Palestine. These ideologies were promoted by the charisma of Egyptian President Gamal Abdel Nasser and other pan-Arab political forces, providing potent sources of legitimacy for many authoritarian Arab regimes. Even after the devastating defeat of Arab forces by Israel in 1967, some legitimacy was still derived from the October 1973 war, from the Arab performance on military and diplomatic fronts in the 1970s and, perhaps most significantly, through the effective use of the 'Arab oil weapon' – all serving to reinforce the spirit of Arab nationalism.

However, the rise of oil as a dominant influence in the Arab economies and the partial peace with Israel ushered the region into a new era of political pragmatism that lasted into the 1990s and, arguably, to the present day. While the oil-rich Arab states were able to enjoy prosperity without extension of the political franchise,[6] this also created unprecedented economic integration of the oil-producing countries in the global economy. Meanwhile, Egypt, the most populous and historically most influential Arab country, became a close strategic and military ally to the United States, along with Saudi Arabia and other traditionally conservative Arab monarchies. The new oil era that resulted in increased wealth and prosperity for countries in the region, along with the greater political dependence of Egypt and the Arab monarchies on the USA, has been accompanied by a major paradigm shift away from the ideals of Arab nationalism that dominated previous decades.

Despite this paradigm shift in the political discourse since the 1970s, there has been no change in the popular legitimacy of the Arab autocracies. While limited forms of political liberalization in some of the Arab countries may be noted, such as formal but controlled parliamentary elections, and a greater but still small degree of freedom in political expression, Arab autocracies have continued to rely on various forms of oppression, legitimacy by default, the engineering of crisis politics and, more recently, the pretext of containing fundamentalist Islamic movements.[7]

In our view, two decades later, this assessment remains, for the most part. Indeed, the very short-lived instances of political freedom under the shadow of civil war in Sudan and Lebanon's partial democracy were exceptions to the general rule over the past five decades. Despite the demise of the Soviet Union, the end of the oil boom, the Gulf wars, the worsening Palestinian crisis, as well as civil wars and other internal conflicts, no regime in the Arab world has extended the political franchise to the point where citizens could exercise effective control over public policy. In virtually all Arab countries, the prospect of a regime losing power in an election is inconceivable.

During this same period, democracy in other regions of the world has been steadily increasing, as demonstrated by trends in the Polity IV index, which provides ratings from −10 (strongly autocratic) to 10 (strongly democratic) for all countries from 1800 to 2003. In Figure 2.1 the average for Arab states is compared to regional comparators East Asia (EAC), Latin America (LAC), Sub-Saharan Africa (SSA), the OECD countries and other countries (non-OECD countries from other areas or regions).

Figure 2.2 illustrates that the Arab world has lagged behind the rest of the developing world with little to no progress in political representation in the past 40 years.[8] The average Arab country entered the 1960s with a polity score of −5.3,

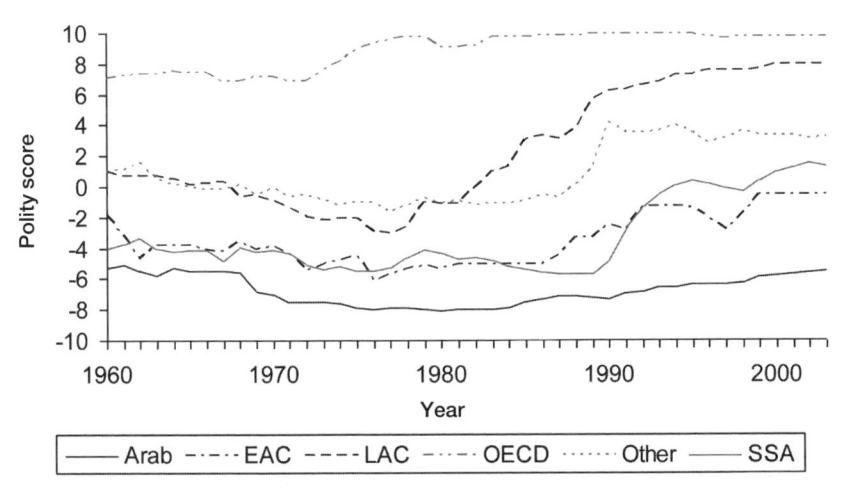

Figure 2.1 Average polity score by region/type, 1960 to 2003.

Source: Polity IV data set.

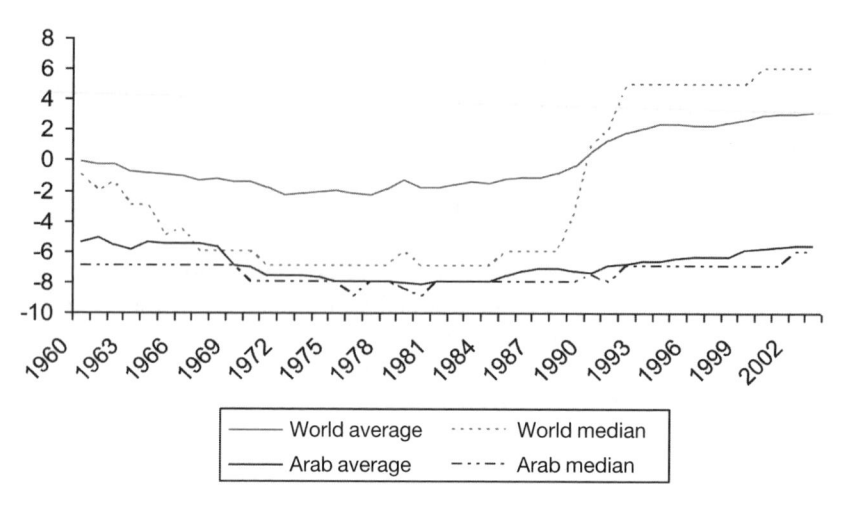

Figure 2.2 Average and median polity for the world and the Arab world, 1960 to 2003.
Source: Polity IV data set.

below that of the average East Asian (−1.9) and Sub-Saharan African (−4.1) country. During the 1970s, a general downward trend in average polity scores is witnessed for all regions, except OECD countries, and the Arab world is no exception. However, for Latin American and other states in the 1980s and in East Asian and Sub-Saharan African states in the 1990s, when, on average, they experienced increasing levels of democracy, the Arab world saw little or no improvement. While the East Asian and Sub-Saharan African averages in 2003 were at −0.6 and 1.35, respectively, the average for Arab states was −5.5, lower than the Arab average from 1960.

Of course, as the foregoing statistics are averages, is it possible that there are outliers driving these results? Unfortunately, for the citizens of the Arab world, the only outliers are the occasional attempts at democracy (see Table 2.1). While the median world polity was low throughout most of the second half of the twentieth century, it increased dramatically in the late 1980s and the 1990s, resulting in the median polity score for the world actually exceeding the average score in 1991. Thus the world average after 1991 was 'brought down' by outliers. In contrast, the median for the Arab world is consistently below that of the mean for the Arab world, suggesting that the average is being brought up by the few Arab countries with better than median polity scores.

The historically differing trends in democratization between the Arab world and other regions are the basis of much conjecture. Following the Second World War and the withdrawal of foreign troops from most of the Arab countries, some of the states that gained their independence at that time experienced certain aspects of democratic progress. However, during the 1960s Arab states witnessed a reversionl to authoritarian rule, with one or two exceptions. Part of this trend observed in the averages can be attributed to the emergence of newly independent states (e.g. small oil-producing countries), the majority of which were ruled by authoritarian regimes. However, the number of countries in the international community has been increasing steadily over the past 50 years. Democratization among new countries, especially following the collapse of the Soviet Union, has been witnessed almost universally, except in the Arab world. Therefore, changes in sample size and composition cannot explain why the global wave of democratization that started in the late 1980s has had such a limited impact on Arab states.

This brings us to the present day and the current challenges to Arab ruling establishments, brought by an unprecedented and sweeping interventionist strategy by the United States. The declared ambitions of the US plan for the region include resolving the Palestinian question, though so far with a strong bias towards the Israeli position; pressing the war on terror by 'fighting them over there'; and, presumably, enforcing democracy, including through the brute force of invasion and occupation, as in the case of Iraq, or through intimidation and acculturation, as in the case of Saudi Arabia. Whatever the real intent of US policy in the region, and even if we assume that the promotion of democracy in the region is the aim of the US agenda, the record of Western and in particular US intervention does not point in this direction.[9] This chapter will demonstrate that no real progress on the question of democracy in the region will take place until the Arab–Israeli conflict is justly resolved and a new social contract is drawn up.

3. Assessing the Arab democracy deficit

To describe the state of democracy in the Arab world, we consider three measures of democracy: the Gastil concept of political rights and civil liberties embodied by the Freedom House Index; a classification system of political regimes proposed by Przeworski;[10] and the Polity IV Index of democracy.

3.1 The Freedom House Index

The Freedom House Index measures both political rights and civil liberties. Political rights refer to the extent to which the people in a regime are able to participate in the electoral process, including voting in free and fair elections, participation in political parties and organizations, competition for accountable public office, and the impact of those offices on public policies. The measure ranges from 1 (high level of political rights) to 7 (political rights absent or virtually non-existent). The civil liberties score is a broader concept, covering four types of rights: freedom of expression and belief; association and organization rights; and rule of law and human rights, including personal and economic rights. This score ranges from 1 (high standard of civil liberties) to 7 (virtually no freedom). The average of these two scores gives the 'freedom' score. Countries with an average score in the range of 1 to 2.5 are referred to as 'free', countries with scores from 2.5 to 5.5 are considered 'partially free', and those with a score of 5.5 to 7 are 'not free'.

Figure 2.3 graphically demonstrates the lack of freedom in the Arab world by plotting percentage of country years of freedom, by country and for the

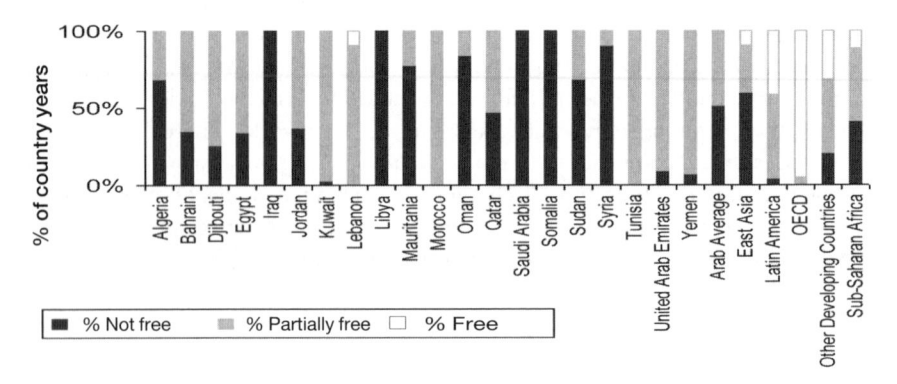

Figure 2.3 Country years of freedom, 1972 to 2002.
Source: Freedom House.

comparator aggregates from Figure 2.1, for the period 1972 to 2002. Only Lebanon among the Arab states qualified as free in any of the years observed, and even then only for 9 per cent of the country years (1972–4). All other Arab countries are partially or not free for the entire sample period, many of them are not free for a majority or all of the period (Iraq, Libya, Mauritania, Oman, Saudi Arabia, Somalia, Sudan and Syria). In comparison, the East Asian and Sub-Sahara African countries were free over 9 and 12 per cent of the country years, respectively. In addition, Latin American countries were free for 41 per cent of the country years and other developing countries were free for 32 per cent.

Admittedly, the Freedom indices are subjective to some extent, dependent as they are on research by a team on the broad concepts defined above. However, effort is made to ensure that the evaluations are not culturally biased and that they are comparable across countries as well as consistent across time. This approach provides one commonly accepted measure of political freedom.

3.2 Democracy and development classification

A global classification of political regime types for 141 countries between 1950 and 1990 using more objective criteria was compiled by a team led by Przeworski and detailed in *Democracy and Development* (Przeworski *et al.*, 2000). According to this system, a regime is classified as a dictatorship if any of the following conditions holds: the chief executive is not elected; the legislature is not elected; there is no more than one party; or if the incumbents unconstitutionally closed the legislature and rewrote the rules in their favour. Even if the regime passed these rules, it will be classified as a dictatorship if the incumbents hold office continuously by virtue of elections for more than two terms. This last rule ensures that, in democratic regimes, opposition has a real possibility to win and assume office.

Dictatorships are further classified within their category as 'bureaucracy' or 'autocracy'. Bureaucracies are a form of institutionalized dictatorship, with a set of rules for operating the government, including rules for regulating the chief executive vis-à-vis the legislature, whereas autocratic regimes have 'neither internal rules nor publicly announced universalistic intentions' (Przeworski *et al.*, 2000: 32).

Classifications of Arab countries from Freedom House and the democracy and development approaches are listed side by side in Table 2.1.

The differences between the results reflect the functional differences between the definitions of 'freedom' and 'political system' as well as the varying degree of subjectivity of the two classification methods. For the Arab world, the one country period in democracy and development that also has observation years in Freedom House is Sudan 1986 to 1988, which is reflected as both a 'democracy' and 'partly free' for those years.

Table 2.1 Two regime classifications, 1960 to 2003

Country	Freedom House classification (1972–2003)			Democracy and development (1950–1990)		
				Authoritarian		
	Not-free	Partly free	Free	Autocracy	Bureaucracy	Democracy
Algeria	1972–87 1992–7	1988–91 1998–2003		1965–76	1962–4 1977–90	
Bahrain	1993–2000	1972–92 2001–2		1971–2 1975–90	1973–4	
Djibouti	1985–8 1992–4	1977–84 1989–91 1995–2003			1977–90	
Egypt	1972–3 1993–8 2001–3	1974–92 1999–2000				1950–90
Iraq	1972–2003			1950 1958–79	1951–7 1980–90	
Jordan	1972–83	1984–2003		1966 1974–83	1950–65 1967–73 1984	
Kuwait	1990	1972–89 1991–2003		1961–2 1976–80 1986–90	1963–75 1981–5	
Lebanon		1975–2003	1972–4			
Libya	1972–2003					
Mauritania	1972–3 1975–97	1974 1998–2003				
Morocco		1972–2003		1955–62 1965–9 1972–6	1963–4 1970–1 1977–90	

continued overleaf

Table 2.1 Continued

Country	Freedom House classification (1972–2003)			Democracy and development (1950–1990)		
				Authoritarian		
	Not-free	Partly free	Free	Autocracy	Bureaucracy	Democracy
Oman	1972–91 1993–9	1992 2000–3		1951–90		
Qatar	1989–2003	1972–88		1971–90		
Saudi Arabia	1972–2003			1950–90		
Somalia	1972–2003			1969–78	1979–90	1960–8
Sudan	1972–6 1984–5 1989–2003	1977–83 1986–8		1958–64 1985 1989–90	1969–84	1956–7 1965–8 1986–8
Syria	1972–6 1980–2003	1977–9		1961–9	1950–60 1970–90	
Tunisia		1972–2003			1956–90	
United Arab Emirates	1972 1993 2003	1973–92 1994–2002		1971–90		
Yemen (N. to 1990)	2001	1990–2000 2002–3		1978–90 1985–8	1989–90	1967–77

Source: Freedom House Index; Przeworski et al. (2000).

The nature of these Arab autocracies is fairly constant. Referring to the Freedom House classification, we see that a few countries are never free over the sample period: Iraq, Libya, Saudi Arabia and Somalia. In fact, freedom is quite rare, with only two countries free or partly free over the entire sample – Lebanon and Tunisia. There are many countries that are classified as one type for the duration of the sample, including the bureaucracies of Djibouti, Egypt and Tunisia and the autocracies of Oman, Qatar, Saudi Arabia and the United Arab Emirates. Periods of partial and no freedom lasted on average 10.8 years for Arab countries, while periods of autocracy and bureaucracy lasted on average 10.8 and 11.9 years, respectively for the sample period. Of course, these statistics are affected by truncation, depending on the beginning and end of the sample as defined in both classification systems. Still, they provide some useful background into the nature of freedom and political systems in the Arab world.

3.3 Polity IV Index

For our present analysis we rely upon the widely used Polity IV Index as a measure of democracy. This measure is somewhat more objective than the Freedom House Index because it uses objective questions with a wider range of measurement and more current data than the democracy and development classifications. The Polity IV Index is based on two concepts: 'institutionalized democracy' (DEM) and 'institutionalized autocracy' (AUT). The DEM score is coded according to four measures of regime characteristics: competitiveness of executive recruitment; openness of executive recruitment; constraints on the chief executive; and competitiveness of political participation. These measures, along with regulation of participation, contribute to the AUT score. The Polity score (POL) is computed by subtracting the AUT score from the DEM score, resulting in a score from –10 (strongly autocratic) to 10 (strongly democratic). As previously demonstrated in Figures 2.1 and 2.2, the Arab world has consistently lagged behind the rest of the world in polity score since 1960.

Delving deeper, the paradox of the Arab democracy deficit grows when comparing annual mean changes in polity in and outside the Arab world (see Figure 2.4).

Mean change in polity was negative for the non-Arab developing world during the 1960s, whereas there was less negative and even some positive change in average polity for the Arab world in the early 1960s. In 1963, Morocco changed from –5 to –2, and in 1964 Sudan changed from –7 to 0 and in 1965 from 0 to 7. This was followed by a large average decrease in polity in 1969. Figure 2.4 suggests that changes in polity were counter-cyclical in the Arab world vis-à-vis the non-Arab world up until the mid-1980s. Still, despite some relative gains in

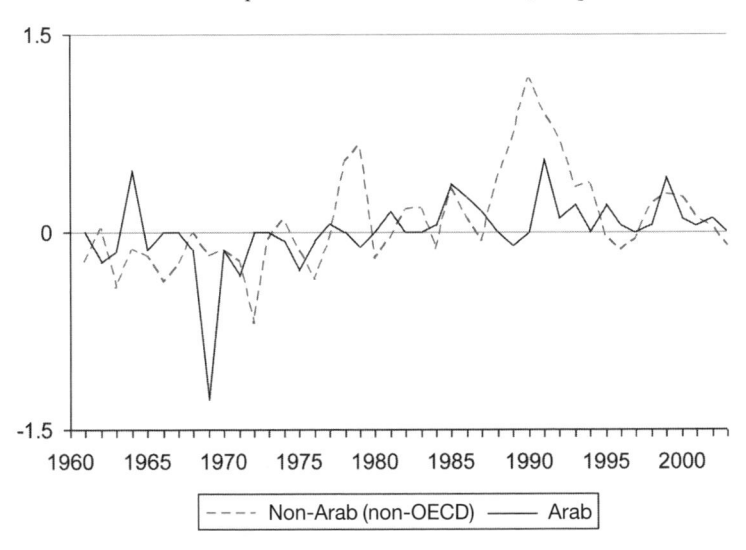

Figure 2.4 Mean change in polity: Arab and non-Arab world.
Source: Polity IV data set.

polity in the 1960s, the Arab world lagged behind the non-Arab world in changes in polity over the past 40 years, especially during the 'third wave' of democratization during the late 1980s and early 1990s.[11]

The trends in the polity scores cohere with the more detailed country-specific assessments of the status of democracy in the Arab world. For example, el-Sayyid argues that even for those countries that have experienced democratic progress in the region, this progress has been neither as deep nor as wide in scope as that in the rest of the world,[12] citing the limited and carefully crafted transitions to multi-party systems in Morocco in 1975 and in Egypt in 1976, followed by similar transitions in Tunisia, Algeria, North Yemen, Jordan and Somalia. In all of these cases only the minimum necessary political rights were ceded by the ruling elites in these countries, resulting in stalled political progress or even occasional setbacks, reflected in continuing negative polity scores (see Figure 2.5). Despite some progress from extreme autocracy of –9 and –10 polity, the upper bound for these reformers is still –2, and there were relapses in Algeria in the early 1990s and Tunisia in 2003.

4. Modelling the democratization process

The positive relationship between levels of development and democracy was advanced by Seymour Lipset and expanded upon by Robert Barro (Lipset, 1959; Barro, 1996). In this worldview, increases in the level of income result in pressures for democratization because a growing middle class demands political representation to ensure that their interests are met through the provision of public goods by the state. This basic explanation, encompassing the Lipset hypothesis and Barro's contribution, is referred to throughout the following text as the 'modernization

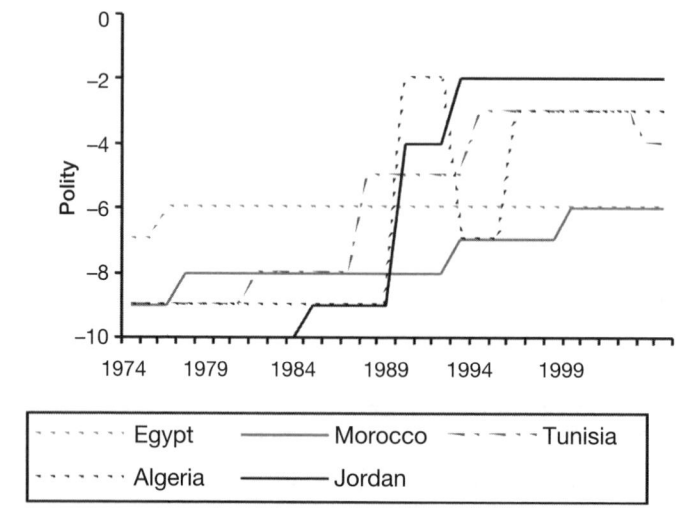

Figure 2.5 Limited democratic progress in the best Arab reformers, 1974 to 2004.
Source: Polity IV data set.

hypothesis' or the 'modernization theory'. Likewise, variables associated with economic and social progress will be referred to as 'modernity variables'.

Despite the lack of a rigorous theoretical foundation to support the modernity view, empirical cross-country evidence lends strong support to the Lipset hypothesis, where measures of standard of living – real per capita GDP, life expectancy and educational attainment – are strongly associated with democratic polity. Moreover, experiences of democratization without economic development, such as those imposed by colonial powers at independence and those imposed through intervention in domestic politics by foreign democracies, tend to be short-lived. It is important to note that, from the perspective of modernity theory, democracy is not an end in itself but instead a means to the end of responsive public policy. This leaves open the question of why there would be pressures for democratization in those autocratic states where there is sufficient provision of public goods. Mancur Olson argues that sufficiently long-lasting and credible autocracies that provide opportunities for investment, both in human and productive capital, can deliver returns in economic and social progress as effectively as any democracy.[13] Daron Acemoglu and James Robinson make a similar argument, citing as their iconic case the one-party rule by the People's Action Party in Singapore since 1963.[14]

As we will show empirically, the modernization hypothesis fails to explain the lack of democratic progress in the Arab world, even accounting for measures of social development such as level of education, in addition to economic development. Despite the limited progress made in reforms (described above) and the abortive attempts at democracy in Sudan and Somalia, we have shown that average and median polity in Arab countries consistently lag far behind the rest of the world (Figure 2.2). Perhaps most telling was the divergence between Arab and East Asian countries over the period 1960 to 2003 (Figure 2.1), because in 1960 the latter seemed to be a reasonable comparator group. Despite similarities in level of development, the average polity score of East Asian countries in 2003 was –0.6, whereas the Arab countries had a mean of –5.5.

In so far as the modernity hypothesis is the leading explanation for democratic progress, the irrelevance of the modernity hypothesis in the Arab world supports claims of a 'freedom deficit' in the region.[15] In search of other theories, we posit and develop alternative explanations, many of which can be found in popular literature or other conventional wisdom, and we test them here empirically. These competing theories for the absence of democratic progress in the Arab world include:

- historical effects of colonization;
- religion as a foundation for the political system;
- social cohesion, including its effect through system of governance;
- type and breadth of social development;
- oil as a source of regime-supporting finance;
- regional wars, international and civil;
- international intervention through aid and strategic support.

The results that follow are based on original empirical tests developed in our earlier works and compiled here (Elbadawi and Makdisi, 2007; Elbadawi, Makdisi and Milante, 2006). To explain the democracy deficit in the Arab world, we employ a pooled panel maximum likelihood estimator accounting for the left and right censored nature of the data using Tobit estimation. To avoid endogenous effects of time in the independent variables and to accommodate small gaps in data, we use nine five-year periods between 1960 and 2003, with the last period being only four years.[16] The dependent variable is the average polity score for the five-year period, for all of the estimates that follow, unless otherwise noted. Before presenting the results, we describe the independent variables that will be used to test the competing theories above.

4.1 The modernization variables

Among the modernization variables suggested by Barro, income and education are employed here. Life expectancy is not used because it is highly correlated with both income and education and is more limited in availability of data. Additionally, neighbour polity scores are included here as a 'modernization variable' to capture spillover effects of political change, further suggesting that the Arab and other regional effects are genuine, even after accounting for these spillover effects. In earlier versions of the chapter, urbanization was also included as a modernization variable; however, data on urbanization are very limited (in availability) and is highly correlated with income, so it is excluded here.

Economic development is proxied by the average of per capita gross domestic product (GDP) in US dollars (base year 2000) over each period.[17] We expect the marginal effect of economic development to be diminishing and endogenous to democratization, so the natural log of this variable is lagged: $(\ln(\text{GDP per capita})_{t-1})$.

Measures of education are often disparate, interrupted and limited in scope. Use of a single measure could mean a halving of the available sample size. Therefore, an education index is constructed from normalizing and averaging three available measures of educational development. The three source measures are average level of school attainment for the population, average literacy of the adult population and secondary school enrolment. These three measures are normalized, and then the average of all normalized measures available for each period contributes to the education index. Correlation between these variables and the education index is presented in Table 2.2. The education index is lagged when used as an independent variable: (Education_{t-1}).

Female percentage of the labour force further reflects the modernity of the economy. In addition, we include this measure as a proxy for political access afforded to women. Better data would reflect suffrage for women and minorities to more accurately measure the extent of the extension of the democratic franchise, however, such measures are not available for the time period. Indeed, female percentage of the labour force is only available after 1980, therefore the 1980 value is used for all periods before 1980.

Table 2.2 Correlation of an education index and measures of education

	Adult literacy	Life expectancy	Secondary enrolment	School attainment
Education Index	0.93	0.81	0.84	0.93
School attainment	0.87	0.71	0.64	
Secondary enrolment	0.63	0.74		
Life expectancy	0.72			

Source: World Bank, 2005.

Note
All measures are averages for 5-year periods. The Education Index is the average of all normalized scores for the period. Life expectancy is included as a comparator and to demonstrate the correlation with education.

Neighbour polity is included as a modernization variable to capture spillover effects from political change in neighbouring countries. This theory suggests that neighbour polity might be influential on a state's polity because of a peer effect, for example, democracies are more likely to encourage local democratization. Alternatively, from a citizen consumer perspective, neighbour polity might be a reservation level of democracy to which citizens could defect if autocracy were too oppressive in the home country; even in the presence of some switching costs this could place pressure on democratization in the home state. In coding neighbour polity, note that island countries do not have neighbours. Since a missing variable would drop all island countries from the sample, the relevant question is: how should neighbour polity be coded for island countries? To avoid this issue, the average world polity per annum is calculated and the world is used as a neighbour to all countries, ensuring that every country has at least one neighbour. The average neighbour polity per annum can then be calculated for the sample. The median for the period is calculated for the country and lagged to measure neighbour polity effect: (Median Neighbour Polity$_{t-1}$).

4.2 Region dummy variables

Four dummy variables are constructed to capture region-type effects. The variable 'Arab' is coded 1 for all Arab states, 0 otherwise.[18] The coefficient on this variable in the estimates that follow reflects the average unexplained effect in the polity scores of Arab states, in other words, the Arab democracy deficit. Regional controls are included for the three regions identified earlier: Sub-Saharan Africa (SSA), East Asia (EAC) and Latin America (LAC). These variables are coded according to geographical location: 1 if in the region, 0 otherwise.

4.3 Historical variables

The historical variables reflect the influence of previous colonial interventions in the political development of the country. These include a dummy variable coded

1 for countries that were former colonies, 0 otherwise. Additionally, former colonies are identified by their colonial masters, Britain, Spain, France and Portugal; countries with other colonial masters are therefore the default and the effect of lineage from these four major colonial powers is the marginal effect beyond that of the dummy variable for being a former colony. Finally, colonial legacy is the inverse of the age of the country since independence for all former colonies.[19] This set of variables is used to test the hypothesis that the colonial experience contributes to democracy deficits.

4.4 Religion

Two variables are constructed to capture the effect of dominant religion on the political system adopted. The variables Muslim and Christian are each coded as 1 if more than 50 per cent of the population practises the respective religion, and 0 otherwise. Because the cut-off of 50 per cent is employed, there are no countries coded as both Muslim and Christian. Countries coded as 0 for both are either not dominated by one of these two religions or have a population where more than 50 per cent practise another religion (e.g. Hinduism, Buddhism, etc.). These variables are used to test the hypothesis that religion serves as the foundation for a political system. These variables are time invariant, like the Arab dummy variable, so they can only capture baseline effects of the dominant religion on level of democracy.

4.5 Social variables

Social cohesion is measured predominantly as ethnic fractionalization. This measure is squared to capture the non-monotonic effects of extreme fractionalization, where beyond a certain threshold high fractionalization could have corrosive effects on democracy. Fractionalization is also interacted with lagged average polity to allow for the possibility that building democracy might be more challenging in socially diverse societies (i.e. negative coefficient for the interaction term), given the level effects of democracy and social fractionalization. Additional measures of polarization and fractionalization are employed to test these effects for robustness. These social variables are used to test the effect that social cohesion might have on the formation of political systems.

4.6 Arab-specific effects

Effects salient particularly to the Arab world, namely, the presence of oil and regional war/international intervention, are proposed to explain the Arab democracy deficit. The choice of these variables is based on the political discourse of major scholars of the Arab world who argue that oil and the creation of the state of Israel are probably the two factors that have influenced the contemporary Arab world more than any other. Both have spurred considerable conflicts in the region as well as attracted intense, sustained and mostly adversarial interests by global powers.

It may be conjectured that the immense oil resources commanded by several Arab countries have facilitated the emergence of repressive militaristic regimes or protected undemocratic, traditionally authoritarian regimes, especially through the lack of citizen oversight or expectations that accompany the collection of taxes. Expectations on public good provision, including political rights, may increase with the level of taxation, suggesting that citizens in oil- and primary resource-dependent countries would have lower expectations of their governments because they pay little to no taxes. Furthermore, we cannot ignore the fact that control of the largest share of global oil reserves is concentrated in the Gulf, among a handful of small countries, ensuring the presence of tremendous foreign influence, which by and large has not favoured democratization. For example, the three major Gulf wars (1980–8, 1991 and 2003 to present) are all linked to the interests of global powers in the oil-rich region and were concurrent with positive changes in global democratization that were not seen in the Arab world.

On the other hand, the ongoing Palestinian crisis has affected the entire region, especially the immediate Arab neighbours of Israel. In particular, the Arab–Israeli conflict and the perceived adversarial global power interventions in the region have provided potent arguments for an authoritarian brand of Arab nationalism for most of the last 50 years or so. Political and civil liberties were violated, in many cases egregiously, and military coups were mounted in the name of Arab nationalism and Palestine.

Measures of these variables are rare and often highly contentious. The variables chosen are used to approximate these effects without sacrificing the scope of the sample. For example, measures of oil production are often interrupted or non-existent, especially for developing countries or those involved in conflict. An alternative measure that is more widely available and which we use is the net export of fuel as a percentage of total trade. This variable is more widely available because trade statistics can be reported by both parties to the trade. Additionally, the value of fuel trade vis-à-vis all trade captures the relative importance of fuel with regard to the country's international trade and terms of trade. However some measures of net exports of fuel are still missing from the observations (119 of 879 observations). For countries with missing observations of net fuel trade, a value of 0 is used and assumed not to bias the results.[20]

To capture the effect of wars in the Arab states, the number of Arab states involved in wars is counted per period. This is similarly used for the other regions identified above. The number of major civil or international wars, according to the International Peace Research Institute of Oslo (PRIO) Armed Conflicts Database, is then added up for all countries in the region and divided by the total number of countries in the region (to account for the different size of regions). This returns a measure of region at war which is lagged to avoid issues of endogeneity (Regional Wars$_{t-1}$). The dummy variables for each region are then interacted with regional war to identify specific regional war effects, coded for the Arab countries and the three control groups: Sub-Saharan Africa, Latin America and East Asia.

4.7 Descriptive statistics

A summary of the (non-binary) variables is provided in Table 2.3 for the entire sample used in the analysis that follows. In addition, summary statistics are provided for the Arab countries. As expected, the average level of democracy reflected by polity score is much lower in Arab states (–6.93) than the whole sample (0.97). For the entire sample, the average per capita income is actually slightly higher in the Arab world (~US $1,800) than the rest of the world (~$1,600), demonstrating that the modernity hypothesis cannot account for the Arab democracy deficit so long as modernity is defined by economic development.

Social development is reflected by level of education, and the average Arab state scores much lower (–0.72) in a normalized score of education indicators than the average country (–0.15, predictably near 0, with a standard deviation near 1). Clearly the Arab countries lag behind the average country in the sample in terms of social development, suggesting that the modernity hypothesis might hold if modernity is defined in terms of social development (though this is shown not to be the case in the analysis that follows). Likewise, the Arab countries lag behind the average country in the sample with respect to gender equality in the labour force, Arab countries have a mean for the sample of 21 per cent versus 37 per cent in the average country (~50 per cent would reflect gender parity in the labour force).

Neighbour polity is much lower for the average Arab state (–4.94) than other countries in the sample (–1.28), owing to the geographical compactness of the Arab world. Since the Arab dummy variable is time invariant, a significant neighbour polity effect would suggest that the Arab democracy deficit is actually larger, since Arab states must overcome the persistent autocratic pressures in their environment.

The other explanatory variables listed in Table 2.3 include ethnic fractionalization, net fuel exports and regional wars. As shown in the table, there is little

Table 2.3 Descriptive statistics

	Entire sample					Arab only				
	# Obs.	Mean	Std. dev.	Min.	Max.	# Obs.	Mean	Std. dev.	Min.	Max.
Polity	889	0.93	7.34	–10	10	110	–6.93	3.23	–10	6
Ln (GDP per capita)$_{t-1}$	889	7.37	1.58	4.32	10.71	110	7.49	1.38	5.32	10.63
Education Index$_{t-1}$	889	–0.16	1.04	–2.35	1.85	110	–0.72	0.75	–2.06	0.91
Female % of labor force	889	36.82	9.59	5	54	110	21.1	8.64	5	41
Neighbor polity$_{t-1}$	889	–1.28	4.93	–9	9.34	110	–4.90	3.10	–9	5.4
Ethnic fractionalization$_{t-1}$	889	0.46	0.26	0	0.93	110	0.44	0.21	0.04	0.80
Net fuel exports$_{t-1}$	889	1.27	25.07	–51.9	98.99	110	25.69	39.30	–25.1	98.99
Regional wars$_{t-1}$	889	0.21	0.12	0	0.63	110	0.31	0.12	0.10	0.48

Sources: As described in the preceding section.

difference in ethnic fractionalization between the average, minimum and maximum values for Arab states and those of the entire sample. As expected, net fuel exports are much higher for the average Arab state (25.69 per cent) than for the average country in the entire sample (1.27 per cent). Negative values of net fuel exports reflect fuel imports. For the Arab states the percentage of countries in the region engaged in war (31 per cent) is a little higher (approximately 1 standard deviation) than the regional wars for the entire sample (21 per cent), reflecting the increased volatility of the Middle East.

5. Results

This section discusses the results of the Tobit analysis presented in Tables 2.4–2.8. Table 2.4 tests the competing explanations for the Arab democracy deficit described earlier, within the context of other comparator regions. Table 2.5 demonstrates how the findings of column (g) in Table 2.4 can be reduced to a more parsimonious version. Table 2.6 explores alternative specifications for the Arab-specific variables, including specification of the Arab war regional variable. Table 2.7 tests for Cold War and international intervention effects on Arab democratization. Table 2.8 introduces two different measures of democracy to test the robustness of the results to alternative measures of the dependent variable.

5.1 Discussion of Table 2.4: a unique Arab democracy effect

The estimation begins with the modernity variables posited by Lipset and Barro. Column (a) of Table 2.4 reports these basic results using a pooled panel Tobit analysis on a sample of 889 period/country observations (141 countries with an unbalanced panel of periods). The empirical evidence supports the modernity hypothesis, as all modernity variables, except for education, are positively and significantly associated with higher levels of democracy. Additionally, the female percentage of the labour force is positive and significantly associated with higher levels of democracy. The evidence also suggests that a legacy of democratic traditions has a positive effect on the future of democracy, though past democracy does not ensure future democratic progress since the coefficient on lagged polity is less than 1 in this basic regression. Moreover, the coefficient on neighbour polity shows that a country surrounded by neighbours with higher levels of democracy is likely to be more democratic, confirming that neighbourhood matters.

Despite the general success of the modernity variables, the basic model fails to explain the Arab democracy deficit. This is evidenced by the significant and negative coefficient on the Arab variable in column (a). This suggests that even this extended version of the modernization theory cannot explain the Arab world 'freedom deficit', though it appears to have accounted for the determinants of democracy in Sub-Saharan Africa, East Asia and Latin America. To comprehend this unique Arab effect we look beyond modernization theory through successive additions of other explanatory variables represented by columns (b) to (g) of Table 2.4.

Table 2.4 Explaining the Arab democracy deficit (dependent variable: polity)

Independent variable	(a)	(b)	(c)	(d)	(e)	(f)	(g)
Income, lagged	0.742***	0.667***	0.660***	0.507***	0.536***	0.654***	0.619***
	(0.144)	(0.150)	(0.155)	(0.157)	(0.157)	(0.159)	(0.160)
Polity, lagged	0.859***	0.850***	0.850***	1.038***	1.025***	1.024***	1.036***
	(0.024)	(0.025)	(0.025)	(0.044)	(0.044)	(0.043)	(0.044)
Education, lagged	0.235	0.205	0.195	0.241	0.267	0.157	0.172
	(0.228)	(0.242)	(0.245)	(0.245)	(0.244)	(0.243)	(0.244)
Neighbour polity, lagged	0.084**	0.091***	0.091***	0.087**	0.090***	0.092***	0.079**
	(0.034)	(0.034)	(0.034)	(0.034)	(0.034)	(0.034)	(0.034)
Female % of labour force, lagged	0.051**	0.069***	0.067***	0.072***	0.066**	0.066**	0.072***
	(0.023)	(0.024)	(0.026)	(0.026)	(0.027)	(0.026)	(0.026)
Regional/type effects							
Arab	−1.737***	−1.840***	−1.797***	−1.479**	−1.370**	−1.838***	−0.779
	(0.577)	(0.596)	(0.616)	(0.634)	(0.635)	(0.641)	(1.146)
Sub-Saharan Africa	−0.523	−0.902	−0.922*	−1.173*	−1.131*	−1.272**	−2.567***
	(0.491)	(0.525)	(0.541)	(0.599)	(0.599)	(0.593)	(0.849)
East Asian	−0.611	−1.172**	−1.196**	−1.162**	−1.102**	−1.233**	−2.548**
	(0.478)	(0.484)	(0.549)	(0.548)	(0.548)	(0.544)	(1.080)
Latin American	−0.498	−1.311**	−1.357*	−0.965	−1.009	−1.013*	−2.386***
	(0.430)	(0.706)	(0.725)	(0.728)	(0.727)	(0.718)	(0.903)
Historical effects							
Former colony		−0.393	−0.382	−0.383	−0.340	−0.427	−0.368
		(0.547)	(0.558)	(0.572)	(0.571)	(0.564)	(0.576)
Colonial legacy		−8.071***	−8.088***	−8.244***	−8.240***	−7.210***	−6.446***
		(1.587)	(1.591)	(1.582)	(1.578)	(1.585)	(1.667)
Former British colony		0.675	0.677	0.862*	0.792	0.813*	0.711
		(0.493)	(0.494)	(0.495)	(0.495)	(0.489)	(0.488)
Former Spanish colony		0.974	0.968	0.876	0.905	0.991	1.012
		(0.755)	(0.764)	(0.763)	(0.762)	(0.753)	(0.750)
Former French colony		0.878	0.882	0.811	0.774	0.855	0.677
		(0.519)	(0.533)	(0.538)	(0.537)	(0.531)	(0.534)

Former Portuguese colony		1.684** (0.744)	1.660** (0.766)	1.448* (0.767)	1.420* (0.765)	1.507** (0.757)	1.301* (0.759)

Effects of religion						
Muslim			−0.112 (0.468)	−0.094 (0.465)	0.026 (0.468)	0.249 (0.467)	0.311 (0.469)
Christian			−0.002 (0.468)	0.054 (0.471)	0.091 (0.470)	0.515 (0.480)	0.378 (0.488)

Social cohesion					
Ethnic fractionalization			1.171 (2.246)	1.000 (2.244)	0.506 (2.220)	1.100 (2.219)
Ethnic fractionalization squared			−1.635 (2.487)	−1.197 (2.492)	−0.511 (2.469)	−1.045 (2.465)
Interaction: ethnic fractionalization * lagged polity			−0.430*** (0.081)	−0.412*** (0.081)	−0.411*** (0.080)	−0.424*** (0.080)

Arab-specific effects				
Net fuel exports				−0.011** (0.005)	−0.011** (0.005)	−0.012** (0.005)
Regional wars					4.368*** (1.238)	0.678 (2.049)
Interaction: regional war and Sub-Saharan Africa						6.900** (3.093)
Interaction: regional war and East Asian						6.155* (3.596)
Interaction: regional war and Latin American						9.292*** (3.312)
Interaction: regional war and Arab						−0.491 (3.441)

Constant	−5.339*** (1.600)	−5.014*** (1.717)	−4.873*** (1.796)	−4.318** (1.885)	−4.400** (1.882)	−6.372*** (1.940)	−5.919*** (1.993)

Notes

Standard errors in parentheses. Significance key: * = $p < 0.10$, ** = $p < 0.05$, *** = $p < 0.01$.

Column (b) of Table 2.4 introduces historical effects as explanation for the Arab democracy deficit. Colonial legacy is significant and negative, not just because of the preponderance of countries that became authoritarian regimes immediately after independence, but also because of the overall trend in democratization over time (inversely related to the year since independence, colonial legacy is by construction inversely correlated with year). Interestingly, the introduction of the historical effects makes the East Asian and Latin American regional dummies significant and negative and strengthens the coefficient of the Arab dummy. This seems to be at the expense of the impact of the income variable, suggesting that the modernization variables may be broadly capturing regional or shared historical factors. As the Arab dummy remains negative and significant, there is little evidence that historical factors can explain the Arab democracy deficit.

Column (c) of Table 2.4 rejects the argument that dominant religion is a significant determinant of democratization. Both Muslim and Christian dummy variables are found to be insignificant and small in scale, suggesting that they have no influence on polity. Additionally, as none of the region-type dummy variables change in significance or scale with the inclusion of the religion variables, religion is rejected as an explanation for the difference between Arab and world democracy.

Next, measures of social cohesion are included to attempt to explain the Arab democracy deficit. As column (d) of Table 2.4 demonstrates, neither ethnic fractionalization nor its squared term is found to have any effect on democratization. Ethnic fractionalization interacted with polity from the previous period is found to have a negative and significant effect on the democratization process. This is particularly interesting because polity ranges from −10 to 10. In highly fractionalized autocracies, this interaction effect is positive, suggesting that the high degree of fractionalization puts pressures on autocratic regimes to democratize. In highly fractionalized democracies, this interaction effect is negative, suggesting that highly fractionalized societies are less likely to experience continuing democratic progress. In other words, ethnic fractionalization reduces the persistence of polity. This reversion towards autocracy (polity = 0) also explains why the coefficient on previous polity is higher than 1 once this interaction term is included. While this effect is significant, comparisons of columns (c) and (d) illustrate that fractionalization and polity interaction have little affect on the Arab dummy variable, implying that social cohesion or lack thereof cannot explain the Arab democracy deficit.

The first of the proposed Arab-specific effects is introduced in column (e) of Table 2.4. The effect of fuel exports on polity is negative and significant, suggesting that there is an oil effect on democratization for the entire sample. This argument supports claims that natural resource wealth can prop up autocratic regimes, keeping them in power much longer than would be expected for a similarly modernized country that does not rely on natural resources. Though the inclusion of fuel does decrease the scale of the coefficient on the Arab dummy variable, it does not decrease its significance, suggesting that much of the Arab democracy deficit remains unexplained even with the inclusion of oil as an explanatory variable. Thus, while the oil effects are significant and, with the importance of oil in the Arab world, may explain some of the persistence of autocracies in the Arab world, oil still cannot fully explain the Arab democracy deficit. With the introduction of the oil effects, the coefficient on female percentage of the labour force decreases slightly and the coefficient on Muslim is still insignificant, corroborating the recent findings of Ross (2008) that oil and female participation, not Islam, are associated with the lagging democratization in the Arab world. Still, it should be noted that the effects on democratization, of female participation and oil, are consistent with all other effects for the rest of the panel, suggesting that they cannot uniquely explain the Arab democracy deficit.

Next, to test the effect of war on Arab democratization, the measure of regional wars is included in the regression in column (f). The presence of regional wars is found to have a significant and positive effect on democratization. This clearly runs counter to claims about Arab authoritarianism, as the higher incidence of conflict in the Arab region (see Table 2.3) has often been proposed as an explanation for the duration of the autocratic regimes. However, a clue to this riddle is suggested by the increase in scale of all of the regional dummy variables (f). With the introduction of the regional war effect, the dummy variables for all regions become more negative and increase in significance (though the Latin American dummy is only marginally significant at the 10 per cent level), offsetting this 'positive' effect of regional wars on democratization. Perhaps for some regions conflicts result in more democratization, while the Arab region responds negatively to regional conflict, becoming increasingly authoritarian in the wake of Arab wars. This is tested in the next column through interaction of the regional dummy with the regional war variable.

The hypothesis of a truly Arab-specific effect of regional war is tested in column (g) of Table 2.4 by interacting region-type dummies with the measures of regional war, and the results are quite striking. For the Arab states, interaction with regional war is insignificant and negative. For the other control regions, Sub-Saharan Africa and Latin America, the coefficient on the interacted measure is positive and significant, and on East Asia the coefficient is positive but only marginally significant (p value = .11). Additionally, the coefficient on regional wars becomes insignificant. These results suggest that there is a profound difference between Arab democratization as a result of regional conflict and other regional democratization. While other regions experience more democratization in the wake of conflict, the Arab regions actually experience less or no democratization. This is especially important since the incidence of regional conflict is higher in the Arab states than the global average (Table 2.3). Finally, the coefficient on the Arab dummy becomes small and insignificant, suggesting that not only is the Arab war effect highly collinear with the Arab dummy variable (as would be expected) but that regional war effects are unique in the Arab world. All other regional dummy variables become significant with introduction of interacted regional war effects – the effect of war in the Arab world is truly unique vis-à-vis the comparator regions. To explore the Arab war effect independent of the collinearity between the Arab dummy and the Arab regional war variable, Arab war is explored further in Table 2.6.

Column (g) of Table 2.4 not only corroborates our argument that regional war effects influence Arab democratization differently than other regions, but turns the argument on its head. Columns (a) to (f) illustrate how thoroughly divergent democratization has been in the Arab world from other regions. As each set of explanatory variables is introduced, the differences between the Arab dummy variable and those of the comparator regions increases. In the final model, in column (g) of Table 2.4, the question becomes not why there is an Arab democracy deficit, since much of it can be explained by oil and regional Arab wars, but, instead, why are the other control regions not more democratic. With the introduction of the interacted regional war terms there remain significant and negative coefficients on the dummy variables associated with all three regions: Sub-Saharan Africa, Latin America and East Asia. This suggests that the modernization variables originally introduced in column (a) gloss over the effect of war by broadly generalizing level of economic development and education. Since we are concerned primarily with Arab democracy, the question about the remaining democracy deficit in these other regions is left open for future research.

To reiterate our results so far, we find that, controlling for the other determinants, oil is robustly associated with the absence of democracy, and Arab wars account for some of the Arab democracy deficit. Moreover, the Arab dummy ceases to be significant as a stand-alone effect once wars are introduced and interacted, discriminating between wars in the Arab region and other regions. These results are refined and tested in the remainder of this section. We begin by testing the results of Table 2.4 for robustness through different specifications of the model and variables.

Our first test investigates the interaction effect introduced in column (g) of Table 2.4. To ensure that our results indicating a unique Arab war effect are not driven by the interaction of the dummy, we ran the regressions again using interaction effects for oil, education, female percentage of the labour force and colonial legacy. These results are reported in Table 2.5. Because the regressions are otherwise identical to column (g) of Table 2.4, we report the results for only the dummy variables, the test variables and the interacted variables in Table 2.5 (each column is identical to the original regression with a different interacted variable, reported at the top of the column).

Interaction of the other four variables indicates that the regional war effect is unique in its interaction effects, as the Arab dummy variable is significant in all four of the other regressions. Additionally, the signs of the interacted terms for oil, education, female percentage of the labour force and colonial legacy are all the same as the other regional dummies, suggesting that the Arab democracy deficit cannot be explained by different interaction effects through these other channels. Thus, even though the sign on oil is negative and the sign on female percentage of the labour force is positive, there is no reason from the interaction or dummy variables to expect that these effects are different in Arab countries than in other countries. Part of the Arab democracy deficit may very well be attributable to the large reliance on oil as a percentage of exports and on the low participation of women in the economy (and by proxy the political sphere), however, those deficits

Table 2.5 Robustness checks with interaction effects

	Interacted variables				
Dummy variables	Regional wars	Net fuel exports	Education	Female % of labour force	Colonial legacy
Arab	-0.779	-1.772***	-2.796***	-5.106***	-2.622***
	(1.146)	(0.654)	(0.769)	(1.745)	(0.713)
Sub-Saharan Africa	-2.567***	-1.308**	-1.285*	-1.728	-2.369***
	(0.849)	(0.600)	(0.665)	(2.012)	(0.671)
East Asian	-2.548**	-1.309**	-1.088**	-1.439	-1.849***
	(1.080)	(0.549)	(0.546)	(2.860)	(0.624)
Latin American	-2.386***	-0.936***	-0.877	-1.071	-1.842**
	(0.903)	(0.730)	(0.720)	(2.513)	(0.817)
Explanatory variable coefficient					
Regional wars	0.678	4.083***	4.959***	4.794***	4.566***
	(2.049)	(1.246)	(1.258)	(1.246)	(1.248)
Net fuel exports	-0.012***	-0.011	-0.010**	-0.009*	-0.011**
	(0.005)	(0.014)	(0.005)	(0.005)	(0.005)
Education	0.172	0.117	0.996***	0.026	0.227
	(0.244)	(0.246)	(0.368)	(0.251)	(0.247)
Female % of labour force	0.072***	0.067**	0.045	0.057	0.075
	(0.026)	(0.026)	(0.028)	(0.040)	(0.026)
Colonial legacy	-6.446***	-7.372***	-7.189***	-6.996***	-20.016***
	(1.667)	(1.582)	(1.590)	(1.586)	(3.971)
Interacted effect					
Arab* interacted variable	-0.491	-0.008	-1.135**	0.127**	16.995***
	(3.441)	(0.017)	(0.502)	(0.057)	(7.355)
Sub-Saharan Africa* interacted variable	6.900**	0.012	-1.039***	0.003	14.974***
	(3.093)	(0.018)	(0.491)	(0.049)	(4.245)
East Asian* interacted variable	6.155*	-0.038	-1.521***	0.000	6.368
	(3.596)	(0.026)	(0.552)	(0.074)	(7.301)
Latin America* interacted variable	9.292***	0.006	-0.670	-0.070	14.349
	(3.312)	(0.018)	(0.603)	(0.068)	(13.706)

Notes
Standard errors in parentheses. Significance key: * = p <0.10, ** = p <0.05, *** = p <0.01.

are 'normal' vis-à-vis other countries in the sample – countries with large oil dependency and economically disenfranchised women have lower polity scores. However, Table 2.5 shows that the war effect is fundamentally different for Arab countries; war in the Arab world in the previous period interacts differently with the extension of the political franchise and democratization.

5.2 Robustness to alternative Arab war and oil specifications

The results in Tables 2.4 and 2.5 are compelling and support the argument that there is something unique to the Arab democracy deficit that cannot be captured by world trends in democratization, namely the presence and importance of oil and the unique relationship between Arab wars and democratization. Here we test these results further with alternative measures of Arab war to confirm that these effects are not artefacts of our initial specification.[21]

We are interested in decomposing this unique feature of Arab states. To single out this effect, we use a parsimonious model derived from eliminating all insignificant terms and retaining the interacted Arab-war variable. Table 2.6 presents select results of estimates for alternative Arab war measures using this parsimonious model.

Here, in the interest of space, we have only reproduced the coefficients for these alternative measures of Arab war effects. The coefficients for other variables and their significance are not changed with substitution of these alternative speci-

Table 2.6 Alternative specifications for Arab war (dependent variable: polity)

Independent variable	(a)	(b)	(c)	(d)	(e)
Interaction: regional war and Arab	−3.473*** (1.420)				
Israeli–Palestinian battle deaths		−0.409 (0.431)			
Arab civil war battle deaths		0.083 (0.218)			
Arab international war battle deaths		0.053 (0.117)			
Arab civil war deaths weighted by distance			−0.083 (0.098)		
Arab int'l war deaths weighted by distance			−0.159* (0.095)		
All Arab battle deaths weighted by distance				−0.156*** (0.072)	
Israeli–Palestinian battle deaths weighted by distance					−1.024*** (0.389)

Notes
Standard errors in parentheses. Significance key: * = p <0.10, ** = p <0.05, *** = p <0.01.

fications. To disaggregate the effect of conflict and determine whether type of conflict affects democratization, column (b) of Table 2.6 introduces three measures of Arab battle deaths: battle deaths from the Israeli–Palestinian conflict, from Arab civil wars and from international wars fought wholly or partly in Arab countries. The results in column (b) suggest that simple measures of battle deaths (a proxy for the scale of the conflict) do not explain authoritarian tendencies in the Arab world.[22]

Column (c) weights the same measures of civil and international battle deaths by distance. Here the battle deaths from civil wars weighted by distance do not seem to have any effect on democratization, however, proximity to large international conflicts does negatively affect Arab democratization, proportional to the scale of the conflict. This would suggest that large-scale interventions such as the current occupation of Iraq and conflicts like the Gulf wars have actually contributed to the resistance to democratization in the Arab world, especially for those countries bordering the conflicts. Similarly, when all Arab battle deaths are summed and weighted by distance as in column (d), the effect of local, large-scale violence is also negative and significant.

Finally, the battle deaths from the Arab–Israeli conflict are weighted by distance to each observation country and included in place of Arab regional war in column (e). The significant, negative results suggest that Arab countries close to Israel and Palestine especially resist democratization following periods of large-scale Israeli–Palestinian conflict.

5.3 *International intervention and the Cold War*

It is arguable that war may not have an effect on Arab democratization so much as geopolitical intervention by world powers in Arab polities. To test this question, we introduce alternative measures that may capture the effect of interventions by world powers from outside the Arab world. The results are presented in Table 2.7. Here again we have only reproduced the coefficients on the variables of interest using a parsimonious model. The effect on the Arab dummy and the interaction effect are significantly unchanged, so the earlier results of interest are carried through.

The Cold War dummy (coded 1 for the first six periods of the sample: 1960–89) has a significant and negative effect on democratization (see column (b) of Table 2.7), suggesting that it was easier for countries to resist democratization during the Cold War, perhaps due to external support and the 'propping up' of autocratic regimes by the United States and the Soviet Union. To test this hypothesis, variables for military intervention by the USA and USSR are introduced in column (c) of Table 2.7.[23] The effect of USA military intervention is found to be negative and insignificant on democratization, whereas the effect of USSR intervention is positive and significant. This latter effect may not imply that the Soviet Union promoted democracy so much as reflect the semi-spurious incidence of the collapse of the Soviet Union and the high levels of democratization in the 1990s (reflected by the significant Cold War dummy), since, by construction, military

Table 2.7 The effect of the Cold War and international intervention

Independent variable	(a)	(b)	(c)	(d)	(e)
Interaction: regional war and Sub-Saharan Africa	7.384*** (2.677)	4.231 (2.765)	7.654*** (2.668)	7.315*** (2.696)	5.925* (3.147)
Interaction: regional war and East Asia	6.243** (2.916)	4.279 (2.922)	6.295** (2.906)	6.153** (2.933)	5.409* (3.066)
Interaction: regional war and Latin America	10.169*** (2.625)	9.310*** (2.597)	10.354*** (2.623)	10.149*** (2.638)	9.881*** (2.784)
Interaction: regional war and Arab	−3.473** (1.420)	−5.052*** (1.460)	−3.303** (1.421)	−3.686** (1.456)	−4.391*** (1.640)
Cold war		−1.229*** (0.319)			
US military intervention			−1.079 (1.350)		
USSR/Russian military intervention			3.374** (1.481)		
US military aid				−0.001 (0.001)	
US official development assistance					−0.001 (0.001)
UK official development assistance					0.017* (0.010)
French official development assistance					0.005 (0.004)
USSR official development assistance					0.002 (0.002)

Notes
Standard errors in parentheses. Significance key: * = $p < 0.10$, ** = $p < 0.05$, *** = $p < 0.01$.

intervention by the Soviet Union was not possible after the end of the Cold War and during the period of post-Cold War democratization.

Intervention by external actors is not experienced only through direct military intervention, but may also be reflected through military assistance and official development assistance. The effects of these variables are tested in columns (d) and (e) of Table 2.7.[24] Aid from the United States, both military and development assistance, is ineffective in promoting democracy. Similarly, development assistance from France and the Soviet Union are both ineffective in promoting significant changes in democracy. Only British foreign development assistance had any significant effect on democratization and this was barely significant at the 10 per cent level of confidence. Meanwhile, in all of these alternative specifications, there was little to no change in the interaction effect of Arab war; in fact, controlling for the Cold War, military aid and development aid, the impact of regional Arab wars is even more pronounced through larger negative coefficients.

5.4 Robustness to alternative measures of democracy[25]

In addition to the above tests on alternative measures of the independent variables, we also test the effects of alternative measures of the dependent variable, using the Freedom House measures of political rights and the Freedom House civil liberties measures, both inverted and rescaled so that they are comparable to Polity scores (i.e. –10 to 10). Both measures are substituted for polity, following the model from column (f) of Table 2.4. In addition, to ensure that the same sample is being used for all three tests, we limit the Polity model in column (a) to only the sample for which Freedom House data are available. The results for all three tests for selected variables are shown in Table 2.8.

The estimates using the two Freedom House measures in columns (b) and (c) behave similarly to the Polity IV results presented in column (a). The main result is that the Arab dummy variable is negative and significant for all three measures, suggesting that the Arab democracy deficit is not an artefact of the polity measure. The results also demonstrate some interaction between the definition of political liberalization and economic and human development, as evidenced by the increases in the income effect and the decreases in the education effect, when the Freedom House measures are used in place of polity. This may reflect the fact that the Polity Index effectively measures political systems whereas Freedom House measures political rights. Additionally, social cohesion is found to have a non-monotonic effect for the Freedom House measures, and this effect is significant in determining the civil liberties scores. Finally, note that the regional war measure is not significant in determining the civil liberties and political rights measures, though when the model is extended to accommodate the interaction effects as in column (g) of Table 2.4, the effects are similar for the Freedom House and Polity

Table 2.8 Alternative measures of democratization

Independent variable	Polity IV (a)	Freedom House civil liberties (b)	Freedom House political rights (c)
Income	0.713***	1.526***	1.695***
	(0.164)	(0.159)	(0.205)
Education	0.134	–0.347	–0.616*
	(0.253)	(0.246)	(0.316)
Arab	–2.215***	–2.019***	–1.669**
	(0.659)	(0.651)	(0.833)
Ethnic fractionalization (social cohesion)	0.567	–6.735***	–4.087
	(2.316)	(2.202)	(2.863)
Social cohesion, squared	–0.293	7.688***	4.931
	(2.576)	(2.491)	(3.212)
Regional war, lagged	3.714***	–0.445	1.024
	(1.288)	(1.237)	(1.605)

Notes
Standard errors in parentheses. Significance key: * = $p<0.10$, ** = $p<0.05$, *** = $p<0.01$.

measures (i.e. the Arab interacted effect behaves differently than the other regional interacted war effects and the significance of the Arab dummy is lost when interacted with war, regardless of whether polity, civil liberties or political rights are used).

6. Democracy and economic growth

While the modernity theory of democratization seems to account for much of the change in democracy in the second half of the twentieth century, the evidence above makes a compelling case that the Arab world is a significant anomaly to the theory. Despite socio-economic development, the Arab democracy deficit has persisted, with the absence of democratic progress in the Arab world attributable to the presence of oil and conflict in the region. Given the persistence of authoritarian regimes in Arab autocracies and the unique challenges to democratization faced by the Arab world, it is difficult to assess what level of democratization will optimize economic growth and what rate of democratization is sustainable. In this section we explore some common trends in growth for those states that have democratized since 1960 and extract some lessons for democratization and sustainable economic development in the Arab world.

In the study of development much has been said on the causes of economic development. Beyond investment, which is itself often endogenous to environments of growth, few macroeconomic variables have been found to be consistent factors in economic growth, especially for developing countries. Much of the current debate centres around three sources colloquially referred to as 'institutions, trade and geography', suggesting that few other conditions have been shown to contribute to sustainable and predictable economic growth. Note that trade is often predicated upon resource endowments and geography, and even if both have an effect on economic growth, there are very few policy implications associated with them, leaving only institutions, possibly including democracy, as an area for real intervention by the state on economic development.

Although there is wide consensus that secure property rights foster economic growth, it is not clear whether democracies or dictatorships have any natural advantages in securing these rights. Numerous arguments for and against the economic advantages of democratization have been extended, with many authors concluding that there are no natural advantages for either, or that anocracies – political systems in transition or with limited features of democracy – can provide the sort of 'creative destruction' necessary for growth. Initial constraints on executive authority can create space for investment and entrepreneurialism, while 'too much' democracy can lead to unproductive political rent-seeking that stems from distributional concerns.[26] Other authors argue that the credibility and consistency of the regime, whether autocratic or democratic, is most important in reducing the volatility and thereby promoting long-term investment and growth.[27] Because anocracies are often countries in transition, the issue of consistency complicates the analysis, suggesting that this growth may only be temporary. In addition, anocracies are often only anocratic because they follow periods of political violence or upheaval which could have been costly and destructive, suggesting that the growth associated with anocracy may only be catch-up growth due to reconstruction, and not necessarily model growth to which democratizing countries should aspire.

To the extent that any non-monotonic effect of democratization is sufficiently robust, increased political rights should also be associated with higher growth in the Arab world, given that most regimes in the region are at the extreme end of authoritarianism. Also, while there is little concern over government repudiation of contracts or the expropriation of property, there are still major concerns over corruption, rule of law and the quality of bureaucracy in the Arab world.[28]

Here we are concerned with how democracy contributes to economic growth. Following the contributions from Rodrik (1998) on the subject there are two effects to consider: the effect of democracy on the growth rate, and on the volatility of growth. In addition, there are two possible ways that democracy might affect growth and volatility: in the short run there may be a shock to the governing system that would be observed in the decade immediately following democratization, and there may be a longer term effect associated with the level of democratization. Combining the two possible causes and effects, we have four possible manifestations that might be paths from democratization to economic growth:

1   The short-term effect of recent democratization that would affect annual growth rates (the recent growth effect of the *act* of *democratization*)
2   The short-term effect of recent democratization on volatility (the recent volatility effect of the *act* of *democratization*)
3   The longer term average effects on growth rates due to the level of democracy (the growth effect of the *level* of *democracy*)
4   The longer term average effects of the level of democracy on volatility (the volatility effect of the *level* of *democracy*)

To identify these different effects, we use the polity scores described earlier to measure level of democracy, and define democratization as an improvement in polity score of three or more points. We allow for the possibility that democratization may take multiple years by defining a dummy variable 'recently democratized' for the ten years following a change greater than two points of polity, including improvements in polity over multiple years. Note that such a definition allows for democratization in one year followed by further democratization from two to ten years later, in which case the 'recent democratization' dummy variable is extended to ten years following the latest year with a positive improvement that qualifies. The state of being recently democratized can be interrupted by a similarly negative change of polity, that is, a change in polity score less than −2. Changes in polity of −1 or −2 do not interrupt coding for recent democratization unless the sum of those changes is greater than the positive democratization (i.e. the state reverts to a level of democracy less than or equal to the original level of democracy). All years that qualify by the definition above are coded as 1 for recent democratization, using the annual data set based on the periodic data used earlier in this chapter.

Once we have defined 'recent democratization' we are prepared to begin to assess the effects of democratization and level of democracy on economic growth and volatility. We employ an unbalanced panel of 117 countries with annual observations from 1960 to 2003 (3540 observations). Using the definition of 'recent democratization' defined above we have a sample of 911 country-year observations for 'democratizing states' and 2629 country-year observations for 'non-democratizing states' used for comparators. We depart from Rodrik here by limiting the sample to only countries that have polity scores less than 7 (countries with higher polity scores cannot democratize by our definition here). In this respect we are comparing democratizers only to states that could conceivably democratize.

To summarize the data on growth for these countries, we collect the annual growth rates for all countries in the sample, separated between those that have democratized and those that have not. Additionally, we break down those that have democratized into successful democratizers (those completely within the sample and those where democratization had not failed by sample end in 2003), and failed democratizers (those that reverse any democratic progress in the first ten years of democratization as above). These results are presented in Table 2.9.

As Table 2.9 demonstrates, there is a statistically significant difference in growth rates between the sample of countries that democratize and those that do not. Countries that did not democratize during the sample period experienced higher growth rates on average, suggesting that there may be a cost in growth associated with the act of democratization. However, delving deeper, Table 2.9 also shows that there is no significant statistical difference in growth rates between those countries that did not democratize and those countries that successfully democratized. Put another way, if the democratization is expected to be successful, there is no reason to expect that economic growth will suffer for the attempt.

Next we consider the volatility of growth for democratizing states versus those states that did not democratize. Because observations of democratization vary by country and many countries attempt democratization more than once in the sample period, the variance of growth between groups cannot be compared as above. Instead, we divide the sample into those countries that had at least one successful democratization, those countries that attempted democratization at least once but did not succeed, and the remaining countries with polity scores below 8 that did not attempt democratization at all over the sample period. Additionally, to separate out the long-term effects of growth between countries,

Table 2.9 Comparison of mean growth rates by democratization attempt

	Mean	*Observations*	*S.E.*
Non-democratizers	0.014	2,431	0.001
Democratizers	0.008	1,137	0.002
Successful democratizers	0.012	738	0.002
Failed democratization	0.001	399	0.003

the variance reported is the variance of detrended growth rates, that is, the variance of growth around the country growth rate for the sample.

Table 2.10 demonstrates that countries with successful democratization attempts showed significantly lower variance in their growth rates than those countries that did not attempt democratization. Note that the average number of observation years for countries that successfully democratized at least once in the sample was 40, while the average for failed democratization attempts was 38, and the number of years for countries that did not attempt to democratize was 31, so the variance is not driven by more observations for successfully democratizing countries. This lower variance, even accounting for trends in growth rates and length of observation, suggests that countries in the sample that successfully democratized enjoyed less volatility in their growth rates. Of course, since this volatility is observed over the entire sample, causality cannot be inferred. We return to issues of causality momentarily.

In addition to the growth and volatility effects of democratization, it is important to consider how these manifest over the post-democratization period. Figure 2.6 plots the average growth profile for 10 years following democratization for the sample of countries described above. For comparison purposes, annual growth rates are included even for those countries that failed at their democratization attempts.

As Figure 2.6 shows, countries that attempted democratization experienced lower than average growth rates for the first few years following democratization. However, those that succeeded at democratizing had higher growth rates for most years than those that failed, and had higher growth rates than the average growth rate of those that didn't attempt democratization. The brackets represent 90 per cent confidence intervals and show that these average growth rates were significantly higher for successfully democratizing states than their non-democratizing and failed democratizing comparators for most years.

To develop our understanding of this complex relationship further, we reduce the sample to only countries that attempted democratization during the period described above. In Table 2.11 we explore the probability of a democratization attempt being successful given growth rates and other variables that might be associated with successful democratization.

The results in Table 2.11 suggest that high growth rates are likely to promote successful democratization when it is attempted. In addition, countries with higher initial levels of income are more likely to be successful in attempts to

Table 2.10 Comparison of variance in growth rates for three types of country

	Variance	*Countries*
No democratization attempts	0.008	42
Democratization attempts		
Successful democratization	0.004	73
Failed democratization	0.005	13

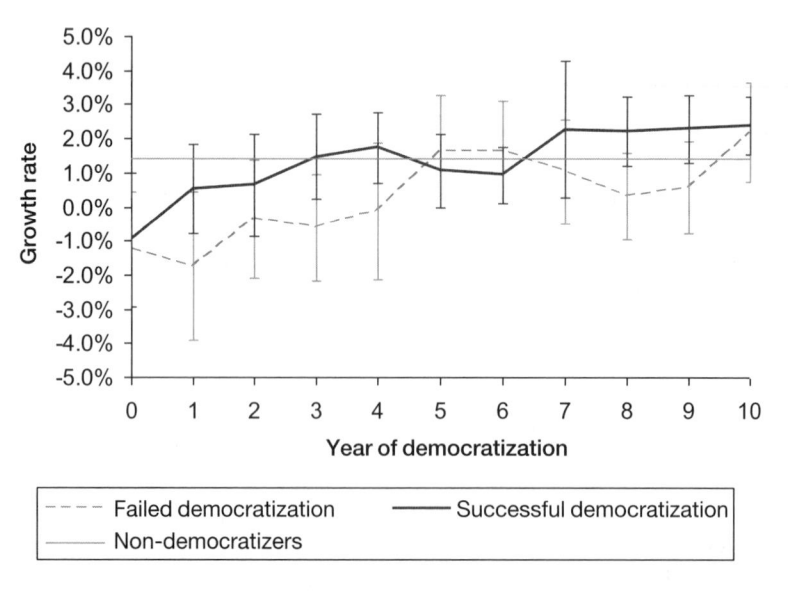

Figure 2.6 Average growth profile in 10 years following democratization.
Source: World Bank 2005; Polity IV data set.

democratize. Also, countries that have recently experienced high levels of growth are more likely to enjoy successful democratization. To address issues relevant to Arab states, we also included regional war measures and fuel exports. We find that war effects do not affect the success rates of democratization attempts (the results are not presented here in the interest of space). Fuel is found to have a negative, but small and not always significant effect on the success rate of democratization. The combination of these results suggests that, although Arab states may be less likely to attempt democratization because of ongoing regional conflicts, there is no reason to expect them to be less successful when they do attempt democratization.

The positive and significant effect of starting year on democratization suggests that those countries that attempted democratization later in the past 40 years have been more successful, which is promising for Arab states; perhaps there are lessons to be learned from other democratization attempts. The extent and type of democratization also affects success rates. Countries that took multiple steps to democratize over a 10-year period or took smaller steps in democratization (the negative coefficient on average step of democratization) were more likely to succeed in their democratization attempts. Finally, we include here the results pertaining to the starting level of democracy and the starting level of democracy squared, both of which are shown to be unrelated to the success of a democratization attempt.[29]

The question that follows from the relationships above is whether democratization can contribute to growth. To test the effects of recent democratization and the level of democracy on growth, in Table 2.12 we conduct fixed (column a) and

Explaining the Arab democracy deficit 73

Table 2.11 Impact of growth on the success rate of democratization

Independent variable	p(successful democratization) (a)	p(successful democratization) (b)	p(successful democratization) (c)
Growth rate during democratization decade	45.08*** (13.761)	36.60*** (12.855)	
Start year of democratization (post-1960)	0.199*** (0.044)	0.235*** (0.052)	0.169*** (0.037)
GDP per capita in year before democratization (ln)	0.991*** (0.331)	1.109*** 0.375	0.924*** (0.289)
# of steps in democratization	0.878** (0.397)		
Growth rate in 5 years preceding democratization	18.845* (9.833)	21.403** 10.478	17.232** (8.371)
Fuel exports as % of total exports	−0.005 (0.011)	−0.021* (0.012)	−0.015 (0.01)
Starting level of democracy		−0.639 (0.572)	−0.065 (0.065)
Starting level of democracy, squared		0.028 (0.023)	
Average step of democratization		−0.255** (0.116)	
Constant	−12.581*** (3.029)	−7.530* (4.33)	−9.265*** (2.380)
Number of observations	104	103	103
Pseudo-R^2	0.45	0.47	0.31

Notes
Standard errors in parentheses. Significance key: * = $p<0.10$, ** = $p<0.05$, *** = $p<0.01$.

random (column b) effects generalized least squares regression on the annual data set described earlier. In addition to including the variables described earlier in this chapter, we include level of democracy, level of democracy squared and recent democratization (as described above) as predictors of growth. Also, we use the predicted probability of the success of democratization for a given year, determined through estimates from column (c) of Table 2.11. This predicted probability is interacted with countries that recently democratized, therefore the level and interaction terms should be interpreted jointly.

Both approaches, comparing the effects within country observations with the fixed effects, and comparing the effects between countries with the random effects regression, suggest that recent democratization is good for growth so long as the probability of the success of democratization is high. Recall that the probability of successful democratization interacted with recent democratization is included as the last independent variable in both models. The positive sign on this interaction

Table 2.12 Impact of democratization on growth

Independent variable	Growth (fixed effects) (a)	Growth (random effects) (b)
Lagged log of GDP per capita	−0.059*** (0.004)	−0.015*** (0.002)
Regional civil wars	−0.001*** (0.000)	−0.001*** (0.000)
Regional international wars	−0.001*** (0.000)	−0.0003 0.0003
Ethnic fractionalization		−0.064*** (0.01)
Level of democracy	−0.005*** (0.001)	−0.003*** (0.001)
Level of democracy, squared	0.0002*** (0.000)	0.0001*** (0.000)
Recent democratization	−0.024*** (0.008)	−0.015* (0.008)
Predicted probability of success in recent democratization	0.035*** (0.009)	0.020** (0.009)
Constant	0.434*** (0.028)	0.165*** (0.016)

Notes
Standard errors in parentheses. Significance key: * = p <0.10, ** = p <0.05, *** = p <0.01.

term suggests that the growth rate will be higher in recently democratized countries if the probability of success is also high. The coefficients for the fixed effects regression suggest that a country with a probability of successful democratization greater than .024/.035 = 68 per cent should expect a higher growth rate if it democratizes, *ceteris paribus*. Likewise, the random effects regressions suggests that a country with probability of successful democratization greater than .015/.020 = 75 per cent should expect a higher growth rate with democratization. The growth rate is actually a function of the probability of success, so countries with higher expected success rates would expect higher growth rates. The estimates of the probability of successful democratization for Arab states based on the most recent data (2003) are presented in Table 2.13.

Taken with the results in Table 2.12, this suggests that the average Arab country is foregoing approximately a tenth of a percentage point of economic growth rate for every year it does not attempt to democratize.

These results explain part of the differences in the growth profiles shown in Figure 2.6. Countries with low probabilities of 'successful democratization' that attempt reforms and revert to autocracy likely experience economic unrest associated with this political reversion. Meanwhile, countries that successfully democratize, such as Thailand (1992–2002), Malaysia (1971–81), Brazil (twice, 1974–95) and Argentina (1983–93) experience higher levels of growth, perhaps in synergy with political reforms.

Table 2.13 Predicted probability of successful democratization per annum

Arab country	Est. p(successful democratization) per annum (based on logit estimation, Table 2.11(c))
Algeria	98%
Djibouti	98%
Egypt	99%
Iraq	n.a.
Jordan	99.5%
Kuwait	99.6%
Lebanon	99.6%
Libya	n.a.
Mauritania	98%
Morocco	99.5%
Oman	99.7%
Qatar	n.a.
Saudi Arabia	99.6%
Somalia	n.a.
Sudan	96.9%
Syria	98%
Tunisia	99.7%
UAE	99.7%
Yemen	94.6%

These results are compelling and suggest that there may be an economic incentive for political reform. The results should be tempered with other results in the literature, where some studies find no systematic relationship between level of democracy and level of growth yet find that democracies perform better in other aspects of economic development. In particular, studies have shown that democracies are more capable of handling adverse economic shocks, that democracies pay higher wages and contribute to lower inequality, and that democracies promote investment and education which can lead to long-term growth (Rodrik, 1998, 1999).

To place Arab growth in perspective, we compare average growth rates for the Arab region and East Asia from 1975 to 2007 in Figure 2.7. While growth in the Arab world collapsed in 1977, the East Asian countries were able to maintain their stellar growth performance for the entire period, with the exception of the East Asian financial crisis. In earlier work, Elbadawi (2002) found three distinct factors that account for the different experiences of the Arab world and East Asia. They are the catch-up associated with initial income and lagged growth in the previous period (1975–84) in East Asia; the quality of institutions (measured by rule of law); and the capacity of a society to manage the impact of exogenous shocks, including oil and conflict.

In addition to slow growth in the 1980s and early 1990s, growth in the Arab world has also been subject to short-term volatility. Clearly the terms of trade, most notably, the price of oil, must be a major contributing factor to this volatility. However, the impact of quality of institutions and the ability to absorb exogenous

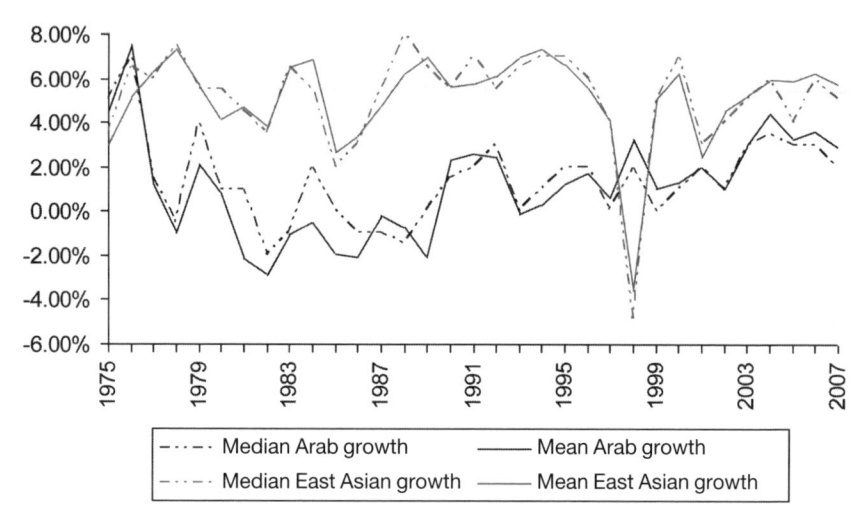

Figure 2.7 Average and median annual growth rates for Arab and East Asian countries.
Source: World Bank 2005.

shocks suggests that these shocks tended to be magnified by the inadequate capacity for conflict management found in autocratic Arab states. As the results in Table 2.10 indicate, those countries that were able to successfully democratize in the period 1960 to 2003 were able to halve volatility, suggesting that democratizing countries are better able to absorb economic shocks.

7. Conclusions

This chapter analyses the widely discussed democracy 'deficit' in the Arab world, popularized by the UNDP Human Development Report of 2002. It empirically corroborates this claim using global quantitative indexes of the level of democracy. The democracy deficit is identified through a significant and negative dummy variable for Arab countries in an extended Lipsetian model of democracy that accounts for the economic, social and historical variables assumed to be associated with democratization in the current literature. This evidence obtains for the polity measure of the standard of democracy as well as for the two Freedom House indicators of political rights and civil liberties. The resilience of the Arab dummy to various alternative specifications suggests that modernization theory alone cannot account for the democracy deficit in the Arab world.

Against this backdrop we argue that region-specific factors, most notably oil and war, may in fact be relevant for explaining the deficit. We find that, controlling for the other determinants, oil is robustly associated with the absence of democracy, and Arab wars account for some of the Arab democracy deficit. Moreover, the Arab dummy ceases to be significant as a stand-alone effect once wars are introduced and interacted, discriminating between wars in the Arab region and other regions. On the other hand, the interactions of the other variables (such as oil, education, female percentage of the labour force and colonial legacy) with regional dummies do not remove the significance of the direct Arab dummy variable. And, very importantly, the sign of the interacted terms for these variables are all the same as the other regional dummies. These findings are robust against a variety of robustness checks: alternative specifications of wars and oil; measures of democracy; and international interventions and Cold War. Other evidence also suggests that socio-religious and cultural factors are either not significant, most notably religion, or that their effects are uniform across regions (e.g. gender and ethnic fractionalization).

The above findings suggest the following several pivotal conclusions:

- First, that the Arab oil dependency has been a hindrance to the region's democracy, confirming the findings of a number of researchers (e.g. Ross, 2001, Nabli and Silva-Jáuregui, 2006).
- Second, the Arab democracy deficit appears to be uniquely associated with inter-state wars (notably the Arab–Israeli conflict) and other violent conflicts, which do not only remove other Arab-specific effects but, unlike other regions, tend to promote autocracy and not democratic transformation, suggesting that the Arab world is different from its comparator regions.
- Third, though part of the Arab democracy deficit may very well be attributable to the large reliance on oil and on the low participation of women in the economy (and by proxy the political sphere), those factors are not specific to the Arab region in that countries with large oil dependency and economically disenfranchised women have low polity scores, regardless of whether they are in or outside the Arab region.
- Fourth, the evidence on the socio-religious and cultural factors suggests that the 'culturalist' theses for explaining the failure of the Arab polity to extend the democratic franchise do not stand the rigorous test of our empirical analysis.

Therefore, while acknowledging the very important influence of oil and the relatively limited political participation of women, among others, in explaining the lagging democratic performance of the Arab region, the above evidence makes clear that the only Arab world 'exceptionalism' regarding the persistence of its democracy deficit is associated with conflicts. As a consequence, it follows that resolving justly and therefore permanently the region's violent conflicts, most notably the Arab–Israeli conflict, would promote the cause of democracy in the region. It also follows that it is very unrealistic to expect that a wide and robust process of democratization will sweep the Arab world in the current pervasive atmosphere of violence engulfing the region.

In addition to the above analysis, which focuses on the long-term determinants of the level of democracy, this chapter also discusses the relatively short-run process associated with the act of democratization. The latter is defined by a dummy variable, 'recently democratized', for the 10 years following a change greater than two points of polity, including a net positive change of three points during the 10 years. In particular, we analyse the subset of successful democratization, which includes those experiences of 'recently democratized' that were not subsequently reversed. We find that, unlike the long-term level of democracy, conflicts and oil do not have robust association with successful democratization. Instead, higher initial income levels or high growth rates are found to be robustly associated with successful democratization. Moreover, late democratizers or those that elected to democratize in smaller and multiple steps are likely to achieve higher rates of successful democratization. Therefore, the above evidence can be taken to suggest that, though the Arab states are less likely to attempt democratization because of ongoing regional conflicts, there is no inherent reason preventing them from achieving successful democratization when they do embark on this process.

Finally, the chapter briefly analyses the growth implications of democratization. First, as indicated above, we develop an indictor variable of 'successful democratization' based on a significant positive change in the polity scale, leading to net positive growth during a course of 10 years and no significant reversals thereafter. Second, we find that countries that have achieved successful democratization have grown faster than those that experienced reversal or those that did not democratize. Third, we also find, in a global panel data model of growth, that recent and successful democratization promotes growth.

These findings have the following two broad implications for the Arab world. First, a major reason for the collapse of economic growth in the Arab region has been the poor capacity of the Arab countries to manage conflicts following external shocks suffered in the region, due to the high levels of oil dependency and the frequency of conflict. If democracies are more capable of handling shocks than their authoritarian counterparts, then as a long-term proposition democratization in the Arab countries would contribute to their longer term economic growth, by allowing them to better manage shocks. Secondly, our findings regarding the robust positive association between (predicted) probability of successful democratization and accelerated economic growth suggests that there is a credible economic argument for democratization in the Arab world. Indeed, greater diversification of Arab economies associated with accelerated growth would help to reduce the impact of external shocks, minimizing the pressure on Arab states to manage domestic social conflicts and saving on economic costs.

Notes

1 A revised and expanded version of 'Explaining the Democracy Deficit in the Arab World', by I. Elbadawi and S. Makdisi, which appeared in the *Quarterly Review of Economics and Finance* 46/5 (Feb. 2007). Permission of the publishers, Elsevier, is duly acknowledged.
2 For examples, see Handoussa and Mikawy, 2002.
3 For a discussion of the obstacles to sustainable development faced by authoritarian Arab regimes, see UNDP and Arab Fund for Economic and Social Development, 2002, and Elbadawi, 2002.
4 The earlier papers (Elbadawi and Makdisi, 2007 and Elbadawi, Makdisi and Milante,

2006) include additional robustness checks and simulations for the Arab states, based on a more parsimonious model.

5 The Lipset hypothesis suggests that with economic development and the associated emergence and growth of an educated middle class, increasing demands for voice and accountability by the middle class result in political liberalization, as described in Lipset, 1959. This theory has been further developed into 'modernization theory' by, among others, Barro, 1996, and revisited by Lipset, 1994. It is important to note that neither of these authors argued that economic growth and development was sufficient for democratization, only that it may be necessary for the demands of political liberalization to be realized. Thus these results augment modernization theory by demonstrating that other factors in the Arab world contribute to the persistence of autocracy.

6 Numerous authors have argued that income from natural resources creates political room for autocracy, because rents from oil and other commodities reduce the tax burden and the expectations from citizenry. Also, these rents can be used to reinforce the state apparatus to secure power or to deliver social goods and development, which obviate the need for political liberalization. Penetrating perspectives on the effect of oil on Arab society are provided by S. Ibrahim, 1982 and Alnasrawi, 1991. An empirical investigation of this relationship is developed in Ross, 2001, and a theory of how capturable resources can contribute to autocratic persistence is developed in Milante, 2007.

7 For a description of the political scene in the 1970s see S. Ibrahim, 1982.

8 This trend is confirmed in other recent empirical work, e.g. Nabli and Silva-Jáuregui, 2006.

9 For a discussion of the perspectives of Arab intellectuals on the USA, and EU commitment to the promotion of democracy in the Arab world, see Al-Braizat, 2003. Recent empirical evidence on the effectiveness (or lack thereof) of intervention by democracies to promote democratization is found in Gleditsch, Siljeholm, and Hegre, 2007.

10 Freedom House measures of political rights and civil liberties are available online at www.freedomhouse.org. The Polity IV index is available under research and data sets at www.cidcm.umd.edu. A classification of regimes is developed in Przeworski, Alvarez, Cheibub and Limongi, 2000.

11 Samuel Huntington (1991) suggests that global patterns of democratization as well as 'reverse' democratization come in waves. He notes that following the first pro and reverse waves of democratization, the 'second wave' of democratization began in 1943 and ended in 1962. He argues that this led to a second reverse wave that started in 1958 and ended in 1975, followed by a third wave of democratization that started in 1974. While debate continues on the validity of these claims, there is evidence from the polity data in Figure 2.3 of a second reverse wave of autocratic consolidation in the late 1960s. The polity data also confirm a general trend in democratization, esp. outside the Arab world, during the 1980s and at the end of the 1980s and into the 1990s, with the collapse of the Soviet Union and the democratization of transition economies.

12 See el-Sayyid, 1995. See also I. Ibrahim, 2000 for a fuller review of democracy in the Arab world, including a detailed discussion of political liberalization experiences.

13 Much of Olson's research focused on the evolutionary success of political systems given assumptions on rational actors. A concise description of the 'stationary bandit' and his potential as benevolent dictator can be found in Olson, 1993: 3.

14 Acemoglu and Robinson (2006) use four iconic cases and a wide range of measures of political progress, contrasting the gradual democratization in Britain to the sudden democratization in South Africa, and compare both to the long-lasting authoritarian regimes in Singapore and the frequent relapses to autocracy in Argentina to explain democratic transitions.

15 See the *Arab Human Development Report 2002* (UNDP, 2002).

16 This approach using five-year periods follows Barro (1996).

17 Data for GDP and population to determine per capita GDP in the five-year periods are taken from the *World Bank World Development Indicators 2005*. Where data are missing for Arab countries, efforts have been made to fill in the gaps through interpolation from surrounding years. Missing data for Lebanon were taken from the Lebanon Ministry of Planning; and Makdisi, 1979.
18 This consists of 16 states composed of more than 50 per cent Arab ethnicity: Algeria, Bahrain, Djibouti, Egypt, Iraq, Jordan, Kuwait, Lebanon, Mauritania, Morocco, Oman, Saudi Arabia, Sudan, Syria, Tunisia and the United Arab Emirates. Three of these countries are also coded as Sub-Sahara African countries: Djibouti, Mauritania, and Sudan. Comoros, Libya, Qatar, Somalia and Yemen are excluded from the data set due to missing data, though they are included in the coding of the independent variable of Arab regional wars, when relevant. Data for Lebanon are sporadically available, so it is excluded from the estimations but was included in simulations run for the case studies that follow.
19 Data for historical and religion variables were taken from the CIA World Factbook.
20 A robustness check of the assumption that missing observations are replaced by 0 is described in Elbadawi, Makdisi and Milante, 2006. These data are collected from the World Bank, 2005.
21 As a robustness check on our measure of oil effects on democratization we use multiple alternative specifications of oil, including running an estimate using only observations where net fuel exports data are available, an estimate with a dummy variable for missing and interpolated values of net fuel exports, and the Arab dummy variable. No significant difference is found with these alternative specifications and the dummy for missing/interpolated data is insignificant and close to zero. See the results in the technical note by Elbadawi, Makdisi and Milante, 2006.
22 We employ data on battle deaths from the Uppsala/PRIO Armed Conflicts Database. Additionally, this battle death data is weighted by distance between Arab states similar to a gravity model, with data on distance from Centre d'Études Prospectives et d'Informations Internationales (CEPII; the French Research Center in International Economics). Lagged values of these measures are employed to avoid endogeneity, and the natural log of the variable is used to reflect the diminishing effect of large-scale violence.
23 US and USSR military intervention are lagged, dummy variables based on military intervention data from the Correlates of War Dataset described in Ghosn, Palmer, and Bremer, 2004: 133–54.
24 Military aid is defined as US 'military assistance, total', measured in million dollars constant 2005 (USAID Greenbook). Official development assistance is drawn from the OECD-DAC Statistics Portal.
25 Elsewhere, Elbadawi, Makdisi and Milante, 2006 have also tested the aggregating rules for polity. In place of average polity we substituted median and minimum polity measures for all countries per period. There is little fundamental effect of the aggregating rule on explanatory power. None of the significant explanatory variables changes in sign, scale or significance by substitution of these variables using differing aggregating rules.
26 See e.g. Olson, 1993: 3; Przeworski and Limongi, 1993: 3; Rodrik, 1998; and Barro, 1996. Elsewhere, Helliwell (1994) finds that democracy only spurs growth through education and investment, which are not unique to democracies (the iconic counter-example is Singapore, developed by Acemoglu and Robinson, 2006).
27 See Wintrobe, 1990: 3.
28 See Ali, 2001.
29 In addition, other variables from previous analysis were used, including ethnic fractionalization, major civil and international wars, regional civil and international wars, former colony and regional effects. None of these variables were found to be significant in determining success of democratization attempts.

References

Acemoglu, D. and Robinson, J. A. (2006) *Economic Origins of Dictatorship and Democracy*, New York: Cambridge University Press.
Al-Braizat, F. (2003) 'Muslims and Democracy: An Empirical Critique of Fukuyama's Culturalist Approach', in R. Inglehart (ed.), *Islam, Gender, Culture, and Democracy*, Willowdale, Canada: de Sitter Publications.
Ali, Ali Abdel Gadir (2001) 'Internal Sustainability and Economic Growth in the Arab States', in Mohamed Salih (ed.), *UNESCO Encyclopedia of Life Support System* (EOLSS), The Hague: International Centre of Social Science Education and Research.
Alnasrawi, A. (1991) *Arab Nationalism, Oil and the Political Economy of Dependency*, Contributions in Economics and Economic History, 120, New York: Greenwood Press.
Barro, R. (1996) *Determinants of Economic Growth: A Cross-Country Empirical Study*, Working Paper, 5698, National Bureau of Economic Research, Cambridge, MA.
Center for International Development and Conflict Management: www.cidcm.umd.edu
Central Intelligence Agency (n.d.) The World Factbook. Online at: www.cia.gov/cia/publications/factbook/index.html
Elbadawi, I. (2002) 'Reviving Growth in the Arab World', background paper for UNDP *Arab Human Development Report 2002: Creating Opportunities for Future Generations*.
—— (2005) 'Reviving Growth in the Arab World', *Economic Development and Cultural Change* 53/2.
—— Makdisi, S. and Milante, G. (2006) 'Technical Note on Democracy and Development in the Arab World', unpublished manuscript.
—— and Makdisi, S. (2007) 'Explaining the Democracy Deficit in the Arab World', *Quarterly Review of Economics and Finance* 46/5 (Feb.).
el-Sayyid, M. (1995) 'The Third Wave of Democratization in the Arab World', in Dan Tschirgi (ed.), *The Arab World Today*, Boulder, CO: Lynne Reinner.
Freedom House: www.freedomhouse.org
Ghosn, F., Palmer, G. and Bremer, S. (2004) 'The MID3 Data Set, 1993–2001: Procedures, Coding Rules, and Description', *Conflict Management and Peace Science* 21: 133–54. Online at: www.correlatesofwar.org
Gleditsch, N. P., Siljeholm, C. L. and Hegre, H. (2007) *Democratic Jihad? Military Intervention and Democracy*, World Bank Policy Research Working Paper, 4242.
Handoussa, H. and Mikawy, N. (2002) *Institutional Reform and Economic Development in Egypt*, Cairo: AUC Press.
Helliwell, J. (1994) 'Empirical Linkages between Democracy and Economic Growth', *British Journal of Political Science* 24.
Huntington, S. (1991) *The Third Wave: Democratization in the Late Twentieth Century*, Norman, OK: University of Oklahoma Press.
Ibrahim, I. (2000) 'Debating Democracy in the Arab World', *Civil Society Democratization in the Arab World*, Ibn Khaldun Center for Development Studies, 9, Cairo, Egypt.
Ibrahim, S. (1982) *The New Arab Social Order: A Study of the Social Impact of Oil Wealth*, Boulder, CO: Westview Press.
Lipset, S. (1959) 'Some Social Requisites of Democracy: Economic Development and Political Legitimacy', *American Political Science Review* 53.
—— (1994) 'The Social Requisites of Democracy Revisited', *American Sociological Review* 59.
Makdisi, S. (1979) *Financial Policy and Economic Growth, The Lebanese Experience*, New York: Columbia University Press.

Milante, G. (2007) *A Kleptocrat's Survival Guide: Autocratic Longevity in the Face of Civil Conflict*, World Bank Policy Research Working Paper, 4186.

Montalvo, J. and Reynal-Querol, M. (2005) 'Ethnic Polarization, Potential Conflict and Civil Wars', *American Economic Review* 95/3.

Nabli, M. and Silva-Jáuregui, C. (2006) 'Democracy for Better Governance and Higher Economic Growth in the Arab Region?', *Proceedings of the International Economic Association World Congress 2006*, Marrakesh, Morocco, Palgrave/Macmillan.

Organization for Economic Co-operation and Development, Development Assistance Committee (OECD-DAC): www.oecd.org/statsportal

Olson, M. (1993) 'Dictatorship, Democracy and Development', *American Political Science Review* 87/3.

Polity IV Project: www.cidcm.umd.edu/inscr/polity

PRIO (International Peace Research Institute, Oslo), Center for the Study of Civil War: www.prio.no/cscw

Przeworski, A. and Limongi, F. (1993) 'Political Regimes and Economic Growth', *Journal of Economic Perspectives* 7/3.

—— Alvarez, M., Cheibub, J. and Limongi, F. (2000) *Democracy and Development: Political Institutions and Well-Being in the World, 1950–2000*, Cambridge: Cambridge University Press.

Rodrik, D. (1998) 'Democracy and Economic Performance', paper presented at the Conference on Democratization and Economic Reform in South Africa, Cape Town, Jan.

—— (1999) 'Democracies Pay Higher Wages', *Quarterly Journal of Economics* 114/3.

Ross, M. (2001) 'Does Oil Hinder Democracy?', *World Politics* 53.

—— (2008) 'Oil, Islam and Women', *American Political Science Review* 102/1.

UNDP and Arab Fund for Economic and Social Development (2002) *Arab Human Development Report 2002: Creating Opportunities for Future Generations*, New York: United Nations Development Program.

USAID, US Overseas Loans and Grants (Greenbook): http://qesdb.cdie.org/gbk/index.html Wintrobe, R.(1990) 'The Tinpot and the Totalitarian: An Economic Theory of Dictatorship', *American Political Science Review* 84/3.

World Bank (2005) *World Bank World Development Indicators* 2005, Washington, DC: World Bank.

Part II

Case studies

Oil, conflict and beyond

MASHREQ COUNTRIES

3 Jordan: propellers of autocracy

The Arab–Israeli conflict and foreign power interventions

Taher Kanaan and Joseph Massad

1. Introduction

Of the variables discussed and examined by the Elbadawi–Makdisi–Milante (EMM) model on the relationship between democracy and development, there is significant evidence that the following 'modernization variables' have, to varying degrees, influenced the democratization process:

- income level/standard of living;
- education;
- neighbouring polity;
- polity of previous period; and
- historical effects of colonization.

Working with a worldwide cross-section model of the behaviour of Polity IV scores of democracy versus autocracy in the different countries and regions, Elbadawi and Makdisi (2007) and Elbadawi, Makdisi and Milante (2006) find that these modernization variables do not satisfactorily explain the democracy deficit deemed to exist in the Arab region as a whole, or in the Arab countries individually. Therefore, they introduce two more considerations specific to the Arab region to examine whether the model then comes closer to explaining the Arab democracy deficit. These are:

- the interaction of oil wealth with democracy, and
- the effects of great power politics and ensuing regional conflicts on the democratization process.

This chapter attempts to examine the specific case of democratic development in Jordan in relation to the predictions resulting from applying the EMM Model to Jordan. In doing this, we probe beyond the main global variables and analyse the potential effects of country-specific factors (history, institutions, culture, etc.) not likely to be captured by the model.

In the Jordanian case, the historical evolution of political institutions was influenced early on by the colonial background of, first, the Emirate of Trans-Jordan, and, later, the Hashemite Kingdom of Jordan. In the aftermath of the First World War, a confluence of events resulted in the formation of Trans-Jordan, with Emir Abdullah of the Hashemite clan of Mecca as its sovereign.

In 1928 the British established the first mechanisms for representation, in an attempt to grant a limited voice to the inhabitants of the country and bring them under the sway of the state. This step was taken after a number of uprisings were staged by Trans-Jordanians against British colonial rule during the first seven years after its establishment. In 1929, representatives were elected to a House of Deputies, which included the appointed cabinet ministers as members. On 25 May 1946 a new treaty was signed with Great Britain whereby the independent Hashemite Kingdom of Jordan was declared. As of 1 February 1947, a new constitution came into force establishing the principle of separation of powers in the state, though the government remained accountable to the King (Mahafzah, 1989: 65–74).

The Hashemite Kingdom of Jordan expanded in 1950 with the inclusion of the relatively more developed Palestinian West Bank. The British colonial regime in Palestine had introduced modern education, created a modern and efficient bureaucracy and enforced the rule of law through a competent judicial system. Similar efforts had taken place in Trans-Jordan, albeit with less intensity.

In 1951, King Abdullah was assassinated and succeeded by his eldest son, King Talal. During King Talal's short reign (1951–2), a relatively liberal constitution was enacted in 1952 by the first Parliament, which represented citizens of Jordan's West Bank as well as the East Bank. This was the same Parliament that in 1950 had ratified 'unification' of the West Bank with the East Bank. However, democratic features of the constitution were seriously deficient until the enactment in 1954 of an amendment that made the executive branch of the government accountable to the parliament (Al-Hiary, 1972: 544–91).

The following sections attempt to review the political and economic developments in Jordan against the 'democracy versus autocracy' theme, in relation to the following:

- First, the historical scores that Polity IV assigned to Jordan between 1951 and 2003, that is, from the inclusion of the West Bank in the Hashemite Kingdom of Jordan to the year of the latest available Polity IV scores for Jordan.
- Second, the ability of the EMM Model to predict the political and economic developments in Jordan by: (a) the modernity variables; (b) the effect of oil wealth; and (c) the effects of great power politics and ensuing regional conflicts.

2. Analysis and critique of polity trends for Jordan

The Polity IV scores for Jordan are given in Table 3.1 and shown graphically in Table 3.1 and Figures 3.1 and 3.2.

The Polity IV data set provides polity scores for Jordan covering the period from the independence of the Kingdom in 1946 up to 2003. The data set shows

88 *Taher Kanaan and Joseph Massad*

Table 3.1 Jordan polity scores, 1951–2003

(1) Periods for 5-year averages	(2) Periods corresponding to remarkable change in polity	Actual polity	Predicted polity	Predicted, without oil effects	Predicted, without war effects	Deviation of actual from predicted (%)	Deviation of actual from predicted, without
	1946–50	–10				n.a.	
	1951	–4				n.a.	
	1952–6	–1				n.a.	
1960–4	1957–73	–9	–9	–9	–9	0.0	
1965–9		–9	–9.31	–9.39	–8.07	+3.1	–9.3
1970–4		–9.2	–9.88	–9.88	–7.24	+6.8	–19.6
1975–9	1974–83	–10	–9.61	–9.82	–6.29	–3.9	–37.1
1980–4		–9.8	–9.26	–9.66	–5.12	–5.4	–46.8
	1984–8	–9					
1985–9		–8	–8.78	–9.49	–3.48	+7.8	–45.2
	1989–93	–4					
1990–4		–2.8	–8.39	–9.40	–1.77	55.9	–10.3
1995–9	1994–2003	–2	–8.37	–9.61	–0.11	+63.7	–19.9
2000–3		–2	–6.84	–8.29	1.74	+48.4	–2.6

Source: Based on EMM data set.

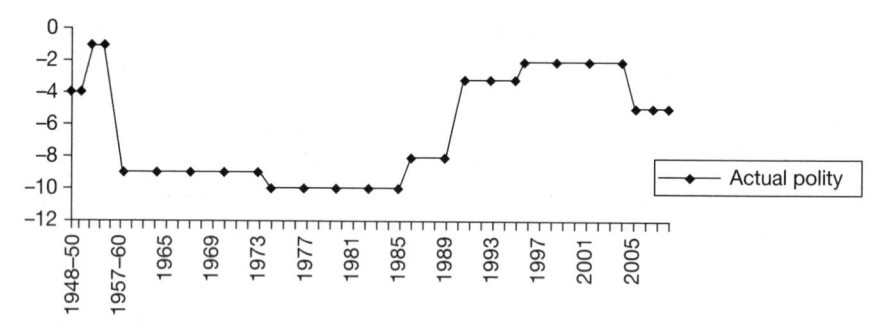

Figure 3.1 Actual polity scores, from yearly data.
Source: Polity IV Index.

uniform scores for several years before a change takes place that continues for several years. Thus, while yearly scores are given for more than 50 years, there are a limited number of variants for which data exist for only eight periods, namely: 1946–50; 1951; 1952–6; 1957–73; 1974–83; 1984–8; 1989–93; and 1994–2003. Moreover, since the EMM Model does not account for the period before 1960, this leaves only five variants, which are then fitted into the five-year periods specified for the EM Model, resulting in nine period observations for each country. Accordingly, Jordan's original five-year period variants are artificially split into the nine period observations of the EMM Model, as shown in Table 3.1. In addition to Polity IV actual scores, the table also shows the EMM Model's predicted scores

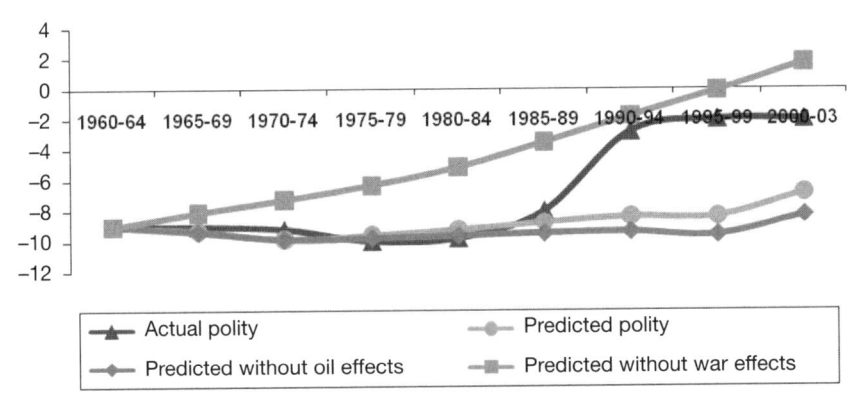

Figure 3.2 Jordan: actual and predicted polity scores in five-year averages, in the EMM Model.

Source: Compiled from Table 3.1, EMM data set.

under different assumptions. We find it useful to extend our analysis to the earlier decade of the 1950s.

With the exception of the period before 1960, where no predictions were attempted, the Polity IV data set and the EMM Model computations provide us with four sets of scores:

- actual scores;
- predicted scores using modernity variables plus oil effects plus regional war/conflict effects;
- predicted scores without oil effects; and
- predicted scores without war/conflict effects.

We examine first the time trends depicted by the scores against the factual record of the political and economic development of Jordan. Then we attempt to examine the predictive/explanatory power of the EMM Model for each of the three categories above.

Actual scores for the period under review, 1950–2003, show that autocratic characteristics outweighed democratic characteristics during the entire period, with some variation. In other words, the net effect of the scores was negative, falling within the autocratic zone denoted by net scores below zero, albeit with certain significant variations.

For most of the period under review, particularly the quarter of a century between 1960 and 1984, the *actual* polity scores for Jordan show that the country remained within levels of the worst percentile in autocracy (–9 to –10). However, in sharp contrast to that unfavourable trend, two exceptional periods stand out:

- The earliest period for which polity scores were compiled, particularly from 1951 to 1956, with the score for 1951 set at –4 and for 1952–6 at –1, the latter

representing the best score on record for Jordan's polity in more than half a century.
- The most recent period covered by the polity scores, namely the 1990s up to 2003: the polity scores for 1990–4, 1995–9 and 2000–3, were set at –2.8, –2 and –2 respectively, just short of actually taking the country over the zero barrier to positive polity, i.e. the democratic zone.

Next, we look at whether the Polity IV ratings are consistent with our own informed judgement concerning the historical record of autocracy versus democracy in Jordan. It will be shown that we find virtually no reason to disagree with the Polity IV ratings for all periods of Jordanian history, with only one exception: the most recent period of 1994–2003, for which Polity IV assigns the relatively favourable rating of –2, the highest since 1960. The EMM Model shows –2 for each of the corresponding two five-year periods, 1995–9 and 2000–3. Because of differences in the electoral law which governed the 1989–93 parliamentary elections, as distinct from the changed, and less democratic, electoral law which governed subsequent elections in 1993, 1997 and 2003, we believe it would have been more meaningful if the ratings for the last two periods, 1995–9 and 2000–3, were relatively lower than –2, particularly as the 1990–4 period, which immediately preceded and was much more democratic, was assigned a score of –2.8.

The following sections also examine the reasons for the exceptionally high ratings for the earliest period (1951–6) and for the most recent period (1990–2003), in sharp contrast to the dismal ratings for the period in between (1960–89).

2.1 Laying the foundations, 1950–56

2.1.1 Political developments

The Polity IV data set shows the earliest score for Jordan's polity, in 1946–50, to be –10, reflecting total autocracy. That appears a fair estimate as the period marks the reign of King Abdullah bin Al-Hussein which, notwithstanding the formal independence of the Jordanian state and the start of certain mechanisms for representation of the people, continued for all practical purposes to be an autocracy not much different from the earlier period from 1921, when political power resided with the Emir and British advisers. The former Emir and now King Abdullah, who had been brought up under the influences of the autocratic Meccan oligarchy, tolerated few constraints to his authority.

The second earliest score shown by Polity IV data set was for 1951, marking a dramatic improvement in the political scene, with autocracy receding to –4. Again, this appears to be a fair score as the period from 1950 marked the election of the First Parliament, giving fair and equal representation to both banks of the Jordan River. As noted earlier, 1952 marked the enactment of the fairly liberal constitution, known as King Talal's Constitution, which remains to this day the governing constitution, albeit with a few amendments introduced to it during the period. Unfortunately, as will be noted later, the more important of these amendments were regressive and ended up significantly weakening its democratic attributes.

The best polity score shown for Jordan in the data set was −1, associated with the period 1952–6. It was the period of momentous political developments characterized by the enactment of a liberal constitution that was the basis for fairly free parliamentary elections, a sustained political mobilization, and by opposition to the British colonial presence. The new young King Hussein, who had acceded to the throne in May 1953, allied himself with the patriotic sentiment that swept the country and culminated in the expulsion of Glubb Pasha, the British head of the Jordanian army, and the 'Arabization' of the Jordanian army command in March 1956. In October 1956 elections were held, marking the fifth parliamentary cycle since 1947. They would be rated as the most free in the country's history up to that time, bringing representation for the first time to a wide spectrum of the Jordanian electorate, including the opposition. That elected parliament was the only one before 1967 to complete its full term, from 1956 to 1960. What made it the most free and representative was, among other things, the enactment of a liberal electoral law designed to assure fair representation. For example, it barred army soldiers from voting while on active duty, to avoid the fraud that accompanied the previous elections in 1952 and 1954, in which soldiers' votes were abused by the British command. The elections, taking place a few months after the formal end of the British presence, brought the popular leader Sulaiman al-Nabulsi to the office of Prime Minister. Patriotic officers were now in control of the army and continuing to press for more democratization.[1]

In the spring of 1949, the war in Palestine ended with the creation of Israel and the expulsion of about 800,000 Palestinians. An armistice agreement was signed and the Central Palestinian territory (renamed the West Bank), which the Palestinians and Arab armies managed to keep upon the creation of Israel, was annexed to Trans-Jordan to form the expanded Hashemite Kingdom of Jordan (which had been declared a kingdom by Abdullah in 1946 upon formal independence from the British). A year later, in the spring of 1950, the First Parliament (lower chamber) of the expanded state was elected to include representatives of the West Bank. The elections were marred by governmental interference through gerrymandering of electoral districts, supporting and opposing candidates according to loyalty criteria, and abusing army votes by providing soldiers with candidate lists marking its favoured candidates. The much more populous West Bank (with 175,000 eligible voters) and the less populous East Bank (with 129,000 eligible voters) were both assigned 20 seats in parliament. The Upper House of parliament had its members appointed by the King rather than elected (Massad, 2001: 187–8).

In the wake of the Anglo-French-Israeli (tripartite) invasion of Egypt, known as the Suez war, Jordan's new parliament recommended in November 1956 the termination of the colonially imposed Anglo-Jordanian Treaty. Early in 1957, on 19 January, Jordan signed an 'Arab Solidarity Agreement' with Egypt, Syria and Saudi Arabia, whereby the three countries undertook to pay Jordan the subsidy previously provided by the British government (Massad, 2001: 190).[2] The formal termination of the Treaty finally came in March 1957. British forces stationed in the country would be withdrawn within six months (Madi and Musa, 1959: 651–60).

In parallel with those events, in January 1957, two months before the implementation of the parliamentary decision to abrogate the Anglo-Jordanian treaty, President Eisenhower had issued the so-called 'Eisenhower Doctrine' which, referring to the power vacuum in the region (resulting presumably from the diminishing British and French presence), offered defence and economic aid to Middle Eastern states that felt threatened by communism. King Hussein immediately expressed interest in the American aid offered, which set him on a collision course with the Nabulsi government, which was then pressing for the recognition of the Soviet Union and communist China, as already agreed by parliament. Faced with such strong resistance from the King, Nabulsi and his cabinet were forced to resign on 10 April 1957 (Massad, 2001: 191; Salibi, 1993: 190–5). The King's embracing of the Americans at this point was due to several factors, particularly his fear of the revolutionist and republicanism of Nasser's Arab nationalism, and his family's traditional friendliness towards Western powers as Hashemite allies dating to the anti-Ottoman Arab Revolt. The King's espousal of the American offer did not implicate him in supporting a former colonial power, as was the situation with Britain, but rather a new Western power whose stance a few months earlier on the tripartite invasion of Egypt seemed to indicate that it opposed the designs of European colonial powers and Israel on the region.

These events mark the direct and thenceforth persistent involvement of the USA in the politics of Jordan. This involvement had initially started with the US operation mission, commonly known as Point Four, 'based on the idea of the transfer and demonstration of technology' (Knowles, 2005: 28). This program started on a low-key basis but funding increased rapidly to JD 2.7 million in 1955, 18 per cent of aid received by Jordan. By 1954 the Point Four program employed 1500 Jordanians at higher salaries than were paid locally, thus weakening the administration of the nascent government. The Point Four officials were concerned about the British domination of the development agenda in Jordan, which resulted in a battle between the United Kingdom, the United States, the United Nations and the Jordanian state, which itself was divided between supporters of the regime and the nationalists (Kingston, 1996, in Knowles, 2005: 25).

2.1.2 Economic development, 1952–56

The period 1952–62 coincided with the first 10 years of modern Jordan. This period was associated with recovery from the tragic effects of the Arab–Israeli hostilities of 1948. A major effect was the influx of about 400,000 Palestinians expelled from 1948 Palestine. The refugees brought with them their savings, together with their relatively superior education, skills and enterprising spirits. This supply of human and material capital augmented the domestic market, creating instant demand for housing and various goods and services. This boost to economic development was fortified with financial resources that continued to be provided by official development assistance.

The overwhelming economic factor that influenced the Jordanian polity during this period was its great dependence on foreign financial aid. At the time, the country had a rather poor, mainly agrarian, economy that had just emerged from a mixed historical background of a teetering Ottoman Empire and the British colonial era that followed its collapse. The country was so poor that the British government had to support its fiscal budget with an annual financial subsidy that amounted in 1956 to £12.5 million sterling, of which £9 million went to the British-led Arab Legion (the Jordanian army), £2 million to development and £1 million for budget support. As noted, in 1957, when the Jordan Parliament decided to consolidate the country's political independence by 'Arabizing' the command of the army, abrogating the Anglo-Jordanian Treaty and joining the Arab Solidarity Agreement with Egypt, Syria and Saudi Arabia, the three countries undertook to pay Jordan the subsidy hitherto provided by the British government.

The capacity of the economy and the quality of governance were enhanced by enriching the civil service with competent and well-trained personnel, educated in the British system under the Palestine Mandate. Economic management was modern and forward-looking.

This was a period of major economic structural adjustment in response to the unification with the West Bank and the influx of the Palestinian refugees. As a result, at the outset of the 1950s the country was suffering from high unemployment. A high population growth rate together with high unemployment meant that a small number of workers had to support a large consumer population. On a somewhat more positive side, Jordan at the time was enjoying increasing development. Domestic industry was still rudimentary; hence it was fairly straightforward and very rewarding to achieve rapid industrial growth by investing in import-substituting industries such as food processing, clothing, household furniture and building materials. The former two industries enjoyed the added stimulation of tariff protection, while the latter two enjoyed the added stimulation of the construction boom caused by population increase and demographic movements that accompanied the refugee influx and unification with the East Bank. Unification also put the expanded country in possession of the great tourist potential represented by the holy shrines in East Jerusalem, Bethlehem and other West Bank sites.

For the period 1954/5 to 1959/60, GDP at factor cost in current prices is estimated to have increased at an annual rate of 11.6 per cent. The estimated inflation rate stood between 3 and 5 per cent at the most. Hence, growth in real terms could have been within the 6 to 9 per cent range, with the construction sector recording the highest nominal growth rate at 22 per cent in current prices (Mazur, 1979: 25–7).

2.2 Reinstituting autocracy, 1957–67

2.2.1 Political developments

The Polity IV data set for the period 1957–67 shows a persistently deep autocratic trend of –9. The political circumstances that explain this trend are outlined in this section. The parallel economic developments are outlined in section 2.2.2.

Although the Jordanian Parliament elected in 1956 was the result of the most free and perhaps most democratic elections in the country's history, as noted earlier, the government that enjoyed its confidence was forced to resign during the second year of its term. The period between 1957 and 1967 was eventful, with regional political turmoil that prompted the Jordanian regime to trade off democracy for stability. The whole Arab Mashreq region was swept up in a cold war between: on the one hand, the Arab nationalist struggle for independence, containment of the Zionist takeover in Palestine and non-alignment in the global East–West cold war spearheaded by Nasserite Egypt; and, on the other hand, the Western imperial powers' insistence on continued hegemony over the region, with the USA taking over the leadership from the British. This took the form of the attempt to align the Arab Mashreq countries in a regional alliance (the Baghdad Pact) as part of the strategy of containment (cold war) against the communist bloc (Soviet Union and China).[3] The landmark political events during this period included the following:

- The (US President) Eisenhower Doctrine of January 1957, which offered defence and economic aid to Middle Eastern countries 'threatened by international communism'.
- The 1958 revolution in Iraq, which destroyed the Iraqi branch of the Hashemite family.
- The formation in 1958 of the United Arab Republic between Syria and Egypt, and its dissolution in 1961.
- The Civil War in Lebanon in 1958.
- The 1962 revolution in Yemen.
- The 1963 Israeli decision to augment its diversion of water from the Jordan River, and Arab counter-plans to divert upstream waters.
- The convening in 1964 of the Palestine National Congress in Jerusalem and the establishment of the Palestine Liberation Organization.
- The Israeli attack on and destruction of the border village of Samu' near Al-Khalil (Hebron) in the West Bank in 1966.
- The 1967 Israeli war on its Arab neighbours, which resulted in it dismembering the Kingdom and occupying the West Bank along with other Arab territories.
- The sentiments of the Arab masses were sharply antagonistic to the pro-West policies of Arab 'conservative' regimes. In Jordan, the democratically elected parliament sided with the policy of independence from Western hegemony and of non-alignment in the global cold war advocated by Egypt and other 'progressive' or 'nationalist' regimes.

When anti-West voices became too loud, the Jordanian regime opted against public sentiment and decided to curtail the democratic process. In 1957, the palace, supported by the US embassy, launched a coup against the elected parliament and government and restored autocracy by declaring martial law, banning all political parties, and rescinding all parliamentary decisions made by the elected parliament that were somewhat progressive, including the granting of suffrage to literate women. Given the corruption of the electoral process with which the regime was periodically engaged at the time, the prospect of expanding the electorate was not necessarily seen as being in its interest.

Newspapers were closed down and a thorough purge of the military and civil service was undertaken, augmented by massive repression. The result was a thorough dissolution of most facets of political life outside government control. All these efforts were undertaken in close coordination with the US Embassy in Amman.[4] Indeed, the American Secretary of State John Foster Dulles spoke on 23 April 1957 of the US government's 'great confidence in and regard for King Hussein', offering assistance 'to the extent that he (Hussein) thinks that it can be helpful' (Satloff, 1994: 171). The King, on his part, had informed the Americans earlier on the night of 24 April of his planned martial law and asked for their help in case of foreign intervention. The White House immediately expressed its support, with a public commitment to 'the independence and integrity of Jordan', which it deemed 'vital' to the United States. The US Sixth Fleet was on its way to Lebanon's shores, technically at the request of Lebanese President Kamil Sham'un, while US military planners considered airlifting troops to Mafraq and Amman. This, however, proved unnecessary as the King informed the Americans that same night that 'I think we can handle the situation ourselves' (Satloff, 1994). In May, the United States provided Jordan with $10 million worth of arms and military equipment, which was followed in June by the signing of an agreement for economic and technical cooperation with Jordan (Murad, 1973: 97). The United States would also help the Jordanian government upgrade its secret intelligence service (General Directorate of Intelligence, or *Da'irat al-Mukhabarat al-'Amah*).[5]

Following the palace coup, which rid the regime of internal threats to the prevailing order, the situation in the Arab world was changing rapidly and the King and his triumphant advisers were becoming more worried about external threats. The unification of Egypt and Syria in what became known as the United Arab Republic (UAR) was declared on 1 February 1958, to the consternation of the anti-Abdel-Nasser rulers in Amman. The regime opted for an immediate federal union with Hashemite Iraq (one that had been long sought by Iraqi strongman Nuri al-Sa'id), dubbed the Arab Federation (*Al-Ittihad Al-'Arabi*), signed on 14 February 1958.[6] On 29 March 1958, the two countries issued a federal constitution. The Arab Federation, which was more of a confederation, had a short life. The Iraqi coup d'état in July 1958 (led by Iraqi army officers) violently eliminated the royal family (and the visiting Jordanian Prime Minister, Ibrahim Hashim, who had declared martial law the year before in Jordan), and declared a republic. The rulers of Jordan panicked. The King asked for immediate British and US help to maintain his throne. Four thousand British troops landed in

Jordan, while US soldiers landed in Beirut. US planes also helped transport oil to Jordan, after it was surrounded on all sides by enemies (the rapprochement with the Saudis, the Hashemites' historic enemies, who had been allied with Nasser's Egypt against the Baghdad Pact, had not yet fully taken place). The British soldiers remained in the country until 2 November 1958. They left only after the Americans pledged to support the throne and to provide the country with US$40–50 million as an annual subsidy, replacing the British subsidy (Murad, 1973: 102; Hussein bin Talal, 1962: 205).

During the period between 1961 and 1967 four parliamentary elections took place. The 1961 (Sixth) parliament lasted just one year before its dissolution. The 1962 (Seventh) parliament lasted for seven months. The 1963 (Eighth) parliament lasted for more than three years before it was dissolved and succeeded by the Ninth Parliament elected in April 1967, shortly before the Israeli war and occupation of the West Bank.

2.2.2 Economic developments

Having weathered the politically tumultuous years of the 1950s, the Hashemite Kingdom of Jordan entered the decade of the 1960s with renewed hope and confidence. The industrial backbone of Jordan's modern economy, including the potash, phosphate and cement industries, was developed during this period. In Zarqa, east of Amman, an oil refinery was constructed. A network of highways linked the country, a new educational system was introduced to the Kingdom, and in 1962 the first university in the Kingdom, Jordan University, was built.

During this period, the investments sponsored by the Development Board (headed by the Prime Minister), whether purely public or mixed with the private sector, were guided by successive development plans that encouraged private industry within an import substitution philosophy, imposing high tariffs or embargos on imports, and restricting market entry to various industries through licensing requirements for new investments under the pretext of avoiding excess capacity resulting from duplication of investments. The overall result of investments and policies of the period was impressive, with rates of economic growth in the 1960s averaging in real terms about 8 per cent for the period 1959/60–1965/6.

The availability of foreign resources, in the form of workers' remittances, official development assistance and, later on, foreign loans, allowed Jordan to maintain a huge foreign trade deficit resulting mainly from investment expenditure on capital formation, but also from non-productive expenditure on defence and for consumption purposes. In all the periods that constituted the economic development narrative of modern Jordan, the productive base of the domestic economy remained too narrow and too shallow to sustain the high levels of consumption and investment.

Two sets of figures illustrate the same point. First, in the period 1950 to 1966, Jordanian exports of goods and services covered only 11–15 per cent of the cost of goods and services imported from abroad. Second, between 1959 and 1966, imports accounted for 28.3 per cent of total GNP (Owen and Pamuk, 1998: 189–90).

Outside the government sector, private enterprise, particularly that by the more prosperous Palestinian business class, characterized the first wave of widespread construction that proliferated in the Kingdom in the years following the 1948 war. During this relatively turbulent period, the Palestinians joined members of the Jordanian commercial elite in setting up a wide range of medium-scale, labour-intensive enterprises, virtually all of which were designed and built in and around the capital city of Amman.

In sum, prior to the 1967 war, Jordan witnessed higher rates of economic growth than most other developing countries. A thriving construction industry provided job opportunities for Jordanians, while tourism to West Bank holy land attractions (Jerusalem, Bethlehem) together with many East Bank attractions (Jerash, Petra) provided the Kingdom with a wellspring of foreign exchange income. The economy was further boosted by remittances from Jordanian expatriates who left to work in the countries of the Gulf.

The progress that Jordan experienced from 1952 gave rise to a new middle class of educated Jordanians keen on building their country. As this group of professionals grew in number and talent, Jordan became more stable and economically prosperous.

2.3 Recovery from war and the formation of a secondary oil economy, 1968–83

2.3.1 Political developments

The Polity IV data set for the period 1967–84 shows that the 1967 war that resulted in Israeli occupation of the West Bank also provided reasons for the ruling regime to persist in its autocratic inclinations, not only preventing the country from improving on the −9 score that prevailed in the previous period, but getting down to −10 or very close to it during the whole period from 1975 to 1984. The political circumstances that explain this evaluation are outlined in this section. The parallel economic developments are outlined in section 2.3.2.

In 1965, eight years after first declaring martial law and the general crackdown on civil society organizations, the government began to relax its repressive measures. In the context of the establishment of the PLO, which vied to represent the largest segment of Jordanian citizens (those residing in the West Bank and those hailing from Palestine but residing in the East Bank), and the rise of the Palestinian guerrilla movement, which sought to recruit among Jordanian citizens, the Jordanian government chose to close ranks by declaring in 1965 an amnesty to all political prisoners, including nationalist army officers who were jailed or exiled in 1957. Two thousand prisoners were released. This relaxation, however, did not last long. Within a year, after the Israeli military raid on Samu' in November 1966 which elicited massive demonstrations against the army's non-confrontational policies towards Israel and its inability to defend its territory, repression ensued.

The army shot at civilians and jailed hundreds, a fate that awaited all army officers suspected of sharing nationalist sympathies with the demonstrators. The Americans were mobilized and sent in arms to prop up the regime. On the eve of the 1967 war, a large number of Jordanian army officers lay in jail.

The 1967 war put the liberalizing opening on hold. It prompted the Jordanian government to curtail the few extant democratic freedoms and to use the consequences of the war as a pretext for the enforcement of emergency laws, which lasted from 1967 until their abrogation in 1989.[7] Following the 1967 defeat, the Jordanian government became more open to the presence of the Palestinian guerrillas in its territory and was forced by popular patriotic sentiment to grant them the right to bear arms, even though it would try to prevent them by force from attacking the Israeli occupation army across the river. This was a period that saw a reduction of US aid to the country due to its signing a mutual defence pact with Egypt and its consequent participation in the 1967 war. This period also saw a brief relaxation of restrictions on the press. The guerrilla presence in the country eventually led to a bloody confrontation with the army which broke out in September 1970. In the wake of the violence in which the army prevailed, the USA significantly increased its economic and military aid to the country. The triumph of the government did not signal a democratic opening but rather, with the increase of US aid, more repression. Following the civil war, a major purge of the army, the civil service and the government was undertaken. Most newspapers were closed down and their editors dismissed. Parliament itself, which had very little power beyond nominally representing East and West Bank citizens, was dismissed in 1974, a month after the Arab League stripped Jordan of its role of representing West Bank Palestinians (Mahafzah, 2001: 40).

The government sought out different representative mechanisms to bring the population into the fold, specifically through the National Union (1971) and, subsequently, through the United Arab Kingdom (1972). Both efforts were soon abandoned. All democratic avenues continued to be closed off. As a result, professional unions came to play an important role in civil society, demanding rights and policy changes.

During this period, we see that the effect of the June 1967 war relaxed autocratic rule in the country and opened up a range of political freedoms, from a less strictly censored press to guerrilla action and more freedom of assembly. This period coincided with a cessation of US aid. The resumption of US aid soon allowed the regime to launch a war against the guerrilla movements with whom it had previously reached an understanding. The result was elimination of the relative freedoms in place from 1967 to 1970 and the inauguration of a new repressive era that closed off all democratic venues. Here again, predicted and actual polity coincide. While predicted polity, however, is low on account of modernization markers, the low actual polity reflected continued US intervention.

The occupation of the West Bank, which was represented by 50 per cent of members of Parliament, prevented the Ninth Parliament, elected shortly before the war, from functioning. Parliamentary life was suspended for the whole period from 1967 up to January 1984 (while Parliament was nominally in place until

1974, it could not hold any meetings in the absence of West Bank delegates and was finally dismissed in 1974) (Mahafzah, 2001).

The rise of professional unions' activism in the country coincided with the Arab world lining up against Sadat's opening of relations with Israel and the distancing of Jordanian foreign policy from US demands to join in the Sadat–Begin peace talks. Once again, the Saudis promised to make up for any loss in US aid, should the USA cut off aid.

It was in this context of declining US influence that the King convened the first National Consultative Council (NCC) in April 1978 as a new representative mechanism of civil society, consisting of a 60-member appointed body. The NCC had a limited mandate, namely to study, debate and render advice on bills drafted by the Council of Ministers. However, it possessed no authority to make policy or to approve, amend or reject any bill. Upon request of the Prime Minister, the NCC provided advisory opinions to the cabinet on general policies of the state. The decree establishing it stated that the NCC would be lawfully dissolved when the House of Deputies was elected and convened. Between 1978 and 1984 three NCCs were formed, consisting of representatives appointed by the King from various sectors of Jordanian society, but none included members from the West Bank.

These were the years of the economic boom and increasing demands for democratic representation from the elites themselves. This agitation continued until the King acquiesced and reconvened parliament in January 1984. Partial elections to fill eight vacant seats from the East Bank were held. Martial law continued, as did US aid, albeit at a substantial reduction, with the conservative Gulf kingdoms making up the difference. This period witnessed the emergence of a new and unlikely ally of Jordan: Saddam Hussein. This new Jordanian alliance and Jordan's support of Iraq in the Iraq–Iran war recemented US–Jordanian relations. If prior to 1981 US policy sought to favour autocratic rule in the country to ensure the stability of the regime to advance its oil interests and its subsidiary support of Israel, by 1981 Jordan's role was to support the USA and the Gulf dictatorships in their anti-Iranian policies.

The conflict between the Gulf countries and the USA with regard to Egyptian peace with Israel was replaced by a unified interest in containing post-revolutionary Iran. In this context, despite the cosmetic opening extended by the Jordanian regime to the elites of the country, its repressive strategy persisted. In 1986, for instance, government troops entered Yarmouk University and shot and killed several student demonstrators, who were demanding more student say in the running of the university and objecting to government policy.

This period witnessed a slow movement toward more liberalization in the brief period of declining US aid and the weakening of the alliance with the USA, followed by a resumption of repression as soon as that alliance was re-established in the context of the war on Iran. Actual and predicted polity continued to coincide in this period. However, when the effect of war and conflict is neutralized in the predictions, that is, when the modernization factors dominate the predictions, the deviation of the actual scores from predicted values increases to a wide gap, averaging more than 40 percentage points. In other words, the coincidence of the actual polity with the predicted polity takes place when the latter includes war/conflict effects (read: the imperial factor in Jordanian politics).

2.3.2 Economic developments

The economic fortunes of the country took a serious turn for the worse with the eruption of the Arab–Israeli war of 1967 and its devastating consequences. Jordan had to cede control over the West Bank (including the eastern part of Jerusalem) which, according to some estimates, was then contributing more than one-third of Jordan's GDP. As a result, Jordan found itself faced with a second wave of refugees, many of them uprooted for the second time in 20 years (Economist Intelligence Unit, 1990/1).

To make matters worse, the loss of the West Bank meant that Jordan lost a large part of its agricultural base (about 40 per cent). Jordanian territory redefined to exclude the West Bank has just over 6 per cent of its area as arable land, and that is dependent on a limited and fluctuating supply of water resources. Rainfall is low and highly variable, and much of the country's available groundwater is not renewable. The defeat in the 1967 war also deprived Jordan of significant amounts of foreign exchange earnings from tourism to Jerusalem, Bethlehem and other West Bank attractions.

Between 1967 and 1973, growth in Jordan's gross domestic product in real terms averaged 1.3 per cent. With a population growth rate that averaged about 4 per cent per annum during the same period, this very low growth rate translated into a decline, in real terms, of about 3 per cent per year in per capita income.

The cushion was provided by an increase in Arab aid, which brought total foreign assistance to just over JD 50 million in 1967/8, compared with an annual average of JD 29 million in 1965/6. With the advent of the oil boom as of 1973, total foreign aid averaged JD 170 million per annum in the period 1975–9; following the Baghdad Arab summit in 1979 and the second oil boom, the figure for financial assistance climbed to an average of JD 344 million per annum for the period 1980–4.[8]

Further stimulation of the high growth rates that characterized the 1973–84 period was provided by:

- The boom in transit trade through the port of Aqaba, to and from Iraq during the eight-year Iran–Iraq war, 1980–8.
- The remittances sent home by Jordanians working abroad. The sums of capital flows transmitted officially through the banking system expanded from an annual average of JD 12 million in 1970–4 to an average of JD 137 million in 1975–9, and JD 368 million in 1980–4 (Central Bank of Jordan, 2004: table 20). This figure falls short of actual flows during that period if one takes into account capital flows remitted 'informally' or in the form of consumer durables and other merchandise (Owen and Pamuk, 1998).
- Jordan benefited, albeit to a limited extent, from the civil war in Lebanon that

began in 1975 and from the war's troubled aftermath, which created a potential role for Jordan to become a provider of banking, insurance and professional services formerly supplied by Lebanon. Fulfilment of this potential has been patchy though, partly because of inadequate infrastructure and partly due to high transaction costs incurred by investors and businesses, including: difficult and time-consuming procedures dealing with the civil service in processing permits, licences, customs clearances, etc.; dead-slow and costly litigation of business disputes, and a far from a level playing field in various markets of goods and services. Accordingly, international and Lebanese companies that moved out of Beirut chose new homes in Cairo, Cyprus, Athens, Paris and London, in preference to Amman, in spite of its geographic proximity.

The average GDP growth rate in real terms for the period 1976–1982 was around 13 per cent, probably one of the world's highest at the time, and certainly the highest on record for Jordan (see Figures 3.3, 3.4, and 3.5, portraying growth rates and trends for GDP, population for the period 1976–2007 and student enrolment for the period 1976–2000).[9]

Economic policy at the time continued on the lines established in the pre-1967 period, that is, using official development assistance to bolster physical and human infrastructure and to lead investment in expensive resource-based projects in collaboration with the private sector. It also continued to support the domestic private-sector investments with tariff protection and monopolistic concessions. Concurrently, it became more and more interested in attracting foreign investment and, in 1972, enacted an Investment Encouragement law for this purpose.

After a record surplus in the account of the Balance of Payments in 1980 (JD 111.6 million), Jordanian net transactions with the rest of the world showed a noticeable decline throughout the rest of the decade (Central Bank of Jordan,

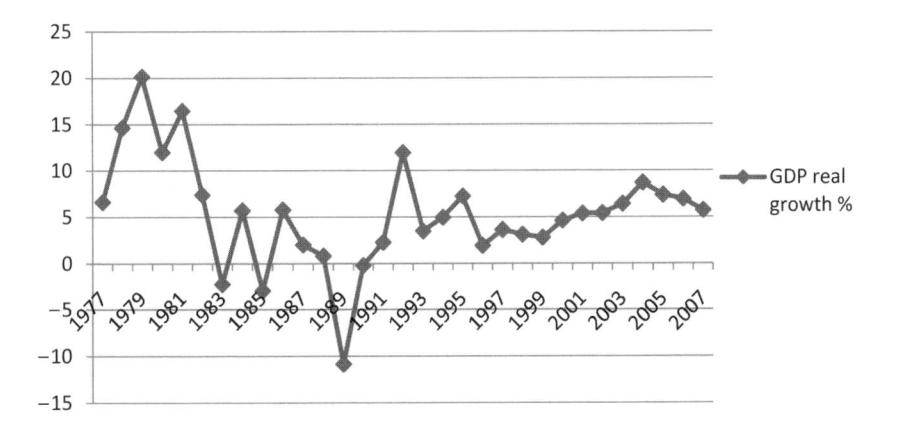

Figure 3.3 GDP annual real growth 1977–2007.

Source: Compiled from official data, Jordan Department of Statistics.

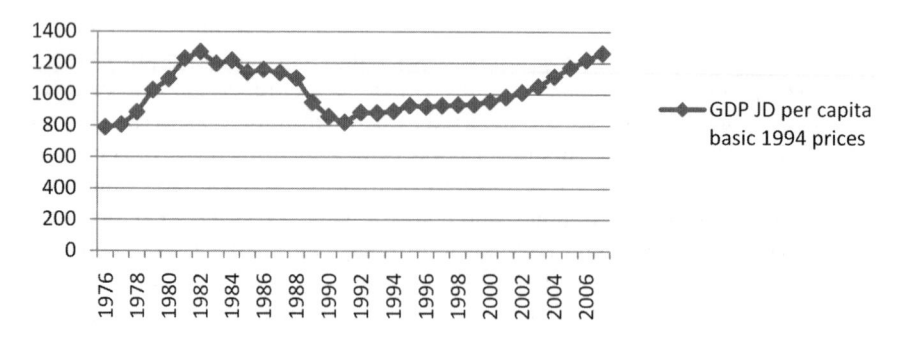

Figure 3.4 GDP per capita at 1994 factor cost, 1976–2007.
Source: Compiled from official data, Jordan Department of Statistics.

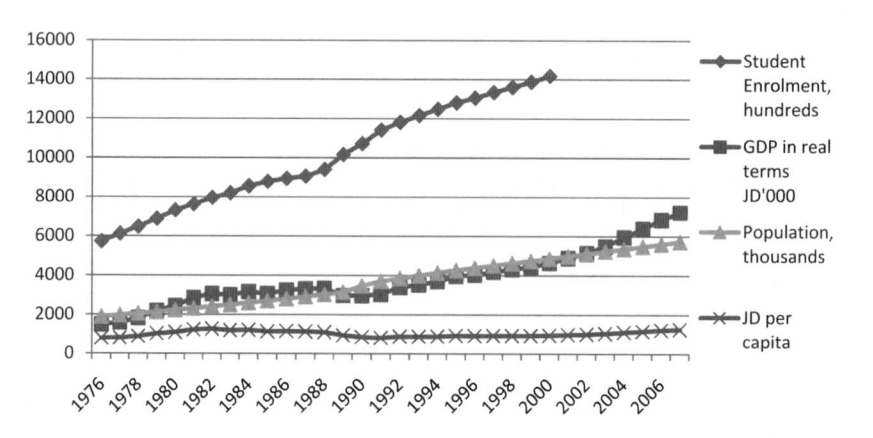

Figure 3.5 GDP, population, and student enrolment trends, 1976–2007.
Source: Compiled from official data, Jordan Department of Statistics.

1980: 71). The year 1980, however, illustrates the spectacular effect of workers' remittances and aid, which allowed Jordan to post a healthy current account surplus despite outspending its GDP by a formidable margin. In that year total consumption, including private and government consumption expenditures, exceeded GDP by JD 90 million, equivalent to 7.6 per cent (Central Bank of Jordan, 2004: table 36).

During the 1970–82 period, public consumption, measured by government recurrent expenditure, had increased at an annual average rate of 10.6 per cent in real terms. Similarly, in the same period private consumption had increased at an average annual rate of 8.8 per cent. Both private and government consumption as a percentage of GDP were above the average of countries at a similar stage of economic development.

Yet despite this flurry of governmental activity, Jordan failed to revive its agricultural sector or to significantly expand the industrial base.

2.4 End of the oil boom: economic hardship as a stimulant of democracy, 1984–88

2.4.1 Political developments

The Polity IV data set for the period 1984–8 shows a significant improvement in polity, moving from the bottom score, –10, to –8. The political circumstances that explain this evaluation are outlined in this section. The parallel economic developments are outlined in section 2.4.2.

To be sure, the democratic improvement referred to above was slight, as shown by polity scores that moved from –9.8 for 1980–4 to –8.0 for 1984–8, improving by less than 20 per cent, but remaining deep in the autocratic zone. A hesitant revival of parliamentary life took the form of reconvening the last pre-1967 Parliament and dismissing the National Consultative Council, the appointed body that was created in 1978 to fill the vacuum created by the suspension of Parliament after the 1967 war. However, no general elections were held.

The King appointed new members to the Senate but recalled those members of the House of Deputies of the Ninth Parliament who were serving when the House had last met in 1976. By-elections were held in the East Bank in March 1976 to fill eight vacancies that had resulted from the deaths of members since the 1967 elections. In accordance with a January 1984 constitutional amendment, the House also voted to fill seven vacant West Bank seats. The newly constituted legislature reflected the demographic and geographical profile of the 1967 Parliament, and was known as the Tenth Parliament.

In March 1986, the Parliament approved a new electoral law that would increase its membership from 60 to 142; 71 members would be elected from the East Bank, 60 from the West Bank, and 11 from Palestinian refugee camps on the East Bank; this law was never implemented. In 1987 the government began registering Jordanians on the East Bank so that they could vote in parliamentary elections scheduled for 1988; these would have been the first national elections in more than 21 years. At the end of 1987, however, registration was halted and the King issued a royal decree that postponed elections for two years.

On 31 July 1988, King Hussein announced the severance of 'administrative and legal ties' with the occupied West Bank, a political move ostensibly consistent with the policy of recognizing the PLO as the 'sole legitimate representative of the Palestinians'. The severance was in contravention of Jordan's constitution and a breach of the oath of office of the government's members.[10] Several nationalist political parties continue to question the constitutionality of this decision and all the legal measures that followed.[11] It marked a defining moment in Jordan's political process. The King dissolved the House of Deputies and in October a royal decree was issued postponing elections for a reorganized legislature indefinitely.

Soon after, mounting economic difficulties led to unrest and violence in certain parts of the Kingdom in April 1989, a date that marked a turning point in the political economy of the country. The favourable economic conditions that created prosperity in the 1970s began to taper off in the early 1980s, reflecting Jordan's dependence on the well-being of the regional economy. With the end of the second oil boom that reached its peak early in the 1980s, an overall curtailment of economic activity in the Gulf countries took place, leading to budgetary cutbacks and a consequent reduction in demand for Jordanian exports and, more seriously, for Jordanian labour. It is estimated that prior to the second Gulf war in 1990/1 the number of Jordanians working abroad was in excess of 300,000 – almost 10 per cent of the population at the time. Employees who kept their jobs often suffered cuts in salaries. The same developments had also a knock-on effect on Arab financial aid. The overall result was a deepening recession in the economy and rapidly mounting foreign indebtedness.

Compared to the robust growth observed up to the opening years of the 1980s, the growth rate of real GDP at 1994 factor cost dropped from an average of 13 per cent during 1977–82 to an average of 3.7 per cent during 1983–7, very close to the population growth rate, before it plunged to about 1 per cent in 1988, then to −10 per cent in the depth of the crisis of 1989. The concomitant inflation was aggravated by removal of subsidies on fuel prices. This immediately led to demonstrations amounting to an uprising in the south and other parts of the Kingdom in April 1989. The King dismissed the incumbent cabinet and appointed a new prime minister who formed a new cabinet. The reformed government went ahead and scheduled parliamentary elections for November 1989. These were the first national elections for the House of Deputies in more than 22 years, ushering in a new era for the institutionalization of Jordan's democratic experience.

2.5 Years of structural adjustment and economic recovery, 1989–2003

Economic hardship resulting from governmental mismanagement would appear to have a political impact different from economic hardship that could be blamed on external misfortunes beyond the regime's control. Economic performance after the severe economic crisis of 1989 saw a hesitant recovery of economic growth from a negative GDP growth of −10.7 per cent in 1989 to a less dismal near zero growth of −0.3 per cent in 1990, to a small positive rate of 1.6 in 1991. To be sure, at the time there were major impediments to economic performance in the form of the continued uprising (intifada) in the Palestinian occupied territories (which had erupted in December 1987), and the first Gulf war in 1990/1. Following six months of robust growth in the first half of 1990, Jordan's stabilization and adjustment plans were thrown off course by Iraq's invasion of Kuwait on 2 August 1990. As a result, the Jordanian economy continued to struggle through another year of economic recession.

The reformed government of 1989 sat down to business with determination, embarking on structural adjustment programs to re-establish fiscal and monetary stability that had been shaken in the wake of the 1988 debt crisis. Reform measures emphasized fiscal discipline and decreasing bias against exports. Salaries and wages in the public sector were frozen and new recruitment was curtailed. Government subsidies were cut and protectionist levels of import duty were scaled down. A sales tax was introduced as a preliminary step to eventual full-scale tax reform based on a system of value added tax.

All these reforms went down well with popular opinion, and contained likely dissatisfaction with the standard of living, which remained below its 1987 levels after two years of reform. Public patience was well rewarded with the remarkable though temporary recovery of the economy during the period 1992–5. The economy made good use of the adverse regional developments resulting from the Gulf war. The sudden influx of about 300,000 returning Jordanians from the Gulf countries, which initially exacerbated unemployment and strained the government's ability to provide essential infrastructure and education, health and other relevant services, on balance proved to be a significant economic stimulant. The returnees came back with their savings (about US$719 million) and, more importantly, with their dynamic working habits, skills and entrepreneurship. As a result, real economic growth shot up by 11.1 per cent in 1992. Gross fixed capital formation (GFCF) rose by 55 per cent in 1992 and 24 per cent in 1993. Massive expansion took place in the form of residential construction, urban infrastructure and investment in various productive activities both directly and via the revived Amman Financial Market. The average GDP growth rate for 1992–5 registered a healthy 6.7 per cent in real terms.

The reform program enabled Jordan to reschedule some debt repayments and have a portion of its bilateral debt forgiven. By the end of the decade (year 2000) the country's debt service ratio to exports of goods and non-factor services fell to 13.6, which was about five percentage points lower than what it was in 1996.

Economic growth slowed to a trickle during 1996–9. The recessionary effects that came with fiscal discipline were not offset by the generous concessions accorded by Iraq on its oil bill or by Jordan becoming the main supply source and supply route to Iraqi imports under the so-called 'oil for food program' that started in 1996 and ended with the second Gulf war in 2003.

The real GDP growth during 1996–9 averaged only 2.9 per cent. With an annual population growth rate of about 3 per cent, this translated into virtual stagnation in the nation's per capita income and in the overall standard of living throughout the late 1990s. Beyond the previous boom period, which lasted for the three years 1992–5, the success of macroeconomic policy reform under the IMF Structural Adjustment Programs did not appear to have helped much in stimulating economic growth during the recession that characterized the subsequent period. Accordingly, Jordan in the second half of the 1990s suffered from a retarded economic performance, notwithstanding the wide range of economic reforms that were being undertaken. The Kingdom's long-term economic outlook appeared favourable in the context of the envisaged reforms, but progress in their implementation was not persistent enough to offset the negative structural flaws in the economy. External factors, over which Jordan had little or no control, such as the financial crisis in Asia and weak demand in the region, exacerbated an already difficult situation. Per capita GDP was on the decline throughout the second half of the 1990s. Real per capita GDP in 1999 was 24.7 per cent below the peak reached in 1984, but 8.3 per cent higher than the corresponding figure in 1991.

Jordan was hoping to cash in on the 'peace dividends' that would have resulted mainly from the peace treaty with Israel in the form of reinstituting profitable trade with the West Bank of Jordan. However, impediments resulting from lack of progress towards terminating Israeli occupation and achieving Palestinian statehood led to a substantial decline in Jordan's exports to Palestine. With the persistent Israeli occupation, the US$3 billion imports market in Palestine remained captive and restricted to Israeli exports.

The Polity IV scores for 1990–4, 1995–9 and 2000–3 were set at the relatively favourable ratings of –2.8, –2 and –2 respectively, just short of actually taking the country over the zero barrier to positive polity, that is, the democratic zone.

Electoral districts had been redrawn to represent East Bank constituencies only, and Jordanians went to the polls on 8 November 1989. Although the ban on political parties, in effect since 1957, remained on the books, candidates ranged ideologically from the far left to the far right. Most of the so-called independent candidates formed loosely organized blocs according to political inclinations.

More than 640 candidates, reflecting the entire spectrum of Jordanian society, including 12 women, competed for seats in the publicly elected House of Deputies, expanded from 60 to 80 members (with the appointed Senate correspondingly expanded to 40 members). The Tenth Parliament ran its full course and parliamentary elections were held again on time in 1993 and in 1997.

Soon after the 1989 elections, King Hussein decided to cancel martial law, in force since 1967. With the easing of tensions, the emergency regulations were frozen in 1989, and formally repealed in April 1992. The new freedoms opened the way for the legalization of political parties and the introduction of new press laws. On 5 July 1992, Parliament formally legalized political parties by passing the Political Parties Law No. 32 of 1992.

King Hussein showed a degree of compliance with the tenets of democracy, civil liberties and human rights, proportionate to the degree of stability prevalent in the regional environment. In order not to relive the difficulties he encountered in the 1950s, he appointed a 60-member royal commission in April 1990 with the mandate of drafting guidelines for the conduct of political life, including party activity, in Jordan. The so-called National Charter Commission comprised members representing all shades of political groupings in the country, and within months produced a written consensus in the form of the National Charter. The Charter, which outlined the main features of political life and the functions of political parties and activities in a democratic Jordan, was adopted by acclamation in June 1991 at a national conference attended by some 2000 leading Jordanians. Along with the Jordanian Constitution, it provided a compass for the national debate on fundamental issues, as well as guidelines for democratic institutionalization and political pluralism in Jordan.

The 1989 parliamentary elections in Jordan were accredited internationally as both free and fair. Subsequently, in 1993, 1997 and 2003 three further parliamentary cycles took place. However, the democratic rating of these three elections did not measure up to the 1989 elections by virtue of regressive changes in the electoral law that governed the later elections.[12] In consequence, the 1997 elections were boycotted by a major party, a number of smaller parties and the major professional unions. The boycott intended to draw attention to a liberal political agenda that called for changing the electoral law and lifting restrictions on the media.

Despite the noted differences between the elections of 1989 and the subsequent elections, we find that Polity IV assigns the relatively favourable ratings of –2.8, –2, –2, to the periods 1990–4, 1995–9 and 2000–3, respectively. However, noting the important differences in the electoral law that governed the 1989–93 parliamentary elections, as distinct from the changed, and less democratic, electoral law that governed the subsequent elections in 1993, 1997 and 2003, we believe it would have been more correct if the ratings for last two periods, 1995–9 and 2000–3, were relatively lower than –2, particularly as the 1990–4 period that immediately preceded this rating, and was much more democratic, was assigned a score of –2.8.

3. Actual versus predicted polity trends, 'oil effects' and 'war and conflict' effects, explaining deviations

In sections 2.1–2.5 above we reviewed the trend of actual polity scores and attempted to relay the events that explain why the country remained within the embarrassingly low levels of the worst percentile, –9 to –10, for not less than the quarter-century of 1960–84, why afterwards, in the period 1985–9, autocracy scores moved up to the next lowest percentile from the bottom, –8, and why from there they jumped dramatically upwards to –2.8 during the 1990–4 period, and to –2 during the latest period (1995–2003). By going back earlier than 1960, to 1951–2, to the early years of the independent Hashemite Kingdom of Jordan, we showed how the polity of that period exhibited a higher polity rating than at any subsequent period.

It was essential to go back to that period, because otherwise we would have jumped to the wrong conclusions about the predictive power of the EMM Model, combining modernity/economic development trends with oil effects and war/conflict effects. The history of the decade of the 1950s clearly illustrates that the limitations on autocracy expressed by the relatively high polity ratings had less to do with economic development, which was then at very low levels, than with the influence of quality education, and of the modern legal framework and institutions such as existed in British-mandated Palestine.

Without considering the earlier period, the model's predicted scores using the modernity variables combined with oil effects and conflict effects showed remarkably little deviation from the actual scores for the whole period from 1960 to 1984. During this time, the range of predicted scores remained within the worst percentile (minimum –9, maximum –9.9) compared to the actual range (minimum –9, maximum –10). The actual polity was better than the predicted polity by not more than 3.1 and 6.8 percentage points during 1965–9 and 1970–4, respectively. Subsequently, while the actual polity worsened relative to predicted polity, their respective scores remained very close, deviating by no more than 3.9 and 5.4

percentage points during 1975–9 and 1980–4 respectively. Afterwards, the scores of actual polity relative to predicted polity showed large deviations in favour of the actual polity, amounting to 56 percentage points in 1990–4, 63 percentage points in 1995–9 and 48 percentage points in 2000–3.

The comparison between actual and predicted trends became more interesting when each of the 'oil factor' effects and the 'regional war and conflict' effects were neutralized. Neutralizing the oil factor made very little difference and kept the predicted values deep into autocratic tendencies. However, neutralizing the war/conflict effect showed a remarkably smooth curve, rising continuously from –9 in 1960–4 to +1.7 in 2000–3. This is clearly the behaviour of polity as it should be when modernity factors are at work without the disfigurements introduced with war and conflict (read: Israeli occupation and American hegemonic interventions). In contrast, actual polity does not show any congruence with the 'normal/peaceful' predicted polity where modernity factors are involved. If these factors had any effect in the case of Jordan, then the actual trend would have shown some tendency to approach the normal/peaceful trend at least during part of the period. In fact, the highest point on the curve as shown in Figure 3.1 appears during the 1950s before our reference period (1960 onwards), at a time when all the modernity variables were at their lowest. Moreover, for three decades, 1960–89, during which economic growth and modernity values had been improving, the actual polity remained stubbornly at its lowest, within the minimum –8, maximum –10 range.

Predicted polity, with or without oil effects but including the effects of war/conflict, was roughly close to actual polity for most of the period 1965 to 1989. In the subsequent, more recent period since 1990, predicted polity under these conditions was much worse than actual polity, with the divergence amounting to an average of 56 percentage points. The mirror picture appears when we neutralize the war/conflict effects, indicating that actual polity, which was widely inferior to the predicted polity in earlier years (1965–89), evolved on a course of conversion which narrowed its deviation from predicted polity (with war/conflict effects neutralized) to a small deviation of $-2.80 - (-1.77) = -1.03$ score levels in the early 1990s, to $-2.00 - (-0.11) = -1.99$ score levels in the late 1990s, and to $-2.00 - (+1.74) = -3.74$ score levels in the early years of the new millennium (2000–3). If we interpret the predicted polity scores for Jordan without the war/conflict effects to mean polity as it is supposed to be when peace and normalcy prevail and modernity factors only are at work, then the scores show that Jordan's actual polity scores came very close to the predicted scores only after the economic crisis in 1988/9. Since then, particularly during the tenure of the Tenth Parliament (1989–92), Jordanian actual polity performed better than the predicted polity, as shown by the wide divergence of their respective curves in Figure 3.2 for the period 1989–2003. The explanation for this divergence for the period 1989–92 is credited to the political relaxation after the 1988/9 economic crisis, as noted earlier.

However, in the following period, 1993–2007, the said convergence was not maintained and a widening divergence reappeared, as the continued regional conflict/war factors gradually dampened the momentum of relaxation which followed the 1988/9 economic crisis.

Is there a particular anomaly in these findings? Not at all. There are perfectly good and satisfactory explanations for the failure of the modernity variables to dislodge autocracy from its stronghold. The educated and materially well-to-do middle class and elite were kept from exercising their inalienable rights and freedoms, not because of retardation of their 'modernity' or their level of economic development, but because of the power and resources enjoyed by the autocratic regime. These were sustained over the years as follows.

1. The regime has been consistently backed by the hegemony of the big powers (Mahafzah, 1989: 20–7):
   (a) Direct British military, financial and political influence from the inception of the Emirate of Trans-Jordan in 1921 through the founding of the Kingdom in 1946, up to the dismissal of British officers and Arabization of the army command in 1956, and beyond it to 1958, in reaction to the Iraqi revolution that toppled the Hashemite regime there.
   (b) The takeover of political and financial influence by the United States, marked historically by the enforcement of the Eisenhower Doctrine in 1957 and 1958.
2. The elite/middle class, which embodied the modernity factors, was subjected to two influences working in opposite directions:
   (a) the co-option by the monarchy of the elite/middle class, allowing it to share in the rents accruing from the power of the state over public contracts, protection tariffs and other dividends of supporting the government, if not directly taking part in government. This negative influence on the modernity factors that had supported democratic tendencies was reinforced by the patronage extended by the regime to what it perceived as its 'power base', within the tribal social structure.
   (b) The influence of political consciousness and ideologies articulated by political movements and parties and supported by the masses, such as anti-imperialism, Arab nationalism, socialism, communism, etc.

It should be noted that the influence of (a) above outweighed the influence of (b) by virtue of the transformation of the ideologically inclined political movements into regimes whose repressive policies ranged from intermittent to ubiquitous. In neighbouring Arab countries the revolutionary regimes became military dictatorships that paid lip service to their programs, such as took place in Egypt, Syria and post-revolutionary Iraq. They particularly failed to accord due priority to democratic freedoms, or at least to show due respect for political or civil rights. Thus, the repression exercised by the 'progressive' regimes of Egypt, Syria and Iraq seemed indistinguishable from the repression of monarchical regimes like that of Morocco, Saudi Arabia and Jordan.

One political analyst has explained the ability of the Jordanian monarchy to overcome the different political and economic storms it was exposed to by the proposition that it managed to weaken 'institutionalized opposition to its rule, relying on the distribution of benefits and privileges to create a cohesive support base and a security establishment loyal to the existing political order' (Choucair, 2006). By and large we agree with this summation except for the adjective 'cohesive' used to describe the support base. It is more to the point to describe the support base as 'balanced' rather than cohesive since it has been skilfully managed by the monarch to keep different segments of society in a state of keen competition for benefits and privileges. To be sure, the Jordanian social structure included one relatively 'cohesive' component of the 'power base', namely the Bedouin and non-Bedouin tribal Jordanians who continued to staff the military and the security apparatus. However, urban Jordanians, who include sizeable numbers of people with Syrian and Palestinian origins and who formed the bulk of the business community and the civil service, were kept on their toes vying for privileges and favours bestowed by the palace and the government.

This was effected through a variety of strategies having to do with national, religious, and ethnic identities. One of the most successful is the regime's continuing ability to persuade all the elites of different communities within the country that the regime's survival alone will ensure the viability of these communities and protect them against other hostile communities in the country. The regime insists that the only way it can accomplish this task is through its less than democratic policies that these elites must uphold. Thus, Jordanian Christian elites believe that the monarchy safeguards them against an Islamist takeover, while Bedouin and non-Bedouin Jordanian elites believe that the regime protects them from a Palestinian takeover based on the Israeli claim that Jordan is the alternative homeland of the Palestinians. Palestinian-Jordanian elites in the country, in contrast, believe that the regime is what protects them from Jordanian chauvinism, while Circassians believe that the regime protects them against Arab chauvinism. Southern elites believe the regime safeguards their interests against northerners, and Bedouins believe the regime protects them against urbanites, etc. The regime was and is able to carry this out through several political, economic and institutional measures, taken over the decades, ensuring the loyalty of all segments of the population to itself and not to one another. Thus unity in Jordan is primarily the unity of elite support for the regime even at the expense of setting the interests of the different communities of Jordanians in rivalry against one another.[13]

The ability of the state, in the Jordan case, to be effective in weakening institutionalized opposition to its rule, relying on the distribution of benefits and privileges to create a balanced support base and successfully co-opting the country's political elite to its less than democratic posture, has been given effective teeth by the rents accruing to the government from aid and official unrequited financial assistance received from foreign and Arab countries, endowing the Jordanian state with 'rentier' characteristics. Thus, the Jordanian treasury was not very dependent on internal taxes, certainly not to an extent where its need for tax revenue would force it to grant significant political concessions to the taxpayers. On the other hand, the political elite, particularly the rising business class, were accorded shares of the rent created through the following channels:

- protection measures against imports of goods that could compete with local industrial products, particularly when the degree of protection exceeded the differential necessary for infant industry encouragement;
- legislation granting monopoly privileges to manufacturing and private service enterprises such as the oil refinery and the tourist transport service; and
- the 'Dutch disease' or syndrome, in the form of the adverse economic consequences of large flows of foreign exchange from both official financial assistance and remittances of Jordanians working abroad. Such foreign exchange flows entice the economy to overvalue the exchange rate and so discourage exports and subsidize luxury consumption of goods (such as Mercedes and Hummer cars) and services (such as travel abroad).

4. Conclusions

Analysing the global polity index, which measures the standards of democracy, we have shown that, like most Arab countries, Jordan has suffered from continued autocratic rule. Though the evolution of the polity score displays an oscillating, U-shaped trend, it remained in the negative zone even at its peak during 1952–6 and after 1995, that is, the regime has not broken through its autocratic fold despite taking occasional steps towards political liberalization. This analysis corroborates the main thesis of the EMM cross-country analysis of the Arab 'freedom deficit' (see Chapter 2), in that the Arab–Israeli conflict, with its attendant foreign power interventions, has clearly affected negatively Jordan's democratic process. To a lesser extent, so have the influences of the oil rich counties of the Gulf, which have supported the Jordanian regime financially, especially in the 1970s and the 1980s. However to fully understand why the modernization factors have failed to promote substantive democratic reforms in Jordan, it is necessary to examine certain country-specific factors that shed additional light on this matter.

It is noteworthy that the oft-cited factors of 'culture' or 'Islam', however defined, have had no obfuscating role to play in the fostering of democratic political life. Rather, the absence of substantive democratic progress is related to the ability of the Jordanian monarchy to impede real political reforms through various incentives and means, largely financed by rentier (non-tax) public revenue, to co-opt the elite and middle class, and by relying on the Western powers (first the British and then the USA) for financial, political and military support that in turn served their regional interests, including their strong support of Israel. With the multiplication of US aid to the country, the corresponding increase in US influence since 11 September 2001, and more so after the US invasion of Iraq in March 2003, the small democratic opening that Jordan knew for less than a handful of years in the early 1990s was effectively ended. Indeed, the growing US influence has been a major factor in maintaining autocratic rule in Jordan.

Furthermore, in the last seven years, the regime has tried several strategies to demobilize the population. Among others, these included: 'Jordan First', a campaign that delegitimized any expression of protest in solidarity with the neighbouring Palestinians and Iraqis as putting the country second or third and threatening its stability; shelving compliance by the regime with the democratic spirit of the constitution as reflected in the National Charter; and carrying on with a demonstrably undemocratic electoral law that nurtured narrow local, tribal and provincial loyalties and interests over national political concerns, leading to deepened fragmentation and a weakening of political opposition. These policies, together with administrative measures restricting the constitutional freedoms of association and expression, were reinforced in particular by the new 'Law for the Prevention of Terrorism, No. 55 for 2006' which allows for heightened repression through provisions that widen the scope of discretion of the Security Administration in ways that may unnecessarily cause citizens, and their businesses and interests, serious harassment or otherwise abuse due legal process.

The regime has been able to fragment and weaken the opposition and win the support of the elites of different communities (tribal, ethnic and religious) by convincing them that their interests are vitally linked to the survival of the regime; and, in turn, that this would require a less than democratic strong central state. The fractionalization of Jordanian society (most notably in terms of Palestinians versus East Jordanians) has facilitated the political machination of the powers that be. This has effectively neutralized the educated middle class, which has rapidly expanded with sustained growth, from becoming the agent for democratization that the Lipsetian modernization theory predicts. These external and domestic factors have combined to perpetuate a trade-off between lesser freedom and democracy and greater national security.

Notes

1 See J. Massad's discussion of this period in Massad 2001: chs 4 and 5. On developments within the military, see Abu Shahut, 1993: 99–100.
2 The arrangements also included the establishment of relations with the USSR and with the People's Republic of China, to express Jordan's gratitude over the stance taken by both countries during the tripartite invasion.
3 See the classic Kerr, 1965. On Israeli aggressions in this period, see Morris, 1997. On the 1956 war, see Neff, 1981.
4 On the intervention of the US embassy, see Satloff, 1994. Satloff documents the relationship by examining declassified State Department documents including correspondence between the US Embassy in Amman and the State Department. On the revelations of the US Embassy intervention, see Murad, 1973.
5 The modernized intelligence service was set up in 1962 and headed by Muhammad Rasul al-Kilani, who had been a minor officer when he interrogated the Free Officers back in 1957 following the palace coup. He also came to prominence in 1959 during the interrogation and torture of Sadiq Al-Shar', who was chief of staff until he was purged on charges of preparing for a coup. Al-Kilani was later sent to the United States for Central Intelligence Agency training. Upon returning to Jordan, Al-Kilani, on the CIA's recommendation, was appointed head of the General Directorate of Intelligence (Murad, 1973:115–16).
6 The Arab Federation Agreement was published in the *Official Gazette*, (*Dustur Al-Ittihad Al-'Arabi*) 1377: 402–13, 1958: 235–8. Also see Aruri, 1972: 151–64.
7 Emergency laws, including martial law, were declared in the aftermath of the 1967

war, and remained in force up to 1989. In effect they abridged certain constitutionally guaranteed freedoms. The martial law authorities and the secret police, popularly referred to as the *Mukhabarat* rather than by its formal name 'General Intelligence Department', were permitted to arrest persons suspected of security offences and to detain them without trial or access to legal counsel for indefinite periods. The emergency laws also authorized the government to censor the press and other publications, ban political parties and restrict the rights of citizens to assemble for political meetings and peaceful demonstrations.

8 Central Bank of Jordan, 2004. Data identified as current public transfers receipts in the current account of the Balance of Payments.
9 Two important observations are in order:

  1 Per capita GDP, which reached a peak in 1984, suffered a slowdown and hit bottom with the major crisis of 1989, and did not recover its 1984 level in real terms until 2006, after a 22-year interval.
  2 Slow economic growth notwithstanding, a major 'modernity variable', namely education, showed steady progress during the interval, surpassing growth in population.

10 Article 1 of Jordan's Constitution stipulates that the Kingdom 'is indivisible and inalienable and no part of it may be ceded'. On the reasons for taking the decision, see Shlaim, 2007: ch. 22, including interview with Taher Kanaan.
11 On the court cases that citizens brought against the government for denationalizing them through the 'severing of ties', see Bakr, 1995. On the unconstitutionality of the decision, see also Massad, 2001: 262.
12 The so-called 'one man one vote' electoral law caused serious distortions in representation; in certain cases electoral victories were made with the winner of highest number of votes scoring no more than 10 per cent of the votes cast, with the remainder of the votes scattered among the rest of the candidates. This is a sign of the weakness of the law, and it also indicates the weakness of the party system in Jordan. See Hammouri, 2004: 1–107.
13 In *Colonial Effects*, Massad (2001) discusses the steps taken historically to ensure the loyalty of the different elites to the regimes. On how the Bedouin were co-opted, ibid., 50–79 and 100–162. On the creation of divisions between Palestinians and Transjordanians, ibid., 204–17 and 222–78. On Circassions and the regime, ibid., 32, 60, 212, 218 and 255. On fostering Christian loyalty, ibid., 32, 41, 60, 234, 265, 268–9, 324n.–325n. On the northern–southern divisions, ibid., 273.

References

Abu Shahut, S. (1993) 'Qissat Harakat al-Dubbat al-Urduniyyin al-Ahrar (1952–1957)', unpublished manuscript, New Jordan Center for Studies, Amman.
Al-Hiary, A. (1972) *Constitutional Law and the Jordanian Constitutional System*, Amman: Ghanem Abdo Press.
Aruri, N. (1972) *Jordan: A Study in Political Development, 1921–1965*, The Hague: Martinus Nijhoff.
Bakr, I. (1995) *Dirasah Qanuniyyah 'an A'mal al-Siyadah wa Qararat Naz' al-Jinsiyyah al-Urduniyyah wa Sahb Jawazat al-Safar al-'Adiyyah* (A Study about the Workings of Sovereignty and the Decisions to Remove Jordanian Nationality and the Withdrawal of Regular Passports), Amman: Maktabat al-Ra'y.
Central Bank of Jordan (2004) *Yearly Statistical Series* (special issue, Oct.), Amman: Department of Research and Studies (1964–2003).

Choucair, J. (2006) Illusive *Reform, Jordan's Stubborn Stability*, Carnegie Papers, 76, Dec., Washington, DC: Carnegie Endowment for International Peace.

Dustur Al-Ittihad Al-'Arabi (Official Gazette) (1958) 1377 (31 March): 402–13.

Economist Intelligence Unit (1990/1) *Country Profile Jordan*, London: The Economist.

Elbadawi, I. and Makdisi, S. (2007) 'Explaining the Democracy Deficit in the Arab World', *Quarterly Review of Economics and Finance* 46/5 (Feb.).

Elbadawi, I., Makdisi, S. and Milante, G. (2006) 'Technical Note on Democracy and Development in the Arab World', unpublished manuscript.

Hammouri, M. (2004) 'Political Development in Jordan', *Jordanian Bar Association Journal* (March).

Hussein bin Talal, King (1962) *Uneasy Lies the Head: The Autobiography of His Majesty King Hussein I of the Hashemite Kingdom of Jordan*, New York: B. Geis Associates.

Kerr, M. (1965) *The Arab Cold War, 1958–1964: Study of Ideology in Politics*, London: Oxford University Press.

Kingston, P. W. T. (1996) *Britain and the Politics of Modernization in the Middle East 1945–1958*, Cambridge: Cambridge University Press.

Knowles, W. (2005) *Jordan since 1989: A Study in Political Economy* (Library of Modern Middle East Studies), New York: I. B. Tauris.

Madi, M. and Musa, S. (1959) *Tarikh al-Urdunn Fi Al-Qarn al-'Ishrin*, Amman: Maktabat al-Muhtasib.

Mahafzah, A. (1989) *Contemporary History of Jordan: The Emirate Era 1921–1946*, Amman: Markaz al-Kutub al-Urduni/Jordan Books Center.

—— (2001) *The Constrained Democracy: The Case of Jordan 1989–1999*, Beirut: Centre for Arab Unity Studies.

Massad, J. (2001) *Colonial Effects: The Making of National Identity in Jordan*, New York: Columbia University Press.

Mazur, M. (1979) *Economic Growth and Development in Jordan*, London: Croom Helm.

Morris, B. (1997) *Israel's Border Wars, 1949–1956: Arab Infiltration, Israeli Retaliation, and the Countdown to the Suez War*, Oxford: Clarendon Press.

Murad, A. (1973) *Dawr al-Siyasi fil-Jaysh al-Urdunn, 1921–1973* (The Political Role of the Jordanian Army, 1921–73), Beirut: Munazzamat al-Tahrir al-Filastiniyah, Markaz al-Abhath.

Neff, D. (1981) *Warriors at Suez: Eisenhower Takes America into the Middle East*, New York: Linden Press/Simon & Schuster.

Owen, R. and Pamuk, S. (1998) *A History of Middle East Economies in the Twentieth Century*, London: I. B. Tauris.

Salibi, K. (1993) *The Modern History of Jordan*, London: I. B. Tauris.

Satloff, R. (1994) *From Abdullah to Hussein: Jordan in Transition*, New York: Oxford University Press.

Shlaim, A. (2007) *The Lion of Jordan: The Life of King Hussein in War and Peace*, London: Allen Lane.

World Bank (1984) *World Development Report 1984*, Washington, DC: World Bank.

4 Lebanon: the constrained democracy and its national impact

Samir Makdisi, Fadia Kiwan and Marcus Marktanner

1. Introduction

Since independence in 1943, Lebanon's national development and political governance have been profoundly affected by the interlocking influences of its sectarian system, geopolitics and regional conflicts and, since 1975, by the impact of a long lasting civil war (1975–90).[1] The political system that emerged on the eve of independence was based on a power-sharing formula among the country's major religious communities that, *inter alia*, applied to cabinet posts and parliamentary representation. Commonly described as 'consociational democracy', it was intended to regulate political life in a country split roughly equally between Christian and Muslim communities, and where religious identification and loyalties were still strong.[2]

The creation of Israel in 1948 and the ensuing inflow of Palestinian refugees into neighbouring countries including Lebanon had a major impact on Lebanon's domestic politics. The persistently sectarian nature and behaviour of Lebanon's political institutions interacted with the Arab–Israeli conflict, eventually leading to the civil war that brought havoc to the Lebanese state and economy. The settlement of the civil war by the Taif Accord (1989)[3] permitted the stationing of Syrian forces in Lebanon and led to Syrian hegemony over Lebanon's political and, to a much lesser extent, economic affairs until the early part of 2005.

In 2005–8, Lebanon witnessed dramatic political, security and military developments that began with the assassination on 14 February 2005 of former Prime Minister and influential Sunni political player Rafic Hariri. This triggered popular protests against Syria which, in combination with mounting Western pressure, forced the withdrawal of Syrian troops in April of that year.[4] On 12 July 2006 Israel waged a full-scale war on Lebanon that lasted until 14 August 2006, ostensibly in response to a cross-border raid by Hizbullah in which two Israeli soldiers were taken hostage a few days before the Israeli onslaught.[5] UN Security Resolution 1701 of 11 August 2006 called for a cease fire (not heeded until a few days later) and for a substantial enhancement of UN peace-keeping forces in South Lebanon. While the immediate outcome of the Israeli war was that it failed to achieve its Israeli-declared objectives, domestically it managed to intensify existing political divisions over specific national issues and to draw external interventions deeper into the affairs of the country.

On 11 November 2006 the Shi'a ministers resigned from the cabinet and the country plunged further into political turmoil that pitted opposition parties comprising Hizbullah and Amal (both Shi'a) and the National Free Movement (primarily Maronite), along with allies from various religious groups, against pro-government parties, including the al Mustaqbal (Future) Movement (Sunni), the Progressive Socialist Party (Druze), the Lebanese Forces (Maronite) and their allies.[6] The government crisis provoked by the resignation of the Shi'a ministers continued to fester, with huge demonstrations and counter-demonstrations being mounted as a show of popular support. When the term of the president of the republic ended on 22 November 2007, no agreement could be reached on the election of a new president, and the post of President became vacant for the first time since independence.

Various Arab League and non-Arab efforts to resolve disagreements between the opposition and loyalist camps over the election of a new president and the formation of a government of national unity did not succeed until mid-May 2008 when the country was on the verge of a new civil conflict.[7] Renewed Arab League mediation led by Qatar resulted in the Doha Agreement (15 May 2008). It was a compromise settlement that specified the immediate election of the chief of the army as the compromise presidential candidate, the overall distribution of cabinet seats in a new government, and the modification of the electoral law that had been a demand mainly of the Christian opposition. The new president of the republic was elected on 25 May 2008 and a new government was formed shortly afterwards. On 7 June 2009 scheduled parliamentary elections took place. The outcome was that the prevailing balance of power between the two opposing camps was more or less maintained.

Clearly this was a period in which Lebanon sank deeper into the quagmire of regional and international political rivalries. The Doha Agreement helped resolve the immediate political disagreements among major politico-sectarian groups and to that extent permitted the resumption of normal political life. For the long term, however, Lebanon has yet to address fundamental weaknesses in its political system and bring about reform that, at once, will shield it from destabilizing sectarian influences and provide the opportunities for sustained and stable long-term development (see section 4 below).

Nonetheless, despite repeated politico-religious tensions, Lebanon's consociationalism has had its positive dimension. It generally tended to promote moderate politics, safeguard freedom of expression and religious beliefs, and protect the pluralism of Lebanese society. However, while nationally agreed, the power-sharing system amounted to unequal political rights among citizens by virtue of belonging to different religious groups, and in practice tended to promote sectarianism and reinforce familiasm and clientelism as the mainstay of Lebanese political behaviour. In fact, consociationalism, based along sectarian lines, could not prevent the outbreak of the civil war, with due recognition of the role of external interventions in its onset.[8] Indeed, sectarian divisions have facilitated these interventions, which more often than not have been of a destabilizing nature. Lebanon has been wide open to the influences of non-democratic regimes in the region, directly or indirectly. According to the simulations in the Elbadawi-Makdisi-Milante Technical Note (Elbadawi et al., 2006),[9] Lebanon would have been more democratic in the absence of the Arab–Israeli conflict, or, alternatively, had that been justly settled, a higher level of governance would have been obtained. And while the direct effects of oil, in this regard, seem negligible, as Lebanon is not an oil country, the region's oil wealth has indirectly influenced Lebanese polity negatively.

From the beginning, the national economy was market-oriented. It experienced an impressive rate of growth in the pre-civil war period, accompanied by relative financial stability, only to be shattered by the outbreak of the war in 1975, with devastating consequences. Lebanon's developmental record in the post-conflict phase is mixed. The growth rate oscillated, averaging well below its pre-war level. At the macroeconomic level some successes were achieved, such as the lowering of the inflation rate, but with major flaws, notably the emergence of persistent macro-fiscal imbalances and the consequent rapid rise of public debt. Overall, the quality of national development suffered. To a large extent, poor political governance, intrinsically, but not solely, linked to sectarianism and clientelism, has been responsible for this outcome. Nonetheless Lebanon achieved a level of real per capita income both in the pre- and post-civil war periods that was relatively high in comparison with other developing countries (see section 2 below).[10] But for all the positive impact of higher per capita income levels on governance, other domestic and external factors (analysed in sections 3 and 4 below) have tended to exert negative influences on Lebanon's polity.

The authors of the Polity IV data set suggest considering countries as autocracies, anocracies and democracies when their polity scores range between –10 and –6, –5 and +5, and +6, and +10, respectively (Marshall, Jaggers and Gurr, n.d.). Lebanon's polity score was 2 between 1950 and 1969 and increased to 5 between 1970 and 1974, the domestic political turmoil unfolding during this period notwithstanding.[11] For the civil war and post–civil war periods no scores were assigned, Lebanon being labelled a case of complete breakdown of central authority and foreign interruption, respectively. For 2006 and 2007, following the withdrawal of Syrian troops in April 2005 and the holding of scheduled parliamentary elections a little later, Lebanon was assigned a polity score of 7, which places it in the democracy category. This score, we submit, may be misleading in that the sectarian political system has remained in place. Other indicators (e.g. the more subjective Freedom House scores) point to a deterioration of Lebanon's democratic practices in the post-civil war period in comparison to the pre-war years.[12] While Lebanon cannot be considered a consolidated democracy but rather a partial or constrained democracy on account of the sectarian nature of its political governance, nonetheless it remains the most democratic in the Arab world, particularly as far as civil liberties are concerned. Perhaps its traditions of civil liberties have helped Lebanon withstand a backslide to a lesser democratic regime than actually prevailed despite the civil war and the strong foreign political influences that came in the wake of the Taif Accord.

The goals of this case study are, first, to discuss, develop and test plausible hypotheses capturing the main explanatory variables that together would explain Lebanon's partial democracy status with the observed deterioration since 1975. In our attempt to do so we go beyond the Arab–Israeli conflict and the (indirect) effects of regional oil wealth, important as they are, and consider additional factors that are relevant to the Lebanese case, such as neighbourhood effects, religious divisions, the civil war, and the familial and clientelist features of the political system. Secondly, we explore ways to enhance Lebanese institutional performance and democratic practices through reforms that, *inter alia*, would consider major issues related to Lebanon's consociational democracy.

Section 2 presents an overview of major developmental trends. Section 3 explores quantitatively the major determinants of Lebanon's polity. Section 4 discusses Lebanon's consociational democracy, its benefits, weaknesses, and the required institutional reform.

2. Development trends

From independence there was political consensus among the major political groupings that the national economy should be market-oriented. This was fostered by the existence of a traditionally influential business class and a political leadership that was close to the business class and that supported liberal economic policies, by generally conservative fiscal and monetary policies, and by the opening of the national economy to the outside world. As early as the 1950s, the Lebanese exchange system became completely free of any restrictions on either currency or capital movements, in contrast with the prevailing exchange systems in the countries of the region and elsewhere that were characterized by exchange controls and other restrictions. Governmental policy was business friendly, mostly non-interventionist, and supportive of private-sector initiatives. The role of the state was thus minimal, whereas in neighbouring Arab countries development was state-led, with most of the major economic enterprises nationalized. In consequence, private capital in these countries tended to seek refuge and investment opportunities abroad, and Lebanon, with its private-sector-oriented and open economy, benefited substantially. This tendency was reinforced by political upheavals in neighbouring countries. At the same time, while experiencing serious domestic political and security tensions of its own (principally relating to national/sectarian divisions over the role played by armed resident Palestinian resistance groups and the readjustment of the sectarian power-sharing formula to render it more balanced between the two major religions groups), Lebanon managed to attract other foreign capital and enterprises, supplemented by emigrant remittances from the Lebanese Diaspora, especially from those living in the US and South America.

The Lebanese private sector, traditionally enterprising, took full advantage of these favourable conditions. In consequence, the pre-war national economy experienced a relatively rapid and broad-based expansion (with high investment rates), accompanied by relative financial stability. The growth rate averaged an estimated 6 to 7 per cent annually, with per capita income reaching $1,200 in 1974 dollars ($4,769 at 2000 prices), one of the highest in the developing world at the time. While the relatively light manufacturing sector expanded, the economy remained trade and services-oriented (about 53 per cent of GDP for 1973). Up to 1970 the annual rate of inflation was estimated at 2 to 3 per cent, and educational standards were also relatively advanced.[13]

This broad-based expansion, however, concealed substantial socio-economic gaps. The distribution of the benefits of the liberal economic system was highly uneven and largely benefited political and business elites, while the income share of factor labour barely increased. The main reason for this lopsided domestic development is the relatively poor institutional performance attributable to the sectarian/familial/clientelist nature of the political system (see section 4). Another reason is that Lebanon's economic and civil freedoms provided it with the opportunity to serve as a safe haven in a geopolitically adverse environment, which in turn provided it with access to strategic rents. In addition, the development of the various regions of the country was strikingly uneven and limited progress was made in narrowing the gap.[14] Further, the social conditions of a sizeable portion of the population were extremely inadequate, being exacerbated by migration from rural areas to urban centres, especially Beirut, which in effect became surrounded with a poverty belt.[15]

The prevailing inequality in income distribution might not have been as skewed as in other developing countries, however, it must be considered against Lebanon's regional inequalities and their confessional dimensions. For example, the position of the middle class was much more prominent in Beirut (dominated by Sunni Muslims and Christians) and the central mountain region (dominated by Christians) than in regions like the south, the Beqa'a, the northeast, and Akkar in the north (dominated by Shi'a and Sunni Muslims) where large land-holdings and class distinctions were common. This gave a clear confessional colouring to the question of inequity in income distribution, particularly in regard to the Shi'a community.

The disastrous impact of the civil war was multifaceted. Apart from the tremendous loss of life (estimated at about 150,000 or 5 per cent of the resident population toward the end of the war), downtown Beirut and whole villages and towns were completely destroyed and the infrastructure of the country was severely damaged. The amount of production lost as a result of the destruction and dislocations the economy had to sustain were huge, though estimates depend upon the assumed rate of growth that would have prevailed in the absence of the war. For example, adopting a reasonable 4 per cent annual rate (in comparison with over 6 per cent of the pre-war rate) would yield forgone output of about $30 billion at 1974 prices (for 1974 GDP was estimated at about $3.5 billion: Makdisi, 2004: 46–8). Estimates of real per capita GDP for 1990 (which, admittedly, may include a wide margin of error) indicate that it was about one-fifth of its level for 1974. In the aftermath of the Israeli invasion of 1982 and the consequent intensification of the political/military conflict, the financial situation began to deteriorate rapidly. Budget deficits increased, the Lebanese pound depreciated quickly, and inflation was on the rise. Real wages suffered and socio-economic conditions worsened.

While a weakened state attempted to counter the deteriorating economic and financial situation, at times successfully, it was the resilience of the private sector, including an expanding informal sector, that prevented a total collapse of the national economy, of course at a substantial social and economic cost.[16]

Since the end of the civil war, four phases of growth may be discerned.

The first, stretching from 1991 through 1994, witnessed an accelerating growth rate peaking at 8 per cent in 1994; it was induced by increasing public-sector expenditure and private-sector investments, led by the construction sector. The increased expenditure took up existing slack in the post-war economy, while private-sector expectations were initially positive regarding future prospects.

The second phase, from 1995 to 2000, saw a gradually declining rate, becoming slightly negative in 2000. This may be partly attributable to continued borrowing by the government at relatively high (though, over time, declining) real interest rates to finance persistent budgetary deficits, with a consequent dramatic rise in public debt (climbing from about 48 per cent of GDP for 1992 to a little over 150 per cent for 2000). This led, in turn, to a 'crowding-out effect' of private-sector investments, and the persistence of generally relatively high borrowing costs for private enterprises. Other factors that contributed to the declining rate of growth were prevailing regional political uncertainties and clashes with Israeli forces occupying a southern part of the country, all of which tended to restrain the flow of private investment. Furthermore, the decline of oil revenues in the Gulf between 1990 and 1999 negatively affected regional investments and remittances from the Gulf region. In addition, while the rehabilitation of the infrastructure had a positive impact on the investment climate, lack of progress in administrative and political reform, not to mention increasing corruption, influenced this climate negatively.

The third phase, from 2001 through 2004, saw a recovery of the growth rate, reaching an estimated 5 per cent in 2004. This improvement is related mainly to post-9/11 developments that caused a reflow of Arab capital towards Lebanon, as well as other Arab countries. The real-estate sector and the tourism industry benefited the most from this development that also contributed to the expansion of bank deposits, easing the pressure on banks in accommodating budgetary deficits.

The fourth phase, 2005 to 2008, witnessed a wave of political assassinations following the assassination of former Prime Minister Rafic Hariri on 14 February 2005, increasing political tensions, and also vast economic destruction (infrastructure, dwellings, factories, other enterprises, etc.) brought about by the war waged by Israel in July 2006. It is not surprising that the growth rate in 2005–6 fell to an average of less than 1 per cent. It picked up substantially in the next two years, averaging about 8 per cent.[17]

The oscillating post-civil war growth trend was accompanied by mixed macroeconomic performance through 2008. On the positive side, anchoring the Lebanese pound to the US dollar beginning late 1992[18] helped restore exchange rate stability and gradually bring down the rate of inflation from its high levels in the immediate post-war years – a peak of 100 per cent for 1992 – to low levels by the end of the decade, estimated at close to 0 per cent for 1999–2001, and to remain at low levels in subsequent years through 2005, but rising in 2006–8 to an annual average of 7 per cent. In the latter years inflationary pressures emanated from the depreciation of the US dollar, and hence the Lebanese pound, vis-à-vis the euro, as well as from the substantial increase in world oil prices.

On the negative side, whatever the reasons, persistent large budgetary deficits led to a continuously rising public debt, reaching about 178 per cent of GDP for 2005, a level that was maintained in both 2006 and 2007, declining to 160 per cent for 2008 (for 2006–8 debt service payments comprised about 50 per cent of budgetary revenues, or over 12 per cent of GDP). These ratios are among the highest in the world. Furthermore, in so far as the fiscal situation was not brought under control, exchange rate stabilization carried with it substantial economic costs. The authorities tended to maintain relatively high real rates of interest on Treasury Bills not only to ensure bank accommodation of the budgetary deficits, but also to defend the pound with consequent high borrowing costs for the private sector from the banking system. Furthermore, adverse domestic political and economic developments were sometimes reflected in heavy and sustained pressure on the pound, which the Central Bank was forced to counter by sustained intervention on the foreign exchange market. At times this was accomplished at the cost of a substantial and threatening decline in its net foreign reserves, prompting the authorities to seek outside financial support to avert a potential domestic economic/financial crisis.[19] Altogether the emerging unhealthy macro-fiscal environment contributed to the overall decline in the rate of growth, particularly after 1995, and exacerbated the unemployment problem, thereby further encouraging the emigration of Lebanese skills.

What should be emphasized is that in the post-war political system the checks and balances that could have prevented the emergence of major macroeconomic imbalances seem to have been weakened at a time when regional economic conditions had become less favourable and when Lebanon was in need of coordination of its economic and reconstruction policies. Budgetary outcomes were not governed by built-in institutional restraints against financial indiscipline. Despite attempts at reform, fiscal policy continued to be embedded in a political environment that did not impose the required accountability, not to mention the conflict of interest on the part of high governmental officials and widespread corruption in the public sector.

However, irrespective of the macroeconomic and growth outcomes in the post-war period, what is equally significant is the quality of development. While in a few areas, such as health and education, progress has been achieved, in other areas little if any improvement was accomplished or else there was noticeable deterioration as in the case of the environment, income distribution and the level of poverty, accompanied by increasing concentration of political and economic power in the hands of the few (Makdisi, 2004: 148–57). This matter is directly attributable to poor institutional performance and to a political setup where the distinction between public and private interest, to say the least, has been blurred.

According to available national income data, per capita income for 2007 is estimated at about $6,000 at current prices ($5,400 at 2000 prices)[20] and of course would have been at a much higher level had the civil war not intervened. Available data show that the 1974 per capita income in real terms was not surpassed until 1998, that is, it took eight years of post-civil war growth before Lebanon could regain its immediate pre-civil war per capita income level.[21] And 16 years after the end of the civil war, the Lebanese economy came to face another challenge of economic recovery and reconstruction, especially in the regions that had been devastated by Israeli aerial attacks. No less important is the challenge of political reconstruction that would permit the dramatic enhancement of the country's institutional performance and level of governance. These challenges have been amply demonstrated by the political turmoil that ensued during the period November 2006–May 2008 noted earlier.

With the above in mind, the following section develops a simple model for the purpose of quantifying the impact of various domestic and external variables on Lebanon's polity. Specifically the model sheds light on how the positive impact on the polity of a relatively high per capita income has been counterbalanced by negative influences related to sectarianism, the impact of the civil war, and, more importantly perhaps, regional factors such as the Arab–Israeli conflict, low-level governance in neighbouring countries and the indirect influences of oil wealth. We are fully cognizant of the fact that because of data and other limitations, the results of the model should not be interpreted as exact quantitative measurements but rather as rough indicators of how the various variables taken into account might have affected Lebanon's polity standing.

3. The determinants of Lebanon's polity: an empirical approach

3.1 The basic model

With the base results of the Elbadawi and Makdisi (2007) cross-country study as a starting point, this section explores quantitatively from a cross-sectional perspective the extent to which certain of Lebanon's major political-economic particularities (for which data are available) are statistically significant determinants of its polity. Several independent variables are considered: income, religious polarization, regional neighbourhood effects (regional oil rents and the Arab–Israeli conflict), civil conflict and vulnerability to outside intervention. The basic hypotheses are summarized graphically in Figure 4.1. Other relevant factors that due to data limitations could not be incorporated in the model are assessed qualitatively in section 4 below, thereby shedding additional light on Lebanon's polity standing.

Estimating the effect of per capita income on polity reflects the modernization hypothesis. According to the modernization theory of political development, higher levels of development correspond to the evolution of civil societies that demand more political participation. Introducing per capita income also serves as a control variable for other indicators of social development.

Lebanon's Muslim–Christian polarization brings to the forefront the question of Lebanon's consociational democracy. Designed as a particular political contract

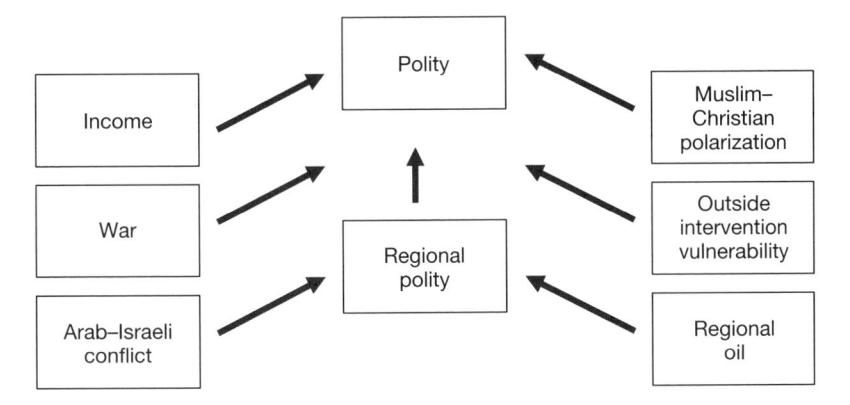

Figure 4.1 Major determinants of Lebanon's polity.

among the various religious groups, the agreed consociational system has imposed certain constraints on the competitiveness and openness of the political decision-making process. In fact, it reflects a trade-off between openness and competition of the political decision-making process on the one hand, and inclusiveness and protection of minority rights on the other.

Additionally, religious polarization renders countries vulnerable to outside intervention by competing third-party interests. Lebanon has witnessed a long history of third-party interventions involving Western and regional powers, especially Syria, Israel and Iran, which would often align themselves with particular religious groups and sectarian oriented parties in order to promote their own interests. Of course, it should be kept in mind that a simple Muslim–Christian Polarization Index is only a useful proxy; it does not capture the full complexity of Lebanon's internal divisions. We argue that, in the presence of religious polarization, neighbouring geopolitical authoritarianism increases a country's susceptibility to outside interventions. And of course the absence of checks and balances, accountability of political institutions and lack of transparency in authoritarian regimes all facilitate such interventions.

However, regional political neighbourhood effects do not only interact with religious polarization, but also have their own direct impact. Regional polity is basically related to regional oil rents and the Arab–Israeli conflict. Oil rents capture the idea of the rentier state, while the Arab–Israeli conflict has been exploited by authoritarian leaders to portray themselves as defenders of the Palestinian cause, in order to justify the need to maintain their authoritarian grip.

War is another prominent variable that we consider. Wars often lead to the negotiation of a new socio-political contract among the warring parties, paving the way for enhanced democratic practices. This is especially applicable whenever the termination of armed conflict is associated with a mutually acceptable and durable settlement. However, as noted by Elbadawi and Makdisi (2007), the Arab world seems to be an exception to this rule. The various Arab–Israeli armed conflicts have not led to any substantial improvements in Arab democratic practices. One major reason is that they have failed so far to bring about a just settlement of the Palestinian question.

3.2 Data and methodology

We use the following variables to approach the model in Figure 4.1.

- The Muslim–Christian Polarization Index is the likelihood of getting one Muslim and one Christian in two random drawings from the population. This index is calculated using data from the *World Christian Encyclopedia* (Barrett, Kurian, and Johnson, 2001). This indicator is assumed to be stable over time.
- The uniqueness of the Arab–Israeli conflict is best captured by the problem of Palestinian refugees. The refugee density expressed as refugees per 100,000 is calculated using data from the 2005 World Bank Development Indicator Database (World Bank, 2005) and the United Nations Relief and Works Agency for Palestine Refugees in the Near East (UNRWA).
- Vulnerability to outside intervention is approached by multiplying the Muslim–Christian polarization figure by an index of prevailing authoritarianism. Thus, a religious split has more adverse effects on domestic political development if it takes place in a non-democratic environment.
- The impact of wars is approached by a dummy variable for armed conflict within a country's territory in a given year. The data was retrieved from the Armed Conflicts Dataset compiled by the Uppsala Conflict Data Program and International Peace Research Institute, Oslo (UCPD/PRIO).
- The polity variable is the Polity 2 score from the Polity IV data set (Marshall, Jaggers and Gurr, n.d.). As already noted, it may take discrete values between −10 and +10. The data set's authors interpret countries with a score between −10 and −6 one as autocracies, countries with a value ranging from −5 to +5 as anocracies, and countries with a score ranging from +6 to +10 as full democracies. The value of zero is reserved for cases in which a country experiences a full collapse of state authority, foreign occupation or a transitional period. In sum, the polity score aims at assessing the degree of competition that a country's political leadership faces. In doing so, it resorts to objective criteria such as, for example, constitutional provisions that limit presidential terms.
- The fuel export share as a percentage of GDP measures national and regional oil rents. The variable is calculated using data available in the 2005 World Bank Development Indicator Database (World Bank, 2005).
- Income is measured as constant per capita income (year 2000, in US$), also available from the 2005 World Bank Development Indicator Database.

Both regional oil rents and regional polity scores are population weighted. Table 4.1 summarizes the data and sources.

Lebanon: the constrained democracy 125

Table 4.1 Data and sources

Variable	Description	Source
Income	Per capita income in 2000, US$	World Bank Development Indicator Database 2005 (WDI, 2005)
Regional oil	Fuel exports as a percentage of GDP, population weighted	
Arab–Israeli conflict	Refugees per 100,000	WDI 2005 and UNRWA
Muslim–Christian Polarization (MCP)	Likelihood of obtaining a Muslim and a Christian by drawing two random persons from a given population	Barrett, Kurian, and Johnson, 2001
Polity	Polity 2 score	University of Maryland, Center for International Development and Conflict Management/ George Mason University, Center for Global Policy
Regional Polity (REGPOL)	Regional Polity 2 score, weighted by population	University of Maryland, Center for International Development and Conflict Management/ George Mason University, Center for Global Policy, and WDI
War 1	Number of armed conflict years during each observation period, lagged by one period of observation	UCDP/PRIO Armed Conflicts Dataset
Arab War 1	Number of armed conflict years of an Arab country during each observation period, lagged by one period of observation	

When approaching empirically the political relevance of the various determinants of national polity, the censored nature of the polity variable poses a problem for regular ordinary least squares which is why, with two exceptions, non-linear estimation techniques are applied to illustrate various bivariate relationships, specifically logistic regression of the form:

$$DV = A + \frac{(B-A)}{1 + \frac{C}{e^{D \cdot IV}}}$$

where DV = Dependent Variable (polity). The first exception is the estimation of the relationship between regional and national polity. Since both variables are bounded between −10 and +10, the trend line is best represented by the cubic function:

$$DV = A + B \cdot IV + C \cdot IV^2 + D \cdot IV^3$$

where A, B, C and D are parameters to be estimated, and IV = Independent Variable. The second exception is the estimation of the impact of the number of war years from the previous on the current period, for which a linear trend line is utilized. Hintze (2001) is used to estimate the models.

The data set consists of a panel of all countries listed in the World Bank Development Indicator Database. Each country has nine observations, collected as follows: eight five-year averages beginning with the 1961–5 period and ending with the 1996–2000 period, while the ninth observation is the average of the 2001–4 period.

3.3 Empirical relationships

Figure 4.2 summarizes in scatter plots the bilateral relationships between polity against income, Muslim–Christian polarization, regional polity, outside vulnerability and lagged wars, respectively. Big dots capture Lebanon's predicted values.

Figure 4.2 indicates that Lebanon is exposed to a high level of Muslim–Christian polarization, a very authoritarian political neighbourhood and substantial outside intervention vulnerability. In terms of explanatory power, regional political neighbourhood effects are the most meaningful, followed by income, outside intervention vulnerability and Muslim–Christian polarization.

Unlike other regions in the world, lagged Arab wars correlate strongly with authoritarianism in subsequent periods, an observation that was first tested empirically by Elbadawi and Makdisi (2007).

Figure 4.3 shows that both regional oil rents and refugee densities correlate strongly inversely with regional polity. Therefore, both are important explanatory factors for political authoritarianism in the Arab world.

Lastly, alternative model specifications are compared in order to assess the overall significance of the model displayed in Figure 4.1. The independent variables are transformed according to the methodology outlined above, displayed in Figure 4.2 and Figure 4.3. The results are summarized in Tables 4.2 and 4.3 for the dependent variables polity and regional polity, respectively. The predicted values for Lebanon and the Middle East and North Africa for the period between 2000 and 2004 are also reported.

Using income as the only predictor for Lebanon's polity yields point estimates that are very close to its actual available polity scores (Model I). The model would predict polity scores of 3.8 while the available values for Lebanon (for the pre-war period only) are between two and five. Adding Muslim–Christian polarization (Model II), political neighbourhood effects (Model III) and outside intervention vulnerability (Model IV) reduces Lebanon's predicted polity by 3.7, 4.0 and 5.9 points, respectively. The country's traditional civil liberties and history of political

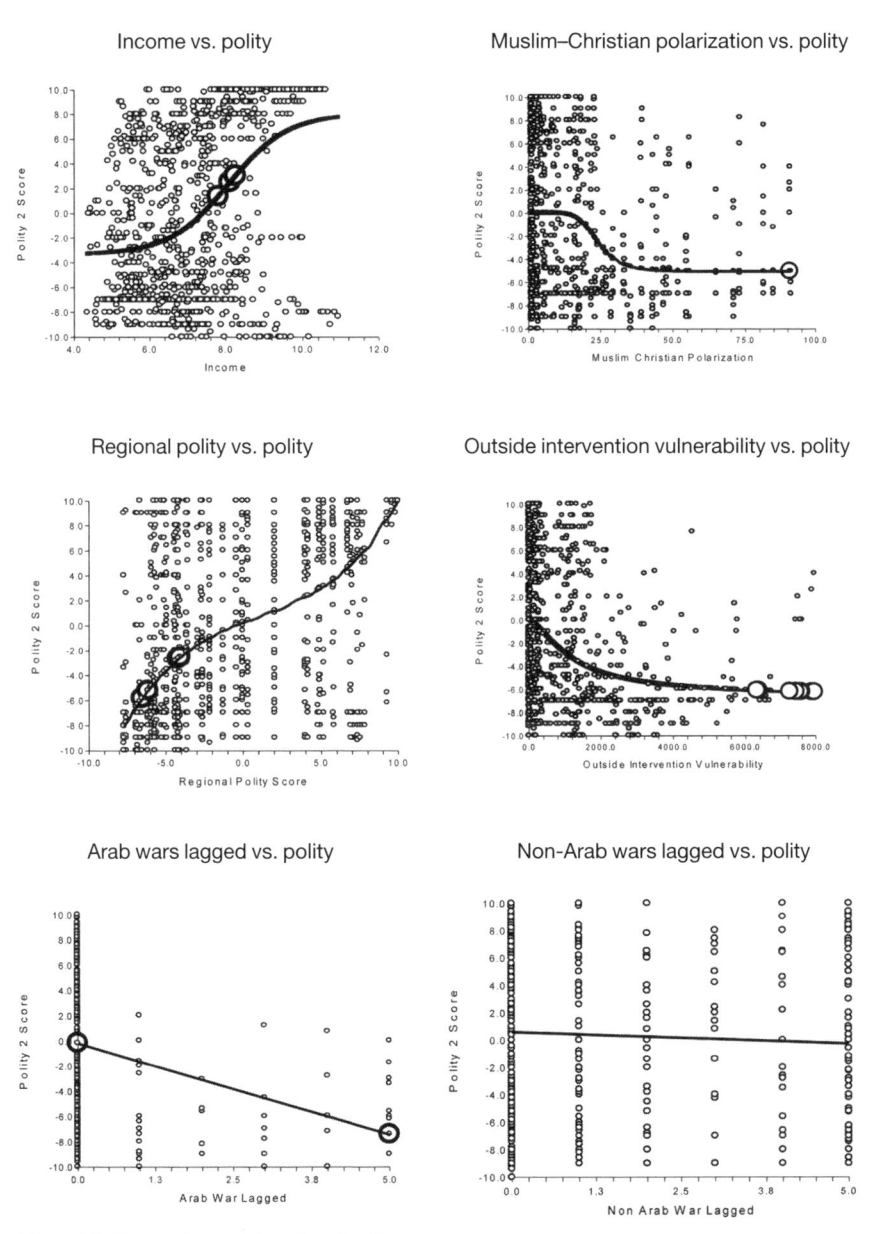

Figure 4.2 Determinants of national polity.

practices explain this wide gap between predicted and actual values and underscore the country's exceptional political position in the region. Model V reconfirms the statistical significance of the perverse polity response to armed conflicts. Table 4.3 eventually shows that regional oil rents and refugee densities, in turn, are very strong explanatory variables for regional polity.

Regional oil export shares vs. regional polity

Refugee densities vs. regional polity

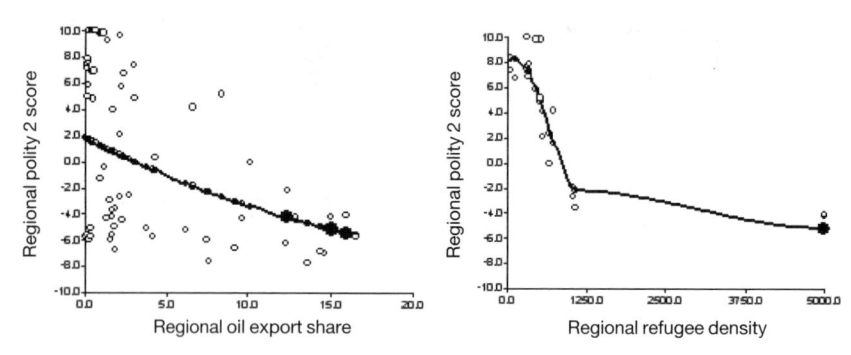

Figure 4.3 Determinants of regional polity.

Table 4.2 Summary regression results, dependent variable: polity

	Model I	Model II	Model III	Model IV	Model V
Intercept	0.03 (0.849)	1.02 (0.000)	0.08 (0.599)	1.95 (0.000)	1.87 (0.000)
Income	1.25 (0.000)	1.08 (0.000)	0.57 (0.000)	0.95 (0.000)	0.94 (0.000)
Muslim–Christian polarization		0.83 (0.000)			
Regional polity			0.79 (0.000)		
Outside intervention vulnerability				1.13 (0.000)	1.19 (0.000)
War (lagged)					0.44 (0.000)
Arab War (lagged)					−1.88 (0.000)
Sample size	1,136	1,133	1,136	1,133	1,044
Adjusted R^2	40.0%	41.2%	47.0%	44.3%	45.8%
Lebanon predicted 2001–4	3.8	0.1	−0.2	−2.1	−2.6

As Muslim–Christian polarization is different from other forms of religious polarization, we also explored the political impact of two additional religious polarizations: The Catholic–Protestant polarization (CPP) and the polarization between the biggest and second biggest religious group, which we refer to as First–Second polarization (FSP).

Regressing polity on income, Muslim–Christian polarization, Catholic–Protestant polarization, and First–Second polarization – with all independent

Table 4.3 Summary regression results, dependent variable: regional polity

	Model I	Model II	Model III
Intercept	0.000 (1.000)	−0.001 (0.994)	0.210 (0.193)
Regional oil	1.000 (0.000)		0.135 (0.023)
Arab–Israeli conflict (refugee density)		1.001 (0.000)	0.966 (0.000)
Sample size	1,872	416	476
Adjusted R^2	15.3%	78.8%	79.0
MENA predicted 2001–4	−5.4	−5.1	−5.5

variables in natural logs – we have the following regression result, with p levels in parentheses:

$$\text{Polity} = \underset{(0.00)}{-19.3} + \underset{(0.00)}{2.1}\ \text{Income} - \underset{(0.01)}{0.4}\ \text{MCP} + \underset{(0.00)}{1.1}\ \text{FSP} + \underset{(0.00)}{0.7}\ \text{CPP}$$

These results suggest that while a Muslim-Christian polarization, which is more likely found in authoritarian regimes, affects polity negatively, the two other polarization indicators carry statistically significant positive signs. One reason for the latter finding is perhaps that the countries concerned happen to be at a more advanced level of development and are situated in a more democratic environment. In other words, neighbourhood effects may contribute to the explanation of the noted discrepancies: it matters as much, if not more so, for a country to be surrounded by a democracy-promoting neighbourhood than for it to maintain a homogeneous community within. This supports our finding that Lebanon's sectarian divisions, while relevant on their own to an explanation of the country's political fragility, assume a much greater importance when taken in conjunction with prevailing regional authoritarianism.

4. Lebanon's consociational democracy: benefits, weaknesses and institutional reform

Given Lebanon's religious divisions, the rationale for adopting the consociational model on the eve of independence was that it would best serve the purposes of stability and democracy in Lebanon and help it withstand external, and generally destabilizing, political pressures. In practice, whereas Lebanon has maintained a generally liberal political environment and civil liberties, especially freedom of expression, the practice of consociational democracy, in particular in the post-civil war period, has been flawed. As the above analysis concludes, the combined negative impact on polity of sectarianism, the Arab–Israeli conflict, regional oil and the civil war more than counterbalanced the positive influence of Lebanon's relatively high per capita income.

In what follows we present a political analysis of why this has been the case, thereby enhancing the empirical results with qualitative insights that help clarify the issues at hand. We begin with a brief outline of what the consociational model implies in the Lebanese context, then move on to discuss its benefits and weaknesses, concluding with a discussion of institutional reforms that we believe ought to be initiated to render the political regime more embracing, equitable and accountable, and thereby strengthen Lebanon's democratic practices.

4.1 The consociational model

In theory, consociational democracy is intended to ensure power sharing among various social groups in a divided or heterogeneous society. It is characterized by four main features.

1 The formation of a large coalition that brings together the political leaders of the social groups in the executive body.
2 Veto power for each social group on decisions concerning vital or fundamental national questions that any group believes goes against their interests.
3 Proportional representation of the different social groups in the society, through a quota system.
4 Social groups are accorded autonomy in specified areas such as personal status laws and establishment of schools.[22]

Being inclusive, accommodating and deliberative, and tending to promote moderate politics, the consociational model has been advocated for countries that are socially divided and/or have emerged from civil wars whose causes, at least partly, are attributed to social divisions. On the other hand, being rooted in proportional representation of social segments in society (rather than political parties), it may not necessarily reflect a full-fledged democracy that mandates equal rights and obligations among citizens.

In the Lebanese case, the consociational democracy model was first embodied in the constitution of 1926 when Lebanon was still under French mandate. Articles 9 and 10 referred to the autonomy and freedom of the religious communities in the management of their beliefs and their personal status, while Article 95 allowed for proportional representation of the various religious communities on a provisional basis in order to ensure equity in power sharing among them. However, the agreed form was not spelled out, leaving it to the mandate authorities to decide.

With independence, a National Pact was agreed in 1943 by the two prominent leaders of the independence movement, Bechara el Khoury and Riad el Solh. The pact specified a division of parliamentary seats among the Christian and Muslim communities on the basis of a six to five ratio, in favour of the Christian community. It also specified that the various Christian and Muslim sects would be represented on a proportional basis. The same principle applied to appointments to major positions in the public sector, especially as concerns the three major religious sects. Veto power by either of the two communities concerning approval of decisions on fundamental questions was provided for by the requirement that such approval was subject to a majority vote of two-thirds.

The Taif Accord of 1989, which was incorporated into the Lebanese constitution (amended and approved by Parliament in November 1990), maintained this veto power but specified the fundamental questions that required a two-thirds majority (Article 65). The Accord readjusted the power-sharing formula among the two main religious communities. It specified equal parliamentary representation (in place of the former six to five ratio in favour of the Christian community), and curtailed the prerogatives of the president while strengthening those of the Council of Ministers and of the Speaker of the House. Most notably, the president could no longer appoint the prime minister at his/her own will but became bound by the outcome of the consultation he/she carries out with members of the parliament on their preferred candidate for the premiership. Furthermore, the president could no longer dismiss the cabinet for any reason whatsoever. In 1995 the bylaws of the recently constituted Constitutional Court gave religious leaders the right to appeal to the Constitutional Court to contest laws they believed were prejudicial to the rights of their communities.

Noteworthy is that Article 95 of the constitution was revisited, whereby the religious quota system for administrative appointments was abolished except for specified senior positions that remained subject to parity between the two main religious communities. Furthermore, Article 95 called for the creation of a National Commission (headed by the president of the republic) to explore ways of eliminating the confessional system other than the personal status laws administered by the respective religious authorities. However no deadline was set for eliminating the confessional system and so far no moves have been taken in this direction.

As already mentioned, the formal consociational framework adopted by the main Lebanese parties was intended to serve the purposes of political stability in a multi-religious country with no one major group constituting a clear majority of the population. Certain studies on social fractionalization (whether ethnolinguistic or religious) point to an inherently high degree of instability or social tension when there exist two groups of almost equal size; the degree of tension declines as the number of social groups increase. Whatever the case, consociational democracy is intended or designed to help reduce tension arising from social cleavages.[23] In the Lebanese context, the interpretation of religious divisions could take one of two forms: a broad Muslim/Christian division or a multi-sect division. We submit that prior to the civil war the first form was more relevant for political analysis, while in the post-war period the second form became more relevant. The existing broad division in the pre-war period contributed to the outbreak of the civil war,[24] while the entrenchment of the multi-sect society in post-civil war years contributed significantly to the political turmoil witnessed in Lebanon, especially in the past few years. In pre-war years, consociationalism and its institutions, while allowing for sectarian proportional representation, could not on their own prevent the outbreak of the war; other internal and external factors intervened to promote conflict (Makdisi and Sadaka, 2005). And in the post-war years, Lebanese consociationalism as practised has yet to prove sufficiently capable of resolving internal conflicts without resorting to outside intervention. Indeed, such intervention has been a constant factor in Lebanon's political development since independence in 1943 and in the settlement of major national conflicts.[25] The dramatic developments since February 2005 have amply demonstrated the great extent to which Lebanon is subject to such interventions.

4.2 Benefits

For Lebanon, the consociational model offered a real opportunity for the various religious communities (numbering 17 in 1936, today 19) to share power, though with clear advantages to politicians of the three main religious communities: the Maronites, the Sunni and the Shi'a. A majoritarian regime could have led to the exclusion of the smaller communities from representation in parliament, from the cabinet and, to large extent, the administration. This of course would remain so to the extent that a secular system is not in place and religious influences prevail in society.

Since the decision-making process in a consociational model is based on negotiation between representatives of different groups of the society, they can and do express their views freely in any debate on public policy. To a large degree (especially before the civil war in 1975) this has been the case in Lebanon, though decisions on basic questions were finally agreed only as a result of consensus, or near consensus, among representatives of the two main religious groups. Of course during the period 1990–2005 Syria's military and political presence in Lebanon was a determining factor, and major public policy decisions were made with implicit or explicit Syrian approval. Syrian influence was felt much less in the economic domain than in the political and security domains.

Other positive attributes of the consociational model in Lebanon are that, on the whole. it has tended to promote moderate politics, as governing coalitions have to accommodate divergent political positions not only as regards internal but also external questions, though under the prevailing circumstances of 2005–8, the moderating influence of consociationalism has waned partly due to mounting but destabilizing outside interventions. Nonetheless, it remains true that Lebanon has traditionally been associated with major Arab causes (especially the Palestine cause) without breaking its friendly ties with the West, despite the West's strong support for Israel. Moderate politics, in turn, promoted freedom of expression and of religious beliefs and permitted relatively free parliamentary elections no matter how imperfect. Finally, one can say the consociational model helped to maintain the pluralism of Lebanese society.

4.3 Weaknesses

Despite its varied positive achievements, in practice the workings of consociational democracy institutions in Lebanon have been marred by major shortcomings.

They have, unfortunately, led, especially in the post-civil war period, to the progressive consolidation of sectarianism: growing allegiance to socio-religious communities instead of a national community bond. Further, religious divisions have facilitated external interventions that more often than not have been of a destabilizing nature. Lebanese political elites have often been beholden to external influences or have tried to exploit these influences for personal gain at home. As discussed in section 3 above, Lebanon has been open to the direct and indirect influences of non-democratic regimes in the region, with ensuing negative influences on its polity. Indeed, as noted, the interaction of sectarianism and external interventions explain to a large extent the onset of the Lebanese civil war in 1975 (Makdisi and Sadaka, 2005).

Sectarianism has led to the emergence of a weak nation-state whose stability is often dependent on indirect external support and, after the civil war until the early part of 2005, on Syrian hegemony over Lebanese internal politics. Syrian influence over the decision-making process has in turn contributed to undermining the proper implementation of the Taif Accord. Political developments since the Syrian withdrawal are still unfolding, with the country remaining partially unstable and held hostage to sharp national politico-sectarian divisions that interact with external, mostly destabilizing, interventions. As noted in section 1, the country was on the verge of a new civil conflict in May 2008, had not a renewed Arab League mediation effort led by Qatar successfully contained it and laid the groundwork for a national agreement on immediate outstanding political issues that had divided the country into two major opposing camps.

Lebanese polity has thus been clearly shown to be fragile and prone to external influences. Noteworthy is that a number of presidential political crises were resolved only after agreeing on the commander of the army as a compromise candidate for president, and again not without outside interventions or threatening the basis of civil power.[26] In other words, the institutions of consociational democracy have so far proved incapable of accommodating political differences over important domestic issues, at least without external intervention.

Being linked to sectarian proportional representation, Lebanese consociational democracy has not only generated, over time, inequities due to demographic changes, but equally importantly has abolished the principle of equal opportunity among citizens in the public sphere. Further, while the logic of the consociational model is that of permanent accommodation, its implementation has been arbitrary and rigid. Public space lacked an institution that could revisit the question of confessional representation and propose measures to render the system more open, equitable and democratic.

Instead, familialism, nepotism, clientelism, and favouritism became entrenched features of political practice. Traditional political elites reliant on sectarian networks have become very resistant to nation-building. No wonder, irregular, let alone corrupt, practices could not be properly controlled and accountability of the government or government officials and public bodies was rarely, if ever, enforced (no government ever lost a vote of confidence in parliament no matter how inefficient or marred with corruption it might have been). Governing coalitions of the representatives of the major religious communities generally managed to hold off any potential opposition that demanded reform and accountability. To them it was and remains mutually beneficial to thwart any reforms that might threaten their political and business interests.

The electoral law has always served the interest of the sectarian leaders by offering them gerrymandering, which extended their predominance in most of the electoral districts and marginalized their opponents in their own community or sect. Criticism of politicians from outside one's own community was often countered by claims that it fostered sectarian feelings, and the significance of any criticism of politicians from one's own religious community was reduced because it was limited to one's community.

Political polarization has frequently followed sectarian lines. Paradoxically, the consociational system, which is supposed to encourage negotiation, came to be based on confrontation and on the principle of yielding as little as possible to others, to the extent that it tended to weaken its moderating influences. The practice of consociational democracy in Lebanon has undermined the institutionalization process of political parties. Certain traditional political families, who continued to play a role in political life, have been eclipsed by a new political elite emerging from militias that prospered during the civil war as well as from the world of business. In consequence of these developments, the emergence of an influential secular opposition has so far been effectively thwarted. The failure to reform the political system helps explain the gaps in national economic management noted in section 2.

Instability of the system and the precarious national polity were the two main characteristics of the decades of national life after independence in 1943. It may be said that the 1975–90 civil war, Syrian dominance from 1990 to 2005 and the tragic events of 2005–7 have constrained the Lebanese from addressing the core question of why the country's political system has failed to promote stability while allowing for a peaceful change towards a higher level of democratic practices.

Whatever the merits of this assessment, initiating fundamental institutional reforms that address the above questions remains the major national issue facing Lebanon today, which is more than ever before exposed to the strong effects of extraterritorial dynamics and imprisoned by the constraints of demography. To this issue we now turn.

4.4 Institutional reform: addressing basic problems of Lebanon's consociational democracy

If reform of Lebanon's political institutions is to enhance the level of governance and provide better safeguards against destabilizing external influences and interventions, three main interrelated challenges would need to be successfully met. The first challenge is how to develop a more embracing democracy, as voiced by civil society associations, women's organizations and other NGOs. In parallel, the second challenge is how to promote a more equitable society at all levels. The third is how to ensure more effective and equitable political participation on the part of major politico-religious groups pending the establishment of a totally secular system, which we regard as one important prerequisite for sustained political stability and development.

In meeting these challenges, a first step would be to enforce those provisions of the Taif Agreement that so far have not been put into practice. Foremost among these provisions is the creation of the National Body for the Elimination of Confessionalism, as stipulated in Article 95 of the new constitution based on the Taif Accord. This step would put aside a potential future controversial question that may be raised by major religious communities (specifically the Shi'a community), namely, the call for a readjustment in the existing power-sharing formula in line with the changing religious composition of the population. So far this question has not been raised, reflecting a realization on the part of the political leadership concerned that it would only lead to unwanted domestic political destabilization.

Another neglected provision in the Taif Accord is the one pertaining to greater administrative decentralization. This step could, on the one hand, weaken the influence of rising (though still not greatly influential) fundamentalist movements and, on the other hand, give greater assurance to various administrative districts, which could very well include multi-religious groups, that they could run their own local affairs without undue or stifling interference from the central authority. It would also help put to rest political strains arising from a continuous search for an acceptable equilibrium in the prevailing system of sectarian power sharing, whether among the major Muslim religious communities or between the broad Christian and Muslim communities. Further, the ability of politicians to dispense favours to their own clients would be greatly reduced.

A related step would be to build greater political immunity from destabilizing regional and external interventions facilitated by Lebanon's sectarian system. Building on the process of de-confessionalism, this could entail taking a stand of positive neutrality vis-à-vis inter-Arab conflicts while maintaining Lebanon's traditional position as concerns the Arab–Israeli conflict. Lebanon's long-term stability hinges on an equitable and acceptable solution to the Palestine question that recognizes declared Palestinian rights. Positive neutrality vis-à-vis inter-Arab conflicts could help Lebanon avoid destabilizing regional interventions whose basic aim has been to serve the vested interests of the regional powers concerned. Removing the confessional element would render such interventions less potent in destabilizing Lebanon's domestic political stability. Of course it should be borne in mind that the principle of positive neutrality vis-à-vis inter-Arab conflicts would require consensual agreement nationally, as well as support from the international community. However, national agreement on this question is unlikely until outstanding border issues with Israel are settled and the question of Palestinian refugees in Lebanon (including the right of return) has been justly resolved, which necessarily would lead to the settlement of other outstanding domestic issues related to the Arab–Israeli conflict (e.g. carrying of arms outside the Lebanese army).

Achieving these objectives would require comprehensive reform based on several related legislative initiatives, as follows.

1. A new administrative reorganization that would give greater autonomy to local communities while aiming at creating districts with religious diversity.
2. A new electoral law that would lead to fairer representation of the country's various political components or parties. Until now a majoritarian system with its 'winner takes all' has been applied. In practice, it has led – especially in the confessional system – to the exclusion of the formation of any sustained opposition that could threaten the majority in power and impose the practice of rotation in governing. Under Syrian influence electoral districts were drawn up arbitrarily, in favour of particular political groups, especially of the traditional political elite, which did not threaten the Syrian presence in Lebanon. We cannot go into the details here of what could be considered an appropriate electoral law, but would like to emphasize that it should serve the purposes of fair representation and prevent the emergence of the hegemony of any particular group. This would help develop political institutions that are more responsive to the questions of governance and socio-economic reform.[27]
3. A uniform civil code for personal status (e.g. civil marriage, divorce, inheritance) to which all Lebanese citizens would be subject, irrespective of their religious affiliation. This would be one important step in the process of de-confessionalizing the political system and promoting a more unified civil society. Its implementation, however, would require accompanying reforms in the educational system, including curricula, and in media outlets, as well as proper monitoring on the part of the national authorities.
4. An important guarantor of the process of de-confessionalism could be the creation of the Upper House, the Senate, as stipulated in the Taif Accord, where the religious communities would be represented proportionally with parity maintained between the Christian and Muslim communities. It is supposed to guarantee Lebanon's religious pluralism and social/cultural diversity by having the power to act on fundamental national questions. Establishing parity among the two main religious communities would alleviate concerns associated with the removal of the confessional system at the parliamentary level. These legislative reforms are expected to facilitate parallel reform in Lebanese public administration and the judiciary. Greater legitimacy of political institutions, with their enhanced accountability, will pave the way for rendering the public sector more efficient and accountable. This would also help lead to the creation of a new social contract that would promote the principles of socio-economic equity.

5. Concluding remarks

Apart from the civil war period, since Lebanon became independent its national record has reflected greater successes in the economic domain (major failures and economic oscillations in the post-civil war period notwithstanding) than in the political domain. Indeed, Lebanon's level of real per capita income should have been associated with a higher level of governance than actually prevailed. The reason why this has not been the case is in large measure attributable to negative domestic and external elements. Specifically, Lebanon's sectarian polarization and regional polity (neighbourhood effects of surrounding authoritarian regimes) have combined to drag Lebanon's democracy status downward. On the other hand, the country's traditional civil liberties and political rights have acted to counter this trend and preserve a certain level of democratic practice, we have referred to as partial democracy by the authors of Polity IV.

Given Lebanon's religious composition, the Lebanese consociational democracy model agreed on the eve of independence was intended to assure a high level of democratic practices. But for all its positive attributes, consociational democracy in Lebanon has, in practice, suffered from major shortcomings. The main (mostly confessionally oriented) political players have failed to build viable national and forward-looking institutions. As a consequence, political life was often marred by major instability fed by the interaction of sectarianism and destabilizing external influences and interventions.

It follows that the fundamental challenge facing Lebanon today is how to develop its national political institutions, with the objective of enhancing democratic practices, strengthening domestic stability and promoting equitable socio-economic growth. This, in turn, would greatly help to shield the country from any adverse neighbourhood effects or destabilizing external influences. Political reform, we submit, calls for modifying the existing consociational model initially by de-confessionalizing it along the lines noted above, and ultimately replacing it with a secular competitive democracy model that would provide the necessary conditions for long-term stability and sustained development.[28] The Taif Agreement incorporates the framework for initiating this process.

Notes

1 For a recent review of these influences see Makdisi, 2007.
2 Lebanon's recognized religious communities currently number 19. The major communities include Maronites, Sunnis, and Shi'a, followed by Greek Orthodox, Druze, and eastern Catholics. For scholarly work on Lebanon's modern history and the question of sectarianism, see, among others, Salibi, 1989; Makdisi, 2000.
3 Under pressure from Western and Arab governments, the war officially ended with an accord of national reconciliation, negotiated under Arab auspices in Taif, Saudi Arabia, in Oct. 1989, and thus known as the Taif Accord. Constitutional amendments were adopted by Parliament on 21 Aug. 1990 and signed into law by the President of the Republic on 21 Sept. 1990. Actual fighting did not end completely end until Oct. 1990.
4 UN Security Council Resolution 1559 of 2 Sept. 2004 had already called for this withdrawal. Following the assassination, the Security Council passed Resolution 1595 (7 April 2005) that established an independent commission to investigate the assassination; and on 30 March 2006 the Council adopted Resolution 1664 which called on the Secretary-General to negotiate an agreement with the Lebanese government for the creation of a tribunal of an international character to try those found responsible for this and subsequent political assassinations.
5 In contradistinction with this declared pretext, the Prime Minster of Israel was reported to have admitted to the Israeli Winograd Commission set up to investigate the conduct of the war that the onslaught had been planned several months before it took place (see *Haaretz*, 17 March 2007).

6 Ostensibly the resignation of the Shi'a ministers (along with one non-Shi'a minister) was due to disagreements with the Prime Minister, who called for a quick adoption of the statutes of the Tribunal as worked out by the Security Council and sent it to the Lebanese government for approval in accordance with Lebanese constitutional procedures. The resigned ministers wished to introduce modifications to the statutes of the Tribunal that, according to them, would safeguard it against misuse for purely political purposes. Failing a national political resolution to this question, on 30 May 2007 the Security Council, acting on a written request by the Prime Minister, created the Tribunal under Chapter 7 of the UN Charter. Since then the country has witnessed persisting political turmoil and conflicts.

7 Domestic tensions reached a climax on 5 May 2008 when the Lebanese government took two decisions that respectively declared Hizbullah's established internal system of military communication to be outside legal bounds and that those responsible should be brought to account, and removed the (pro-opposition) head of internal security at the airport from his post. Responding to what they regarded as 'acts of war' on the resistance movement in Lebanon, Hizbullah and its allies in West Beirut and nearby Shouf mountains acted quickly on 7 May to gain control on the ground, especially in areas of West Beirut politically dominated by the pro-government parties of al Mustaqbal and Progressive Socialist Party. Dozens of casualties in Beirut and other regions were suffered. Fear of a pending civil conflict with all its regional repercussions prompted the Arab League to actively renew mediation efforts.

8 For an analysis of the causes of the civil war see Makdisi and Sadaka, 2005.

9 Elbadawi *et al.* (2006) elaborates further on the variables chosen, data set used, econometric techniques employed, and the assumptions made for the purposes of the analyses and simulations.

10 According to World Bank data on per capita GNI for 2006, Lebanon ranked, on the basis of the Atlas methodology, at 51 over 180 (28th percentile) of all countries excluding the OECD countries.

11 This included repeated clashes between the Lebanese army and armed resident Palestinian resistance groups over the infringement by the latter on Lebanese national sovereignty (not to mention interference in Lebanese domestic affairs), while struggling for the Palestinian cause.

12 Freedom House scores rank Lebanon as free in the immediate pre-civil war years, partly free in the war period up to 1988; not free in 1988–91, partly free in 1992–5, not free during 1996–2005, partly free in 2006–8. The basis for such rankings is not available. However the different rankings for the civil war after 1982 and post-civil war period could stand closer scrutiny.

13 For 1974, gross school enrolment for the first and second levels stood at 74 per cent. Again, this was a higher level than prevailing at the time in neighbouring Arab countries, as well in many other developing countries. National health standards also improved, though mainly in urban centres and especially the city of Beirut. See Makdisi, 2004: 14–29.

14 Available empirical studies indicate that over the pre-war period the percentage of the very poor/poor groups in the total population may have declined from the 1950s to the early 1960s but thereafter remained the same at roughly one half of the total. A study conducted in the mid-1970s indicates that for 1973–4, the middle class accounted for 25 per cent of the population, the well-to-do and very rich for about 20 per cent, and the remaining 55 per cent the poor and very poor. See Schmeil, 1976.

15 For a review, see Makdisi, 2004: 23–8.

16 For a detailed analysis of the war period, see Makdisi, 2004: ch. 2.

17 For the whole period 1992–2008 the annual rate of growth averaged about 3.8 per cent; if 2006 is excluded the rate would increase to about 4 per cent. In late Sept. 2005, the government published a new national account series for the 1997–2002 period (see Lebanese Ministry of Economy and Trade, 2005). For this period the new estimates for

GDP are on average about $0.65 billion or 4 per cent greater than the previous estimates. However, the trend of the real rate of growth is basically similar, except for 2001. According to the new series, for the period 1998–2002, the average rate of growth was 2 per cent compared with the previous estimate of 1.5 per cent.

18 The exchange rate was initially pegged to the US dollar with a crawling-up policy, i.e. gradual upward adjustment of the pound against the dollar throughout 1993–8. In late 1998, this policy was discontinued in favour of a fixed rate vis-à-vis the dollar, which has since been maintained at 1 US dollar to 1,507 Lebanese pounds, with very narrow margins around parity. Whereas this exchange rate policy had its favourable effects, as noted below, given persistent large macro-fiscal imbalances, it also carried with it substantial economic costs. This is not the place, however, to discuss the most appropriate exchange rate policy for a country such as Lebanon, with an open capital account and its heavy reliance on capital inflows.

19 Major Lebanon donor meetings called by President Chirac (Paris II and Paris III) were held, respectively, on 23 Nov. 2002 and 25 Jan. 2006, resulting in billions of dollars in pledged aid. They were intended to help the Lebanese authorities stabilize the debt dynamics and shore up confidence in the Lebanese pound. Persisting political infighting and governmental inefficiencies and constraints have so far not permitted the attainment of the objectives of these meetings. In any case, in attempting to attain sustainable growth, donor aid does not substitute for the implementation of appropriate domestic policies and good institutional performance. This was and remains the major challenge facing Lebanon in the post-civil war period.

20 The UN National Income Accounts indicate a higher level of per capita income for this year. The difference could be due to varying population estimates.

21 According to UN national income estimates, the catching up period was shorter by one year, i.e. taking place in 1997.

22 See Lijphart, 1984; Andewig, 2003.

23 See e.g. Reynal-Querol, 2002.

24 See Makdisi and Sadaka, 2005.

25 To cite some examples: the resolution of the 1958 conflict needed the intervention of both the USA and Egypt; the Cairo Agreement of 1969 that settled the conflict between the Lebanese army and Palestinian armed groups was brokered by Egypt; the settlement of the Lebanese civil war in 1989 (the Taif Agreement) was brokered by the Saudi Arabia with the support of the US and the French governments; and, until its withdrawal in 2005, Syria imposed a settlement (in accordance with its own interests) on any domestic political or sectarian conflict. Since the withdrawal of Syrian troops and the ensuing dramatic political turmoil that has followed the Hariri assassination in Feb. 2005, domestic conflicts are yet to be settled and indeed settlement is awaiting the agreement of the concerned outside powers.

26 We are referring to the elections of Presidents Fouad Chehab (1958–64), Emile Lahhoud (1998–2007) and Michel Suleiman (elected 25 May 2008 for a six-year term, almost six months after Lahhoud's term had ended with no new presidential elections being carried out). In 1952, Fouad Chehab, then commander of the army, was appointed as head of a transitional government following the forced resignation of the first president of independent Lebanon, Bichara el Khoury, in the middle of his second six-year term. Chehab's government paved the way for the election of Camile Chamoun, a member of parliament, as president later in the same year. Also in 1988, towards the end of the civil war, when the Lebanese Parliament failed to elect a new president to succeed Amin Gemayel, the latter appointed the then commander of the army Michel Aoun to head a new government pending the election of a new president. However, this move was accompanied by a *de facto* government in Western Beirut that did not recognize the Aoun government. This odd situation persisted until October 1990 when Aoun was forced to leave the country by a joint Syrian/Lebanese military operation with the tacit agreement of Western powers, mainly the USA, after which

the country was effectively reunified. Earlier, the Lebanese Parliament had met on 5 Nov. 1989 in the town of Chtoura, and elected Rene Mouawad, a member of parliament, as the first post-Taif president. On his assassination on 22 Nov., Elias Hrawi, also a member of parliament, was elected to succeed him (1989–98).
27 The provisions of the Taif Accord relating to electoral reform are quite significant. They call for a fair parliamentary representation with the Muhafazat as the electoral district, but after implementing a new administrative reorganization as to the number and size of the Muhafazat.
28 This theme is developed in Makdisi and Marktanner, 2008.

References

Andewig, R. (2003) 'Consociational Democracy', *Annual Review of Political Science* 2003/3.

Barrett, D. B., Kurian, G. T. and Johnson, T. M. (2001) *World Christian Encyclopedia: A Comparative Survey of Churches and Religions in the Modern World*, Oxford: Oxford University Press.

Elbadawi, I. and Makdisi, S. (2007) 'Explaining the Democracy Deficit in the Arab World', *Quarterly Review of Economics and Finance*, 46/5 (Feb.).

——, —— and Milante, G. (2006) 'Technical Note on Democracy and Development in the Arab World', unpublished manuscript.

Hintze, J. (2001) *NCSS and PASS, Number Cruncher Statistical Systems*, Kaysville, UT. Online at: www.ncss.com

Lebanese Ministry of Economy and Trade (2005) *Lebanon's Economic Accounts, 1997–2002*, Beirut: Author.

Lijphart, A.(1984) *Democratic Patterns of Majoritarian and Consensus Government in Twenty-One Countries*, New Haven, CT: Yale University Press.

Makdisi, S. (2004) *The Lessons of Lebanon, the Economics of War and Development*, London: I. B. Tauris.

—— (2007) 'Rebuilding without Resolution: The Lebanese Economy and State in the Post-Civil War Period', in L. Binder (ed.), *Rebuilding Devastated Economies in the Middle East*, New York: Palgrave/Macmillan.

—— and Sadaka, R. (2005) 'The Lebanese Civil War, 1975–90', in P. Collier and N. Sambanis (eds), *Understanding Civil War: Evidence and Analysis* vol. 2, Washington, DC: World Bank.

—— and Marktanner, M. (2008) *Trapped by Consociationalism: The Case of Lebanon*, Institute of Financial Economics Lecture and Working Paper Series, 1, American University of Beirut, Lebanon.

Makdisi, U. (2000) *The Culture of Sectarianism, Community, History and Violence in Nineteenth Century Ottoman Lebanon*, Berkeley, CA: University of California Press.

Marshall, M., Jaggers, K. and Gurr, T. (n.d.) *Polity IV Project: Political Regime Characteristics and Transitions, 1800–2008*. Online at: www.systemicpeace.org/polity/polity4.htm

Reynal-Querol, M. (2002) 'Ethnicity, Political System and Civil Wars', *Journal of Conflict Resolution* 46/1.

Salibi, K. (1989) *A House of Many Mansions: The History of Lebanon Reconsidered*, London: I. B. Tauris.

Schmeil, Y. (1976) *Sociologie du Système Politique Libanais*, Grenoble: Universitaire de Grenoble.

United Nations (2007) *National Income Accounts*. Online at: unstats.un.org/unsd/snaama/dnllist.asp

United Nations Relief and Works Agency for Palestine Refugees in the Near East (UNRWA). Online at: www.un.org/unrwa/publications/index.html

University of Maryland, Center for International Development and Conflict Management, and George Mason University, Center for Global Policy. Online at: www.systemicpeace.org/polity/polity4.htm

Uppsala Conflict Data Program/International Peace Research Institute (UCDP/PRIO) Armed Conflicts Dataset. Online at: www.prio.no/CSCW/Datasets/Armed-Conflict

World Bank (2005) *World Bank Development Indicators 2005*, Washington, DC: World Bank.

—— (2006) *World Bank Development Indicators 2006*, Washington, DC: World Bank.

5 Syria: the underpinnings of autocracy

Conflict, oil and the curtailment of economic freedom

Raed Safadi, Laura Munro and Radwan Ziadeh

In this chapter we investigate the factors that have led to the persistence of autocracy in Syria since at least 1949, when political instability provided the stage for a series of coups d'état that ended when the late Hafez Assad assumed power in 1971 through a bloodless coup. The autocratic regime he established survived his death in 2000 and has continued under the regime of his son, President Bashar Assad. In parallel, Syria has followed a state-led economic development model. While it has achieved a notable overall rate of economic growth and rising living standards, its national economy has been marred by significant inefficiencies and periods of stagnation, despite occasional cosmetic attempts at economic reforms. Indeed, Syria's economic landscape is a mirror image of its political reality: highly centralized and dirigiste.

Building on the findings of Elbadawi and Makdisi (2007), hereafter EM, and Elbadawi, Makdisi and Milante (2006), hereafter EMM, we seek to provide additional insights into the factors that have impeded the democratization process in Syria, despite the economic achievements since it gained independence in 1946. Section 1 presents an overview of the Syrian model of economic development and achievements that prompt the question as to why the Syrian democratization process has lagged behind its economic development. Section 2 gives a snapshot of the command and control system that President Hafez Assad built during more than three decades in power. Section 3 presents the results of an econometric model that, building on the EMM model, investigates the extent to which lack of economic freedom in Syria explains the observed gap between actual and predicted values of polity. Section 4 draws on these findings and proposes an agenda that could serve to promote change and democracy in Syria.

1. An overview

The post-Second World War model of economic development in Syria and across the Arab region was anchored in a strong interventionist-redistributive mentality that included heavy reliance on state planning, import substitution policies, nationalization of private and foreign assets, and a social contract whereby the state provided education, housing, health care and food subsidies (Richards and Waterbury, 1996; Yousef, 2004). This statist, inward-looking model was embedded in the post-independence constitution, laws and public policies that saw the state as an instrument of social transformation, political mobilization and economic distribution. One important consequence of this model was the establishment of the state as an agent of public welfare, which to this day continues to define state–society relations (Safadi, 2006).

Syria's economy was relatively developed when it gained its independence in 1946. Thereafter, and until the mid-1970s, it enjoyed unprecedented levels of economic growth (average annual GDP growth rates of 6.3 per cent in constant 1963 prices) and social development fuelled by public investments in infrastructure, health and education, as well as state-owned enterprises operating behind high and opaque protective walls, all of which benefited from rising oil prices, intra-regional flow of capital, and labour and workers' remittances. By the end of the 1970s, the Syrian economy had shifted from its traditional agrarian base to an economy based on commercial, service and industrial activities. The main sources of Syria's income were oil and tourism. Nevertheless, the economy continued to rely heavily on foreign aid and grants to finance both its budget and trade deficits; Arab aid transfers and Soviet assistance also supported mounting defence expenditures.

By the mid-1980s, Syria's sclerotic interventionist-redistributive model ran out of steam as the economy's past prosperity all but disappeared, and was even negative (–2 per cent GDP growth rate in 1982–3) in the wake of a rapid decline in oil prices, lower export revenues, drought that affected agricultural production, and falling workers' remittances. This prompted the government to rethink its economic management approach and to adopt policies to achieve macroeconomic stability, a larger participation of the private sector in economic activity, and a higher degree of integration into global markets. The government reduced its spending, cut down on imports, and launched anti-corruption campaigns against black market currency dealers. However, the measures taken did not go far enough in addressing the deep-rooted structural problems of the economy, nor did they seriously tackle governance and institutional reform issues.

The government also began to reform its state-led economy, with initiatives such as liberalizing the agriculture sector and privatizing several state monopolies. This paved the way for Syria's considerable economic development and significant capital accumulation in the early 1990s. Growth rates accelerated in part due to oil revenues (and discoveries of new oil deposits) and to initial domestic liberalization measures. By the end of the 1990s, however, the pace of economic liberalization had slowed, favouring members of the powerful elite; during the period 1997–9 Syria's economy grew by an average 1.5 per cent per annum, and in 1999, the economy actually shrank (see Table 5.1). In 2000 and 2001 the Syrian economy recovered, owing to increases in oil exports and cooperation with Iraq, which was under UN-imposed economic sanctions at the time. At the same time, earlier reforms proposed by the regime of Hafez Assad stalled, and the country's infrastructure deteriorated.

Indeed, the Syrian economy has been going through a roller-coaster ride since

Table 5.1 Syria, selected economic indicators, 1997–2006

	1997	1998	1999	2000	2001	2002	2003	2004	2005	2006
Exports of goods and services (% of GDP)	32.42	30.53	32.32	35.39	35.38	38.07	31.39	40.57	41.47	39.42
GDP growth (annual %)	1.80	6.34	–3.55	2.74	5.20	3.96	1.64	5.83	4.50	5.10
Imports of goods and services (% of GDP)	33.80	30.90	31.99	28.58	29.24	30.54	28.59	37.78	39.50	35.56
Inflation, GDP deflator (annual %)	6.01	–0.30	7.44	9.70	4.56	0.54	2.16	8.30	12.94	9.06
Merchandise trade (% of GDP)	54.77	44.64	45.96	43.72	47.39	51.08	48.41	61.17	64.63	55.14
Population growth (annual %)	2.40	2.38	2.43	2.53	2.62	2.69	2.73	2.73	2.71	2.68
Services, etc., value added (% of GDP)	41.21	41.84	41.18	38.31	39.73	40.99	40.78	42.81	44.97	49.48

Source: World Bank, 2007a.

the late 1990s. During the period 2000 to 2006, the annual rate of growth averaged close to 3 per cent in tandem with the growth in the population and, as a result, standards of living have deteriorated, poverty has become more widespread and unemployment levels have risen. Syria's public sector is bloated, employing roughly one quarter of the total workforce in money-losing state-run companies that are kept afloat under the pretext that their privatization would generate great social disruption.

Liberalization measures have been further hindered by the business community's allegiance to the regime. Involved with influential members of the regime in rent-seeking activities (oil, foreign trade, mobile phones, etc.), the Syrian business community has sided with and reinforced the autocratic regime, indicating little interest in fostering democratic development. Indeed, reforms have failed to develop without the business community's support. Foreign companies across all sectors have operated in Syria for decades through middlemen (sponsors) in the power system, weakening the strength of Western pressure to liberalize. Western oil companies, in particular, have invested heavily and have begun operations in cooperation with the Syrian authorities, the only way to gain access to the Syrian market. This issue is not unique to Syria but leads to the question as to whether market liberalization and reform on their own could promote a business community interested in a genuine democracy, or simply give rise to crony capitalism.

As a direct result of the policies adopted from the 1960s to the late 1980s, the Syrian economy remains relatively isolated from the global markets for goods and services. International trade is highly restricted by both tariff and non-tariff barriers, and all the efforts at liberalization have left in their wake a web of protection that distorts economic incentives and discourages competition. Syria's tariff regime is one of the most complex and opaque both in absolute terms and in comparison to other countries at similar levels of economic development.

While tariff rates have been reduced from their historically high levels, they are still very high compared to those of other developing countries, ranging from 6 to 235 per cent. The tariff schedule is also marred by a complex web of exceptions and special rates that are determined according to the origin of the import and the entity that is importing it. Around 200 state-owned companies enjoy different levels of subsidy and protection; many also have either the exclusive right to import some goods, or have the exclusive right to grant licenses for key imports. Syria bans the import of certain final goods that compete with Syrian enterprises. There are also goods whose importation into Syria is prohibited. One may argue that quite legitimate public policy objectives (security, health or protection of the environment) may lie behind these prohibitions, however, in Syria, the list is fairly extensive and the criteria are not publicly known. Not only have these practices injected further distortions into the economy, but, equally importantly, they have given rise to a culture of rent-seeking. According to the World Bank, quantitative restrictions add up to the equivalent of a 19 per cent across-the-board tariff on all imports (World Bank, 2005).

Since Bashar Assad took over the presidency in 2001, the fundamental aspects of the Syrian economy have remained unchanged: strong dependence on volatile oil markets, limited private-sector activity, limited employment creation and declining integration into the world economy. This is perhaps not surprising in view of the influence of entrenched interests and the regime's power base that have combined to offer, at best, cosmetic touches of reform (Richards and Waterbury, 1996; Lust-Okar, 2006).

Bashar Assad inherited an economy that had been facing grave economic challenges, including restoring economic growth (–3.6 per cent GDP growth rate in 1999), addressing rising population growth (Syria's annual population growth stood at 2.5 per cent in 2000), alleviating poverty, providing jobs (unemployment was close to 20 per cent in 2000), attracting investment, and tackling a large external debt. The government initiated modest economic reforms, starting with a rethink of the regulatory environment in the financial sector, including cutting lending interest rates, licensing private banks and consolidating multiple exchange rates. Other reforms saw a reduction in subsidies on some items, most notably gasoline and cement, and the establishment of the Damascus Stock Exchange, which is set to begin operations in 2009. In addition, President Assad signed legislative decrees to encourage corporate ownership reform, and to allow the Central Bank to issue treasury bills and bonds for government debt.

Partly as a result of these and other reforms, the economy made a remarkable turn and registered impressive performances from 2004 onwards, the rate of growth averaging about 4 per cent during 2004–7 (lower oil exports were offset by higher prices, leading to higher budgetary and export receipts). However, the main drivers of growth were domestic demand augmented by the influx of Iraqi refugees and private investment, both domestic and foreign, particularly from the Gulf States.

Despite these reforms, competition in Syria remains limited and substantial barriers to entry continue to plague many economic sectors. Some productive sectors remain firmly in the hands of the government, while for others foreign entry remains subject to certain types of restrictions. Public-sector monopolies control cement, sugar refining, fertilizers, oil refining, port operation, water distribution, air transportation, electricity, telecommunications and insurance (World Bank, 2005). Inefficient state-owned enterprises and public authorities play key roles in many value chains through, for example, exclusive control of the procurement and sale of cotton and wheat, exclusive control of yarn-making, and through the provision of infrastructure. In summary, Syria's economy continues until today to suffer from deep-rooted structural weaknesses and a business environment plagued by bureaucratic red tape, governance weaknesses and a lack of corporate transparency. Unsurprisingly, the World Bank's ease of doing business rankings for 2008 ranked Syria at 137 out of 178 countries (see Figure 5.1).

These, together with continued security and stability concerns across the region, argue for deeper and more sustained economic reform efforts, including a fundamental reassessment of the role of the state in the economy and the creation of a rules-based regulatory environment.

Equally important, the progress noted above along the development front has failed to generate any breakthrough on the democracy front, as the political landscape in Syria, and indeed across the Arab world, remains dominated by authoritarian regimes (Elbadawi *et al.*, 2006), reflecting what is now commonly referred to as the Arab 'freedom deficit' (UNDP and Arab Fund for Social and Economic Development, 2002). This defies conventional wisdom that has long established that economic development undermines repressive regimes.[1]

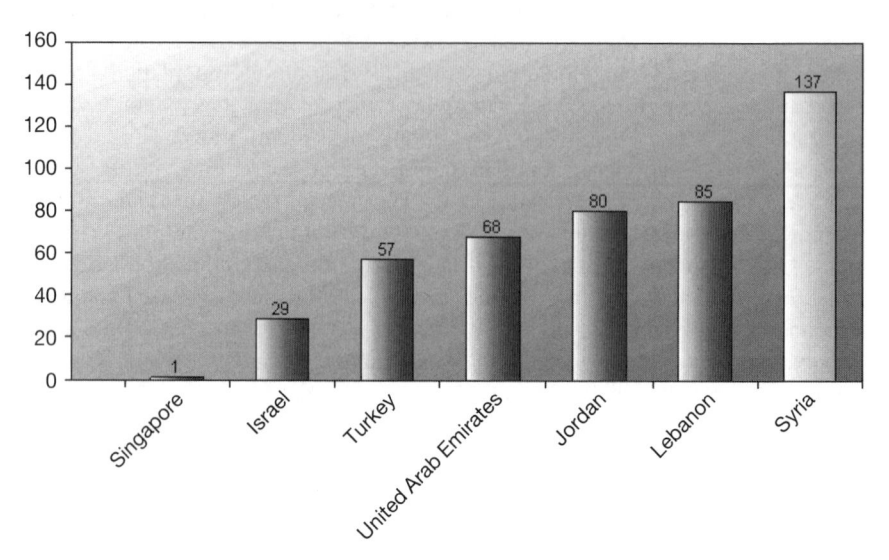

Figure 5.1 Ease of doing business in Syria – global rank.
Source: World Bank, 2007b.

What explains this (lengthy) lag between the onset of economic growth and the emergence of an Arab liberal democracy? The innovative work of Elbadawi and Makdisi (2007) and Elbadawi et al. (2006) provides some of the answers. Their study presents estimates for an extended 'modernization' model of democracy that takes into account country and region-specific social, economic, political and historical conditions. However, on their own these variables do not fully explain the Arab freedom or democracy deficit. This prompts them to add region-specific factors, namely, the influence of oil and conflict, to their model, which greatly enhances its explanatory powers. These additions pave the way for some strong analytical conclusions, though a depressing reality: despite the notable progress the region has achieved in development, oil wealth and conflicts (most importantly the Arab–Israeli conflict, but also domestic conflicts) have retarded the development of democracy. The absence of a positive correlation between development and greater democratization stands in contrast to experiences in other regions.

Building on these findings, we seek to provide additional insights into the factors that have impeded democratic development in Syria. In particular, they find a gap between the observed polity (democracy) and the predicted polity in Syria as well as the other Arab countries. In the case of Syria, predicted polity is above actual polity, implying that Syria was actually less democratic than predicted by the model. Moreover, under the two separate counterfactuals of no conflicts or no oil dependence, simulated democracy in Syria would have been much higher than the actual for the case of conflict and to a lesser extent for the no oil scenario. However, the polity scores would still fail to reach the positive zone in the case of oil, and would just turn positive in the case of conflict. Thus, while oil and regional conflicts have contributed to Syria's democratic deficit, on their own they do not fully account for this deficit.

Here we search for additional explanatory variables by focusing on the broad role of government in Syria's economy, and conclude that lack of economic freedom is an additional explanatory variable of the democracy deficit in Syria.

It is important to note that the empirical finding of a freedom deficit is not particular to the Arab region; indeed, we can find the same phenomenon in China and Russia. China's economy has grown by an average annual rate in excess of 10 per cent during the last 25 years, yet its politics have remained essentially repressive. In Russia, the economy has recently been improving even as the authorities have been tightening the political reins. These are but two examples where autocratic and/or illiberal governments of various stripes are managing to at least delay democracy. Moreover, economic freedom in both of these countries still leaves much to be desired, though less so in the case of Russia than China.

2. Syria's autocratic regime: resistance to significant political change

In this section, we first describe the strong and stable autocratic regime that has emerged since 1970 following a period of instability marked with coups d'état. We then analyse why neither the business community nor outside pressure have managed to effect any significant change in the prevailing autocratic political system. We conclude with a brief comment on the failure of external forces to generate change.

2.1 The command and control system

The authoritarian regime of the late President Hafez Assad and his son the current President Bashar Assad has reinforced Syria's political freedom deficit since 1971 (albeit with occasional liberalization measures). Between 1946 and 1970, 21 coups and counter-coups took place until Hafez Assad assumed power in the aftermath of a bloodless intra-party coup, known as the Corrective Movement. Assad moved quickly and organized his rule along one-party lines, the Ba'ath Party. His era marked the beginning of stability and strong control of Syria. Aware of the fleeting power of his predecessors, Hafez Assad developed a power system based on the presidency, where key decisions regarding foreign policy, national security, internal politics and the economy are made by the President himself. All three branches of government (executive, legislative and judiciary) came under the control of key figures in the Ba'ath Party, whose dominance in state institutions was mandated by the constitution. Hafez Assad would rule Syria for close to three decades with an iron fist.

In Assad's Syria, ministers and senior staff members of the state are nominated by the President and assigned limited executive rights. The Regional Command of the Ba'ath Party and other secondary circles of the power system propose candidates for government posts and key civil service positions, but the final selection is always made by the President. The Syrian experience demonstrates that, under the prevailing autocratic regime, the government does not govern according to any specific programme, but rather takes decisions according to the interests of the power system. Any dissent risks political detention, and there are ever present random detention campaigns.

The regime uses the need for 'security' as a pretext to silence dissent. The state of emergency imposed in 1963 remains in force, allegedly to ensure political stability and national security. Freedom of association, expression and assembly continue to be strictly limited. The authorities still treat Kurds, Syria's largest non-Arab minority, as second-class citizens subject to systematic discrimination.

Independent media workers and correspondents, including bloggers, face arrest and harassment, while the regime continues to monopolize all forms of large-scale media and restrict access to the internet. The regime also uses the pretext of national security in an attempt to justify its stranglehold on the judicial system. Torture and ill-treatment of prisoners is carried out with total impunity.

The Assad regime did not completely consolidate its power until early 1982, when it violently suppressed a Muslim Brotherhood insurrection in the city of Hama. Thousands were killed and whole segments of the city were obliterated. This action followed a series of violent incidents and clashes between the Brotherhood and the regime dating back before Hafez Assad had assumed full power in 1970.[2] Subsequently, the regime introduced several measures to further strengthen its authoritarian hold. Director generals of various ministries (i.e. the senior civil servants who guarantee the continuity of public-sector institutions) were replaced by assistants to the minister who could be changed at will. All public political discussions were henceforth monitored and activities by opposition groups banned. Furthermore, all political parties were subjected to Ba'ath Party rules and prohibited from opening offices or publishing newspapers and newsletters (George, 2003). As Assad and many of his aides belonged to the Alawite sect, his assumption of power gave rise to hidden grievance on the part of the Sunni majority, who saw power resting exclusively in the hands of a minority sect with all the privileges that go with it. The fact that the ruling Ba'ath Party was secular did not alter these feelings.

Over time, the party's monopoly of power over all major public-sector decisions has given rise to systemized corruption and kickbacks, with key decision-makers taking advantage of their position to extract illegal profits. Suffering from low salaries, the army as well as the judiciary system has fallen prey to corrupting influences (Lust-Okar, 2006).

In his March 1999 inauguration speech, President Hafez Assad signalled a limited relaxation of the authoritarian approach of the prior three decades. He emphasized the importance of responsibility in the context of 'the people's democratic system'. He also noted that the enlargement of the decision-making circle and freedom of discussion and public participation would facilitate the democratic process and strengthen the country. Furthermore, he called for various economic reforms and described the public sector as the basis for the national economy, being instrumental in maintaining economic and social balance (Assad, 1999).

During the 1998 parliamentary elections that preceded the 1999 referendum to re-elect President Assad to a fifth term, public political debates were authorized, within prescribed limits. This prompted a heated rivalry for parliament's assigned independent seats (83 out of a total of 250) and gave rise to calls to fight corruption, modernize the administration and expedite reform of the public sector. The Arab press referred to the period as 'elections for change' (*Al Hayat*, 26 Nov. 1998).

The motivation for this move, after three decades of strict authoritarian rule, was the President's wish to rearrange the political and security landscape in anticipation of his death and the assumption of power by his son. Towards this objective, a number of key security officials were replaced by personnel closer to his son.[3] Parallel preparations for the takeover by Bashar Assad included his undertaking official and public tours under wide media coverage. Though he had no formal status in the state, he gave extended political interviews, in which he demonstrated a strong understanding of key international shifts and currents, especially of the important Lebanese portfolio at a time when Syrian troops were still deployed in Lebanon. Potential contenders (mainly his uncle Rifaat Assad) were kept at bay.[4] The media began to focus more closely on Colonel Bashar Assad's campaign to modernize the state and reduce corruption through economic and administrative reforms.

Soon after peace negotiations with Israel stalled in early 2000, Hafez Assad fell terminally ill. Given his strict control of the regime, legislative and executive institutions virtually collapsed during his illness (Wedeen, 1999; Seal, 1998; Maoz, 1998). Only the security forces maintained their effectiveness. State paralysis ensued, bringing in its wake another wave of deep economic and social crises. Nonetheless, party and state apparatus were mobilized to assure a smooth succession after Hafez Assad's death on 10 June 2000. Potential constitutional hurdles were overcome and exactly one month later by popular referendum Bashar Assad was elected to succeed his father. At the same time, he assumed the positions of general commander of the Armed Forces, secretary-general of the Party and leader of the Progressive National Front, thus, like his father, holding monopoly power over state and party.

Bashar stated in his inaugural speech that there could be no democracy without the development of institutions and without administrative reforms. The speech gave intellectuals and dissidents a whiff of hope and they began calling publicly for economic and political reforms (popularly referred to as the Damascus Spring). This 'freedom' was short-lived, and the regime reversed course in early 2001. Now, eight years into his presidency, the power system remains as closely knit as under Hafez. The strong separation between the power system and state structure continues to hinder democratic reform.

2.2 The Syrian business community: distancing itself from domestic politics and accommodating the regime

The Syrian business community has generally distanced itself from domestic politics since 1963, when the political parties with which it had been associated were dismantled by emerging military dictatorships accompanied by a wave of enterprise nationalization.[5] At the time a good number of business owners opted to leave the country, and those who remained chose not to be involved either in public-sector enterprises or domestic political issues. With the loss of its political power, whatever influence the business community had on public policies disappeared. The command system described in the previous section became the primary mover in the political as well as the economic field.

Nonetheless, there were attempts from the early 1970s to engage select business leaders in specific fields, notably tourism, by proposing attractive investment opportunities and later opening the door for them to benefit from huge public investments and remittances from Syrians abroad (particularly from those in the Gulf States).[6] Additional opportunities emerged in the late 1980s, when barter trade with the Soviet Union collapsed, leading to a broadening of wealth and capital accumulation.

These moves, however, did not in any way diminish public-sector control over economic policy and developments. Rather, they were intended to mobilize private-sector support under the aegis of the state. In that sense there developed an alliance between business interests and the state.

It was only in the 1990s that the role of the business sector began to expand. The business community benefited from activities connected to oil revenues and oil construction contracts as well as the subsidization of main agriculture crops.

Also stimulating economic growth were: Investment Law No. 10 of 1991, which transferred foreign trade from state organizations to the private sector; protection of local industries; contracts for the reconstruction of Lebanon; and trading with Iraq in the last years of Saddam's reign.

Nevertheless, the new business community did not share power and was generally not involved in domestic politics. The business community's most powerful members, those who seized the original opportunities, had family ties to important members of the ruling body. As the regime could easily crack down on any illegal practices, most of the business community avoided benefiting from financial advantages extended to it by the regime.

As of early 2000, two main groups have emerged in the business community. The first, with direct links to the power base, has positioned itself in profitable rent-seeking activities such as oil and gas, mobile phones, real estate and advertising. This group favours limited liberalization of media and free speech, on the condition that it controls sufficient media sources to defend its interests. The second, larger group favours the acceleration of liberalization, rationalization of the administration, and equal opportunities for all. It views the establishment of democracy and the rule of law as a precondition to developing its business activities and investments. While both groups favour business growth and expansion, they also both fear instability and have historically stood up against any foreign pressure aimed at destabilizing the regime.

It can be concluded that, while the business community in general has favoured the liberalization of the national economy, it has not engaged in activities aimed at fostering the pace of democratization in Syria. Rather, it has accommodated the regime and defended its stability, which it has regarded as necessary for its own business interests.

2.3 Outside influences: failure to influence change

In certain regions of the world (e.g. Eastern Europe), Western interventions and pressures might have helped the initiation of the democratic process. In the case of Syria, this has not been so. The objective of foreign, principally US, pressure on Syria has related more to its role in the region and in the Arab–Israeli conflict, Syria being a major actor, than to any push for democratic reform, foreign rhetoric in this regard notwithstanding. Since the US invasion of Iraq in 2003, Syria's relation with the USA has been strained.[7] It has, however, managed to develop a more positive relationship with the European Union (EU), but not one free from emerging strains.

The European Union and Syria have been engaged in discussions for a Euro-Syrian partnership under the Barcelona Agreement, and the European Union has launched several large assistance programmes for administrative and economic reforms over the last decade.[8] However, though the partnership agreement was initialled in 2004, the European Union has so far chosen to postpone ratification as a way of exerting pressure on Syria to modify its political course (i.e. to become more accommodating of Western interests in the region, including Syria's stance on the ongoing crises in Lebanon, in Iraq and an eventual reconciliation with Israel). While human rights issues are also raised, in practice, they do not occupy a high priority on the Western agenda.

The Syrian regime has proven to be steadfast in the face of Western pressure, no matter what objectives were being sought. Its hold on power has remained strong, all the while pursuing additional measures to liberalize the economy and open it up to direct investment (Lust-Okar, 2006). Indeed, Syrian political activists advocating political reform have generally distanced themselves from close contacts with Western governments, in particular the USA. One reason is their fear of domestic persecution by the authorities on grounds of complicity with foreign powers. Another reason is that many Syrian activists do not believe that the real aim of foreign pressure is to foster a change in Syria's political climate to allow for the initiation of a democratic process, but rather, as noted above, that their interest lies elsewhere.[9] In practice, economic or political sanctions imposed on Syria have produced a negative effect. Even pro-reform Syrians have considered them as unjust acts aimed not at promoting domestic reform but at extracting concessions from the Syrian regime on the Iraqi, Lebanese or Palestinian fronts, where Syrian and Western interests have diverged. The USA invasion of Iraq, for example, by ending favourable Syria–Iraq economic relations, generated discontent among the Syrian people and promoted further support for the regime (Lust-Okar, 2006).

Noteworthy is the reluctance of Western powers to engage the Ba'ath Party itself or employ systematic pressure to encourage democratic practices. Even the Euro-Syrian partnership, which deepened Syria's involvement with the West, did not set any practical modality for fostering democracy in the country. Possibly Western pressure could have been more effective if instead it had relied 'on conditional aid and diplomatic pressure to convince the Syrian government to improve human rights' (Lust-Okar, 2006: 16). But this has not been the case.

3. Accounting for the democracy deficit: oil, conflict and beyond – the role of economic freedom

Cross-national quantitative research on the social and economic conditions that are most favourable to the transformation of political systems has long established that the level of economic development is positively correlated with democracy. In an early ground-breaking paper, Lipset suggested that democracy was both created and consolidated by a broad process of modernization that involves changes in 'the factors of industrialization, urbanization, wealth, and education.... The factors subsumed under economic development carry with it the political correlate of democracy' (Lipset, 1959: 80). More recent literature, including Lipset (1994), has empirically established that economic development can act as a force for democratic change in autocratic states.[10] Until recently, few have questioned this correlation.

In important research on the relationship between development and democracy, Adam Przeworski and Fernando Limongi disputed this notion (Przeworski and Limongi, 1993, 1997; Przeworski, 2004). They found that, while wealth has a measurable effect on the survival rate of democracy, it has no impact on the emergence rate of democracy. In other words, certain wealthy autocracies remain so despite rising wealth, while wealth above a certain level has a powerful and unambiguous impact on the durability of democracy. More concretely, entries into democracy are determined by non-economic factors and are hence random with respect to level of development.

In his classic book, *Capitalism and Freedom*, Nobel economics laureate Milton Friedman wrote: 'Historical evidence speaks with a single voice on the relation between political freedom and a free market. I know of no example in time or place of a society that has been marked by a large measure of political freedom that has not also used something comparable to a free market to organize the bulk of economic activity' (Friedman, 1962: 9). Friedman openly gave primacy to economic freedom over political freedom. Later on, and in his 1994 introduction to the 50th-anniversary edition of Hayek's *Road to Serfdom*, Friedman went beyond his original line of thought and stated: 'The free market is the only mechanism that has ever been discovered for achieving participatory democracy.' Taken to its limit, Friedman seems to imply that economic freedom is both a necessary and sufficient condition for political freedom. Empirically, Barro (1999) analyses a panel of over 100 countries from 1960 to 1995 and finds that increases in various measures of the standard of living predict a gradual rise in democracy. Barro also finds that democracies that arise without prior economic development – sometimes because they are imposed by former colonial powers or international organizations – tend not to last.

Fukuyama also lent his support to Friedman's thesis and Barro's empirical findings. In his book, *The End of History and the Last Man* (1992), he predicted that economics and politics will come together, with liberal democracy standing at the end of history. Fukuyama argued that, economically, only capitalism could deliver the goods, while politically, only democracy could satisfy our desires for respect. These findings matter a great deal in our present context, and as will be seen in section 4 below, they hold the key to unshackling Syrian society.

Despite the econometric difficulties of establishing beyond doubt that development promotes democracy, the weight of the evidence is quite clearly in that direction. Certainly, there is no coherent body of evidence that it is bad for democracy. This point is important in our present context, where we focus on the case of Syria and adopt the seminal approach of Elbadawi, Makdisi and Milante (2006) that has examined the relationship between economic development and democracy in the Arab world.

Syria's standing in terms of democracy, as measured by the polity index, is abysmal by any account. Though its polity score was bad enough in the first half of the 1960s (see Figure 5.2), it slipped to −7.0 during the second period (1965–9) and then dipped even further to −9.0 for the following three decades (1970–99); for all practical purposes, this outcome is not distinguishable from the worst record of −10.0. By the turn of the current century, the country had experienced some hesitant economic and political opening, but still remains deeply autocratic, with a polity score of −7.0 during 2000–4. The fact that Syria has experienced a major

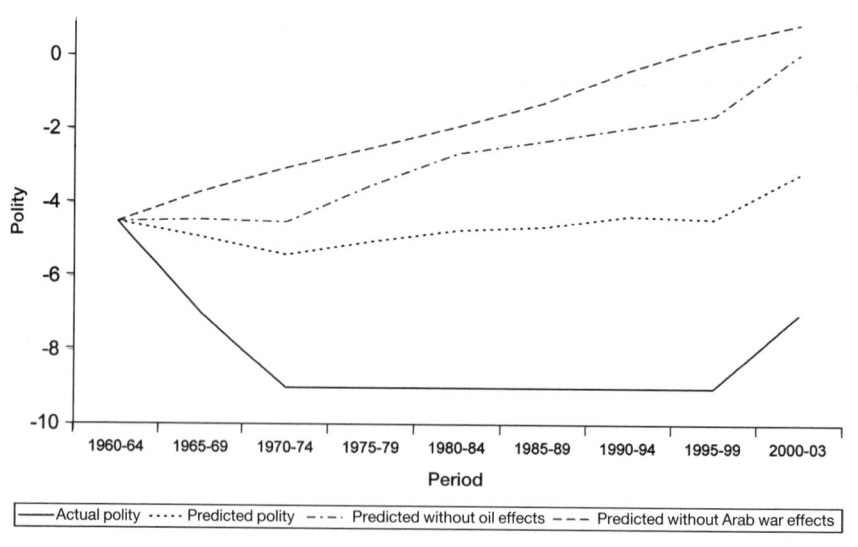

Figure 5.2 Democratization in Syria, or lack thereof.
Source: EMM, 2006.

'democracy deficit' can be demonstrated even in the context of the basic EMM extended modernity model. Predicted polity scores for Syria according to this model range from –5.0 during the 1970s to about –3.0 by the first half of the current decade. Though this suggests that Syria would continue to be autocratic under this basic model, its predicted polity nevertheless reflects significant and steady improvements relative to the prevailing polity in the last 40 years or so.

When the two pivotal factors of oil and conflict are taken into account, much more pronounced freedom deficits emerge. If in addition to controlling for modernity and other historical and socio-cultural characteristics we also account for the oil and conflict effects (the full EMM model), we can generate two further counterfactual simulations. First, under the scenario of no oil effect, the simulated polity for Syria would average less than –5.0 for 1960–74, precipitously rise to less than –2.0 in the 1990s and to a positive but small score of 0.06 in the first half of the current decade. The story is even more dramatic under the no-conflict scenario, where the simulated score is initially higher and rises at a faster rate to reach almost 1.0 during the first half of this decade. Noting that the score of 3.0 is widely considered to be the threshold for attaining democratic transition, this simulation suggests that, in the absence of conflicts, Syria should, by now, have been within striking distance of this goal.

Both oil and conflicts appear to have created an enabling environment for autocracy to prevail; indeed, these two factors may have also served to co-opt and even pre-empt the inherently democratizing role of the educated middle-income professional and entrepreneurial class. One key theme developed here is that the ability of the regime to curtail 'economic freedoms' has rendered economic actors completely dependent on the power relations that define the state; hence this class should, for all intents and purposes, be regarded as a by-product and a beneficiary of the state. Indeed, the premise of this chapter is that the lack of economic freedom has played an additional critical role in retarding democratic reforms in Syria.

The most comprehensive empirical study on the relationship between a country's economic policies and institutions and a country's level of prosperity is the Fraser Institute's report on Economic Freedom of the World. The institute constructs a summary index of overall economic freedom for each country during a particular year, based on raw scores on a variety of factors relevant to economic freedom, including: size of government; legal structure and security of property rights; access to sound money; freedom to trade internationally; and regulation of credit, labour and business and personal choice. This reflects the essence of a free private market where ideally a government focuses on protecting private property rights and safeguarding the private market for individuals to freely engage in exchanges. The index directly assigns scores to all component variables on a 0 to 10 scale (a higher number indicating higher degree of economic freedom) and applies formulas to convert original data on component variables into scores. Principal component analysis is used to construct weights for each component variable in calculating the final scores of economic freedom.

The economic freedom index is constructed for 130 countries, beginning in 1970 and with the most recent data covering the year 2004. The latest report (2007) finds a strong relationship between economic freedom and prosperity. The freest economies have an average per capita income of US$24,402 compared with $2,998 in the least free countries. It also finds that free economies grow faster than less free ones: growth in per capita incomes in the past 10 years in the countries that are more economically free was 2.1 per cent compared with –0.2 per cent for the least free countries.

In what follows, we use the Fraser Institute economic freedom index to first test the hypothesis that the 'economic class' in Syria is no more than a by-product and a beneficiary of the state. We then examine the simultaneous influence of economic freedom, incomes and various non-monetary measures (essentially, neighbourhood effects, colonial heritage, religious and ethnic heterogeneity) on democracy in Syria.

To test this hypothesis, we generate a scatter diagram showing the residual of the full EMM model (Elbadawi and Makdisi, 2007; Elbadawi, Makdisi and Milante, 2006) against the orthogonal component of the Fraser index of economic freedom (Figure 5.3).[11] The results reveal that there is no discernible pattern, suggesting that more economic freedom does not in general lead to higher democratization over and above what is explained by the EMM model. On the other hand, Syria appears to be an outlier, with very low (residual) Fraser scores associated with very low (residual) polity index. Therefore, at least qualitatively, it can be argued that increased economic freedom should bring up the polity score in Syria to the higher levels observed for some Arab countries.

To see the extent to which the addition of the economic freedom index narrows the gap between observed and predicted polity of Syria, we first run the

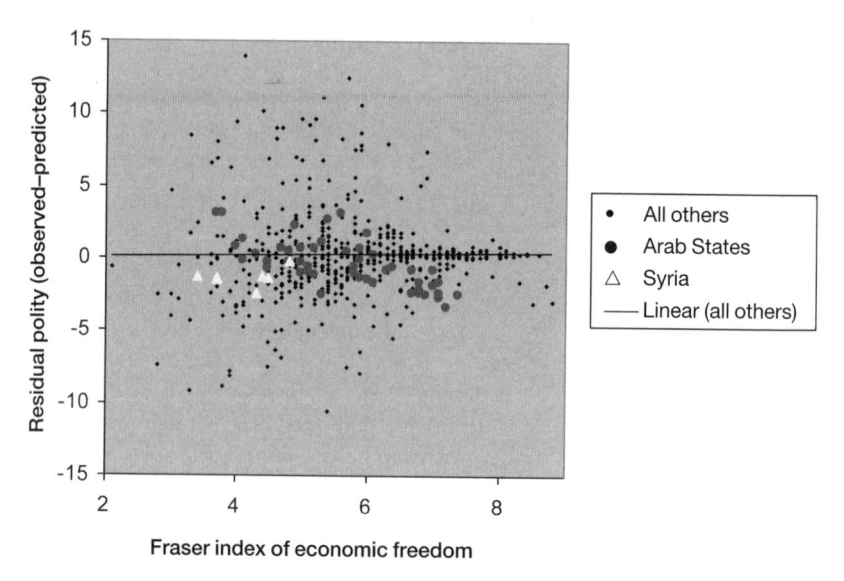

Figure 5.3 Polity residual and index of economic freedom.
Source: Authors.

EM model including all countries for which Polity IV data are available. Since the dependent variable is censored, we use the Tobit model to estimate the coefficients using the entire data set, and we then fit them into the equation concerning Syria to arrive at the predicted value of polity in Syria.

Panel A in Figure 5.4 charts the observed and the predicted value of polity using the EM parsimonious model, but excluding economic freedom as an additional explanatory variable. Panel B includes the economic freedom index. As can be seen, this inclusion narrows the gap between observed and predicted polity in Syria during the period under review. Model details are provided in the Annex at the end of this chapter. These results also confirm many found in EM: Arab neighbourhood, colonial heritage and religious divisions all have a negative impact on polity in Syria. However, the most critical result we find is that there is a greater coherence between the predicted and the observed polity scores for Syria when the economic freedom index is added to the model. This finding adds to those of EM and makes clear that promoting economic freedom in Syria would also promote democratic change. In fact, given the Arab–Israeli conflict and its destabilizing political effects, its settlement would help create a domestic political environment that is more conducive to the process of economic and political reforms in Syria.

It is worth noting in this context that the Syrian regime is not averse to economic and administrative reforms; however, it has always taken the position that such reforms should take place in a slow and predictable manner that would not lead to the loss of political control. The regime appears to be leaning away from a Soviet style perestroika and towards a Chinese model of reform where the

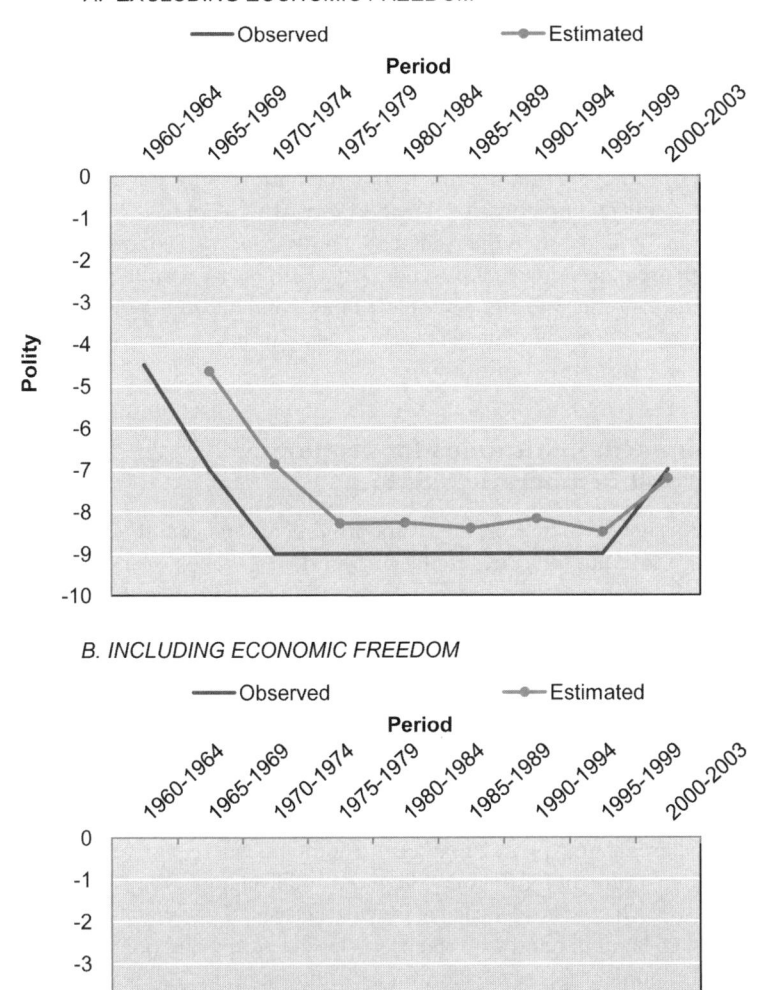

Figure 5.4 Observed and estimated polity in Syria.

Source: Authors.

government has promoted economic reform, openness and modernization of the economy while simultaneously preserving complete political control. Perhaps this explains why, so far, economic reforms in Syria have not had a significant impact on the government's control over the economy, and why space for the private sector, while growing, remains limited. For example, where the private sector has had an increasing role, this was the direct result of new monopolies being created and controlled by members of the governing elite, rather than being broad-based and inclusive. Also to note is that the much touted plan to reduce the size of the public sector has not been implemented. Furthermore, where political reform has been introduced in Syria, the steps that were taken have in fact served to reinforce, not undermine the regime's power (Lust-Okar, 2006). In Syria, despite promised and implemented economic reforms, personal relations and informal power structures, all coloured by sectarian allegiances, remain far more important than formal governmental structures or institutions.

4. Moving forward: institutions for economic development and democratic build-up

Understanding this new evidence on the relationship between economic freedom and political transformation is critical to the current debates taking place in Syria and in the Arab region. If economic freedom is an essential element in the democratization process, then the debate should actually focus on the most critical ingredient of economic freedom: private property. Without securing private property and independent sources of wealth, the exercise of political rights loses its effectiveness. Hayek (1944) maintains that 'economic control is not merely control of a sector of human life which can be separated from the rest: it is the control of the means for all our ends'. The material foundations for political freedom lie in the ability to create wealth, and we know of no other system to achieve this than through free (albeit regulated) private markets. In addition, where people continue to depend on the government for their employment and livelihood, they have little capacity to oppose it. Of course advocacy of free markets and the sustenance of real political freedom go hand in hand with the promotion of equity and political institutions that protect human rights and allow for a genuine participatory democracy.

We believe that supporting the establishment and the strengthening of domestic economic institutions in Syria would place it on a steadier path towards democracy than any direct or indirect pressure designed to force the regime to change its behaviour. The outside pressure that has so far been applied on Syria to democratize has been at the very least counterproductive. Indeed, in view of the current strengths of the regime, the stakes that are involved, the weakness of the opposition and the perception of the Syrian population that has clearly shown it prefers the devil it knows to the one it does not, it looks unlikely, if not impossible, to effect a peaceful democratic change overnight. The prospects for a paradigm shift in the short term are non-existent. On the other hand, institution-building, without threatening the existence of the regime, may in the medium to long term yield better results. The questions are, what institutions and how to build them?

Early contributions on these issues came from Douglass North and Mancur Olsen among others, but in our current context the main protagonist has been Rodrik (2000), who addresses the question of what institutions matter and how to achieve them. On the former issue he identifies five critical areas:

- property rights – strictly speaking, control over property rather than legal rights *per se*;
- regulatory institutions to correct externalities, information failures and market power, such as anti-trust bodies, banking supervision and, more controversially, coordination of major investment decisions that, as Rodrik argues, the Korean and Taiwanese developmental experiences demonstrate;
- institutions for macroeconomic stabilization, e.g. a lender of last resort;
- social insurance – these are often transfer programmes, but Rodrik argues that other institutions such as jobs-for-life can also play the same role; and
- institutions to manage social conflict.

On the latter issue of how to acquire institutions, Rodrik makes two observations:

- There is no single optimal set of institutions – there are many ways of achieving the same objectives.
- Moreover, the interactions between institutions mean that the package needs to be considered as a whole (or at most in a few broad parts) rather than piece by piece.

Institutions can be adopted from abroad or evolved by trial and error locally. Rodrik prefers the latter, although he recognizes that it often provides political cover for an unwillingness to reform, and that it takes time and can involve blind alleys. The critical issue here is the legitimacy of the institutions. Adopting foreign institutions can often be an efficient way of short-cutting the learning process and, indeed, good policy-making will always seek to learn from others' experience. The requirement, however, is that the institutions are sought as solutions to locally identified problems and are adapted to local needs and conditions in quite subtle ways. There is a world of difference between a society facing a problem and looking abroad for something to adapt to its own needs, and an external force declaring that a certain institution will be good for it. Syria's institutions, however, have resisted pressure for change, whether the pressure was external or internal.

At least part of the job of institutions is to codify solutions to distributional conflicts – to codify trade-offs. Institutions help to ensure that the same rules apply through time, and thus make it easier for losers in 'Issue A' to accept their losses because they believe that on future 'Issue B' they will reap corresponding gains. But institutions can only assist in finding such solutions if, broadly speaking, they push in the direction in which society wishes to go anyway.

Rodrik goes on to argue that while, in particular, international financial institutions should not impose specific institutional structures on countries, it would be reasonable to insist on basic human rights and democracy. He adduces some evidence that, while democracy neither significantly raises nor reduces mean rates of economic growth, it is associated with greater stability in growth, investment and consumption, better responses to negative shocks and more equal distributions of (a) personal income and (b) rents between labour and capital. He concludes on democracy that '[i]f there is one area where institutional conditionality is both appropriate and of great economic value . . . this is it' (2000: 34).

There are two caveats to this conclusion. First, while participatory government and democracy are to be lauded, it is not clear that the international community, let alone international financial institutions, have the right to insist on them. If, in Rodrik's phrase, democracy is a 'meta-institution', this would be meta-conditionality; it would be interference of the deepest kind, and it could undermine the legitimacy of governments and their willingness to interact with the international community at all. Second, other scholars have worried more than Rodrik about the causality in all this. Clague *et al.* (1997) observe that the factors associated with lasting democracy – e.g. equality, racial harmony, clean bureaucracy – are also directly associated with better economic policy. Clague *et al.* identify regime stability as an important dimension of the pro-growth environment. What matters most in our present context is how to follow the above prescriptions in an environment that is politically repressive and averse to change.

The question of institution-building, thus, is a matter that has to be tackled by Syria itself. Civil society, the business class and Syrian intellectuals all had and have a role to play in pushing for institutional reform along the lines mentioned above. In the past, the authorities have been reluctant to respond to calls for substantive reform. In recent years, however, they have indicated a greater understanding of the benefits of integrating the Syrian economy into the world economy, attracting foreign investment and achieving stable development, and thus they may now be more responsive to calls for institutional reforms, not least because of self-interest in perpetuating the survival of the regime itself. This potential window for domestic institutional reform should be complemented by a different stance on the part of Western powers in their dealings with Syria.

At the external level, emphasis should be placed first and foremost on fostering economic freedom by providing direct support for social and economic development programmes that help the population. That also means promoting Syria's engagement in international markets for goods and services, and supporting its entry into multilateral institutions such as the World Trade Organization (WTO). The West, and in particular the European Union and the USA, rather than blocking even the consideration of Syria's application to the WTO, as has been the case, should actually accelerate the process and use this opportunity to promote economic reforms in Syria and help it reform the institutions that are needed to build its prosperity. These are small and achievable steps that will also go a long way in calming Syrians' perception that the West is just promoting its own interests and completely disregarding Syria's. Within the current mindset, the West's support of Syrian opposition parties has in fact served to undermine rather than promote the cause of democracy in Syria. Indeed, the very legitimacy of the opposition in Syria has been compromised, if not to say totally discredited.

In promoting social and economic development, Western countries and international organizations should offer more carrots to Syria than sticks, and learn to be more patient, rather than demanding dramatic and immediate change that will not happen. Constructive engagement, built on mutual trust in areas that do not threaten the very existence of the regime, should be favoured. These include economic and social development programmes that improve the lives of Syrians. The Syrian population needs to be convinced that engagement with the West can be turned into a positive-sum game. Conditions in the provision of technical and financial support should therefore be confined to the economic sphere, and should not impinge on the regime power base.

Finally, it is worth mentioning that even President Bashar Assad recognizes the role of institutions in promoting democracy. In his inaugural address eight years ago he emphasized the need for democracy and its linkages to institutional development and administrative reforms. However, eight years on, with international sanctions and blockades, the situation remains basically unchanged. It is time to take another route, one that bears reward rather than sanctions or threats, but we should all be mindful that 'rich gifts wax poor when givers prove unkind' (William Shakespeare, *Hamlet*).

5. Concluding remarks

Authoritarian rule in Syria is as entrenched today as when President Hafez Assad consolidated his power in the early 1980s. The goal of democracy continues to elude the Syrian population despite notable, though unstable, economic development since independence. The Ba'ath regime that seized power and appropriated the state in the early 1970s has been ruling Syria with an iron fist for close to four decades now. This it has managed through a strict command and control system where dissent is severely punished. In the process, the regime has succeeded in co-opting the business sector, whose members have chosen to play by the regime's rules rather than risk losing their business and/or face persecution.

Oil and regional conflicts, especially the Arab–Israeli conflict, have provided an enabling environment for Syrian autocracy to prevail. We also find evidence that lack of economic freedoms has played a critical role in retarding democratic reforms in Syria. While the settlement of the Arab–Israeli conflict awaits a just regional/international solution to the Palestinian question, the cause of democracy in Syria could be well served with incremental doses of institutional and economic reforms. Reforms that benefit the wider segments of the population should be favoured. These have to be conceived and developed at home; they can neither be imported from, nor imposed by, the outside. Nonetheless, Western countries can help promote the democratic process by supporting domestic institutions and economic reform programmes that are of broad benefit, rather than imposing sanctions or attempting to deny Syria access to international economic bodies.

Annex

Table 5.2 Parameter estimates using EM parsimonious model

Independent variable	A	B
Income	0.453***	0.569
	−0.138	0.209
Polity	1.054***	0.942
	−0.042	0.052
Education	0.470***	0.271
	0.21	0.279
Neighbour polity	0.087***	0.052
	−0.032	0.038
Fraser Index of Economic Freedom		0.246
		0.18
Regional effects		
Sub-Saharan Africa	−1.704***	−8.685
	−0.705	1.821
East Asian	−0.336***	−3.525
	−0.948	1.069
Latin American	−0.207***	−2.833
	−0.584	0.77
Historical effects		
Colonial legacy	−0.151***	−8.455
	−1.531	4.148
Interaction: ethnic fractionalization * lagged polity	−0.418***	−0.265
	−0.076	0.093
Arab-specific effects		
Net fuel exports	−0.016***	−0.013
	−0.005	0.005
Regional wars		
Interaction: regional war and Sub-Saharan Africa	7.384***	31.521
	−2.677	6.64
Interaction: regional war and East Asian	6.243***	8.391
	−2.916	3.221
Interaction: regional war and Latin American	10.169***	12.569
	−2.625	3.39
Interaction: regional war and Arab	−3.473***	−7.555
	−1.42	1.887
Constant	−1.475	−2.904
	−1.101	1.496
Number of observations	596	596

Source: Authors.

Notes
A: Global EM estimation, without the Fraser Index of Economic Freedom.
B: Global EM estimation, with Fraser Index of Economic Freedom.
***With 95% confidence.

Notes

1 The idea that prosperity stimulates democracy is referred to in the literature as the Lipset hypothesis. Lipset (1959) credits the idea to Aristotle: 'From Aristotle down to the present, men have argued that only in a wealthy society in which relatively few citizens lived in real poverty could a situation exist in which the mass of the population could intelligently participate in politics and could develop the self-restraint necessary to avoid succumbing to the appeals of irresponsible demagogues.'
2 For details see Carré, 1983.
3 Between July 1998 and early 2000, the Army chief of staff, director of the General Intelligence Department, chief of Internal Security at the General Intelligence Department, commander of the Air Forces, and chief of Military Intelligence were all forced into retirement. As the majority of these 'security pillars' had reached the legal age for retirement, these moves could have been seen as part of a normal process of change. Historically, however, Hafez had not changed his political, military, security or even administrative staff when they reached the legal retirement age. Only when a staff member committed a notable error would he be discharged from the power circle, but with due respect to his status and role in exchange for political loyalty. The stability of Hafez's regime was strongly dependent on the loyalty of his security staff, and thus the release of numerous key security officials indicated an underlying motive of surrounding his son with key personnel deemed to remain loyal to him once he assumed the reins of power.
4 Bashar employed his rising power to eliminate Uncle Rafaat Assad from competing for the presidency, by demolishing his illegal port in Tartous and announcing his imminent trial should he return to Syria.
5 In 1963 commercial banking and insurance were completely nationalized, and in 1965 most large businesses were wholly or partially nationalized. By 1966 the public sector included natural resources, electric power and water; the bulk of industrial plants, banking and insurance; part of transportation; and most international commerce and domestic wholesale trade.
6 Estimates of Syrian expatriates' assets abroad amount to approximately US$80 billion.
7 US–Syrian relationships have undergone several turnarounds. Suffice it to mention here their cooperation in ending the Lebanese civil war in 1990 and the subsequent stationing of Syrian troops there with the presumed objective of helping the Lebanese authorities implement the Taif Accord brought about the settlement of the war.
8 The implementation of this programme has been hindered by the complexity of EU procedures. Direct state-to-state cooperation, such as the French approach of sending experts for consultation, may be a better avenue to tackle specific reform issues.
9 The USA did support the Reform Party of Syria established by a Syrian businessman living in the USA. Calling for the change of the Syrian regime and peace with Israel, this party has failed to grow, lacking both political credibility and local support.
10 See also Bilson, 1982; Huntington, 1991; Burkhart and Lewis-Beck, 1994; Feng, 1997; Barro, 1999.
11 The orthogonal component of this index is the residual of the regression of the Fraser index on all of the right-hand-side variables of the full EMM model (including oil and conflicts variables and their interaction terms).

References

Assad, President Hafez (1999) Inauguration speech, *Al Munadhil* (internal magazine of Al Ba'ath Arab Socialist Party) 295 (March–April).
Barro, R. (1999) 'Determinants of Democracy', *Journal of Political Economy* 107 (suppl.) (Dec.).
Bilson, J. (1982) 'Civil Liberty: An Econometric Investigation', *Kyklos* 35.
Burkhart, R. and Lewis-Beck, M. (1994) 'Comparative Democracy: The Economic Development Thesis', *American Political Science Review* 88.

Carré, O. (1983) *Les Fréres musulmans: Egypte et Syrie (1928–1982)*, Paris: Gallimard.
Clague, C., Philip, K., Stephen, K., and Mancur, O. (1997) 'Democracy, Autocracy, and the Institutions Supportive of Economic Growth', in Christopher Clague, ed., *Institutions and Economic Development*, Baltimore, MD: Johns Hopkins University Press.
Elbadawi, I. and Makdisi, S. (2007) 'Explaining the Democracy Deficit in the Arab World', *Quarterly Review of Economics and Finance* 46/5 (Feb.).
——, —— and Milante, G. (2006) 'Technical Note on Democracy and Development in the Arab World', unpublished manuscript.
Feng, Y. (1997) 'Democracy, Political Stability and Economic Growth', *British Journal of Political Science* 27.
Friedman, M. (1962) *Capitalism and Freedom*, Chicago: University of Chicago Press.
Fukuyama, F. (1992) *The End of History and the Last Man*, New York: Free Press.
George, A. (2003) *Syria: Neither Bread Nor Freedom*, London: Zed Books.
Hayek, F. (1944) *The Road to Serfdom*, London: Routledge & Kegan Paul.
Huntington, S. (1991) *The Third Wave: Democratization in the Late Twentieth Century*, Norman, OK: University of Oklahoma Press.
Lipset, S. (1959) 'Some Social Requisites of Democracy: Economic Development and Political Legitimacy', *American Political Science Review* 53 (March).
—— (1994) 'The Social Requisites of Democracy Revisited: 1993 Presidential Address', *American Sociological Review* 59 (Feb.).
Lust-Okar, E.(2006) *Reform in Syria: Steering between the Chinese Model and Regime Change*, Carnegie Papers, 69, Washington, DC: Carnegie Endowment for International Peace.
Maoz, M. (1998) *Assad: The Sphinx of Damascus. A Political Biography*, New York: Weidenfeld & Nicolson.
North, D. (1991) *Institutions, Institutional Change and Economic Performance*, Cambridge: Cambridge University Press.
Olsen, M. (1982) *The Rise and Decline of Nations: Economic Growth, Stagflation and Social Rigidities*, New Haven, CT: Yale University Press.
Przeworski, A. (1997) 'Modernization: Theories and Facts', *World Politics* 49/2.
—— (2004) 'Capitalism, Development and Democracy', *Revista de Economia Politica* 24(4).
—— and Limongi, F. (1993) 'Political Regimes and Economic Growth', *Journal of Economic Perspectives* 7(3).
Richards, A. and Waterbury, J. (1996) *A Political Economy of the Middle East*, Boulder, CO: Westview Press.
Rodrik, D. (2000) *Institutions for High-Quality Growth: What they are and How to Acquire Them*, Cambridge, MA: NBER Working Paper, 7540 (Feb.).
Safadi, R. (2006) *The Legacy of Trade Reforms in the Arab Countries*, Vienna: OPEC Fund for International Development.
Seal, P. (1998) *Assad of Syria: The Struggle for the Middle East*, London: I. B. Tauris.
UNDP and Arab Fund for Economic and Social Development (2002) *Arab Human Development Report 2002: Creating Opportunities for Future Generations*, New York: United Nations Development Program.
Wedeen, L. (1999) *Ambiguities of Domination: Politics, Rhetoric and Symbols in Contemporary Syria*, Chicago: University of Chicago Press.
World Bank (2005) *Syrian Investment Climate Assessment: Unlocking the Potential of the Private Sector*, Washington, DC: World Bank.
—— (2007a) *World Bank World Development Indicators 2007*, CD-Rom, Washington, DC: World Bank.
—— (2007b) *Doing Business 2008*, Washington, DC: World Bank.
Yousef, T. (2004) 'Development, Growth and Policy Reform in the Middle East and North Africa since 1950', *Journal of Economic Perspective* 18/3 (Summer).

OIL-DEPENDENT COUNTRIES

6 The Gulf region: beyond oil and wars

The role of history and geopolitics in explaining autocracy

Sami Atallah

Introduction

The six Gulf countries – Bahrain, Kuwait, Oman, Qatar, Saudi Arabia and United Arab Emirates (UAE) – have the highest standard of living in the Arab world, yet they are the most authoritarian. For the period 1960 to 2003 per capita income of the Gulf States as a group averaged US$13,600 in constant 2000 prices, more than 13 times the rest of the Arab world and its per capita income of under $1,000. However, the Gulf's accumulated wealth has not led to democratization, as the modernization theory would predict (Lipset, 1959). The polity score, a raw measure of democracy, of the Gulf averaged –9.2 (the lowest possible score being –10 and the highest 10), compared to –5.5 for the rest of the Arab world for the same period, 1960 to 2003.

Economic development in the Gulf region did not unleash any significant social or cultural pressure to democratize, despite rising levels of urbanization, education and occupational specialization. According to the resource curse literature (Luciani, 1987; Ross, 2001), oil wealth tends to inhibit the democratization process by enabling the ruling classes in oil-producing states to trade off economic welfare for political rights. This argument has merit: oil wealth has been used to maintain authoritarian regimes. However a closer examination of the politico-historical evolution of the Gulf region would seem to indicate that oil wealth does not, on its own, explain this phenomenon. In particular, Kuwait, with a historically active merchant class, is a good example of how political dynamism manifested in the creation of an elected assembly (albeit with limited powers) as early as 1938. Kuwait citizens have gone to the polls at least twelve times since 1962 to elect a national assembly.[1] In other Gulf states, fundamentalist religious groups in Saudi Arabia, and British colonial interests in the lower Gulf states of Oman, UAE, Qatar and Bahrain have played an important role in fostering authoritarianism over and above any impact oil wealth may have had in this regard. The recorded polity scores of the Gulf States indicate differences in terms of change over time between Kuwait on the one hand and the rest of the Gulf States on the other. The reasons for these differences, as will be demonstrated, precede the discovery of oil.

The purpose of this chapter is threefold. The first is to examine empirically the determinants of the democracy deficit in the Gulf States. Building on the Elbadawi, Makdisi and Milante (EMM) model (Elbadawi and Makdisi, 2007, and Chapter 2 above), the extent to which the alternative theories of democracy explain the democracy deficit is tested. Second, key factors, beyond oil and wars, that are responsible for producing a polity different in Kuwait than the other Gulf States, are identified. Third, mechanisms are assessed through which oil and wars affected polity in these countries.

The key findings are as follows: empirically, the various theories of democracy including modernization, oil and war hypotheses do not fully explain the persisting autocracy in the Gulf States. While oil and conflicts help in understanding this phenomenon, the story of why autocracy has persisted needs to be complemented by a comparative historical approach. Specifically, Britain's occupation of India in the nineteenth century led to an expansion of its influence over the Gulf region in order to protect its interests in that country. As a result, the regimes that emerged in the Gulf States in the early twentieth century were, in large measure, determined by their proximity to India: the closer to Mumbai (Bombay), the more likely Britain had to intervene to protect its interests. In consequence, rulers loyal to Britain were empowered at the expense of other influential groups. States that were further away came under relatively less British influence and the domestic balance of power was more the outcome of the relative political strength of various local groups. This was notably the case in Kuwait and Saudi Arabia. In Kuwait, the fiscal dependence of the ruler on the merchants compelled the former to give up political power and to agree to set up a national assembly in return for fiscal support. In Saudi Arabia, the continued reliance of the ruling family on the support of fundamentalist religious groups (the *mutawwa*) to stay in power contributed to the persistence of a strict religious/autocratic regime.

In this chapter section 1 examines empirically alternative explanations of democracy in the Gulf countries. Section 2 discusses how the formative years of the Gulf States in the nineteenth century explain the regimes that emerged in the twentieth century. Section 3 examines the mechanism through which oil and wars affected the regimes of the Gulf States. Section 4 concludes.

1. Do hypotheses of democracy explain the regimes in the Gulf states? An empirical investigation

Building on the EMM model, the purpose of this section is to empirically assess the determinants of the democracy deficit in the Gulf region as a whole and in Kuwait separately. Unlike the rest of the Gulf, the polity scores for Kuwait vary sufficiently to allow for a separate examination. For this purpose the roles of modernization, colonialism, religion, social cohesion, the resource curse and wars are respectively tested[2] and the main findings are then discussed.

These tests are based on hypotheses found in the literature. The standard hypothesis of democratization is that of Lipset (1959), who argues that modernization leads to democratization. In other words, as countries develop, they witness higher rates of urbanization, education and occupational specialization. Consequently, their citizens demand more political participation, which eventually leads to democracy. We use three variables to measure modernization: the first is income, measured as the average GDP per capita in US dollars using the year 2000 as a base year. To deal with endogeneity of income and democracy, we lag by one period the natural log of GDP per capita. The second variable is education, lagged by one period, which is composed of the average level of school attainment, average literacy of the adult population and secondary school attainment. The third variable is the neighbour polity, to account for the effects of the regime type of the states that neighbour the country.

Hypotheses concerning the historical legacy of colonialism have two variants. The first argues that countries that have been colonized are less likely to be democratic, either because the colonial experience disrupted economic growth and, hence, reduced the prospects for democracy to survive (Gasiorowski, 1995), or because it has drawn arbitrary borders for the newly created states and, hence, exacerbated ethnic fractionalization (Abernethy, 2000). Countries that have formerly been colonized are coded as 1, and 0 otherwise. Another measure of colonialism used in the analysis is colonial legacy, which is the inverse of the number of years since the country became independent.

Other scholars have distinguished between the identity of the colonizers and their relationship to democracy. Lipset (1959) and Laporta *et al.* (1998) have argued that different European empires established different regimes in their respective colonies. For instance, competitive democracies in newly independent states are attributed to British colonialism, whereas French, Portuguese and Spanish colonies are associated with autocratic regimes. The hypothesis stipulates that British colonialism has a positive effect on democracy, whereas French, Portuguese and Spanish colonies have negative effects on democracy. In our empirical analysis, former British colonies are coded as 1, and 0 otherwise; former French colonies are coded as 1, and 0 otherwise; former Spanish colonies are coded as 1, and 0 otherwise; and former Portuguese colonies are coded as 1, and 0 otherwise.

The effect of religion on democracy has received growing attention in the literature. Certain writers, such as Kedourie (1994), argue that Islam fosters authoritarian regimes, since its legal codes or their interpretation are not compatible with the notion of democratic governance. Other writers, such as Mark Tessler (2002), Stepan and Robertson (2003) and Plateau (2008), argue that religion as such does not determine the nature of political regimes. In our analysis the Muslim variable is coded 1 if more than 50 per cent of the population is considered to be Muslim. Similarly, the Christian variable is coded 1 if more than 50 per cent of the population is Christian.

On the effect of social cohesion on democracy, the conventional literature has argued that ethnically heterogeneous societies find it more difficult to resolve conflict and achieve consensus (Horowitz, 1993). Thus it is argued that ethnically diverse societies are more prone to violence and conflict and consequently are less able to sustain democracy. Following the literature, our measure of social cohesion is based on the ethnic fractionalization index. Ethnic fractionalization squared captures the non-monotonic effects of high level of fractionalization. We also introduce an interactive term of ethnic fractionalization and lagged polity to account for the difficulty that democratization might be harder to attain in diverse societies.

The resource curse literature attributes authoritarian regimes to oil. Countries that produce and export oil are more able to sustain autocratic regimes since they are able to use oil rents to buy off the opposition and hence sustain autocratic rule. Thus it follows that high oil rents from exports should have a negative effect on democracy. Oil is measured by net fuel exports to GDP.

The EMM model reaches the conclusion that the above modernization, historical, social and religious factors do not on their own explain the persisting democracy deficit in the Arab world. Rather it is regional wars, along with oil, that account for this phenomenon. The authors make the case that wars in the Arab world, unlike other regions, have sustained authoritarian rule, that is, they have had a negative effect on democratization. Regional wars are measured as the number of international and civil wars in the region divided by the number of countries in the region. Alternative measures of wars include the following: the number of battle deaths in the Israeli–Palestinian conflict, measured as the natural log; Arab civil wars, measured in the number of battle deaths in civil wars in the Arab region per period; and Arab international wars, measured as the number of battle deaths in wars in the Arab region that involved a foreign power. All the war measures are lagged by one period.

1.1 An empirical assessment of the Gulf countries

With the above in mind, we first look at the polity scores that serve as a proxy measure for democracy over time. What these scores indicate is that the Gulf countries are not only more authoritarian but have experienced little change in polity score, especially between 1960 and 1990. For the same period, non-Gulf Arab countries also slid into greater authoritarianism between 1960 and 1980, with limited recovery in the polity scores since then. Although both groups have witnessed political liberalization, the rate of change for the Gulf countries is much lower than the non-Gulf Arab countries.

To examine the determinants of the regime in the Gulf States, the hypotheses elaborated above are tested. But first, a dummy variable is created for the Gulf countries that takes the value of 1 if the country is Bahrain, Kuwait, Oman, Qatar, Saudi Arabia and United Arab Emirates, and 0 otherwise. The Gulf dummy represents only 3.75 per cent of the observations. A second dummy variable is created to measure non-Gulf Arab states. It takes the value of 1 if it is an Arab country but not a Gulf state. The Arab non-Gulf dummy includes the following countries: Algeria, Djibouti, Egypt, Iraq, Jordan, Lebanon, Mauritania, Morocco, Sudan, Syria, Tunisia and Yemen. These make up 10 per cent of the observations. Both dummies are interpreted in reference to non-Arab countries. The goal is to empirically explain the Gulf dummy by making it statistically

170 *Sami Atallah*

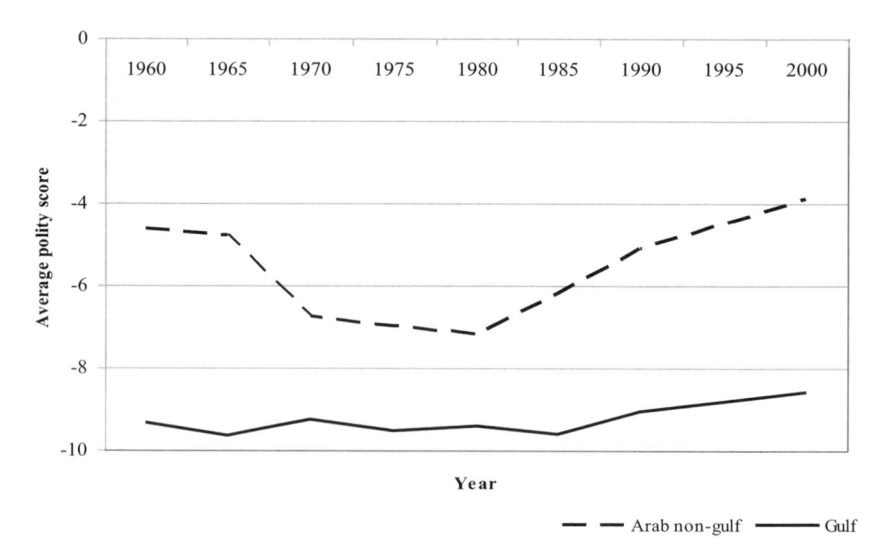

Figure 6.1 Polity score for Gulf and Arab non-Gulf countries, 1960–2003.
Source: Polity IV data set.

insignificant. Substantively speaking, once the Gulf dummy variable is no longer considered significant, then one can conclude that the regime type in the Gulf States is accounted for by the theory (and its respective variables) that led to this outcome.

A Tobit model is run with group fixed effect, to take care of both censoring and truncation of the data, with 893 observations, which include all the counties in the world from 1960 to 2003, using the EMM data set. The data are a five-year panel asymptotic in N (number of units), with T equal to nine periods, since little change in the political institutions is taking place from one year to the next.[3] In addition to the explanatory variables, we control for three regions: Sub-Saharan Africa, East Asia and Latin America.

Table 6.1 presents the results. A common finding among the seven models is that modernization measured by income levels, democratic tradition in the country and the polity of neighbouring countries – all lagged one period – have positive and significant effects on democracy. However, in Model A we observe that none of these variables along with education can explain the democracy deficit in the Gulf countries. The Gulf dummy is not only negative and significant but its coefficient is more than three times that of its non-Gulf Arab countries. Adding historical conditions in Model B (measured by colonial legacy or origin), religion in Model C (Islam and Christianity), social fractionalization in Model D (social cohesion interacted with polity) and oil in Model E (measured by net fuel exports, lagged one period), reduces the coefficient of the Gulf dummy from –5.9 in Model A to –5 in Model E, but remains statistically significant, and with higher coefficient, than the non-Gulf Arab states.

Table 6.1 Dependent variable polity scores 1960–2003, with robust standard error

	Model A	Model B	Model C	Model D	Model E	Model F	Model G
Income	0.907	0.779	0.764	0.605	0.62	0.771	0.751
	(0.226)***	(0.224)***	(0.225)***	(0.216)***	(0.215)***	(0.214)***	(0.208)***
Polity	0.836	0.835	0.836	1.022	1.014	1.011	1.024
	(0.035)***	(0.038)***	(0.038)***	(0.067)***	(0.068)***	(0.067)***	(0.067)***
Education	0.322	0.35	0.327	0.389	0.399	0.272	0.291
	(0.254)	(0.267)	(0.272)	(0.254)	(0.254)	(0.245)	(0.244)
Neighbour polity	0.088	0.094	0.093	0.089	0.091	0.093	0.078
	(0.042)**	(0.046)**	(0.045)**	(0.044)**	(0.045)**	(0.045)**	(0.042)*
Gulf	−5.954	−5.758	−5.602	−5.413	−5.071	−5.862	−4.878
	(0.916)***	(1.014)***	(1.036)***	(0.912)***	(0.876)***	(0.979)***	(1.05)***
Non-Gulf Arab	−1.654	−1.866	−1.775	−1.527	−1.443	−1.912	−0.584
	(0.429)***	(0.483)***	(0.486)***	(0.485)***	(0.469)***	(0.526)***	(1.009)
Sub-Saharan Africa	−0.049	−0.118	−0.144	−0.346	−0.37	−0.521	−2.01
	(0.499)	(0.478)	(0.501)	(0.517)	(0.511)	(0.538)	(1.003)**
East Asia	−0.505	−0.935	−0.871	−0.824	−0.801	−0.94	−2.203
	(0.698)	(0.640)	(0.669)	(0.606)	(0.602)	(0.606)	(1.102)**
Latin America	−0.884	−1.323	−1.385	−1.019	−1.049	−1.039	−2.404
	(0.431)**	(0.476)***	(0.52)***	(0.554)*	(0.583)*	(0.551)*	(1.002)**
Former colony	—	−0.301	−0.346	−0.372	−0.341	−0.445	−0.427
		(0.609)	(0.649)	(0.615)	(0.615)	(0.595)	(0.609)
Colonial legacy	—	−7.34	−7.351	−7.499	−7.545	−6.345	−5.219
		(2.194)***	(2.172)***	(2.141)***	(2.167)***	(2.052)***	(2.111)**
Former British colony	—	0.278	0.307	0.484	0.458	0.476	0.334
		(0.487)	(0.510)	(0.470)	(0.476)	(0.478)	(0.470)
Former Spanish colony	—	0.297	0.285	0.154	0.224	0.311	0.27
		(0.473)	(0.472)	(0.482)	(0.528)	(0.494)	(0.467)
Former French colony	—	0.427	0.492	0.458	0.457	0.51	0.291
		(0.416)	(0.474)	(0.490)	(0.484)	(0.488)	(0.500)

Table 6.1 Continued

	Model A	Model B	Model C	Model D	Model E	Model F	Model G
Former Portuguese colony	—	1.559	1.613	1.392	1.375	1.471	1.231
		(0.821)*	(0.868)*	(0.889)	(0.909)	(0.89)*	(0.762)
Muslim	—	—	−0.035	−0.029	0.057	0.311	0.393
			(0.418)	(0.420)	(0.416)	(0.402)	(0.397)
Christian	—	—	0.199	0.286	0.3	0.767	0.666
			(0.572)	(0.557)	(0.547)	(0.540)	(0.514)
Ethnic fractionalization	—	—	—	1.946	1.774	1.287	2.04
				(2.452)	(2.417)	(2.487)	(2.463)
Ethnic fractionalization squared	—	—	—	−2.385	−2.014	−1.28	−1.955
				(2.750)	(2.714)	(2.785)	(2.775)
Ethnic fractionalization	—	—	—	−0.425	−0.413	−0.412	−0.428
*Lagged polity	—	—	—	(0.115)***	(0.117)***	(0.115)***	(0.115)***
Net fuel exports	—	—	—	—	−0.008	−0.008	−0.01
					(0.005)*	(0.005)**	(0.005)**
Regional wars	—	—	—	—	—	4.927	1.158
						(1.497)***	(2.890)
Regional wars* Gulf	—	—	—	—	—	—	−1.256
							(3.101)
Regional wars* Non-Gulf Arab	—	—	—	—	—	—	−0.924
							(3.558)
Regional wars* Sub-Saharan Africa	—	—	—	—	—	—	8.291
							(4.196)**
Regional wars* East Asia	—	—	—	—	—	—	6.288
							(4.206)
Regional wars* Latin America	—	—	—	—	—	—	c.559
							(4.47)**
Constant	−4.59	−3.178	−3.154	−2.521	−2.697	−5.062	−4.551
	(1.701)***	(1.788)*	(1.797)*	(1.632)	(1.63)*	(1.663)***	(1.723)***
N	893	893	893	893	893	893	893

The introduction of regional wars in Model F raises the Gulf dummy coefficient to −5.86, which remains statistically significant. When we interact the Gulf dummy with regional wars to assess whether regional wars have different effects on the Gulf countries, its coefficient drops to −4.88, but remains negative and significant, indicating that on its own it does not explain the persisting democracy deficit in the Gulf region. This stands in contrast to the non-Gulf Arab dummy, which upon interaction with regional wars in Model G sees the coefficient drop from −1.9 to −0.58 and becomes no longer statistically significant. Similarly, while oil does not seem to account, on its own, for the democracy deficit, it has played a significant role in fostering authoritarian rule. We take up this matter in section 3 below. It is also worth noting that regional war effects interacted with the Gulf countries and non-Gulf Arab countries have a negative, albeit not statistically significant, effect on democracy. This is in contrast to the positive effect on democracy of regional conflicts for other regions of the world like Sub-Saharan Africa or Latin America.[4]

To further refine the above tests and achieve a parsimonious model, Model G is rerun without the non-significant variables. The results, which remain unchanged in terms of scale and significance, are shown in Table 6.2, column A. The absence of a regional conflict effect on the Gulf's polity may be due to how regional wars are measured. To make sure that the lack of effect is not due to a measurement problem, Model A in Table 6.2 is replicated by substituting regional wars with different measurements and types of war, as per the EMM model. In Models B, C and D of Table 6.2, the natural log of the Israeli–Palestinian battle deaths, Arab civil wars, Arab international wars, all lagged by one period, are used as alternative proxies of conflict.[5] The results confirm the two earlier findings. First, conflicts in the Arab world fail to fully explain the Gulf dummy. Although the Israeli–Palestinian battle deaths (Model B) and Arab civil wars (Model C) have separately reduced the significance of the Gulf dummy, it remains statistically significant at the 10 per cent level. Even when we control for all three types of conflict, the Gulf dummy in Model E retains its significance, suggesting that other supplementary factors are needed to explain the resilience of authoritarianism in the region. Second, none of the three conflicts, when interacted

Table 6.2 Dependent variable polity score 1960–2003: robust standard error in a parsimonious model with alternative war measure

	Model A	Model B	Model C	Model D	Model E
Income	0.863	0.861	0.769	0.766	0.866
	(0.18)***	(0.191)***	(0.182)***	(0.182)***	(0.192)***
Polity	1.026	1.019	1.017	1.017	1.019
	(0.064)***	(0.064)***	(0.065)***	(0.065)***	(0.064)***
Neighbour polity	0.086	−0.001	0.095	0.097	−0.004
	(0.039)**	−0.045	(0.042)**	(0.042)**	−0.046
Gulf	−5.003	−4.474	−9.604	−4.822	−8.095
	(0.963)***	(2.701)*	(5.048)*	(0.751)***	(4.25)*

Table 6.2 Continued

	Model A	Model B	Model C	Model D	Model E
Non-Gulf Arab	−0.742	−2.395	−3.853	−1.504	−8.891
	(0.986)	(2.834)	(2.054)*	(0.716)**	(4.795)*
Sub-Saharan Africa	−2.364	−0.806	−0.611	−0.606	−0.812
	(1.021)**	(0.499)	(0.486)	(0.485)	(0.500)
East Asia	−2.449	−0.78	−0.792	−0.787	−0.783
	(1.082)**	(0.619)	(0.583)	(0.582)	(0.621)
Latin America	−2.282	−0.609	−1.036	−1.035	−0.607
	(0.893)**	(0.426)	(0.432)**	(0.432)**	(0.426)
Colonial legacy	−5.183	−5.161	−7.431	−7.432	−5.174
	(2.127)**	(2.072)**	(2.163)***	(2.159)***	(2.081)**
Ethnic fractionalization	0.067	−0.232	−0.16	−0.152	−0.233
	(0.734)	(0.734)	(0.728)	(0.729)	(0.735)
Ethnic fractionalization *Lagged polity	−0.407	−0.416	−0.389	−0.389	−0.417
	(0.11)***	(0.111)***	(0.112)***	(0.112)***	(0.111)***
Net fuel exports	−0.01	−0.01	−0.009	−0.009	−0.01
	(0.005)**	(0.004)**	(0.005)*	(0.005)**	(0.004)**
Regional wars	0.938	–	–	–	–
	(3.005)				
Regional wars*Gulf	−1.077	–	–	–	–
	(3.176)				
Regional wars *non-Gulf Arab	−0.784	–	–	–	–
	(3.662)				
Regional wars *sub-Saharan Africa	8.743	–	–	–	–
	(4.406)**				
Regional wars *East Asia	6.499	–	–	–	–
	(3.878)*				
Regional wars *Latin America	9.558	–	–	–	–
	(4.434)**				
Israeli–Palest. bd *Gulf	–	−0.233	–	–	−0.083
		(0.401)			(0.440)
Israeli–Palest. bd *non–Gulf Arab	–	0.1	–	–	0.53
		(0.384)			(0.519)
Arab civil wars *Gulf	–	–	0.406	–	0.237
			(0.433)		(0.369)
Arab civil wars *non-Gulf Arab	–	–	0.213	–	0.36
			(0.200)		
Arab international wars *Gulf	–	–	–	−0.051	0.004
				(0.038)	(0.056)
Arab international wars *non-Gulf Arab	–	–	–	−0.01	−0.034
				(0.060)	(0.067)
Period	–	0.377	–	–	0.382
		(0.073)***			(0.075)***
Constant	−4.527	−6.329	−3.204	−3.19	−6.397
	(1.576)***	(1.611)***	(1.413)**	(1.41)**	(1.629)***
N	893	893	893	893	893

The Gulf region: beyond oil and wars 175

separately and jointly with the Gulf dummy, are statistically significant, indicating that wars did not have an effect on their regime type.[6]

Before turning to an examination of the supplementary factors, let us move from the regional level to an examination of the case of Kuwait. Unlike the other Gulf States, its polity, that is, the dependent variable, varies sufficiently enough over the years to obtain meaningful results. The object is to see whether we can have a better understanding of the factors underlying its regime type, which seems to be different from the rest of the Gulf States.

1.2 An empirical assessment of Kuwait

Looking inside the Gulf States, we observe some variation in the median and dispersion of the polity score. For one thing, not all the countries in the Gulf are equally authoritarian. For instance, Kuwait has a median polity score of −8 (mean of −8.36) compared to −10 median polity scores for Oman, Qatar, Saudi Arabia and UAE. Also, Kuwait, and to lesser extent Bahrain, have the largest dispersion in their polity score, measured in standard deviation of 1.15 and 0.78, respectively, compared to no dispersion for Qatar, Saudi Arabia and UAE. Over time, the polity score in the six countries has also varied (Figure 6.2). For instance, Qatar, Saudi Arabia and UAE have experienced no changes in their political institutions in the last 43 years. The political institutions in Bahrain and Oman improved only after 1990. It is only in Kuwait that democratic attempts from the mid-1970s on have led to lesser forms of authoritarian rule, especially after the liberation of Kuwait from the Iraqi occupation in 1990. Kuwait's polity has the highest median (and mean) and the largest dispersion.

Building on the aggregate analysis, I examine more closely the polity in Kuwait. A Kuwait dummy is introduced that takes the value of 1 for Kuwait and 0 otherwise. Also included in the regression are the Gulf dummy and the non-Gulf dummy, which includes all the other Arab countries. Following the same specification as in Table 6.1, all seven models are run for Kuwait. Table 6.3 which

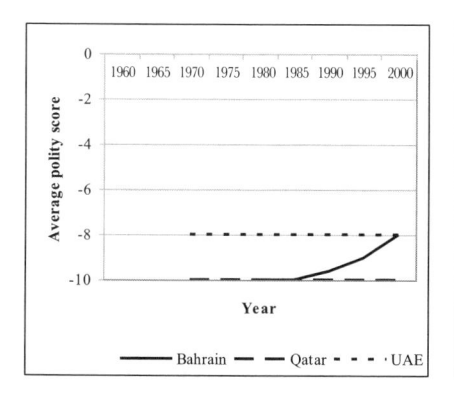

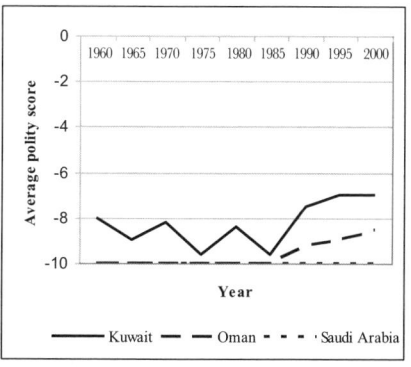

Figure 6.2 Polity scores for the Gulf countries, 1960–2003.

Source: Polity IV data set.

Table 6.3 Dependent variable polity score 1960–2003, with robust standard error for Kuwait

	Model A	Model B	Model C	Model D	Model E	Model F	Model G
Kuwait	1.33	1.797	1.829	1.144	1.179	1.02	0.341
	(0.802)*	(1.021)*	(1.032)*	(0.771)	(0.712)*	(0.679)	(0.831)
Gulf	−6.351	−6.257	−6.104	−5.742	−5.408	−6.152	−4.964
	(1.037)***	(1.13)***	(1.15)***	(0.992)***	(0.924)***	(1.023)***	(1.147)***
Non-Gulf Arab	−1.658	−1.833	−1.74	−1.515	−1.431	−1.9	−0.572
	(0.428)***	(0.482)***	(0.483)***	(0.484)***	(0.468)***	(0.525)***	(01.009)
Net fuel exports	—	—	—	—	−0.008	−0.009	−0.01
					(0.005)*	(0.005)*	(0.005)*
Regional wars	—	—	—	—	—	4.907	1.15
						(1.498)***	(2.895)
Regional wars* Kuwait	—	—	—	—	—	—	2.201
							(1.233)*
Regional wars* Gulf	—	—	—	—	—	—	−1.928
							(3.145)
Regional wars* Non-Gulf Arab	—	—	—	—	—	—	−0.919
							(3.562)
N	893	893	893	893	893	893	893

presents the results shows only the relevant coefficients. The other variables are not reported.

Two major observations are made. The first is that the Kuwait dummy is positive and statistically significant in Models A, B, C and E, which suggests that there is something about Kuwait that makes it different from other Gulf countries. Second, although modernization theory, historical conditions and religion do not explain its polity, social cohesion and regional wars have reduced its dummy to non-significance. For instance, upon adding regional wars, the Kuwait dummy coefficient decreases from 1.17 in Model E to 1.02 in Model F and, consequently, becomes statistically insignificant. Furthermore, when regional wars are interacted with Kuwait, the Kuwait dummy coefficient drops further to 0.34 in Model G, and the interactive dummy is positive and significant, unlike the EMM general result for the Arab world, indicating that regional wars have had a positive effect on Kuwait's polity.

To examine whether different types of wars have had a different impact on Kuwait, various proxies of wars are tested: Israeli–Palestinian battle deaths and Arab civil and international war battle deaths are interacted with the Kuwait dummy on the parsimonious model.[7] Table 6.4, which presents the findings, does not report all the coefficients for the sake of brevity. Unlike the Israeli–Palestinian and Arab civil wars, the Arab international wars, when interacted with the Kuwait dummy, have a positive and statistically significant effect on the polity at the 1 per cent level. This indicates that certain wars in the Arab world have served democracy in Kuwait. This finding is robust even when we control for the other two types of wars in Model E.

So far, we conclude that unlike the non-Gulf Arab states, the polity in the Gulf countries is not fully explained by modernization, colonial history, religion, social cohesion, oil and regional wars (and its various measures). However, Kuwait seems to be an exception in the region; regional wars explain the polity in Kuwait, and Arab international wars have had a positive impact on its political liberalization. In the next section, we examine what accounts for the persistence of the authoritarian regimes in the Gulf countries. Section 3 explores further how oil and wars have influenced the polity in Kuwait.

2. How geopolitics and local conditions shaped the regimes in the pre-oil era

The purpose of this section is to offer a supplementary explanation for the persistence of the democracy deficit in the Gulf region as a whole and for the variation in the evolving regime type among the Gulf countries. Methodologically, a comparative historical approach is used to understand how key players interacted and resolved conflict when sovereignty over territories began to take shape in the nineteenth century, how the balance of power shifted among groups, and what forces caused the changes in the regime type. It is also comparative because only then can we begin to infer the changes of the polity across states and time. Holding several variables constant, such as tribal mobility and tradition across the Arabian

Table 6.4 Dependent variable polity score 1960–2003: robust standard error in a parsimonious model with alternative war measures for Kuwait

	Model A	Model B	Model C	Model D	Model E
Kuwait	0.407	−2.585	6.604	0.189	5.24
	(0.760)	(3.823)	(8.299)	(0.633)	(6.099)
Gulf	−5.115	−3.225	−12.018	−4.913	−8.47
	(1.064)***	(3.904)	(8.458)	(0.826)***	(6.256)
Non-Gulf Arab	−0.755	−2.401	−3.851	−1.51	−8.851
	(0.986)	(2.837)	(2.056)*	(0.717)**	(4.798)*
Net fuel exports	−0.01	−0.01	−0.009	−0.009	−0.01
	(0.005)**	(0.004)**	(0.005)**	(0.005)**	(0.005)**
Regional wars	0.921	–	–	–	–
	(2.996)				
Regional wars *Kuwait	1.843	–	–	–	–
	(1.181)				
Regional wars *Gulf	−1.631	–	–	–	–
	(3.194)				
Regional wars *Non-Gulf Arab	−0.765	–	–	–	–
	(3.654)				
Israeli–Palestinian bd *Kuwait	–	0.575	–	–	−0.201
		(0.572)			(0.615)
Israeli–Palestinian bd *Gulf	–	(0.476)	–	–	−0.231
		(0.579)			(0.610)
Israeli–Palestinian bd *Non-Gulf Arab	–	0.101	–	–	0.526
		(0.385)			(0.519)
Arab civil wars *Kuwait	–	–	−0.504	–	−0.345
			−0.744		(0.667)
Arab civil wars *Gulf	–	–	0.599	–	0.337
			−0.749		(0.668)
Arab civil wars *Non-Gulf Arab	–	–	0.212	–	0.359
			(0.200)		(0.205)*
Arab international wars *Kuwait	–	–	–	0.122	0.135
				(0.039)***	(0.077)*
Arab international wars *Gulf	–	–	–	−0.082	−0.06
				(0.04)**	(0.074)
Arab international wars *Non-Gulf Arab	–	–	–	−0.01	−0.34
				−0.06	−0.067
Period	–	0.378	–	–	0.382
	–	(0.073)***	–	–	(0.075)***
N	893	893	893	893	893

Peninsula, Islamic religion and culture, oil, we can try to gauge or tease out the real factors that made the polity differ.

I argue that the variation in the regime type in the Gulf region is a function of two factors: geostrategic location of the newly created states in mid-nineteenth century, and the strength and composition of the religious and economic classes during the formative years of these states. Briefly, the closer the Gulf state is to India, which Britain wanted to protect from its European rivals and ensure maritime peace in the vicinity to serve its interests, the more Britain intervened in the affairs of that Gulf state. Consequently, this tended to shift the balance of power in favour of the local ruler who sought British recognition and support. With British military and fiscal support, favoured local emirs had little incentive to bargain with various groups in the population for fiscal support and this allowed them to ignore any demands for political participation. This was the case in Oman, Trucial Oman (now UAE), Bahrain and Qatar.

The further away the states are from India, the less was the incentive for Britain to intervene in their domestic affairs, at least in their formative years. Consequently, the polity that emerged came to be influenced by the strength of the internal players, for example, the *mutawwa*, the Wahhabi religious leaders in Saudi Arabia, and the merchants in Kuwait. In the first case, Abd Al Aziz ibn Saud (1902–53) formed a convenient alliance with the *mutawwa*, who provided him with the needed legitimacy given the family's lack of a strong association with tribal confederations; in return he gave them a platform through which they could impose their religious interpretation of Islam while he was expanding his hegemony over the territories of Arabia. The state was thus formed on the basis of a military-religious alliance, where no checks or demands by other groups (merchants, *ikhwans*, tribal military force or other tribes) survived the state-formation process.

As for Kuwait, in the pre-oil era the ruler was dependent on the merchants for revenues. This dependence held the emirs' autocratic tendencies in check. Kuwait emerged out of this experience with a different polity outcome than other Gulf countries. Being in need of revenues, the ruler had to bargain with the merchants, at times giving them political power in return for fiscal backing. No such outcome emerged in the other Gulf States. Saudi Arabia relied on the *zakat* (pilgrimage taxes) and British subsidies to deal with its conquest. As for the remaining states, given their strategic location and British subsidies, their rulers did not need to compromise with domestic groups in exchange for fiscal support. Hence, except for Kuwait, the rulers of the emerging Gulf States could ignore political or economic demands and, if need be, resort to violent means to deal with any internal challenges.

The experience of state formation and, particularly, how rulers dealt with internal demands for political participation, influenced the set of strategies to which they resorted in later years when facing emerging challenges and crises.

2.1 Political costs of falling within the vicinity of British India: the case of Bahrain, Oman, Qatar and UAE

Upon colonizing India, Britain's main policy objectives were twofold. The first was to protect British India mainly from its rival European powers, which effectively transformed the lower Gulf region into India's western frontier. The second was to impose maritime peace in the Gulf to serve its own economic interests. To achieve these two objectives, Britain often resorted to two alternative strategies. On the one hand it imposed treaties on local rulers, preventing them from conceding any rights or concessions to any foreign power or engaging in any

180 *Sami Atallah*

foreign policy without consulting Britain. On the other hand, it used force or sanctions to enforce the treaty or to subjugate tribes that would challenge Britain's influence. These two strategies complemented each other; treaties either preceded or succeeded the use of force. A classic example of the first strategy is Britain's relationship with Muscat,[8] whereas the second strategy was applied to Bahrain, Qatar and UAE.[9] In other instances, the use of force preceded the signing of treaties. This was the fate of the Qawasim tribe of Ras Khayma and Sharjah (currently both are emirates in UAE), accomplished traders (other sources refer to them as pirates), who threatened Britain's shipping interests.[10]

Britain's goal of protecting its interests had domestic political repercussion in the lower Gulf States. It tipped the balance of power in favour of rulers, who were allied to Britain, in three ways: one, in return for serving Britain's interests, local emirs were militarily protected by Britain; two, because they became dependent on British subsidies and rents, the rulers did not have to bargain with the commercial class for fiscal support that may have compelled them to give up some political power; and three, Britain's economic penetration in these states weakened directly the commercial class and hence reduced their bargaining power. The outcome was a pliant ruler serving Britain's interest, a domestically strong state due to the military and fiscal support by Britain, and a weak commercial class with little bargaining power.

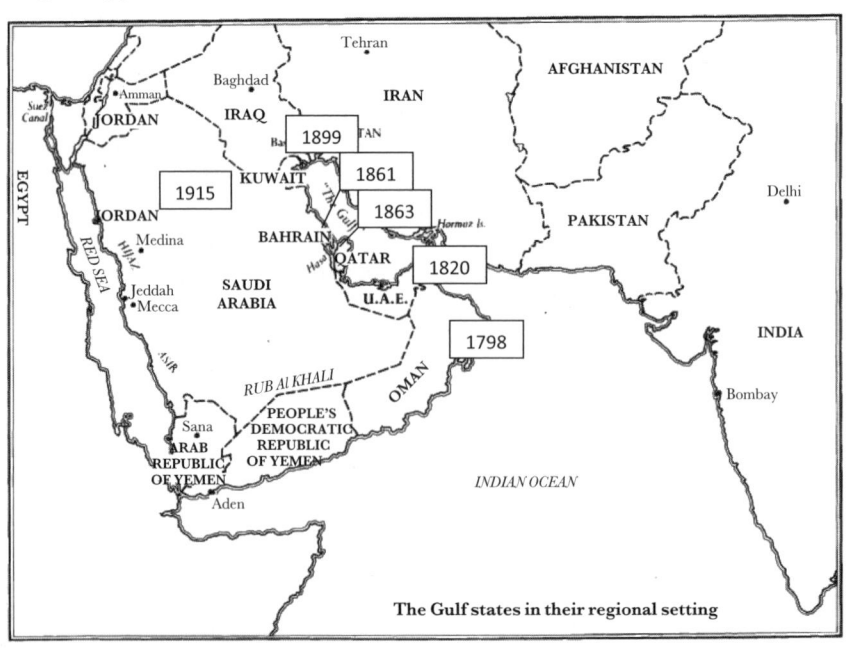

Figure 6.3 The Gulf states.

Source: Adapted from Said Zahlan (1998).

Note: The year in each box indicates the date in which each Gulf country first signed a treaty with Britain.

Oman, the closest of all the Gulf States to British India, exemplifies Britain's involvement in its domestic affairs, which often led to sending troops to Muscat either to prevent internal threat or to claim back the throne. For instance, in 1868, Britain sent Indian troops to claim back the city after the Imamate, tribal leaders from the inland mountains, occupied it. In 1913, Britain, to pre-empt attack on the emir, sent British Indian troops to protect the city. Not all of the interventions were defensive. In 1922, it bombed the port in Sur, south of Muscat, to quell opposition to the ruler (Owtram, 2004). In other instances, Britain had the power to remove rulers if it served British interests. For example, in 1923, Britain deposed Bahrain's Sheikh Isa bin Ali and replaced him with his son (Zahlan, 1998). To ensure compliance, Britain stationed its political agent in Bahrain to run its internal affairs for almost 30 years from 1926. Following the assassination attempt on the ruler of Dubai by his two cousins in 1934, Britain armed the surviving Sheikh Said al Maktoum, and flew its aircraft over the town to express its support for the family. Four years later, when the merchants established a consultative council to introduce reforms, the Sheikh, with British support, disbanded the movement with force[11] (Davidson, 2005).

Britain's policies also made the emirs fiscally dependent on Britain. When Zanzibar defaulted in 1857 in paying Muscat 40,000 Marie Theresa dollars (annually, as agreed when the two states split up), Britain took up the payment and thereby increased Muscat's rulers' dependence on Britain (Owtram, 2004). In return for granting landing rights and refuelling facilities for military aircraft heading to India, Britain offered to Sharjah's ruler in the late 1920s a personal income of 500 rupees per month and an additional 5 rupees for every aircraft.[12] The ruler of Dubai also became a beneficiary to these air concessions in 1937 by permitting the landing of flying boats on Dubai Creek (Davidson, 2005).

Furthermore, Britain's policies weakened the commercial class by prohibiting slavery and gun trading – profitable business – in Oman and Trucial Oman. It also prevented the exchange of German and French equipment in return for the pearl concession in Arabia, by policing pearl banks and forbidding the local population to accept foreign assistance. Consequently, the Gulf was turned into a 'British lake', preventing merchants from expanding their economic activities. In response to the peripheralization of the economy, Dubai's merchants attempted to introduce reforms by setting up a consultative council.

In summary, to protect India from European rivals and to ensure maritime peace in the Gulf, Britain neutralized or brought under its wing the rulers of Oman, Qatar, Bahrain and Trucial Oman. The consequence of its foreign policy was the shift in the balance of power in these states in favour of local emirs. British involvement made rulers less willing to bargain or negotiate with opposition groups, since they neither relied on them for fiscal support nor were their threats credible or life threatening. In other words, the internal politics of these states and the balance of power that emerged thereafter was a consequence of the geostrategic location of these states.

2.2 Bargaining power of the mutawwa in Saudi Arabia and the merchants in Kuwait

Unlike the lower Gulf States, the balance of power in Kuwait and Saudi Arabia in the domestic arena was a product of the strength and composition of economic and religious groups. In the latter country, it was the military-religious alliance of Al Saud with Al Wahhab that formed the backbone of the state. In the former, it was the tacit agreement between the ruler and merchants that shaped political development. Before we explain how the internal dynamics shaped the polity, we briefly present Britain's role.

Kuwait and Saudi Arabia were not immediate threats to British India due to geography. For one thing, Saudi had no significant port on its eastern front to cause any concern to the British. As for Kuwait, it was further north. In fact, Britain signed treaties with these states as late as 1899 with Kuwait and 1915 with Al Saud, more than hundred years after signing the treaty with Oman in 1798, and much later than with the other lower Gulf territories. Both Al Saud and Al Sabah sought the treaties with Britain for their own interest. By then, the internal dynamics in both Kuwait and Saudi Arabia that shaped the balance of power had superseded British intervention.

Britain's policy towards Saudi Arabia became active during the First World War. In 1915, it formalized its alliance with Al Saud through the Anglo-Saudi treaty, which effectively prevented the Al Saud from entering into any agreement with any foreign power, and made them refrain from violating the territories of Kuwait, Bahrain, Qatar and Oman. In return, Britain acknowledged that the regions of Najd, Hasa, Qatif and Jubayl were Al Saud territories, and any aggression on these regions would lead to British intervention. Effectively, Britain supported the Al Saud–Wahhabi conquest of Arabia,[13] and in later years it played a crucial military role in assisting the Al Saud to quell the rebellion of the *ikhwan*, a tribal military force that played a major role in the expansion of the Saudi state.

As for Kuwait, it was Mubarak who, upon killing his brother to assume leadership in 1896, made contacts with the British to protect him from an Ottoman attack.[14] This resulted in the treaty of 1899 whereby Britain offered protection in return for giving up his right to 'cede, sell, or lease any territory to any other power' (Crystal, 1995: 23). Unlike other Trucial states, the treaty was not the product of a foreign threat to India or to maritime peace. The treaty allowed Britain to station a political agent in Kuwait. However, Britain's influence was constrained; the political agent did not have a formal status, his advice was not always heeded and Britain's formal jurisdiction was narrower than in other Gulf States. In sum, the role of the political agent remained in the background and played a very limited role in domestic politics.[15]

2.2.1 Political–religious alliance defining polity in Saudi Arabia

Two key domestic players helped Al Saud in creating and expanding its conquest of Saudi Arabia. The first were the *mutawwa*, who formed a convenient alliance with Al Saud.[16] Al Saud, lacking tribal depth, gained legitimacy through his alliance with the *mutawwa* as long as he 'championed the cause of the religious specialists' (Al-Rasheed, 2002: 51). Al Saud, according to Al-Rasheed (2002: 16), lacked 'an identifiable tribal origin that would have guaranteed a strong association with a tribal confederation', and significant resources as they collected tribute from settlement. The *mutawwa* found in Al Saud the 'politico-military figure, a symbolic Imam to endorse their cause'. In other words, to impose their interpretation of Islam, they needed a political authority that applied the Shari'a law.[17] The *mutawwa* helped the Al Saud in their conquests by preaching to the population the Quran, before raids took place, and how they must submit and obey the *wali al amr*, the leader of the Muslim community. Their obedience had to manifest itself in paying *zakat*, an Islamic tax, and jihad. Through this, they were able to domesticate the population by having it submit to God. In practice, this was materialized through submitting to Al Saud, or otherwise the 'faith and deeds of Muslims would be threatened' (Al-Rasheed, 2002: 52).

The second key player to Saudi expansion and consolidation of the state were the *ikhwan*. In response to a rebellion by the Araif branch of Al Saud family in 1907–8, Al Saud, whose conquests began in 1902 with the capture of Riyadh and south and east Najd between 1902 and 1906, became alarmed by the fragility of his conquests. In order to overcome the tribal confederations' practice of nomadism and political autonomy, he organized a military force, known as *ikhwan*, which had the 'mobility of the Bedouins and the loyalty, bravery, dedication, and stability of the townsmen' (Al-Rasheed, 2002: 60). With this force, Al Saud were able to overcome the tension between central power and the tribal periphery that often resulted in the collapse of any consolidation attempts of the whole of Arabia. While the *mutawwa* coerced the population mentally to submit to Al Saud, the *ikhwan* did so militarily. This combination exercised 'a system of terror' that was difficult to avoid. This holy alliance did not last long. Upon successfully expanding the state through Madina, Mecca, Taif and other Hijazi towns, several *ikhwan* leaders hoped to be rewarded for their successes by sharing the bounty and being elevated to emirs.[18] In 1925, upon capturing Hijaz, the *ikhwan* began to question Al Saud's leadership. With the threat of rebellion by *ikhwan* leaders, Al Saud first got the *ulama* and the *mutawwa* on his side before launching a military attack to silence their demands. While the *ikhwan* refused to be instruments of Ibn Saud and demanded participation in governing, the Al Saud utterly rejected the sharing of political power. To deal with the threat, they resorted to what they had mastered the most: the use of force.

2.2.2 Merchants' fiscal support in return for political participation in Kuwait

The creation of the polity in Kuwait differed markedly from that in the lower Gulf States and Saudi Arabia. With the first group falling under the protection and spell of Britain, local rulers found little need to bargain with opposition groups. In contrast to Saudi Arabia, from the arrival in the eighteenth century of the Bani Utub in Kuwait where they settled, polity was marked by consensus and agreement between the tribes (Salem, 2007). The rise of Al Sabah as a ruling family was neither accomplished by force nor backed by Britain. According to Crystal (1995), there are two versions of how Al Sabah came to power. The first says it was through the division of labour among the three major tribes: in 1716 Al Sabah was assigned to administer the area, subject to consultation with the Al Khalifa, who were assigned commercial affairs, and the Al Jalahima, maritime trading. Another version is that Al Sabah, known for his diplomatic skills, was elected by the tribes to lead a delegation to Basra to relay their peaceful intentions in settling in Kuwait. The Al Sabah tribe, known for its caravan trade, was able to reach the desert and become tax collectors. Both versions indicate that consensus was the primary factor for the emergence of the family at the apex of the political system, and that their comparative advantage was not wealth, piety or military skills but diplomacy and negotiation skills.

Lacking any rents or subsidies, the ruling family was fiscally dependent on the sizeable merchant class, a coherent and active community in the pearl business. Three factors contributed to their strength. The first was their geographical location. In addition to being outside the immediate realm of British India's interest, the merchants, after the pearl crash during the First World War, became involved in caravan trading between Basra and Aleppo (Crystal, 1995). In the absence of a complementary economic activity, the merchants could have suffered the same fate as their counterparts in Qatar who ended up migrating because of the declining pearl business. Here geography was again in Kuwait's favour. Also, the workers were tied to the merchants through debt, which effectively enhanced the merchants' bargaining power vis-à-vis the ruler. Finally, the merchants were a closely knit group through marriage, allowing them to maintain an identity as a group. This became particularly useful when they needed to mobilize to protect their interests.

This dependence on the merchant class meant that the Al Sabah could not rule unchecked and had to accommodate their interests. In response to an increase in taxes[19] to finance Mubarak's military adventures, the merchants threatened to leave Kuwait. With mobile assets, they boarded their ships with their workforce, demanding that the ruler withdraw the tax increase, which he did.[20] This credible threat was a clear case that the Al Sabah could not rule unchecked. Indeed, in 1921, the merchants, wary of the ruler's attempt to encroach on their interests, called for the creation of an assembly to preserve their wealth. This was a first instance of the merchants demanding the institutionalization of their power through an assembly. Upon becoming ruler, Ahmad Jabir promised the merchants to consult with the council 'on all important matters'. However, he never called the council into session and the attempt to institutionalize their power collapsed.

Facing economic problems spearheaded by the Saud blockade, competition from Japanese cultured pearls, world depression and the emir's higher taxes, the merchants began to organize politically.[21] Their efforts finally culminated in the creation of a national assembly in 1938. The merchants petitioned the ruler for an elected assembly, and drew up an electorate of 150 notables who elected an assembly of fourteen members.[22] Although the emir initially refused to sanction the assembly, he finally conceded. An important source of pressure on the emir to concede to the demands of the merchants was the division within the ruling family. Abdalla Salim, who had been bypassed in the succession but who eventually succeeded Ahmad in 1950, was sympathetic to the merchants' demand, possibly to curb the power of the emir.

The merchants' demand for political participation was not an end to itself. The assembly was meant to be an instrument through which the merchants could preserve their economic interests by passing favourable legislation or vetoing unfavourable laws. Despite its short life of six months, they managed to cancel the pearl tax, export duties, the import tax on fruits and vegetables and monopolies. They also prepared a basic law where, among other things, the people and their elected representatives, as a source of authority, extended its responsibility over the budget, justice and public security. They also extended their power to include collecting and distributing state revenues. It was only when they attempted to have control over the 'next oil check' that Ahmad Al Sabah dissolved the assembly. Still, the emir felt compelled to call for new elections, but with a larger electorate (400) and an elected assembly of 20 members, hoping that the outcome would be in his favour. It was not. When he tried to make the body sign up to a constitution that enhanced executive power at the expense of the legislative assembly, it was rejected, and in March 1939 the assembly was dissolved and its members arrested.[23]

Despite the brevity of this experience, it elucidates an important point in the relationship between ruler and merchants. The former was unable to rule totally without constraints. The 1938 *majlis* (assembly), which was itself the product of years of contestation for political power that began formally in 1920s and transformed itself in the 1930s into elected councils for the municipality, education and other government administration, formally contributed to the democratic capital of the country. After all, it was through the education and, later, the municipality councils that the idea of creating a national assembly coalesced. Even after its dissolution, many of these councils remained in place until the mid-1950s. In fact, in 1951 and 1954, the ruler held elections for these committees which administered health, education, religious endowment departments and the municipality, with a total electorate of 5000. The consequence of this experience was immense: it formalized the efforts of the opposition into an assembly that became thereafter a minimum demand for political rights. But as is shown in the next section, it provided the emir, given his constraints, with a political instrument to fend off internal and external threats to ensure his survival.

It is worth mentioning how Britain responded to these events. According to Tetreault (1991), Britain initially supported the democratic movement of the merchants both in 1918–21 and in 1938, not to enhance democratic participation but to curb the role of the emir. Actually, whenever the responsibilities of the *majlis* were widened to include either oil or security, two areas of concern for the British sphere of influence, it withheld its support for the merchants. Britain was worried that the assembly, although pro-British, would eventually turn against its interests.

According to Crystal (1995), when the emir informed the political resident that he planned to dissolve the parliament, deGaury's response was that he should 'risk no failure'. After that, the political resident informed the British office in India that 'balance of power as between Sheikh and Council has been readjusted in favor of the former which suits us' (Crystal, 1995: 51).

In brief, the nature and composition of the alliance between the ruler and other domestic groups, in the relative absence of Britain, shaped polity in the formative years. In Saudi Arabia, the military-religious alliance spearheaded the formation and expansion of the Saudi state without the need to compromise politically other groups. In Kuwait, the fiscal dependence of the ruler on the merchants, and the latter's ability to organize and demand political participation, led to the creation of the assembly. Note that the assembly of 1938 was the institutionalization of years of efforts and lobbying by the merchants to have a say in the decision-making process. Even after its dissolution, several elected councils remained active until the 1950s. With the different groups becoming politicized, their demands converged on bringing back the assembly. The success of the merchants in 1938 provided the impetus for various groups at a later stage in the political history of Kuwait to demand no less than an assembly.

3. From transit states to geopolitical states: how oil affected the Gulf regimes

The discovery of oil in the Gulf in the early 1930s was a major turning point in the political history of the Gulf States. Holding two-thirds of the world's oil reserves, its geostrategic importance intensified foreign intervention and led to wars in the Arab region for the purpose of controlling oil resources as well as its transit routes to Europe and Asia. From the Suez crisis in 1956 to the US occupation of Iraq in 2003, oil was a key factor.

But while oil strengthened the rulers by reducing their dependence on local taxes, it did not change the nature of the relationship between rulers and citizens in several Gulf States, in that oil replaced other types of rents – British subsidies and rents from other economic activities. The effect of oil wealth in trading off the political loyalty of citizens for their economic welfare had its limitations. In fact, it created grievances within certain segments of the population, which often came to the surface during regional crises such as the Suez crisis and the 1967 Arab–Israeli war. The rulers often responded with repression, exiling and deportation. It is only in Kuwait that the emir, in addition to employing these strategies, resorted to the assembly as an expedient political tool to deal with the opposition.

3.1 Oil strengthened the power of rulers, but only relatively

Three theories trace how oil fosters authoritarian regimes. The first is through taxation. Where normally taxation leads to representation (Tilly, 1975), according to Luciani (1987), oil rents break this link as governments no longer rely on taxes to finance spending, which effectively dampens attempts for political participation. The second mechanism is through spending. Oil revenue provides the state with an effective tool to buy the loyalty of the population through the provision of services (Lam and Wantchekon, 1999; Ross, 2001). The third is through obstructing the formation of independent social groups that would demand political participation (Putnam, 1993)

Gulf oil has empowered rulers through their fiscal independence from the population, as epitomized in the case of Kuwait. In pre-oil Kuwait, due to the emir's fiscal dependence on the merchants, they were successful in forcing him to grant them political rights through the creation of the assembly in 1938. But as soon as oil became a significant source of revenue, the emir felt strong enough to break the tacit understanding between the ruling family and the merchants, by dissolving the assembly. Awash with cash, the emir not only became autonomous but also paid off the ruling family's debt to the merchants.

In the other Gulf States, the dependence of the ruler on the merchants or other economic groups was non-existent in the first place. Most of them either relied on other types of rents such as British subsidies (Saudi Arabia, Trucial Oman), landing rights, refuelling facilities, guano concessions, red oxide mining authorization (Trucial Oman), religious indirect taxes such as pilgrimage tax or *zakat* (Saudi Arabia), or the ruler's own investment (Qatar). None of these taxes compelled the ruler to bargain with any domestic groups. In Saudi Arabia, the merchants were forced to pay taxes to finance the military conquests of Al Saud. Because of the military's ability to coerce them, the merchants could not extract any political representation in return for fiscal resources. In Qatar, after the crash of the pearl industry, many of the merchants left the territory searching for profitable opportunities elsewhere, and the remaining ones were too small a group to demand any political rights (Crystal, 1995). In Oman, the economic policies of the British led to economic stagnation and, eventually, to the depopulation of the coast (Owtram, 2004).

Secondly, by way of buying political loyalty, the rulers developed welfare programmes including housing and health services for their population at large. In Kuwait the services, which also included rent, water and electricity subsidies, as well as monthly allowances, targeted middle- and low-income families, the elderly, the disabled and single women (Tetreault and Al-Mughni, 1995). They paid off the merchants through preferential treatment, monopolies, granting them dealerships, state contracts and land (through the acquisition programme) (Tetreault, 1991; Crystal 1995).[24] In addition to buying off the loyalty of the population and merchants, the most important group that benefited from oil rents was the ruling family. To pacify family members, most rulers of the Gulf resorted to three types of benefits: allowances, state jobs and land. The ruler had to please them to avoid any rebellion while at the same time containing their demands lest they bankrupt the state's finances. In Saudi Arabia and Kuwait, the ruler not only resorted to money, but also institutionalized the family members into government positions, partly to give them a stake in the system and partly to monitor them. In Qatar, the ruler, Abdalla, whose succession in 1913 was challenged by twelve brothers, found it hard to please them or to discipline them.[25]

Oil revenues have also been used to buy old tribal nobility, particularly in Saudi Arabia. However, one ought to be cautious not to overstate the importance of oil in transforming the states from extractive to distributive functions. In fact, oil rents replaced Ottoman and later British subsidies in Saudi Arabia used for distribution to different tribes in return for their loyalty. According to Al-Rasheed (2002), oil consolidated a mechanism of distribution that was in place before its discovery. The real change was in the magnitude and diversity of benefits.

However, oil was not trouble free. Oil rents were neither able to buy off a group permanently or to avoid creating tensions and conflicts due to it. In other words, oil, as an instrument of power, quickly proved to have limits. The maldistribution of rents created grievances within certain groups, who were able to politically mobilize and challenge the state, either peacefully by demanding rights or by demonstrating and rioting (Okruhlik, 1999).

This brings us to the third mechanism, where oil rents give governments the power to prevent from organizing groups that may eventually demand political rights. In practice, there is no strong evidence to show that oil-producing states have been totally successful in doing so. On a number of occasions, opposition groups, when banned from public organization and meetings, resorted to alternative venues. In Bahrain and Kuwait, Shiite groups met in *ma'atim*, funeral homes, or *husaniyat*, meeting places. Secular opposition in Kuwait found refuge in *diwaniyat*, forums for discussing political and social issues (Ghabra, 1991).[26] In the 1950s in Kuwait, opposition groups met in various clubs such as the Graduate Club, the Teachers Club and National Culture Club. In response to major riots between Sunnis and Shiites during Ashoura, members of both communities set up a Higher Executive Council demanding political participation in Bahrain. The inability of opposition groups to organize in Saudi Arabia has been attributed to pre-existing social hierarchies (regional, tribal) rather than to oil rents (Al-Rasheed, 2002).

Dissatisfaction and grievances of dissent groups were often triggered by regional events such as wars and revolutions. Two groups have challenged the state from 1930s to the present. The first were the secularists, nationalists and Nasserists who joined the other group – oil workers – in their strikes and riots and were all radicalized by regional events such as the partition of Palestine, the 1956 Suez crisis and 1967 Arab–Israeli war. These groups were often deprived economically and politically. Oil workers often went on strike to improve their conditions and to end the racist discriminatory policies of US and British companies. This was particularly the case of oil workers in Saudi Arabia's ARAMCO and in Qatar (Vitalis, 2007; Crystal, 1995). In 1953 and 1956, Bahraini oil workers, with students and intellectuals, demanded political participation and the end of British influence over the island. In 1967, students at ARAMCO, galvanized by the Arab–Israeli war, attacked the company's installation.

From the late 1970s, regional events that impacted the Gulf shifted from the Mediterranean to the periphery of the Gulf States. The Iranian revolution radicalized groups that were up to then supporters of the regimes. The Shiite Islamists rebelled in 1979 in Saudi Arabia against the discriminatory policies of the Saudi state. Sunni groups mobilized against their government for not having implemented Islamic codes of conduct strictly enough. They considered the government's modernization drive, the consumerism in society and the corruption in the ruling families to be un-Islamic. The 1979 Mosque siege in Saudi Arabia exposed the tension between Islamic fundamentalist values, the basis of the legitimacy of the Saudi state, and the modernization effect brought to the surface by oil. The period after the Iraqi invasion of Kuwait brought conflict and tensions between the secularist and nationalists, on the one hand, and the Islamists on the other, both demanding reforms from the Saudi Arabia's government.

The government's response to these challenges oscillated within a narrow set of options. At best, but infrequently, they would set up elected committees to address health, education and labour issues, as was the case in Bahrain in the 1950s, or they would promise to set up a national assembly, as did the Saudi government after the 1979 Mosque rebellion, but never delivered. At worst, and often, they used military force to suppress the opposition groups. In 1956, Britain sent its navy to suppress oil strikes in Qatar. During 1957–60, Britain again sent its army and Royal Air Force to suppress the rebellion both in Dhofar and the interior of Oman, in order to pave the way for oil companies to begin oil exploration (Owtram, 2004). In 1979–80, the Saudi government used force to end the Mosque rebellion and the Shiite uprising. In response to the ability of the Arab expatriate workforce to mobilize Gulf citizens, the governments often resorted to their marginalization and eventually to their deportation. Crystal (1992) argues that Arab workers were more of a threat to the state because of their sense of entitlement as members of the Arab nation. Consequently, the Kuwaiti government removed non-Kuwaitis from voluntary organizations in the 1960s in order to limit the influence of Arab nationalists. In other instances, the government passed several laws to that end. This included the nationality law to distinguish between nationals and Arab non-nationals, labour law in 1964 which limited expatriates' contracts to five years and required them to be registered with the state and, most importantly, forbade them from striking. If all else failed, the governments would deport expatriates.

3.2 An assembly to control the opposition?

In addition to the above strategies used by the rulers to deal with the opposition, Kuwait and Bahrain responded to the opposition's demands by creating a national assembly. Although Bahrain's assembly lasted only two years, the Kuwaiti parliament had a longer life span, though often with interruptions.[27]

Both Kuwaiti and Bahraini leaders found it politically expedient to set up a national assembly in order to confront internal demands for political participation, compounded by the external claims of Iraq in 1961 and Iran in 1971, respectively, on the eve of their independence. Both countries have had an active civil society since at least the 1920s, demanding a say in the decision-making process. Giving in to these demands was perceived by the ruling families to be the best strategy to enhance legitimacy at home and provide some power to internal groups like the merchants and nationalists. It also prevented any potential backing or support by foreign countries to different domestic groups. For example, in 1938, while the merchants were fighting for a national assembly, they made contacts with Iraq to support them against the emir. In order to prevent such a situation in 1962, the emir pre-empted such contacts and opted to give these groups some political power. British interventions in both countries – militarily in Kuwait and politically in Bahrain – were not enough to keep them in power.

However, the assembly in Bahrain did not last for more than two years. The emir dissolved it after a major confrontation between the government and the People's Bloc, a group of nationalists, socialists and communists, over security issues. The first issue involved a security bill that the assembly rejected, since it gave the government the right to arrest and imprison anyone without charge up to a period of three years. The second issue dealt with the Jufair agreement, which provided the US navy with military facilities for a yearly amount of $4 million. Given that these two issues were at the core of the emir's ability to stave off internal and external threats, he opted for authoritarian rule rather than give in to the assembly.

In Kuwait, the situation was different. For one thing, the merchants, who were the first to demand political participation, struck an economic bargain with the emir in 1953. They gave up their political demands in return for sharing the economic benefits that oil was bringing into the country (Crystal, 1995).[28] With the merchants pacified, the rise of Nasserism galvanized Kuwaitis and expatriates in the 1950s.[29] Calls for political participation were at first ignored by the emir. But then he opted to confront the internal opposition along with the Iraqi claims for annexation, by resorting to the assembly in 1962, to which he conceded certain powers. In 1980, a year after the Iranian revolution, which radicalized the Shiites in Kuwait,[30] the emir found it politically convenient to bring back the assembly to contain again the opposition by transferring the demands from the streets to the parliament.[31] By legislating national issues in the parliament, the emir was also able to discriminate between the demands of Kuwaiti versus non-Kuwaiti citizens, which served to divide the Kuwaiti and Iranian Shiites.[32] The policy of splitting the opposition, which was often enmeshed with non-national groups through the assembly, has roots in the 1960s when the emir split the pan-Arab Kuwaitis from their Arab nationalists. In 1992, the emir, who was still dealing with a legitimacy crisis brought about by Iraq's invasion in August 1990, brought back the assembly.[33] In every instance in which the emir faced external and internal threats simultaneously, he resorted to reviving the assembly to contain the internal opposition, either to prevent external threats or deal with its consequences. In this case, he fended off threats to his survival.[34]

The strategy of bringing back the parliament did not always pay off for the emir. It often was a short-term one. After the reactivation of the assembly, the opposition would soon flex its muscles in an attempt to shape policies, especially regarding oil-related issues. The response of the ruler was to often dissolve it, as he did in 1938, 1976 and 1986. For instance in 1938, when the assembly asked the emir to transfer the next oil check to the parliament for financial control, the emir dissolved it. We observe a similar situation in 1986 when the parliament was again dissolved after it forced the resignation of the justice and oil ministers.[35]

Between convening and dissolving the assembly, the emirs resorted to other measures to contain their power. In the 1960s and 1970s, they politicized the Bedouins and Shiites, respectively, to offset the opposition of the merchants and nationalists. On other occasions, the ruler tried to rig the election in 1967 to get a pliant assembly that would not question the policies of the executive.[36] In another instance, the government tried to change the electoral law to produce a docile assembly, by increasing the number of districts from 10 to 25. In 1980 and again in early 1990, the government attempted to reduce the power of the assembly through a change in the constitution.

The relationship between the emir and parliament has thus been frequently marred with tensions and tests of the authoritarian limits of the ruling family. Reviving the assembly was a convenient tool used by the Kuwaiti emirs in response to external and internal threats. When the threats subsided, they attempted to manipulate the assembly by politically mobilizing other groups, rigging the elections or attempting to reduce its power, not always successfully. The liberation of Kuwait from Iraq in 1991 changed the calculus: the disgrace of the emir by the Iraqi invasion has led to a more active national assembly, but still within the prescribed authoritarian framework.

4. Conclusion

The persistence of autocracy in the Gulf States has been largely attributed to oil. Holding the world's largest oil reserves, these states have been able to buy off their population through various welfare programmes and suppress the opposition by exiling, deporting or ultimately using military force. Although the resource curse theory captures the cases of Qatar, Saudi Arabia and United Arab Emirates, the Kuwait case does not fall in the same category in that it has had an elected parliament since 1962, though with limited powers.

This chapter argues that the roots of the persistence of autocracy go back to the formative years of the Gulf States. The closer the states were to British India, the more likely that Britain intervened in their polity to secure its own economic interests. This was particularly the case of Oman, Bahrain, United Arab Emirates and Qatar. Kuwait and Saudi Arabia were initially less prone to British influence because they were further north. Hence, their polity was largely the product of domestic factors. In Saudi Arabia, religious fundamentalist groups allied with Al Saud imposed an autocratic religious regime, which was reinforced after the discovery of oil. In Kuwait, on the other hand, the rulers who were dependent on the merchants for fiscal support had to give up some political power in return, which culminated in a parliament as early as 1938. Although oil inhibited the development of democracy, threats (Iraq's claims in 1961, the Iranian revolution in 1978) and wars (the Gulf war in 1991) made the ruling family aware that they could not go back on the political gains, the elected assembly, that had been achieved earlier.

In brief, to understand the autocratic nature of polity in the Gulf region, it is necessary to go beyond oil and certain types of conflicts for all their negative influences. The politico-historical background of the Gulf offers major supplementary insights that help explain the persistence of autocracy in the Gulf countries despite their significant socio-economic development since the Second World War.

Notes

1 The Kuwait Assembly exercised its power as early as mid-1960s, forcing the resignation of the justice and oil ministers. When it was unconstitutionally dissolved, the opposition was able to maintain its political activity and successfully managed to defeat the emirs' attempts to change the constitution and dilute the power of the assembly.
2 The sources of the measures are found in Ch. 2 of this volume.
3 White's standard errors is used to deal with panel heteroskedasticity where the errors for different units may have different variance or may be contemporaneously correlated. In other words, the errors for one country may be affected by the errors for other countries in the same year. To deal with such errors, one ought to use panel corrected standard errors if T is large (above 15), which is not the case here where the T is only 9 (Beck and Katz, 1995). Even after correcting for heteroskedasticity, the observations in the model are not temporally independent, which leads to optimistic inferences. In other words, the errors in the model are serially correlated, which makes the standard errors invalid. To deal with the temporal dependency, a lagged dependent variable is added in the specification. This makes intuitive sense since the propensity that there is a democracy in time, t, is influenced by whether there was a democracy in time, $t-1$.
4 In addition to the above, Models E, F, and G are run with two interactive variables: income and oil and Gulf dummy and oil. The first is to capture the rise in income due to oil and the second to examine the Gulf countries' specific effect of oil (given by the oil–Gulf interaction term). No major changes are observed in the coefficients of the Gulf dummy and hence the results are not reported.
5 Because the Palestinian–Israeli conflict covers the duration of the sample, there is a high probability that the battle deaths from the conflict trend upwards with time. To deal with this issue, I control for time trends in Models B and E.
6 An F test for all three conflicts interacted with Gulf of .14 shows that we cannot reject the null hypothesis, which means that three interactive terms are jointly insignificant in the polity.
7 Note that like the Gulf model (Model A in Table 6.2), a parsimonious model for Kuwait is run by removing from the regressions all non-significant variables. As a result, the coefficients do not change in scale or significance.
8 In response to France's contact with the ruler of Muscat in 1798 following its invasion of Egypt, Britain imposed the Anglo-Omani treaty (ratified and confirmed in 1800), which states that the relationship between Britain and Oman would 'remain unshook till the end of time, and till the sun and moon have finished their revolving career' (Owtram, 2004: 36). To enforce the treaty, Britain threatened the ruler of Muscat to impose a commercial blockade from India in 1803 if he kept in contact with the French. In 1839, Britain, which by then had lost interest in Oman after capturing Ile de France (Mauritius), felt compelled to renew its alliance with Muscat 'to offset American commercial encroachment in the Indian Ocean area' (Owtram, 2004: 38). This strategy of imposing treaties that would confine local rulers' action was repeated again in 1891 when Sultan Faisal bin Turki promised 'never to transfer Omani territory except for the British government' (Owtram, 2004: 39) In 1899 Sultan Faisal withdrew his commitment to build a French coaling station at Bandar Jissah in response to British threats to bomb his palace (Owtram, 2004).
9 In response to shipping attacks and taxes on British Indian traders, in 1861 Britain forced the ruler of Bahrain to sign a maritime truce in exchange for protection from

Persian and Ottoman claims to the island. It is through this treaty that Britain also succeeded in containing any threats from both the Ottomans and the Persians on India. In the same decade, Britain resorted to the same strategy by signing a treaty with the Al-Thani in Qatar to ensure maritime peace. The agreement came about as a result of the attack by Bahrain and Abu Dhabi on Qatar and the counterattack by the latter on Bahrain, resulting in 1000 deaths and the destruction of 600 ships (Crystal, 1995). This warfare had to be brought to an end as it threatened the maritime truce made by Britain in 1835.

10 According to Davidson (2005), the Qawasim were accused of sinking three British Indian merchant ships in 1816 and for attacks 70 miles from Bombay in 1819. Britain responded in 1819–20 by launching an attack on Ras Khayma and the Trucial Oman coast with 3000 soldiers, battleships and eight cruisers, hence neutralizing any threat to British Indian shipping and competition to the British East India Company. Britain followed its military victory with a treaty to the ruler of Sharjah to surrender all vessels and fortified towers in return for protection and economic incentives such as granting access to British ports. Opposition to the treaty by the rulers of Ajman and Fujairah led to naval shelling which forced them to toe the line. The outcome of British military intervention was a series of maritime peace treaties of 1835 and 1853. Lord Palmerston succinctly stated that Britain's goal is trade rather than to control land.

11 The imposition of limits on his personal income (of 10,000 rupees) triggered Sheikh Said's use of force to dissolve the council and attack its members.

12 In 1932, the agreement was extended to civilian aircraft.

13 They also armed Al Saud with 1000 rifles, a sum of £20,000, a monthly subsidy of £5,000 and further shipments of machine guns (Al-Rasheed, 2002).

14 The first official contact took place in 1775, when the East India Company had their mail sent through Kuwait as plague and then Persians struck Basra. According to Crystal, 'The East Indian Company also sent a ship to Kuwait to evaluate it as an alternative port for Basra and the captain noted its excellent harbor. Although no action was taken, these inquiries forged the first political link between Britain and Kuwait . . . Relations were good, but for some time limited. When Stocqueler visited Kuwait in 1831, he was told no Europeans had been there for years. Britain had as yet no enduring interests in Kuwait' (Crystal, 1995: 22).

15 According to Crystal, 'Because of Kuwait's late entry into the trucial system, its distance from the trucial "piracy," and the minor leverage it enjoyed through playing off Ottoman Iraq and Arabia, it maintained greater independence' (Crystal, 1995: 42).

16 Once the *mutawwa* studied with *ulama* in Najd and Qasim, they became specialists in jurisprudence and Islamic rituals. As a result, they became enforcers of obedience to Islam.

17 This alliance, however, has roots that date back to 1744 when the first alliance was struck between Muhammad ibn Saud and Muhammad ibn Abd al-Wahhab, a religious scholar. Muhammad Abd al-Wahhab's goal was to purify Islam and to impose a strict implementation of the Shari'a which included adherence to monotheism, refusing mediation between God and believers, the payment of *zakat*, launching holy wars on those who fail to adhere to these principles. This alliance produced the first Al Saud–Wahhabi emirate in Najd between 1744 to 1818, followed by a second attempt between 1824 and 1891.

18 According to Al-Rasheed (2002), Al-Duwaysh and ibn Bijad, both *ikhwan* leaders, were expecting to become emirs of Madina and Taif, respectively.

19 In 1909 Mubarak imposed new taxes on imports, pearls, houses and pilgrimage as well as price controls.

20 In fact, some rich pearl buyers migrated to Bahrain, followed by traders on 17 ships. To strengthen their threat of secession, the richest merchant, Hilal al-Mutairi, promised to forgive the debts of all those who followed him (Crystal, 1995).

21 Prior to the assembly, the merchants had set up an elected education council and a municipality through which they were able to organize, debate and mobilize politically.

22 When the merchants met secretly to draw up a list of reforms to address their economic grievances, the government overreacted by arresting and beating a dissident who confessed the names of the leading merchants organizing the movement. This served as a catalyst for the merchants to demand an elected assembly.
23 Following the dismissal of the assembly, the emir found a letter in the possession of the one of the assembly members, and signed by other members, requesting King Ghazi of Iraq to integrate Kuwait with Iraq.
24 In 1961, the government of Kuwait introduced a commercial law ensuring that any foreign investment project must be 51 per cent owned by Kuwaiti nationals, hence ensuring that merchants enjoy the benefits of oil. This policy was followed by all the other Gulf States.
25 Note that the succession in Qatar since the turn of the twentieth century was always contested. Both Abdalla (1913–48) and Ali (1949–60) abdicated and Ahmad (1960–72) and Khalifa (1972–95) were overthrown.
26 The term *diwaniyat* refers to a room in a house where family members meet with relatives and friends. Tetreault (1993) argues that the *diwaniyat* served as a 'plausible substitute for civil society in the public space . . . can be held without the government permits'.
27 The Kuwaiti national assembly was established in 1962, dissolved in 1976, reconvened in 1980, dissolved again in 1986, but brought back again in 1992.
28 To this end, the emir commissioned the private sector to undertake development projects that became feasible as a result of oil windfalls.
29 Responding to Nasser's call to demonstrate in 1956, 4,000 convened in Kuwait at the National Culture Club.
30 The Shiites, who were politicized by the emirs in previous years to offset the power of the merchants in the 1960s, then became a mass political movement. Before the revolution, the Shiite population was essentially under the control of established Shiite leaders and merchant families.
31 The assembly had been dissolved in 1976.
32 It is estimated that Kuwaiti Shiites make up 20 per cent of the population, and that there were 30,000 Iranian Shiites residing in Kuwait in the mid-1980s (Crystal, 1995).
33 Meeting in Taif in Saudi Arabia, where the ruling family resided during the period of occupation, the emir promised the opposition to reconvene the assembly in return for standing up to Kuwait. Since 1992, the government has not unconstitutionally dissolved parliament.
34 In fact, the robustness of the effect of regional wars and Arab international wars on Kuwait's polity in section 1 (Model G in Table 6.3 and Models B and E in Table 6.4) may be capturing some of these threats where the emir revives the assembly in light of external wars and threats. The analytical narratives confirm the empirical results.
35 The oil minister, Ali Khalifa, resigned after being subjected to interrogation by the assembly over financial and security concerns of the oilfields.
36 In response to the assembly's unwillingness to ratify oil agreements in 1966, the emir sought to produce a rubber-stamp parliament in 1967 that would approve the agreement.

References

Abernethy, D. (2000) *The Dynamics of Global Dominance: European Overseas Empires, 1415–1980*, New Haven, CT: Yale University Press.
Al-Rasheed, M. (2002) *A History of Saudi Arabia*, Cambridge: Cambridge University Press.
Beck, N. and Katz, J. N. (1995) 'What to Do (and Not to Do) with Time-Series Cross-Section Data', *American Political Science Review* 89/3: 634–47.
Crystal, J. (1992) *Kuwait: The Transformation of an Oil State*, Boulder, CO: Westview Press.
—— (1995) *Oil and Politics in the Gulf: Rulers and Merchants in Kuwait and Qatar*, Cambridge: Cambridge University Press.

Davidson, C. (2005) *The United Arab Emirates: A Study in Survival*, Boulder, CO: Lynne Rienner.

Elbadawi, I. and Makdisi, S. (2007) 'Explaining the Democracy Deficit in the Arab World', *Quarterly Review of Economics and Finance* 46/5 (Feb.).

Gasiorowski, M. J. (1995) 'Economic Crisis and Political Regime Change: An Event History Analysis', *American Political Science Review* 89: 882–97.

Ghabra, S. (1991) 'Voluntary Associations in Kuwait: The Foundation of a New System', *Middle East Journal* 45/2 (Spring).

Glaeser, E., Porta, R., Lopez-De-Silanes, F. and Shleifer, A. (2004) 'Do Institutions Cause Growth?', *Journal of Economic Growth* 9: 271–303.

Horowitz, D. (1993) 'Democracy in Divided Societies', *Journal of Democracy* 4 (Oct.).

Kedourie, E. (1994) *Democracy and Arab Political Culture*, London: Frank Cass.

Lam, R. and Wantchekon, L. (1999) 'Political Dutch Disease', Working paper. Online at: www.nyu.edu/gsas/dept/politics/faculty/wantchekon/research/Ir-04-10.pdf

Laporta, R, Lopez-de-Dilances, F., Shleifer, A., and Vishny, R. (1998) 'Law and Finance', *Journal of Political Economy* 106: 1113–55.

Lipset, S. (1959) 'Some Social Requisites of Democracy: Economic Development and Political Legitimacy', *American Political Science Review* 53 (March).

Luciani, G. (1987) 'Allocation versus Production States: A Theoretical Framework', in Hazem Beblawi and Giacomo Luciani, *The Rentier State*, London: Croom Helm.

Okruhlik, G. (1999) 'Rentier Wealth, Unruly Law, and the Rise of the Opposition: The Political Economy of Oil States', *Comparative Politics*, April.

Owtram, F. (2004) *A Modern History of Oman: Formation of the State since 1920*, London: I. B. Tauris.

Plateau, J.-P. (2008) *Religion, Politics and Development: Lessons from the Land of Islam*, Economic Research Forum, Working Paper, 438, Cairo, Egypt.

Putnam, R. (1993) *Making Democracy Work: Civic Traditions in Modern Italy*, Princeton, NJ: Princeton University Press.

Ross, M. (2001) 'Does Oil Hinder Democracy?', *World Politics* (April).

Salem, P. (2007) *Kuwait: Politics in a Participatory Emirate*, Carnegie Papers, 3, Washington, DC: Carnegie Endowment for International Peace.

Stepan, A. with Robertson, G. (2003) 'An "Arab" More than "Muslim" Electoral Gap', *Journal of Democracy* 14.

Tessler, M. (2002) 'Islam and Democracy in the Middle East: The Impact of Religious Orientations on Attitude towards Democracy in Four Arab Countries', *Comparative Politics* 34.

Tetreault, M. (1991) 'Autonomy, Necessity, and the Small State: Ruling Kuwait in the Twentieth Century', *International Organization* 45/4 (Autumn).

—— (1993) 'Civil Society in Kuwait: Protected Spaces and Women's Rights', *Middle East Journal* 47/2 (Spring).

—— and Al-Mughni (1995) 'Gender, Citizenship and Nationalism in Kuwait', *British Journal of Middle Eastern Studies* 22/1–2: 64–80.

Therborn, G. (1977) 'The Rule of Capital and the Rise of Democracy', *New Left Review* 30 (May/June).

Tilly, C. (1975) *The Formation of National States in Western Europe*, Princeton, NJ: Princeton University Press.

Vitalis, R. (2007) *America's Kingdom*, Palo Alto, CA: Stanford University Press.

Zahlan, R. S. (1998) *The Making of the Modern Gulf States: Kuwait, Bahrain, Qatar, the United Arab Emirates, and Oman*, Reading: Ithaca Press.

7. Algeria: democracy and development under the aegis of the 'authoritarian bargain'

Belkacem Laabas and Ammar Bouhouche

1. Introduction

The main objective of this chapter is to study the relationship between democracy in Algeria and the economic and social development achieved since independence in 1962, using the modernization theory of democratization and models of elite behaviour, focusing particularly on the role of rents and conflicts on the democratization process. Despite the relative political liberalization introduced after the watershed October 1988 riots and the relative political competitiveness introduced in 1989, Algeria is still regarded as non-democratic, according to major indices of democratic performance around the world.[1] It is worth noting that the Polity IV index ranks democracy in Algeria more favourably than the Gastil and EIU indices. In fact the Polity IV index in 2004 raised Algeria to +2, the highest among Arab countries, up from –9 in 1989 when multi-party politics were introduced.[2] The crucial question to be addressed is why the Algerian political regime proved to be so persistent and slow in democratization, despite the country's substantial economic and social development.[3]

Using an extended modernity model, Elbadawi, Makdisi and Milante (2008), hereafter EMM, argue that Arab countries are characterized by a persistent 'democracy deficit' that is primarily the result of oil rents and regional wars and conflicts. The oil rents and conflicts shielded Arab countries from global democratization waves. Even though the model presents an eloquent explanation of the Arab freedom deficit, it needs to be fine-tuned to make it account for Algeria's specific performance, as is clear from the model simulation presented in Elbadawi and Makdisi (2007). Indeed oil and conflict are at the heart of the 'authoritarian bargain' between the elite and the population. Oil rents are extensively used to maintain the incumbent regime, however not sufficiently to fully trade off all political rights against economic welfare. Because the Algerian political regime is deeply nationalist, it never resorted to the external conflict doctrine in order to stay in office. The war of liberation (1954–62) and the ensuing 'revolutionary legitimacy' was the main argument of the regime for monopolizing power. The decline of oil prices in 1986, the worsening of the external debt problem and the collapse of economic growth, coupled with the waning appeal of revolutionary legitimacy among the younger generation, pushed the regime to opt for liberal political

Algeria: the 'authoritarian bargain' 197

reforms as an exit from the economic and political deadlock. Despite the fact that Algeria avoided open and lasting regional wars relating to border tensions and to the Western Sahara problem, internal conflict is very prominent and reflects the dynamics of the authoritarian bargain.

There are no easy or obvious answers to the puzzle of the persistence of the authoritarian regime, but some elements can be found in understanding the nature of the regime, its factional structure, its economic (rents distribution) and political means (repression and cooptation), and survival strategies used by the elite to control the masses. On the other hand, modernity theory regards democracy as the outcome of economic and social development. The accumulated empirical cross-country evidence is informative concerning the factors that help to set up a framework for analysing democratic performance at the country level. Using Polity IV data of democratic scores between 1962 and 2004, we try to establish a relationship between democracy and economic and social development, taking into consideration major political events and the role of oil rents and conflicts.

When looking at the historical data on Algerian polity, reflecting different facets of economic development, it is difficult to assert that economic development alone had a strong and consistent effect on democratic development. Rather, the political system proved resilient and sluggish after independence. The sharp jumps in polity score (see Figure 7.1) were the result of emerging political pressures, as well as economic and social upheavals, and not directly a consequence of sustained economic development. Put differently, the narrow version of the modernization model does not seem to fully explain the discontinuous change in Algeria's polity. This is probably due to many interrelated factors. Algeria is a primary goods exporter and the economic development it has achieved since 1962 was the result

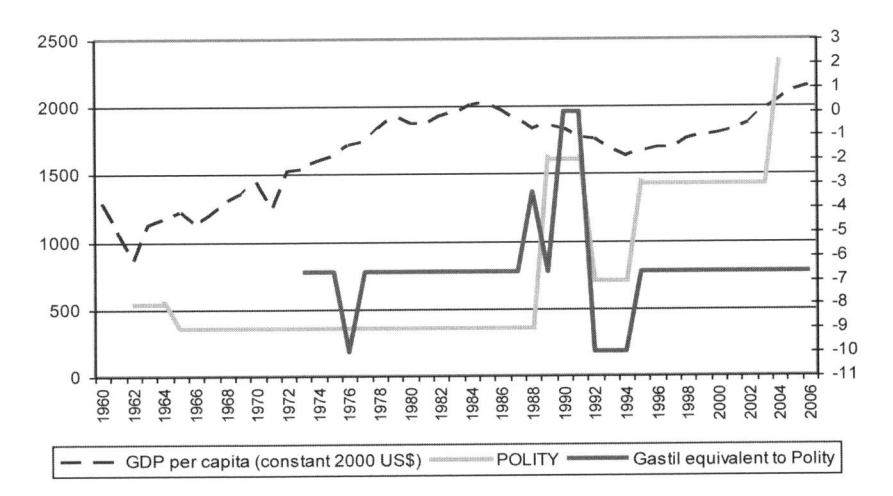

Figure 7.1 Democracy and development in Algeria, 1962–2006.

Source: World Bank, Freedom House, Polity IV data set.

of using oil windfall (rents) and contracting external debt, almost entirely by the public sector. Large-scale government intervention in the economy produced a state of economic monopoly that buttressed the political monopoly of the incumbent regime, which since the liberation war relied on the support of the army and had a non-liberal, paternalist vision of polity. As reforms became needed to jump-start the stalled economic engine, political reforms were also introduced in an effort to soften the impact of political and economic deadlock (e.g. in 1988 and 1999). Hence the downturn in GDP between 1986 and 1995 due to lower oil prices and deteriorating political environment and the rise of internal conflict coincided with improved polity scores.

We argue that whereas modernity, economic or social, tends to promote democracy, in the case of Algeria this trend is countered by the strong persistence of the incumbent political system, which has created a freedom deficit. The level of this deficit, in turn, depends on the size of the oil rents and the intensity of internal conflict in society. Citizens are forced to trade off part of their freedom in exchange for economic benefits. Given the fact that the size of the rents to be distributed is not considerable, a sustained decline of the oil price leads to an increase in the level of internal conflict that threatens to break down the 'authoritarian bargain' struck by the three main political actors in the country: the president, the army and the bureaucracy. To avoid this possibility, a reconfiguration of the political system is engineered, as happened in 1989.

2. Democracy, authoritarianism and development

Development is a complex process of structural transformation (Chenery and Syrquin, 1975) and maturity of a society that ultimately leads to the emancipation and freedom of the human being. In this respect Sen's (1999)[4] larger definition of development puts economic,[5] social[6] and political[7] development under the umbrella of human development. However this definition does not help to study the interactions between economic, social and political development, because they are regarded as one process that makes up human freedom. To simplify matters and study the relationships between development and democracy, one can adopt the UNDP definition of human development embedded in their Human Development Index (HDI). The HDI excludes political freedoms and concentrates only on economic and social development, measured by GDP per capita, health and education. Democracy is usually taken as synonymous with liberal political systems based on the promotion and guarantee of personal freedoms and political rule through competition, and sustained political freedoms. The Schumpeterian (Schumpeter, 1947) model of procedural political organization[8] is the workable form of democracy compatible with liberalism. In this context we can consider both Polity IV and Gastil indices as measuring such democracy, although the former emphasizes electoral competition and constraints on executive discretion, whereas the latter focuses on political rights and civil liberties.[9]

In a seminal paper Lipset (1959) argued that democracy is positively related to economic development. He argued that countries witnessing development would gradually democratize. As they transform from poor to rich, education level rises, demography and family patterns change, society becomes more secularized, and the population values more independence and freedoms. Since then, political scientists and economists alike, such as Burkhart and Lewis-Beck (1994), Huntington (1991), Dahl (1989), Jackman (1973), Leblang (1997), Bollen (1983), Barro (1996, 1999), Snyder and Kick (1979), have argued that a relation between economic development and democracy does exist. To them, the populace's demand for democracy grows with higher levels of economic development.

However, it is not well known why development would lead to more democracy. Przeworski and Limongi (1993), and Glaeser and Ponzetto (2007), among others, argue that education is the channel that links development to democracy, through its impact on political attitudes responding to the demand for more freedoms. Education and an enlarged middle class are key elements in civic activity that lead to democracy (Putnam, 1993). Other authors such as Fukuyama (1992) argue that social capital is detrimental to democracy because social ties and interactions consolidate freedom values that become difficult to suppress in the event of high social capital. However, Jackman and Miller (1996) found little evidence of social capital effects on democracy. Rice and Ling (2002) argue that cultural issues such as religion, ethno-linguistic composition, colonial history and dependence are thought to exert some effect on democratic performance. Most of the cross-country regressions include these as control variables. Despite efforts and advances in modelling democracy, as noted by Bardhan (2005), the literature based on cross-country regression is not conclusive as studies reached different conclusions.[10] Robinson (2006) argued that democracy and income are weaker than previously believed when controlling for initial democracy and fixed effects. Huntington (1968) and Bollen (1990) argued that autocratic regimes are better suited for developing countries because of their ability to achieve order and stability needed for development. This is thought to be so because democracy is sustainable only in high-income economies. In fact Testas (2005) argued that the authoritarian regime is better for Algeria and Tunisia in order to keep the same level of labour productivity. Had it adopted greater political rights after independence, Algeria would have lost 20 per cent of labour productivity. On the other hand, Kraska (2005) severely criticized the modernity model as an apology to authoritarianism and argued that poor countries should not wait for preconditions or income thresholds to introduce democracy, instead it should be promoted as a way to accelerate development. Despite the shortcomings[11] of the modernization model, it is nevertheless a very helpful tool that allows us to synthesize the determinants of democracy and how they interact.

The authoritarian model of Acemoglu and Robinson (2006) assumes that the elite control society by manipulating the judicial and security apparatus using a combination of repression (coercion) and redistribution policies. Citizens are disenfranchised and trade off their welfare/security for political participation. If this equilibrium is fundamentally disturbed, citizens can engage in political activity in order to drive the elite out of office and restore a democratic political regime. The elite can respond either by concessions or by further repressions in order to put down the citizen movement. The degree and mix of repression and redistribution depends very much on the political configuration of the elite, and on the political maturity and values of the citizens. Democratization occurs when collective actions are credible, and concessions insufficient, and when the elite consider that the cost of repression is higher than the cost of democracy.

The type of authoritarian regime, as well as intra-elite competition and factional conflicts within the regime, may contribute to democratic transitions, as happened in Latin America, Greece, Spain and Portugal. Transitions come in different ways in different parts of the world (Van de Walle *et al.*, 1999). Intra-elite factionalism is different in different authoritarian regimes, and deals with opposition and citizens in different ways. All these affect democratic transition. Geddes (2000, 2004) found that military regimes are relatively more easily destabilized by intra-elite conflict, and that regime breakdown usually begins by splits within the military establishment. Single-party regimes are resilient to pressures and have mostly been brought down by external pressures. Party cadres value unity and regard survival of the party as their own survival. Single parties usually co-opt rival factions and tend to respond to crisis by granting modest political participation. For these reasons single-party regimes like the Front of National Liberation (FLN) in Algeria tend to last longer and survive economic and political crises. However, dictatorships based on personalized leadership regimes repress factions and collapse, either by the death of the dictator or in times of severe economic problems, and usually end in bloodshed. Hybrid regimes like the Algerian political system that combine aspects of a single party, personalized leadership and military regime are the strongest of all. The FLN has been in command since independence in 1962 and today still holds on well to power.

Many authoritarian regimes felt the heat of global democratization and embarked on a process of political reforms by introducing some limited and controlled political freedoms. However this incomplete form of transition created hybrid regimes based on a combination of democratic rule and autocratic governance. Levitsky and Way (2002) labelled it competitive authoritarianism.[12] Desai *et al.* (2007) proposed a testable quantitative model of authoritarian behaviour. They assume that dictators survive by striking a bargain in which they trade off political rights against economic benefits. According to the authors the data confirm the generality of such bargains and explain the durability of non-democratic regimes.

The democracy and development literature surveyed above provides some guidance for understanding the survival and persistence of Algerian authoritarianism despite the rapid social development since 1962. First, history[13] and colonial cultural heritage played a decisive role in the emergence of an authoritarian and highly factional elite after independence. For more than a century Algerians were subject to a colonial rule based on settlements and exclusion of the indigenous population: by independence in 1962 illiteracy was very high, and human and formal social capital was very limited. The elite, though deeply divided and fragmented, was radicalized into a very strong nationalist current that still has deep roots in Algerian society, although today is highly challenged by Islamist movements (Hill, 2006; Quandt, 1998; Zoubir, 1996). Civil society and the democratic movement in Algeria are led by a secular, westernized elite (Maddy-Weitzman, 2006) sympathetic to the Berber cause and their parties. The democratic movement, however, greatly to mobilize the masses around a democratic political agenda. The primacy of unity required by the national liberation movement as a consequence of the hard line of colonial rule helped to cement a triangular regime based on the alliance of the military, the single party and bureaucracy. Collegial decision-making and factional arbitration within the regime was always necessary for maintaining regime equilibrium. The configuration of this political build-up was changed only artificially by the adoption of multi-party elections in 1989.

Algeria is a rentier state. Most of the nation's wealth is extracted from oil and gas. Controlling the state institutions means controlling this wealth (Bendib, 2006). The Algerian economy is highly controlled by the state and the private sector remains marginal and active only in the rent-seeking sphere of the economy (Ali, 2006). Redistribution of the rent is detrimental to the survival of the incumbent regime. Despite prolonged economic development difficulties and slow economic growth, redistribution of the wealth kept poverty, inequality and social indicators at acceptable levels. The regime conceded some democratic changes only after oil revenues per capita declined sharply after the mid-1980s. Oil revenues per capita (in constant 2000 prices) declined from US$1,144 in 1985 to just US$726 in 1997. The predominance of the youth in the society, along with rapid urbanization, created a severe housing and employment problem that is the major source fuelling social tensions in Algeria The combination of rapid population growth, the collapse of oil prices and a mounting debt service burden created social tensions (Thieux, 2003) and put pressure on the authoritarian bargain, causing the regime to concede some political rights (Lowi, 2004). The population, aware of the importance of the bargain for the survival of the regime, has often resorted to popular riots (Roberts, 2002) to force larger rent distribution in terms of jobs and infrastructure projects. The regime, too, is highly aware of the importance of the bargain, and consistently engages in the distribution of local infrastructure project funds during electoral campaigns.

The economic reforms undertaken since the 1990s, especially those related to foreign trade liberalization and financing and privatization of public enterprises, encouraged members of the regime to convert into a new class of businessmen. Given their established networks of influence in terms of access to finance and to government procurements, there was increased interest in perpetuating the political status quo and in blocking genuine reforms, leading to the creation of a façade democracy (Volpi, 2003, 2006). This is bound to increase the level of corruption in government and make democratization even more difficult. The vertiginous increase of the oil price since 2000 to a level beyond US$100 per barrel, and the build-up of foreign reserves to more than US$100 billion by the end of 2007, will certainly give more room for the elite to better manage the authoritarian bargain that consists of trading off political rights with redistribution.

3. Roots and practices of Algerian authoritarianism

The Algerian experience of democratization differs from that of other Arab states. Algerians experienced a brutal colonial French rule based on a settlement that excluded the masses from development for more than a century. They liberated their country after a costly seven-year war, which led to independence in 1962 and the establishment of a revolutionary system of government, led by the FLN, comprising several political groups. Soon after obtaining independence, 'factionalism and deep antagonism among nationalist leaders quickly surfaced' (Entelis, 1986: 58) because the competing factions were unable to create a consensus on national policies, which, in turn, explains why the Algerian leaders have never succeeded in defining the relationship between state, party and the army that brought the first president of Algeria to power in 1962. The insistence of Mr Ben Bella (1962–5) on strengthening the FLN vis-à-vis the army resulted in his imprisonment until 1981. Under Houari Boumediene, who became the chairman of the pseudo-military Revolution Council (1965–78), military power was consolidated and political leaders were marginalized. This position was supported by left-wing groups in and outside the FLN. Like Boumediene, they wanted to block political parties from gaining power and at the same time impose a secular Western model of governance (Ahdjoudj, 1992: 19). However, in effect, Boumediene's regime suspended the constitution, dissolved the parliament and transferred its power to a revolutionary council which ruled the country until 1978[14] without a constitution, parliament or independent political parties (Nellis, 1980: 491).

The death of Boumediene marked the end of an era of charismatic leadership. He was deeply committed to socialist policies and was not willing to revise his economic strategy. However, many politicians within the FLN supported his policies, which enabled them to receive a share of the national wealth. Boumediene's colleagues selected a moderate, Colonel Chadli Bendjedid (1979–92), who had accepted the principle of collegial leadership, to succeed him. The biggest problem he faced was not how to use the party as an instrument to curb and control the bureaucracy, but rather how to deal with his colleagues in the political leadership (Entelis, 1986: 36). The political reforms undertaken at the 1979 congress of the FLN, when it was decided to modify the constitution and establish new rules, opened the way for him to assert his authority, enjoying the support of the military officers.[15]

From the beginning Bendjedid wanted to rectify some of the anomalies he saw in the economy.[16] He decided to shift from the policy of heavy industrialization to one that gave priority to agriculture and basic infrastructure. The new government focused on improving productivity in agriculture and on providing better services in housing, medical care and education. He also aimed at making state enterprises more efficient and productive; it was hoped that industrial restructuring would make state enterprises more efficient and self-reliant. However, this policy negatively affected the operation of the state companies, which were encumbered by overstaffing, lack of skilled technicians, appointment of administrative managers by the state and state monopoly over raw materials, all of which had led to inefficiency and low productivity. Moreover, without state subsidies, most companies would have been forced out of business. A turning point occurred in 1986 when the price of oil dropped drastically and the state suddenly found itself unable to generate funds for the basic needs of the people.

At the same time, there was a fierce power struggle within the regime. Resistance to Bendjedid's reforms came from the state bureaucrats who disliked the growing political strength of the party. On 5 October 1988, people took to the streets in the first major rioting since independence. Social grievances associated with economic mismanagement had intensified with the dramatic drop of oil revenues in 1986 and severe international debt service. State revenues, which came mainly from oil, were no longer sufficient for importing intermediate industrial products and food (Entelis, 1986: 149). Seizing on the October events, Benjedid made sweeping changes. At the sixth congress of the FLN, held in November 1988, he proposed that the FLN should no longer remain the party of the state and that it should not have the right to control social and professional organizations. He also proposed that divergent political views be tolerated within the party in the hope that they could be harmonized. The strategy of trying to create unity among diverse political groups did not work out. However, despite opposition, especially by barons of the party, in 1989 Bendjedid was able to introduce a multi-party system and allow the media to criticize corrupt government practices, which they hastened to do. This, in turn, stimulated a popular desire for radical change in the political system. The objectives of the political reforms were to strengthen the incumbent elite by creating a multi-party system, allowing a free press, writing a new constitution, calling for new parliamentary elections and making the president share his power with the prime minister.

In the midst of all this, FLN infighting among its various wings increased, breaking the party apart. By the time the first multi-party municipal elections were held on 12 June 1990, many Algerians were prepared to vote for newly emerging political parties and to oppose the FLN. The new Islamic Front of Salvation (FIS) obtained 55.5 per cent of the votes and the FLN 31.6 per cent (Kapil, 1991: 45). This perhaps was not a surprising result as, over the years, the Algerian elite had gradually distanced itself from the people. Most of them were educated in French schools and universities and were highly committed to European values and culture. As Francophiles, they looked down upon the rest of the population. This tended to drive many of the young men to embrace the Islamist movements in order to fight a regime that provided them with education but at the same time excluded them from political participation.

The new grass-roots leaders, who despised officials of the one-party system and their material wealth, promised to meet the needs of the people and to speak for the poor (Mortimer, 1991: 577). They thought that elections would help rid the country of the entrenched politicians of the old system. The FIS understood that and focused on this matter as a part of its political strategy. The Islamists took full advantage not only of the new political openings but also the economic crisis that served as an ideal opportunity for them to provide social services for the unemployed youth and the poor. Their social activities helped build sympathy and support. They attracted large audiences, and their political message was effectively delivered. The FIS benefited greatly from animosities and power struggles that were taking place among various FLN factions. The political offensive of the FIS disrupted the economy and created disorder in many parts of the country.

The army again intervened, on 5 June 1991, to re-establish order and security in Algiers. This intervention was followed by the imposition of martial law, the dismissal of the prime minister and the postponement of the legislative elections that were originally scheduled for that month. These fast-paced events led to a *de facto* political dominance of the army. They grew impatient with the failure to end the crisis and consequently decided to put pressure on Bendjedid to dismiss Prime Minister Hamrouche who they blamed for contributing to the Islamist unrest and violence. He was replaced by Ghozali, a holdover form Boumediene era. The optimistic mood generated by the appointment of Ghozali did not last, however. Soon after he took office, tension with FIS mounted again. On 28 June the FIS leaders threatened to call for jihad (holy war) if the state of siege, martial law and the curfew were not lifted. The government reacted to this threat by arresting, on 30 June, the two leaders of the FIS, Abbassi Madani and Ali Belhadj; they were later tried by a military court and sentenced to 12 years in jail.

On 29 September 1991, the government announced the lifting of the curfew and the scheduling of parliamentary elections for 26 December. In spite of the fact that its two leaders were in jail, the Islamists party decided to participate in the vote. The FIS won 44 per cent of the seats, whereas the FLN, which had ruled Algeria alone, came in third with only 15 seats. The army opposed the transfer of power to the Islamists. They asked Bendjedid to resign from power on 11 January 1992. Two days later, a High State Council (Haut Comité d'État, or HCE) was established to assume presidential powers. The historical exiled leader, Mohammed Boudiaf, was invited to return to Algeria from Morocco and head the HCE. In April 1992, Boudiaf inaugurated a new Consultative Assembly of sixty members, which replaced the dissolved parliament. On 29 June 1992, he was assassinated by one of his security men.

Boudiaf's successor, Ali Kafi, and Prime Minister Ghozali were both unable to deal with the crisis effectively. Ghozali was replaced by Mr Belaid Abdesselam in the summer of 1992, in hopes that the latter could win back the support of the FLN. In the end, however, he antagonized most party leaders, the press and most groups from the left who had previously supported him. In the summer of 1993, he was replaced by Redah Malek, who wanted to create a national consensus on a solution to end the political crisis and to address the international debt problem. In October 1993, the HCE created a National Dialogue Commission, whose main task was to develop, on the basis of consultations with all parties and civic associations, a platform for a three-year transition back to the democratic process (1994 to 1996). The platform for transition was debated and approved by the national conference held on 25 and 26 January 1994. The National Security Council appointed Defence Minister Liamine Zeroual as the new President of Algeria, for a three-year transitional period.

Mr Zeroual acknowledged from the beginning that security measures alone would not bring about a solution to the crisis, and that only a political dialogue among all social forces (including the Islamists of the FIS) could save the country. In the mean time, political violence had gained momentum, and thousands of security personnel and civilians were killed. On the economic front, negotiation with the Paris Club and the IMF continued for an agreement that would ease Algeria's heavy debt-servicing burden. Even though he seemed committed to finding a political solution to the crisis, Zeroual faced great political and economical challenges. He had to continue the military pressure on the Islamists' armed groups while seeking a negotiated solution. However, the hardliners within the regime pursued a policy of eradication of the Islamists. Sooner than expected by many observers, Zeroual decided to end the transition period by calling for a presidential election that was held on 16 November 1995. The vote was boycotted by opposition parties who met in Rome in January 1994 and proposed a new National Platform for solving the crisis. With voter participation close to 75 per cent, Zeroual won the election with 61 per cent of the vote. Feeling strong after his electoral victory, President Zeroual did not respond to calls from the FIS to enter into negotiations over the future of the country. In the summer of 1996 he even called the FIS question a 'closed issue' and invited all other opposition parties to participate in a conference of 'National Entente', held 14–15 September. Some parties refused the invitation, claiming that the real intention of the regime was not a democratic opening, but rather a consolidation of authoritarianism under a democratic façade. The final outcome of the conference was a 'Platform for National Entente', which outlined which political reforms were going to remain, including the rejection of parties or movements based on religion, ethnicity or regionalism, and the affirmation of Islam as the religion of the state. On the basis of these principles and others, President Zeroual organized a referendum on a constitutional revision on 26 November 1996. New parliamentary elections were held on 5 June 1997 according to a proportional representation system, and produced Algeria's first multi-party parliament. In spite of this, political violence continued. The legitimacy of the current regime would come to rest not on reforms alone, but more on the ability to end the political violence that had claimed the lives of over 200,000 people since 1992.

In September 1998 President Zeroual announced that he would step down for health reasons,[17] paving the way for selection of a civil leader, namely Abdelaziz Bouteflika, who emerged as the leading candidate during the electoral campaign of 1999. Mr Bouteflika was elected President of the Republic, winning with 73.8 per cent of the votes cast. Despite his denials, he was widely seen as the candidate of the *Pouvoir*.[18] The same scenario took place on 22 February 2004 when Mr Bouteflika announced that he would run in the presidential election and won the vote cast on 8 April 2004 with 85 per cent.

What is important to note here is the new approach of Bouteflika to changing the political system of Algeria. He sought to strengthen his position by encouraging leading parties to constitute what he called a Presidential Alliance, composed of four parties with varied political outlooks.[19] The underlying strategy was to create a consensus on policies among different factions, being based on the notion that democracy cannot take root in a society divided by ideologies, political antagonism and distrust among various groups. Each party committed itself to the president's programme. Since the four political parties work together to execute the programme, there are no reasons for disagreement on any policy or bill to be presented to the two legislative authorities. The source of change and influence is the president, who has the power to allocate national resources. With a reserve of more than US$100 billion at his disposal in the state treasury, the president can influence the course of events as he wishes. The accumulated wealth in the treasury has made the president the most influential political actor in the country.

4. Democratic, economic and social performance

Since 1988 Algerian political reforms have been undertaken as a response to economic and political upheavals. They have been designed as a regime exit strategy to ensure the survival of the incumbent political elite, which has been in power since 1962. The economic reforms implemented since the 1990s, including those associated with IMF structural adjustment programmes (Nashashibi et al., 1998),[20] were intended to deal with the requirements of the Paris Club for the rescheduling of Algeria's external debt,[21] and were seen as a route to break the international isolation imposed by most Western governments, who did not overtly supported the military-backed government. The pace of liberalization these reforms entailed was slow, however. Economic freedom indices published by the Heritage Foundation (2007) and the Fraser Institute (2007) reveal that progress was very limited. The Heritage Foundation index of economic freedom for 2007 ranked Algeria at 134th worldwide, and 14th in the Middle East and North Africa region.[22] The economy is ranked as partially free. It is worth noting the low scores for the financial sector and for corruption. Both factors are highly related to rent distribution and explain the recent proliferation of financial and banking scandals related to corruption. The scandal of the Khalifa Bank is a perfect illustration of the complex web in place used to divert oil money by illegal means. The Heritage index of corruption declined from 50 in 1995 to just 28 in 2007, whereas that of financial freedom deteriorated from 50 to just 30 for the same period. The House of Fraser (HF) index ranks Algeria 127th out of 141, though the level of economic freedom increased from 3.9 in 1980 to 5.3 in 2005. Thus the level of government intervention and control of the economy remains very high and hampers the emergence of a transparent system of governance.

The political reforms that accompanied economic reforms centred around shifting political activity from monopoly of the FLN to a controlled multi-party system (Volpi, 2006). As a consequence of the introduction of multi-party politics, the polity index increased from –9 in 1988 to +2 in 2004. On the other hand, the Freedom House (FH) index did not take such constitutional changes into consideration in their evaluation of democracy in Algeria. According to the subscores in the FH index, the electoral process is still far from being fair and transparent. Despite the introduction of multi-party politics, participation and pluralism are still very weak.

Freedom of expression and personal autonomy scored highest, at nearly half the maximum (see Table 7.1), while rule of law and functioning of government are the highest impediments to freedom. By converting the Gastil index into polity using the formula suggested by Paldam (2005),[23] we see a democracy gap of two points compared to the polity index before 1988. The gap widened to four points after resumption of the electoral process in 1995, and increased to nine points in 2004 as polity appreciated the presidential election of 2004 as competitive. Democracy was upgraded by five points from –3 to +2, whereas for HF it did not represent any improvement. Algeria is ranked as non-free by HF, therefore according to Levitsky and Way (2002) it could not be considered as a form of competitive authoritarianism. However, the large gap between the Gastil and polity indices could be regarded as a presumption that procedural democracy, which consists of introducing multi-party elections, may not necessarily reflect improvements in political rights and civil liberties. This situation could be described as façade electoral authoritarianism.

Other aspects of Algerian political reforms pertain to the strikingly weak level of political and economic institutions and the deterioration of political and economic governance. In this unstable, non-enabling environment for democracy, liberal political reforms leading to more freedom and government disengagement implemented since the end of the 1980s could have contributed to the weakening of institutions and signal difficulties for sustaining future democratization. Reforms resulted in a shallow and cosmetic democratic configuration. Looking at the scores of the Institutional Credit Rating Guide (ICRG) published by Political Risk Services Group on political risk assessment in Algeria (1984–2007), given in Table 7.2, one notes the generally weak and declining level of

Table 7.1 Gastil Index, 2006

				Political rights			Civil liberties			
				Electoral process	Political pluralism and participation	Functioning of government	Freedom of expression and belief	Associational and organizational rights	Rule of law	Personal autonomy and individual rights
Country	Political rights	Civil liberties	Status							
Algeria	6	5	Not-free	5	3	3	8	6	4	7
Min	1	1		0	0	0	0	0	0	0
Max	7	7		12	16	12	16	12	16	16

Source: Freedom House.

Table 7.2 Institutions and polity, Algeria 1988–2007

ICRG Components	1988	1992	1995	1999	2003	2005	2007	Correlation with polity (1984–2004)	Correlation with Gastil	Trend rate of change 1984–2007
Government stability (11)	8.8	4.5	6.3	10.0	8.1	9.8	9.4	0.2	−0.3	1.0
Socio-economic conditions (11)	6.0	4.8	5.2	3.1	4.0	5.4	6.0	−0.7**	−0.1	−1.5
Internal conflict (12)	6.7	5.6	5.4	6.0	8.0	9.2	8.5	−0.5**	−0.4**	1.5
External conflict (12)	10.0	12.0	10.2	9.0	11.0	10.5	10.5	0.1	0.4	0.4
Corruption (6)	4.0	3.5	3.0	2.0	1.5	1.5	1.5	−0.5*	−0.3	−5.0
Military in politics (6)	3.0	1.0	0.0	0.0	0.0	3.0	3.0	−0.4**	−0.5**	−1.7
Religion in politics (6)	4.8	2.0	0.1	0.0	0.0	2.5	2.5	−0.7**	−0.1**	−5.0
Law and order (6)	2.8	1.4	3.0	2.0	2.0	3.0	3.0	0.0	0.1	1.4
Ethnic tensions (6)	4.0	3.0	4.0	2.0	2.0	3.4	3.5	−0.2	−0.1	−1.4
Democratic accountability (6)	2.1	2.1	3.0	1.8	2.0	5.0	5.0	0.5**	−0.6**	1.8
Bureaucracy quality (4)	2.1	1.0	1.0	2.0	2.0	2.0	2.0	0.6**	−0.6**	2.2

Source: ICRG, PRS Group.

Notes
Figures between brackets represent maximum possible score. *T test significant at 5%, ** at 1%.

governance and the quality of institutions. Most of the ICRG components declined between 1988 and 1995, the period that witnessed dramatic political events. However, after then some improvements in the quality of institutions could be detected and particularly concern government stability, internal conflicts and democratic accountability. Intervention of the military in politics, and the use of religion in the political discourse reached bottom scores and improved only after 2003. Corruption scores deteriorated throughout the period and could be regarded as a serious impediment to further democratization. In fact, looking at the correlation between ICRG components and the polity index, one should expect a positive and significant correlation as improvements in institutions and polity are reinforcing factors. However, the correlation figures given in Table 7.2 indicate that the democratization process was implemented in a context of deteriorating institutions.

For example, bad socio-economic conditions, further internal conflicts and more military and religious intervention are significantly and negatively correlated with polity. Under these conditions political reforms that led to the introduction of multi-party politics and general elections did not result in a genuine change in the Algerian political system. These results are a simple reflection of the peculiar behaviour of Algerian polity and reinforce the idea that political reforms are a result of the breakdown of the authoritarian bargain under the pressure of mounting domestic conflict and economic meltdown.

It is thus apparent that, despite a turbulent social and economic environment since independence in 1962, the Algerian political regime has been able to survive turmoil, and political and economic crises. For more than 40 years the FLN ruled Algeria without real power sharing. Political stability of the authoritarian nationalist regime from 1965 until the mid-1980s permitted it to set a priority of nation-building from above and to accelerate economic and social development. The Polity IV score was very stable, unchanging at –9 from 1965 to 1988. However this period coincided with noticeable economic and social structural change, and economic growth was robust. For the period 1960–79 GDP per capita increased by 3.6 per cent and GDP by 6.7 per cent annually, in contrast with the period 1980–2005, when the average annual growth rate of the GDP per capita was only –0.1 per cent and GDP growth was 2.11 per cent per annum.

Boumediene's era (1965–78) of revolutionary single-party and autocratic rule coincided with political stability and rapid economic development. Development policies, based on central planning, concentrated on agricultural reforms and rapid, heavy inward-looking industrialization, financed by oil rents and supplemented by external resources. Real GDP per capita doubled between independence and the end of President Boumediene's era. It increased in 2000 prices from US$838 for 1962 to US$1,800 for 1978. Also, social policy was generous and redistribution policies played a major role as a trade-off for political rights. Education and health were free for all,[24] and consumption prices were tightly controlled and highly subsidized.

On the other hand, the noted economic development notwithstanding, the concentration on heavy industries, along with market control and mismanagement of the agricultural collectivization programme, repressed the economy and created widespread shortages in the consumer markets. These conditions, along with a rapid population growth and increasing urbanization,[25] tended to keep unemployment levels high, averaging over 20 per cent of the workforce. Nonetheless, there occurred a reduction in poverty despite the deterioration in income inequality during this period.[26] Rapid expansion of the public sector and central government jobs provided job security and relatively better standards of living, thereby creating strong support for the political elite. Poverty was essentially rural, at 41 per cent, compared to 12 per cent in large towns.

As a consequence of the above developments the HDI increased from 0.28 to 0.43.[27] This increased welfare was mainly financed by the oil rents and external debt. Fuel exports increased from 66 per cent in 1965 to 98 per cent of the total in 1978, while external debt increased from less than US$1 billion at the end of 1970 (20 per cent of GDP) to more than $15 billion at the end of 1978 (60 per cent of GDP). The share of the mining industry also increased considerably, from 25 per cent to more than 42 per cent. Thus, despite rapid industrialization, the manufacturing sector was overshadowed by the mining sector, leading to a decline of its contribution to GDP from 13 per cent for 1965 to just 11 per cent for 1978.

The rise in oil prices (and government revenues) caused by the Iranian revolution of 1979 gave the new Algerian elite (headed by Bendjedid) an opportunity to cope with emerging national economic strains, including widespread shortages in consumer markets, which became a source of popular discontent. The reform agenda approved by party congress in 1980 aimed at placating the population by loosening the central planning system and increasing the imports of consumer durables at affordable prices. The investment programme in new projects was halted and priority was given to finishing projects that were under way. Public corporations were restructured and broken down in order to facilitate their management, giving them autonomy of decision-making. The public investment programme was refocused on housing projects and basic infrastructure. Price and marketing controls on agricultural products were lifted and private-sector investment was encouraged.

However no significant political reforms were undertaken. Bendjedid's entourage needed time to consolidate his position and neutralize the anti-liberal reforms. While the rate of economic growth during 1980–5 averaged 5.1 per cent annually, GDP per capita increased only by 1.7 per cent annually, that is, less than half the growth rate recorded in the Boumediene era, with real GDP per capita for 1985 reaching US$2,020 at 2000 prices. This modest growth was very costly, as external debt increased rapidly from US$15.8 billion at the end of 1984 (30 per cent of GDP) to US$ 22.65 billion for 1986 (36 per cent of GDP). Nonetheless, the social welfare programme was not reduced but rather consolidated by expanding the social housing programem. Unemployment was not controlled and continued running around 20 per cent; however poverty levels continued to decline, reaching 16 per cent for 1988, while adult literacy increased to 41 per cent, and life expectancy to 64 years for 1986. HDI increased from 0.42 for 1978 to 0.53 for 1986.

With the collapse of international oil prices in February 1986 to as low as US$10 a barrel, total exports declined from US$14 billion in 1985 to just $9 billion the following year. In parallel, external debt service reached US$5.15 billion for 1986 (8.2 per cent of GDP) and increased steadily to US$9 billion for 1993 (18 per cent of GDP). Imports had to be restricted, declining from US$15.3 billion for 1981 to $11 billion for 1987. Despite the oil price rally in the second half of the 1980s, exports were not sufficient to finance the import bill and meet debt service obligations. More debt was contracted and increased to US$26 billion at the end of 1988 and to $28 billion at the end of 1991. The contraction of imports was very harmful to growth, initially relating to the import of intermediate goods and various inputs, and halting new investments. As a consequence, development lost steam. Economic growth collapsed by an average of –1.9 per cent annually during the period 1985–90. For 1988, GDP per capita had declined to its 1978 level.

Deep divisions among antagonist factions within the ruling FLN prevented the government from carrying out deep economic reforms, and internal feuding within the ruling party, coupled with popular discontent at the deteriorating economic and social situation, spilled outside the closed regime circles. As noted earlier, angry mobs took to the streets in October 1988. Violent demonstrations put down by the military ended in a heavy death toll.[28]

The violent October 1988 events allowed the ruling elite to go ahead with deep political and economic liberal reforms, consisting mainly of multi-party politics and engaging in a structural adjustment and stabilization programme as well as negotiations of debt restructuring with the main creditors of Algeria. These reforms resulted in the polity score rising to –2. Freedom House upgraded its score from 7 to 4 for 1989 and regarded the country as partially free. The regime, however, had grossly underestimated the strength of the radical Islamists under the banner of the FIS.[29] In January 1992 the army stepped in and cancelled the second round of the first multi-party parliamentary elections. The polity score deteriorated to –7 for that year. With the return of general elections in 1995 the polity index improved to –3; however the Freedom House index improved only by one index point, from 7 to 6. The improvement in the polity index between 1988 and 2003 (except for the period 1992–4) was accompanied by the disruption of the economy due to political instability and the rising debt burden. Real GDP per capita continued its slide, reaching US$1,631 for 1994, equivalent to 80 per cent of its pre-crisis level in 1985. GDP per capita declined between 1989 and 1994 by –2.7 per cent annually, and for 1995 unemployment increased to 28 per cent and the head count poverty ratio to 21 per cent (Laabas, 2001), with inflation averaging 27 per cent annually between 1991 and 1994. As the total debt service continued to rise, its ratio reaching more than 70 per cent of exports in 1991, the government was compelled to accept debt rescheduling and an IMF stabilization and structural adjustment programme. However, the three Stand By programmes signed in 1989, 1991 and 1994, external debt reprofiling with some creditors and massive public-sector retrenchment through the cessation (asset sales) of local public enterprises proved to be insufficient to redress the economic situation.

Resort was again made to the Paris Club to reschedule outstanding external debt, followed by new agreements with the IMF[30] whereby liberal and contractionary policies were implemented to bring about macroeconomic balance (Nashashibi *et al.*, 1998). Though such reforms were carried out under conditions of political violence, growth resumed, per capita income increased by 1.7 per cent annually between 1995 and 2000, and inflation declined steadily from 30 per cent for 1995 to just 2.6 per cent for 1999. However, unemployment increased from 24 per cent for 1994 to 28 per cent for 1998, and poverty reached more than 30 per cent in 2000 (see e.g. Laabas, 2001). Though progress in acquiring human capital slowed down, HDI increased from 0.56 for 1988 to 0.59 for 1994 and to 0.62 for 1998.

Despite violence and economic difficulties, the electoral process was resumed in 1995 with the election of General Zeroual as president. This was followed by parliamentary elections in 1997 that brought the RND a parliamentary majority in a highly contested round of elections. Election management became the efficient instrument of keeping the regime factions in power, though some competition was allowed and a vocal private press was tolerated (Volpi, 2006). The election of Mr Bouteflika in 1999 permitted the army to disengage from the political forefront. The Islamist insurgency of the FIS ended by signing an agreement that was later approved by a referendum and followed by reconciliation law in 2004. By the end of 1999 the oil price started to improve considerably to a point that the rescheduled external debt was paid ahead of schedule, reducing the level of the external debt to less than US$5 billion at the end of 2007. A major investment plan in infrastructure and housing was launched. The government continued the economic liberalization programme by further attracting foreign investment, beginning the process of joining WTO and signing a partnership accord with the European Union. GDP per capita increased by more than 3.6 per cent between 2000 and 2005, and unemployment declined steadily, to 12.3 per cent in 2006. The FLN captured the parliament by a comfortable majority in the 2002 and 2007 parliamentary elections. The political status quo of FLN hegemony that was forged during the 1970s and early 1980s was restored, but this time in a pseudo-democratic decor.

5. Explaining the Algerian democratization experience

From the analysis of the political history and institutions of Algeria, it is evident that the role of economic and social development in democratization cannot be understood in isolation from political events and the will of the elite to introduce democratic reforms. Economic and social development only increases the potential demand for human freedoms. These demands are usually met in a sluggish way, creating an 'authoritarian bargain' between the citizens and the incumbent elite, whereby freedoms are traded off for some economic benefits. This bargain is maintained by a complex system of benefits/patronage/repression depending on the size of the rents to be distributed. Given the fact that Algeria is a rentier state with limited resources to be distributed, this bargain is inherently unstable. Internal conflict and oil rents are among the main drivers of the pressures to democratize the political system in Algeria. In this context the modernization model should integrate explanatory variables that summarize major political events as well as oil and conflict, which in essence reflect the dynamics of the 'authoritarian bargain'. It is worth noting that using the modernization model at the country level may not permit a test of 'fixed' structural characteristics of society such as religion, colonial history and other cultural features that are prominent in cross-country modernization models. Also, the role of oil rents and conflicts may not be well captured by the time-series single-country approach, since they are almost constant permanent phenomena throughout the sample period.

In the context of Arab countries, the impact of oil and conflict is better captured by cross-country modernization models such that developed by EMM (2008) where oil rents and conflicts are found to robustly account for the Arab democratic deficit. Although the model does not neatly reproduce Algerian polity, as indicated in Table 7.3, because of the peculiar behaviour of Algerian polity, the relatively limited rents to be distributed and the limited impact of external conflicts and Arab–Israeli war on Algerian polity. When controlling for polity shifts, the EMM model simulations for Algeria indicate that conflict and oil rents had strong impacts on polity over the sample period. While the Arab–Israeli war effect might be appealing in certain Arab countries, such as the case of Iraq as documented by Davis and Yousif (2008) on the basis of EMM model simulations, it is very hard to carry over the same argument for the Algerian case, given the distance of Algeria from Palestine and, initially, the preoccupation of the Algerians with their own war of liberation, as well as the fact that the incumbent regime never linked the question of democracy to the resolution of the Arab–Israeli conflict. Internal conflict as opposed to external conflict is central to the democratization in Algeria. In fact, monthly data from ICRG over the period 1984 to 2008 shows the index of external conflict scored on average 10 index points, with a minimum value of 8 out of maximum of 12. On the other hand, internal conflict deteriorated significantly during periods of economic hardship, reflecting the struggle between citizens and the elite in modifying the status quo bargain. Additionally, ICRG data show that the score of internal conflict is correlated positively with oil price and negatively with Polity IV.

Table 7.3 Polity simulation, EMM Model

Period	Actual polity	Predicted 1985	Predicted 1990	Predicted 1990, without oil effects	Predicted 1990, without oil or Arab war effects
1980–4	–9.0	–9.0	–9.0	–9.0	–9.0
1985–9	–7.6	–7.6	–7.6	–7.6	–7.6
1990–4	–5.0	–9.9	–5.0	–5.0	–5.0
1995–9	–3.0	–10.0	–6.9	–5.4	–3.8
2000–3	–3.0	–10.0	–7.6	–4.5	–2.6

Source: EMM (2006).

The role of oil rents in explaining the democratic deficit in Algeria is very pertinent and represents the central question in the struggle for democratization as proposed by EMM. However, some issues related to oil rents in Algeria are worth discussing. Oil was discovered back in the 1950s, and became a major source of finance only after the first oil shock in 1973. The Algerian authoritarian regime emerged after a bitter struggle between FLN factions in the summer of discontent that nearly plunged the country into a prolonged civilian war (Haroun, 2000). Oil was not the reason for establishing an autocratic regime in the first instance. In fact oil revenues represented only 12 per cent of budget revenues in 1963 and a meagre US$5 per capita, and only surpassed 50 per cent of budget revenues after the first oil shock in 1973. However, the incumbent elite found in oil rents the optimal tool to create and maintain an authoritarian bargain in which political freedoms are traded off for economic benefits. The status quo is not as stable as in the Gulf oil-exporting countries, because the size of the rent is not considerable. Size of oil rents when measured as the ratio of mineral exports to GDP reveals that Algeria (39 per cent in 2000) is highly dependent on hydrocarbons, even higher than the level in Saudi Arabia (37 per cent in 2000). However, when these rents are calculated per capita, reflecting the ability to distribute such rents, the Algerian elite have relatively limited resources at hand. Fuel exports per capita in 2000 reached only US$700 compared to more than US$3,400 in Saudi Arabia or US$17,150 in Qatar.

Using the EMM model to assess the impact of oil rents on Algerian polity, compared to a base run solution initialized in 1990, and after taking into account the sharp increase of 1989, polity would have improved by three index points for the average during the period 2000–3. The model also predicts an improvement of the polity by a further 1.9 point index if Arab regional wars end and the region becomes conflict-free.

Improvement in polity occurred because a sustained decline in oil prices deeply altered the authoritarian bargain as the harsh economic realities stemming from low rents triggered a wave of internal conflicts. Given the relatively limited amount of rents to be distributed, a significant decline of rents forced the elite to trade off welfare with some political rights, as happened in 1989. Thus, a decline in rents would normally lead to an increase in polity. Up to now the elite have engaged in reforms that only re-establish the authoritarian bargain and do not fully engage in democratization. The decline in oil prices did not lead to lasting, improved polity because during the time of the precipitous decline in oil rents, conflicts and external influence also came to play a role. The military cracked down on FIS and were rewarded with massive debt restructuring and direct bilateral support.

Democracy is usually measured by scores such as the Polity IV or Gastil index, whereas GDP per capita is often taken as a measure of the level of economic development. However this money-based welfare metric is not, on its own, a sufficiently good indicator. It does not reflect the extent of inequality nor the extent of structural transformation of the economy (Chenery and Syrquin, 1975). It also excludes the social development that accompanies economic development. We should bear in mind that per capita income in a partially rentier state such as Algeria could change significantly in that it is influenced by rapid changes of primary commodity prices in international markets. Income per capita declined between 1988 and 1995 from US$5,934 to $5,227 purchasing power parity (PPP), exactly the period where the polity index increased from –9 to –3. Structural social modernity variables, on the other hand, reflect less erratic behaviour. The Algerian case demonstrates this contrast. Whereas per capita income levels changed significantly over time, the growth rates of urbanization, adult and youth literacy, female participation in the labour force and life expectancy tended to change more gradually and with a very strong trend (see Table 7.4).

To test the modernity hypothesis we shall thus supplement GDP per capita data by an array of structural economic and social indicators that together more appropriately reflect the evolution of Algeria's level of development. Political events are captured by a series of dummy variables that represent the introduction of multi-party politics in 1989, the cancellation of the electoral process in 1992, and the resumption of elections in 1995. We found that these events when modelled as single-event (one-period) dummies had insignificant impact on polity. However when these events are modelled as permanent shocks, their explanatory power and significance increases tremendously. This probably reflects the fact that elite behaviour has a huge long-term impact on polity.

Table 7.4 Causality test between polity and modernity variables

Granger Causality Tests
Sample: 1962–2004
Lags: 2

Null hypothesis:	F-statistic	Probability
POLITY Does not Granger Cause Rents	2.27	0.08
RENTS does not Granger Cause POLITY	0.80	0.53
POLITY does not Granger Cause Agriculture share of GDP	0.4	0.67
AGR does not Granger Cause POLITY	4.38	0.02
POLITY does not Granger Cause FUEL exports % exports	0.03	0.96
FUEL does not Granger Cause POLITY	0.51	0.6
POLITY does not Granger Cause GENDER	0.72	0.49
GENDER does not Granger Cause POLITY	4.03	0.02
POLITY does not Granger Cause HDI	2.41	0.1
HDI does not Granger Cause POLITY	4.05	0.02
POLITY does not Granger Cause INCOME	0.75	0.47
INCOME does not Granger Cause POLITY	2.3	0.11
POLITY does not Granger Cause Adult Literacy	0.62	0.54
ADULT LITERACY does not Granger Cause POLITY	5.36	0.01
POLITY does not Granger Cause Youth Literacy	2.4	0.1
YOUTH LITERACY does not Granger Cause POLITY	3.71	0.03
URBAN does not Granger Cause POLITY	5.06	0.01
POLITY does not Granger Cause URBAN	0.38	0.68

Source: World Development Indicators (2007), Polity IV data base and Penn World table 6.2.

In the literature there is a debate as to whether democracy and development are intertwined processes: no development without democracy and no democracy without development. Of course this view clashes with the evidence that some non-democratic regimes have registered good, if not impressive, economic progress. We have attempted to test this two-way causality in the Algeria case by applying the Granger (1988) causality test between polity and social and economic modernity variables in Table 7.4. As the table shows, causality runs almost exclusively from modernity to polity and not the other way around. This is so because polity is very sluggish and does not entirely follow the path of modernity variables. The government engaged in political reforms only when the economic environment was very bad. In other words, improvements in polity were used as a compensation for economic difficulties in order to minimize potential unrest. In contrast with social modernity variables, which had a strong causality impact on polity, the test shows that GDP per capita and the share of fuel in total exports are not significant. Only the share of agriculture output had a causal impact on polity, which is further strengthened by the strong causal effect of urbanization. Thus, generally in the Algerian case, little or no evidence is found for the reverse Lipset theory.

Given the fact that polity index is limited to the interval −10 to +10 and that democracy will level off with further development, we use a quadratic semi-logarithmic regression equation representing a logistic curve between polity and GDP per capita PPP (see Table 7.5). As the dependent variable is limited to [−10, +10] the model was also estimated as a censored dependent variable. In addition, the income variable was lagged one period in order to control for endogeneity between explanatory variable and polity. The endogeneity of income should not be an issue in our case, given that polity does not cause income.

The model is useful is simulating the impact of a long-term structural transformation of the economy as well as assessing the impact of further gains in education and its impacts on polity. The strict version of the modernity model (Model 1) using income as the sole explanatory variable of polity gave a highly significant positive relationship between democracy and GDP per capita, however the explanatory power of the model was only 0.27. By adding the income squared (Model 2) the explanatory power of the model increased to 0.40 and the null hypothesis of redundancy of the squared income was strongly rejected. On the other hand, political events of 1989 (introduction of multi-party politics), 1992 (nullifying of the electoral process) and 1995 (resumption of elections) exert a strong influence on polity when modelled as permanent-impact dummy variables. Single-event dummy variables were not significant. The parameters of the dummy variables (Model 3) are highly significant and of the expected sign. The explanatory power of the model is understandably high because the coding of the dummies mimics the evolution of polity. The dummy model indicates that average polity was −8.8, and the introduction of multi-party politics in 1989 added 6.8 points to the index, whereas the freezing of elections in 1992 reduced the index by 5 points. The resumption of elections in 1995 added 4.5 points to the index. Several trials with the rents variable showed that this variable is highly correlated with the political events dummies.

Table 7.5 Estimation results of the modernity model, 1962–2004[1]

	Model 1 Income	Model 2 Income	Model 3 Dummy	Model 4 (Income)	Model 5 (HDI)	Model 6 (PC)	Model 7 (Income)	Model 8 (HDI)	Model 9 (HDI)
Constant	−80.97 (4.52)[2]	1735.96 (2.97)	−8.88 (57.49)	430.71 (2.09)	−2.22 (0.58)	226.71 (3.22)	3.39 (6.167)	3.98 (6.16)	16.06 (3.15)
$Ln(X_{t-1})$	8.75 (4.14)	−424.95 (3.04)	—	−104.74 (2.12)	15.77 (1.77)	−109.34 (3.38)	1.60 (3.57)	1.37 (4.93)	33.91 (2.25)
$Ln(X_{t-1})^2$	—	25.88 (3.11)	—	6.23 (2.11)	8.81 (1.88)	12.64 (3.41)	—	—	27.07 (2/05)
DUM_{89}	—	—	6.88 (14.09)	6.77 (12.83)	6.26 (11.04)	5.50 (7.26)	—	—	—
DUM_{92}	—	—	−5.00 (7.62)	−4.97 (7.89)	−5.23 (30.82)	−3.69 (4.88)	—	—	—
DUM_{95}	—	—	4.50	4.46 (8.50)	4.12 (8.77)	—	—	—	—
Log (rents)[3]	—	—	—	—	—	(14.57)	0.69 (3.57)	0.46 (2.42)	0.62 (2.61)
Log (internal conflict)[4]							−0.17 (2.65)	−0.18 (3.25)	−1.87
$\bar{R}^2$	0.27	0.40	0.93	0.94	0.94	0.90	0.69	0.75	0.79
F	17.22	15.2	192.13	125.79	132.73	73.13	31.87	42.06	20.34
AIC	4.83	4.63	2.48	2.44	2.39	2.82	0.92	0.72	0.56
Elasticity	4.37	14.30	—	2.22	4.34	7.70	1.60	1.37	5.0
RMSE	2.55	2.28	0.76	0.72	0.69	0.83	1.73	1.68	1.65

Notes
1 For Model 1 to 6 the dependent variable is polity, whereas in Model 7, 8 and 9 the dependent variable is log (polity +11). T-statistics are between brackets.
2 T-statistics.
3 Rents are calculated as oil revenues per capita in real prices deflected by the consumer price index.
4 Internal conflict is taken from ICRG database.

The rents variable performed significantly only with the level of income, or, alternatively, HDI, and the 1995 dummy. The strong multicollinearity between the square of income, the dummies on one hand, and the rents on the other hand prevented estimation of the full model. In Model 7 and 8 rents are found highly significant and negatively related to polity; a 1 per cent decline in rents would increase polity by 0.17–0.18 per cent. However, the strength of income impact on polity is higher than rents and the elasticity was 1.6 per cent for income and 1.3 per cent for HDI. Model 7 explained 69 per cent of polity variation for income and 75 per cent for HDI (Model 8).

It was difficult to assess the impact of internal and external conflict on polity due to data limitations and to strong correlations between different explanatory variables included in the regression model, particularly with the polity dummies and oil rents data. This correlation is natural in the case of Algeria, given the fact that considerable decline of oil rents triggered a wave of sustained internal conflict and a shift in polity. The index of conflict measurements were taken from ICRG data which are available only from 1984 onward, which considerably reduces the sample of estimation. After extensive experimentation with different model specifications it was found that external conflict has no impact on polity because no significant impact was detected in all estimation experiments. However, internal conflict was found in most cases strongly significant, and consistently had a negative impact on polity. Model 9 gives the results of the best regression equation, where polity variations are highly explained by almost 80 per cent by the HDI and a dummy for 1995 and internal conflict. Other variables were dropped from the equation because of multicollinearity between explanatory variables of the model. The model indicates that a 1 per cent increase (improvement) in the internal conflict index reduces polity by 1.87 per cent.

Despite the fact that GDP per capita was highly significant in the strict modernity model (Model 1 and 2), it explained only a small proportion of sample variability of polity. The augmented modernity model with political events (Model 4) produced a far better fitting of the polity data than the strict modernity model. The income parameters are significant at less than 5 per cent and the parameters of the dummies produced the right signs and are highly significant. The political break of 1989 that signalled the end of single-party rule represents a genuine structural change in the polity. Using recursive OLS the estimates of income and the squared income show signs of considerable structural break; no structural break around 1989 was significantly rejected and recursive OLS estimates of the income parameters show a clear break after 1989. The augmented modernity model shows that, despite economic development exerting a long-term positive effect on polity, the elite can impact the path of polity evolution by blocking the political institutions that would otherwise develop in accordance with economic and social development.

Introducing social modernity variables in the equation proved to be difficult, because most of these variables are highly correlated and show a strong common trend. The best strategy was either to use a principal component analysis (Model 6), that is, using the components that explain most of the variability in the data, or to use the UNDP's HDI as a proxy of economic and social development. In the case of principal components it turned out that 95 per cent of the social modernity matrix (gender gap in primary education, life expectancy, youth and adult literacy, urbanization, female fertility) variability was explained by the first component. Model 6 performed well and the component explained some 75 per cent of the variations in the polity variable. The principal components' impact on polity resembles that of the income model because as is clear from the correlation matrix (Table 7.5) the social modernity variables are highly correlated with the income variable.

Despite data limitations we computed time series of human capital according to the standard formula UNDP uses in their HDI. Human development is more appropriate to link to polity because, as noted earlier, it includes both social and income dimensions of modernity and also gives a meaning to the interpretation of development as freedom (Sen, 1999). According to our computations, HDI increased from a low level of 0.23 in 1962 to medium level (0.67) in 2004, and increased annually by 2.1 per cent between 1962 and 2004, which is roughly equal to one and a half of GDP per capita growth of 1.3 per cent per annum for the same period. HDI explained almost 95 per cent of the variations, however HDI parameters were less significant than income and the principal components of social modernity variables.

In conclusion, the modernity model showed that the level of economic development in Algeria does affect democracy directly, though only moderately, despite a sluggish economic record and the discontinuous shifts in the polity variables, which normally took place when growth collapsed. The EMM model showed that oil rent and conflicts explain the Arab deficit freedom. In the Algerian case, oil rents were used to lengthen the life of the incumbent regime in office and changes were made only as a direct response to pressure brought by the shrinkage of oil windfalls. Internal conflicts were more related to polity than Arab regional wars, however the resolution of such conflicts by neutralizing the distribution of rents through transparent budget operation would reduce tensions in society. In line with modernity models, social variables showed a strong correlation with polity and proved to be a strong predictor of polity in Algeria. As Algeria achieves advanced stages in urbanization, fertility, literacy and life expectancy, further pressures on democratic reforms will be exacerbated by the increasing education levels of the population. Combined education enrolment rates increased from 21 per cent in 1970 to more than 70 per cent in 2004. Adult literacy increased rapidly from 16 per cent in 1962 to more than 60 per cent in 2005, and youth literacy reached more than 90 per cent in 2004.

All the estimated models show that the elasticity of polity with respect to modernity variables is quite high, ranging from 2.2 per cent for a 1 per cent increase in GDP per capita, to 4.24 for a 1 per cent increase in HDI and 7.7 per cent for the principal components, assuming that no adverse political events come to considerably affect polity. The forecasting performance of the models is good and the human development model produced the lowest RMSE at 0.69. Assuming that the components of the HDI increase in the future at their historical rates of change, GDP per capita would reach around US$9,000 PPP, and HDI 0.86, in 2030. By using the human development equation in predicting future polity it turns out that when the values of the dummies are extrapolated, assuming the perpetuation of the political configuration, future income and human development would have little impact on future polity. However, when modelling political events as transitory, economic and human development would strongly drive polity, and according to the model Algeria would have become fully democratized. This, unfortunately, means that under the actual political configuration development does not lead to democracy, and would only force the elite to distribute even more rents, and that genuine change would happen only when the economy shifts from a rentier state to non-primary commodities export, or when rents declines substantially as happened in 1986.

6. Conclusion

The current Algerian political regime was moulded during the bitter war of liberation (1954–62) and was based on an alliance between the FLN, the army and the bureaucracy, and up to the end of 1980s its authoritarian rule and monopoly of the polity derived from its revolutionary legitimacy. Soon after independence the provisional government was overthrown by Mr Ben Bella, who had the backing of the army. The authoritarian rule was even further strengthened by the rule of Mr Boumediene (1965–78), who concentrated on state-building through implementing an ambitious socio-economic development plan financed mainly by oil rents and foreign debt. Despite healthy economic growth and strong social development achieved during the Boumediene era, inefficient bureaucratic political and economic management and concentration on large-scale heavy industry created huge shortages in the consumer and housing markets, and there was an absence of civil liberties and political rights. Mr Bendjedid (1979–92) tried in the first half of the 1980s to reform the economy and to loosen the grip of the state. However the decline in the price of oil in 1986 and the worsening of the external debt ratio brought the economic machine to a halt. The incumbent regime was very slow to respond to the economic downturn due to the lack of consensus among the main factions of the regime as to which reforms to pursue. Popular discontent grew rapidly and reached its climax on 5 October 1988 when the mob took to the street and destroyed public property and attacked state symbols. The bloody events gave Mr Bendjedid the opportunity to abandon single-party rule and introduce multi-party politics in 1989, and to organize plural local elections in 1990 and parliamentary elections the following year. The success of the radical Islamists in these elections prompted the army to intervene to halt the political process in 1992. This decision triggered 10 years of civil conflict that resulted in a heavy human toll. Although the electoral process was resumed in 1995, it was carried out to the exclusion of the radical Islamists, and thus was by no means a free and competitive election. As to the recorded rise in the polity score for 2004, this was more a reflection of a formalistic than a substantive or free electoral process.

The sharp jumps in polity scores on these landmark dates render validation of the modernization theory, as far as Algeria is concerned, a difficult task. This theory predicts a smooth political transition, likely over a long period of time, as a result of economic development leading to a growing middle class and increased demand for freedom. The regression results carried out in this study show that the impact of economic development, as measured by GDP per capita on polity, was not very strong. The sluggishness of polity and its sharp jumps in a discontinuous manner reflect the fact that the incumbent elite have been very slow to respond to the pressures of democratization. The elite, in fact, established an 'authoritarian bargain' by which they trade off economic benefits for political and economic freedoms. When political events are modelled as dummy variables the explanatory power of the modernization model increases sharply, thereby giving some credence to the model that explains democratization by elite bargain. In this context it is argued that oil rent and internal conflict are the main drivers of this bargain, which ultimately corroborates the thesis developed by EMM in explaining the democracy deficit in the Arab world. However it also argued that the oil rent to be distributed is very small compared to the size of the population and, hence, the bargain is inherently unstable, and polity shifts positively when the oil price declines substantially. In this case it is found that internal conflicts increase sharply, causing the incumbent regime to reconfigure the authoritarian bargain. External conflict and the Arab–Israeli war contribute little to the survival of the incumbent regime. More importantly, it is found that a sharp increase in oil rents, as has happened since 2000, eases internal conflicts, but does not reverse the democratization process; rather it preserves the status quo.

Since the end of the 1980s Algeria has engaged in political reforms in a violent environment and with a very poor institutional setup. Both elements tend to weaken the prospects for further democratization, if not render it unsustainable. Although political violence and insurgency have more or less been brought under control, the quality of institutions remains low and hinders development. Indeed, the spectacular increase of oil rents and the ensuing reduction in the level of internal conflict in the past few years will enable the elite to strengthen the status quo authoritarian bargain by permitting them to alleviate the housing shortage and address the unemployment problem, along with other needs of the population at large. This trend conforms with the finding of the Economist Intelligence Unit (2008) based on their global democracy index for 2008, which observed that the world in undergoing a sort of 'democratic recession', where little progress in democratization has been made across countries. Given the comfortable economic position of Algeria today, if not reversed by the current global turmoil, with almost no external debt and very high foreign exchange reserves, little or no pressures from Western powers, and, more importantly, no willingness from the incumbent elite to push democratization forward, the democratic recession in Algeria may continue for a long time. The key to a substantive process of democratization in Algeria that could reverse this trend lies in disengaging the confrontational process between the elite and citizens. This would require making development work for democracy, mainly by reducing the impact of oil rents on the economy through a resumption of non-oil growth, and by building strong and trustworthy political and economic institutions in order to combat corruption and pacify the turbulent relation between the elite and the citizens. According to the regression models given in Table 7.5, future enhancements in human development would have little impact on democratization given the actual political configuration. Development for democracy will work only in the event of peaceful, fundamental political reforms.

Notes

1. Gastil Index (Freedom House) benchmarks Algeria as 'non free', with a score of +2 in the polity index (range –10 to +10). In the Economist Intelligence Unit democracy index for 2006 Algeria was considered as authoritarian regime and was ranked 132 out of 167.
2. The 2004 rise in the polity score is due to the holding of the presidential elections that year. They were not, however, truly competitive elections and the basic nature of the political regime, as later discussed, remained essentially the same.
3. Despite the fact that economic growth is not very high due to the resource curse, averaging only 3.11 per cent (0.5 per cent for GDP per capita) for the period 1965–2005, social development was more considerable in terms of education and literacy, health, urbanization and gender.
4. See also Clark, 2002: 22.
5. Economic development is the process of economic structural change from a poor, agrarian, rural-based economy to an industrial, urban-based economy, leading to an increase of GNP per capita.
6. Social development means the expansion of people's entitlements or command over goods and services. It implies the reduction of absolute poverty, unemployment and inequality, and improvement in social indicators such as rates of life expectancy, adult literacy and infant mortality.
7. Political development is the growth of political freedom and democratization.
8. Huntington (1991: 120), inspired by Schumpeter (1947), stated 'the central procedure of democracy is the selection of leaders through competitive elections of the people they govern'.
9. Both indices differ considerably in assessing democracy. For example the Gastil Index considers Algeria as authoritarian and non-democratic, and does not discount the political changes registered in Algeria. However Polity IV upgraded the Algerian score to +2 in 2004, thereby making it the most democratic Arabic country. This is equivalent to 3 points in the Gastil index. However the Gastil index equivalent to polity was –7 for 2006.
10. To illustrate, Campos (1994) found a positive correlation between democracy and development, Sirowy and Inkeles (1990) found a negative correlation, the study of Prezowski and Limongi (1993) was inconclusive, and Burkhart and Lewis-Beck (1994) found a casual relationship between development and democracy.
11. The Barro (1999) model forecasts a democracy level for Algeria one-third of a full democracy in 2000. This is of course very different from the reality, as the effective 2000 score was 6.
12. Descriptions of these hybrid regimes include, among others, semi-democracy, virtual democracy, semi-authoritarianism and electoral authoritarianism.
13. It is beyond the scope of this chapter to dwell on the political history of Algeria, but it should be mentioned that autocratic rule was apparent in the Ottoman rule of Algeria. For a succinct analysis of Algerian political history see e.g. Rudy 2005.
14. In 1976, Boumediene decided to set up the Popular National Assembly, the country's

Algeria: the 'authoritarian bargain' 223

unicameral legislature where members elected only FLN candidates by secret, direct and universal suffrage.
15 In March 1979, Bendjedid formed a new government that retained only four ministers (out of twenty-eight) from the previous government. Influential personalities in the Boumediene era were removed from the cabinet.
16 Immediately after starting to tackle economic reforms, Bendjedid was challenged by his former colleagues on the Council of the Revolution. They put pressure on him to liberalize the economy and to promote the private sector, and to strengthen the party by establishing its political control over the administrative apparatus of the state. To deal with the crisis, in June 1980 Bendjedid called for an extraordinary meeting of the congress of the FLN. He succeeded in persuading the delegates to revise the party statutes and get rid of most of his opponents. The party had, thus, acquired the upper hand in policy-making, while the local governor served as the executive authority. Bendjedid also induced the Central Committee to create a Discipline Commission that would discipline members who did not conform to party decisions. As its chairman, Bendjedid used this commission to dismiss his opponents from the party and send their files to the economic state tribunal (*Cours des Comptes*) which specialized in trying officials suspected of corruption.
17 However, most Algerian newspapers revealed that his partners in the leadership put pressure on him to dismiss his closest political and military adviser, General Mohamed Betchine.
18 Ibid.
19 These are: the FLN Party, for Nationalists; the RND party, or Democrats; the HAMAS party, for Islamists; and the Labor Party, for the left wing.
20 Algeria implemented three one-year Stand By Arrangements in 1989, 1991 and in 1994, as well as a three-year Extended Fund Facility in 1995.
21 Algeria concluded two rescheduling agreements with the Paris Club in 1994 and in 1995. The first treated US$5.3 billion, and the second rescheduled $7.3 billion. The spectacular increase in the oil price since 2000 permitted Algeria to negotiate a premature payment of the scheduled debt, thus reducing the total debt stock drastically from US$33 billion in 1995 to just $5.58 billion in 2006.
22 According to ONS (2006), the private sector share of GDP was 47 per cent in 2003, concentrated in agriculture (11.8 per cent), services (22.4 per cent) and light industries (35.3 per cent). The Gini Index of private sector sectoral output distribution was 0.75.
23 Gastil (G) index is equivalent to polity (P) according to the following formula $P = (40 - 10G)/3$
24 Life expectancy at birth increased from 47 years in 1962 to 58 years in 1978, and adult literacy increased from less than 17 per cent in 1962 to more than 30 per cent in 1978.
25 Population growth during this period averaged 3 per cent annually, while the urban population increased from 30 per cent in 1962 to more than 40 per cent of total population in 1978.
26 Income inequality, measured by Gini, deteriorated from 30.5 in 1966 to 34.3 in 1980. Poverty head count declined from 54 per cent in 1966 to 28 per cent (Laabas, 2001).
27 HDI was computed by the author according to UNDP methodology and data compiled from WDI (2007) and ONS (2005).
28 It is still not known whether the demonstrations represented genuine popular uprising, or if they were manipulated in order to settle scores within the ruling factions.
29 The exact reasons for legalizing the FIS have yet to be known.
30 An IMF Extended Fund Facility provided a sum of 2.2 billion SDR between May 1995 and 1998.

References

Acemoglu, D. and Robinson, J. (2006) *Economic Origins of Dictatorship and Democracy*, Cambridge: Cambridge University Press.
Ahdjoudj, A. (1992) *L'Algérie, Pouvoir et Société*, Algiers: Epigraphie.
Ali, A. (2006) 'State and Private Sector in Algeria: The Politics of Rent Seeking and Failed Development', *Journal of Third World Studies* (Spring) 23.
Bardhan, P. (2005) *Democracy and Development: A Complex Relationship*, Berkeley, CA: University of California.
Barro, R. (1996) 'Democracy and Growth', *Journal of Economic Growth* 1: 1–27.
—— (1999) 'Determinants of Democracy', *Journal of Political Economy* 107: 158–83.
Bendib, R. (2006) *L'état rentier en crise: éléments pour une économie politique de la transition en Algerie*, Algiers: Office des Publications Universitaire.
Bollen, A. (1983) 'World System Position, Dependency, and Democracy: The Cross-National Evidence', *American Sociological Review* 48: 468–79.
—— (1990) 'Political Democracy: Conceptual and Measurement Traps?', *Studies in Comparative International Development* 7–24.
Burkhart, R. and Lewis-Beck, M. (1994) 'Comparative Democracy: The Economic Development Thesis', *American Political Science Review* 88: 903–10.
Chenery, H. and Syrquin, B. (1975) *Patterns of Development, 1950–1970*, Oxford: Oxford University Press.
Clark, D. (2002) *Visions of Development: A Study of Human Values*, Cheltenham: Edward Elgar.
Dahl, R. (1989) *Democracy and its Critics*, New Haven, CT: Yale University Press.
Davis, E. and Yousif, B. (2008) 'Understanding the Iraq Autocracy: Oil and Conflict in a Historical and Sociopolitical Context', paper presented at dissemination conference, Institute of Financial Economics, American University of Beirut, 24–25 Oct.
Desai, M., Olofsgrd, A. and Tarik, Y. (2007) *The Logic of Authoritarian Bargains: A Test of a Structural Model*, Global Economy and Development Working Paper, 3, Washington, DC: Brookings Institution.
Duteil, M. (1991) ' l'avenir en cinq questions', *Le Point*, 981 (July): 21.
Economist Intelligence Unit (2008) *The Economist Intelligence Unit's Index of Democracy 2008*. Online at: http://a330.g.akamai.net/7/330/25828/20081021185552/graphics.eiu.com/PDF/Democracy%20Index%202008.pdf
Elbadawi, I. and Makdisi, S. (2007) 'Explaining the Democracy Deficit in the Arab World', *Quarterly Review of Economics and Finance* 46/5 (Feb.)
——, —— and Milante, G. (2006) 'Technical Note on Democracy and Development in the Arab World', unpublished manuscript.
——, —— and —— (2008) 'Explaining the Arab Democracy Deficit: The Role of Oil and Rents', paper presented at dissemination conference, Institute of Financial Economics, American University of Beirut, 24–25 Oct.
Entelis, J. (1986) *Algeria: The Revolution Institutionalized*, Boulder, CO: Westview Press.
Fraser Institute (2007) 'Economic Freedom of the World 2007 Annual Report', Economic Freedom Network, 2007, a Fraser Institute publication, Canada. Online at: www.freetheworld.com/2007/EFW2007BOOK2.pdf
Fukuyama, F. (1992) *The End of History and the Last Man*, London: Penguin.
Gastil, R. (2003) 'Freedom in the World', Gastil Index. Online at: www.freedomhouse.org
Geddes, B. (2000) 'Authoritarian Breakdown: Empirical Test of a Game Theoretic Argument', unpublished manuscript, University of California, Los Angeles, Department of Political Science.

—— (2004) 'Authoritarian Breakdown', Los Angeles: University of California Department of Political Science.
Glaeser, E. and Ponzetto, G. (2007) 'Why does Democracy Need Education', *Journal of Economic Growth* 12: 127–99.
Granger, C. (1988) 'Some Recent Developments in a Concept of Causality', *Journal of Econometrics* 39: 7–21.
Haroun, A. (2000) *L'été de la discorde: Algérie 1962*, Algiers: Casbah Edn.
Heritage Foundation (2007) 'Index of Economic Freedom 2007'. Online at: www.heritage.org
Hill, J. (2006) 'Identity and Instability in Post Colonial Algeria', *Journal of African Studies* 11/1: 1–16.
Huntington, S. (1968) *Political Order in Changing Societies*, New Haven, CT: Yale University Press.
—— (1991) *The Third Wave: Democratization in the Late Twentieth Century*, Norman, OK: University of Oklahoma Press.
Jackman, R. (1973) 'On the Relations of Economic Development to Democratic Performance', *American Journal of Political Science* 17: 611–21.
Jackman, R. and Miller, R. (1996) 'The Poverty of Political Culture', *American Journal of Political Science* 40: 607–716.
Kapil, A. (1991) 'Portrait statistique de élections du 12 Juin 1990', *Les Cahiers de l'Orient* 23: 45.
Kraska, J. (2005) 'International Law, Economic Development, and Democracy', *Whitehead Journal of Diplomacy and International Relations* 6/2: 73–88.
Laabas, B. (2001) 'Poverty Dynamics in Algeria', *Journal of Development and Economic Policies* 4/1: 43–99.
Leblang, D. (1997) 'Political Democracy and Economic Growth: Pooled Cross-Sectional and Time-Series Evidence', *British Journal of Political Science* 27: 453–66.
Levitsky, S. and Way, L. (2002) 'Elections without Democracy: The Rise of Competitive Authoritarism', *Journal of Democracy* 13/2 (April).
Lipset, S. (1959) 'Some Social Requisites of Democracy: Economic Development and Political Legitimacy', *American Political Science Review* 53: 69–105.
Lowi, R. (2004) 'Oil Rents and Political Breakdown in Patrimonial States: Algeria in Comparative Perspective', *Journal of North African Studies* 9/3: 83–102.
Maddy-Weitzman, B. (2006) 'Ethno-Politics and Globalization in North Africa: The Berber Culture Movement', *Journal of North African Studies* 11/1: 71–84.
Mortimer, R. (1991) 'Islam and Multi-Party Politic in Algeria', *Middle East Journal* 445/4: 69–70.
Nashashibi, K., Alonso-Gamo, P., Bazzoni, S., Feter, A., Laframboise, N., and Horvitz, S. (1998) *Algeria, Stabilization and Transition to the Market*, IMF Occasional Papers, 165, Washington, DC: International Monetary Fund.
Nellis, J. (1980) 'The Algerian Socialism and its Critics', *Canadian Journal of Political Science* 13/3 (Sept.): 491.
Office Nationale des Statistiques (ONS) (2005) *Retrospective Statistiques 1962–1991*, Algiers: Office Nationale des Statistiques.
—— (2006) *Rétrospective Statistiques 1970–2004*, Algiers: Office Nationale des Statistiques.
Paldam, M. (2005) 'The Big Pattern of Development: A study in the Gastil Index', Working Paper, School of Economics and Management, University of Aarhus, Denmark. Online at: www.artin.paldham.dk

Przeworski, A. and Limongi, F. (1993) 'Political Regimes and Economic Growth', *Journal of Economic Perspectives* 7/3.

Putnam, R. (1993) *Making Democracy Work: Civic Traditions in Modern Italy*, Princeton, NJ: Princeton University Press.

Quandt, R. (1998) *Between Riots and Bullets: Algeria's Transition from Authoritarianism*, Washington, DC: Brookings Institution.

Rice, T. and Ling, J. (2002) 'Democracy, Economic Wealth and Social Capital: Sorting out the Causal Connections', *Space and Polity* 6: 307–25.

Roberts, H. (2002) *Moral Economy or Moral Polity?: The Political Anthropology of Algerian Riots*, Working Paper, 17, London: Development Research Centre, London School of Economics and Political Science.

Robinson, J. (2006) 'Economic Development and Democracy', *Annual Review of Political Science* 9, June.

Rudy, J. (2005) *Modern Algeria: The Origins and Development of a Nation*, Bloomington, IN: Indiana University Press.

Schumpeter, J. (1947) *Capitalism, Socialism, and Democracy*, New York: Harper.

Sen, A. (1999) *Development as Freedom*, Oxford: Oxford University Press.

Sirowy, L., and Inkeles, A. (1990) 'The Effects of Democracy on Economic Growth and Inequality: A Review?', *Studies in Comparative International Development* 25: 126–57.

Snyder, D. and Kick, E. L. (1979) 'Structural Position in the World System and Economic Growth, 1955–70: A Multiple Network Analysis of Transnational Interactions', *American Journal of Sociology* 84: 1096–1126.

Testas, A. (2005) 'The Economic Costs of Transition to Democracy in the Maghrib: Quantitative Results for Algeria and Tunisia', *Journal of North African Studies* 10/1: 43–59.

Thieux, A. (2003) 'Political Standstill, Economic Dependence and Social Tension', *Papeles de Questiones Internacionales* 81, CIP-FUHEM (Spring). Online at: www.cipresearch.fuhem.es.

UNDP, HDI: http://hdr.undp.org/en/statistics/indices/hdi/

Van de Walle, N. and Butler, K. (1999) 'Political Parties and Party Systems in Africa's Illiberal Democracies', unpublished manuscript, Michigan State University.

Volpi, F. (2003) *Islam and Democracy: The Failure of Dialogue in Algeria*, London: Pluto Press.

—— (2006) 'Rethinking Models of Security and Cooperation between Europe and North Africa', UACES Workshop, Foresight Centre, University of Liverpool, 22 May.

World Bank, *World Development Indicators*: http://devdata.worldbank.org/dataonline/

World Bank (2007) *World Bank World Development Indicators*, Washington, DC: World Bank.

Zoubir, Y. (1996) 'Algerian Islamists' Conception of Democracy', *Arab Studies Quarterly* (Summer) 18/3.

8 Iraq: understanding autocracy
Oil and conflict in a historical and socio-political context

Bassam Yousif and Eric Davis

1. Introduction

This chapter examines the relationship between development and democracy in Iraq. We examine in particular the two variables that Elbadawi and Makdisi posit as critical in explaining the 'Arab democracy deficit'. The first variable emphasizes the pervasive impact of war and conflict in the Arab world as an impediment to democratic rule, while the second argues for the negative impact of oil wealth, understood as 'rentierism' (Elbadawi and Makdisi, 2007). Here, we survey and analyse trends in economic growth and development over the past half-century, and evaluate trends in democratization and political rights. We then assess the effects of oil, notably in relation to the theory of the rentier state, and the impact of war – especially the Iran–Iraq war (1980–8) and the Gulf war of 1991 – on democratization. If considered in isolation, oil and war possess only limited ability to explain why Iraq has not experienced greater democratization, so we attempt to expand the Elbadawi–Makdisi model. We conclude by offering a number of supplemental hypotheses, such as the manner in which the Iraqi nationalist movement of the pre-Ba'athist era and the political economy of identity have intersected with the two variables emphasized by the Elbadawi–Makdisi model. By placing the model in a larger context, we seek to enhance its ability to account for the lack of democratization in Iraq.

We frame our analysis of Iraq by posing two main questions. First, what is the relationship between economic growth and democracy? Is there a certain level of GDP that must be achieved before democratization can occur? Further, once a substantial level of economic growth has been achieved, does that promote the consolidation of democracy? Second, does democracy foster economic growth? Are technological innovation and entrepreneurship possible if subject to the whims of authoritarian rulers? Given that all economic activity entails a certain level of uncertainty, why would economic actors expose themselves to further risk if the 'rules of the game' are constantly subject to change?

Early social science literature asserted that there is a positive effect between economic growth and democracy. The classic 'Lipset hypothesis' (Lipset, 1959) states that there is a direct relationship between rise in GDP and democratic governance. In a more recent formulation, Przewroski *et al.* (2000) tested Lipset's hypothesis and discovered that nation-states that maintain a median annual income of at least US$5000 are likely to sustain democratic rule.

At the same time, observers have noted that a number of relatively poor nation-states below the threshold suggested by Pzreworski *et al.* have been able to meet the minimum requirements of democratic rule since the fall of communism. The abilities of states such as Mali, Ghana, Bolivia and others to pursue a democratic agenda challenges the hypothesis that democracy requires a certain level of economic prosperity before it can take hold.

Iraq challenges the Lipset model in a different respect. Between 1970 and 1980, Iraq achieved a very high level of economic growth and development through a twentyfold increase in oil revenues. By 1980, it had established the most advanced health care system in the Middle East, dramatically expanded the national education system, and electrified much of the rural sector. Nevertheless, there was an inverse correlation between economic growth and prosperity on the one hand, and democratic change on the other. As the 1970s progressed, political repression increased, especially after Saddam Husayn[1] ousted President Ahmad Hasan al-Bakr in August 1979 and asserted total control over the Ba'athist regime. Although economic growth continued through the early years of the Iran–Iraq war, we demonstrate here that the Iraqi economy actually contracted, even though there was continued improvement in some development outcomes – notably health and education – while political repression intensified as Saddam built what one Iraqi analyst has termed the 'family-party state' (*dawlat hizb al-usra*) (Abd al-Jabbar, 1995).

Clearly, the Iraqi experience does not substantiate the Lipset hypothesis. However, when discussing economic growth in Iraq, an important qualification needs to be made on the problematic nature of treating the concept in a one-dimensional manner. Economic growth and development have been almost entirely based on oil wealth, pointing to the rentier quality of the Iraqi economy. It is well known that rentierism has been associated with authoritarian rule. The basic hypothesis argues that the state's ability to derive rents from the sale of commodities in high demand allows it to circumvent the populace at large as a source of revenues, while likewise ignoring pressures for political reform and change.[2]

While the rentier state hypothesis may help explain the lack of democratic change during the 1970s, it raises more questions than it answers. First, oil was discovered in Iraq in the 1920s. Is it then possible to speak of Iraq as a rentier state prior to the 1970s? Second, how and when did the rentier state come into being, and what were the conditions that led to its decline? Third, which social and political elites controlled the rentier state? How were they able to acquire control of the state? Fourth, why have some rentier states, for example, the Arab Gulf oil producers, developed a more benign form of rule in contrast to the highly repressive quality of the Iraqi Ba'ath? Why have other nation-states that are major oil producers, such as the United States, Canada, Norway and the United Kingdom, not developed authoritarian rule? What explains the variation between oil wealth and forms of political rule?

One argument highlighting the need for a historical analysis suggests that a critical variable is the extent to which a particular society had already developed a functioning civil society, the rule of law, democratic institutions and diversified economies, prior to the discovery of oil. The United States, Canada, Norway and the United Kingdom were all well established democracies at the time when oil became a significant part of their respective economies. Thus 'history matters' when invoking the rentier hypothesis. In other words, the hypothesis has the potential to lose validity if divorced from the specific historical context of the nation-state to which it is applied.

Finally, rentierism has not always immunized the state from popular pressures, as the overthrow of the Pahlavi regime in neighbouring Iran demonstrates (Davis, 1991: 10, 13). It can also be argued that rentierism can undermine the state by creating an illusory sense of power, such as that which led Saddam Husayn's Ba'athist regime to initiate two devastating wars that ultimately led to its demise. Under what conditions does rentierism strengthen authoritarian rule, and under what conditions does it undermine it? In short, how do we avoid the static quality and a historical quality that is often inherent in the use of the concept of rentierism?

2. Democracy and economic growth in Iraq

When studying the relationship between democracy and development in Iraq, insights can be gained from the extensive literature that examines whether democracy (or authoritarianism) promotes or hinders development or economic growth.[3] Initial skepticism in development economics about whether developing countries could 'afford' democracy – often viewed as a costly luxury – has been replaced with the growing realization that there is little empirical evidence to suggest a robust relationship (either positive or negative) between forms of political rule and economic growth. In other words, the effect of democracy on growth in per capita income or development is contingent, weak or indeterminate.

Nevertheless, as suggested by the Lipset hypothesis, there is a statistically robust correlation between the existence of democracy and certain 'modernization' variables, such as per capita income, as well as education, health care and other indicators of development (Lipset, 1959). In particular, rising incomes per capita tend to generate increased demand for democratization and promote the development of civil society.[4] Although Elbadawi and Makdisi recognize that theorizing how precisely these indicators promote democracy is somewhat tenuous, they use the hypothesis as a platform for a thorough econometric study that explores the factors that account for the 'Arab democracy deficit' (Elbadawi, Makdisi and Milante, 2006). They conclude that oil and regional conflicts are the main explanatory factors for the lack of democratic governance in Arab countries.

3. Trends in economic growth and income distribution

Income per capita rose steadily in Iraq between 1950 and 1980, but declined thereafter. In fact, incomes collapsed (Yousif 2001, 2007) after the Gulf war of

1991 when economic sanctions limited the export of oil. The Oil for Food Program, starting in 1998, revived Iraqi exports and consequently improved incomes in the late 1990s. However, as we shall see, GDP statistics no doubt overstated the extent of the recovery of the late 1990s.

Although the time series of GDP estimates (in 1990 prices) are unavailable for the period before 1970, there is good reason to believe that incomes increased between 1950 and 1970. According to calculations made by K. G. Fenelon, per capita national income (in 1950 prices) increased from Iraq Dinar (ID) 32 in 1950 to ID 49 in 1956 (Central Statistical Organization, 1970: 17). Our own calculations indicate that per capita GDP (in 1975 prices) increased from ID 675 in 1960 to ID 885 in 1970 (Yousif, 2001:79).[5] Per capita GDP estimates are presented, along with estimates of oil output and value added in the oil sector, in Table 8.1,[6] and show that GDP per capita doubled between 1970 and 1980. However, with the onset of the Iran–Iraq war (1980–8), there was a sharp reduction in oil exports, which recovered only very slowly in a decade of declining oil prices. The result was declining per capita income after 1980.

The state attempted to insulate the public from the decline in incomes during the 1980s by the continued subsidization of food as well as education and health services, in part through massive borrowing (Yousif, 2001). Consequently, according to the UN,[7] household consumption continued to increase during the 1980s, while human development outcomes continued to expand (sometimes at an unreduced pace).

Table 8.1 Per capita GDP, oil output and value added in the oil sector

Year	GDP per capita, in constant (1990) US$	Oil output (million barrels/day)	Value added to oil sector, as percentage of value added in all economic activities
1950	n.a.	0.14	n.a.
1955	n.a.	0.07	n.a.
1960	n.a.	1.0	41
1965	n.a.	1.3	37
1970	898	1.5	32
1975	1161	2.3	50
1980	1749	2.6	61
1985	1152	1.4	24
1990	1244	2.1	15
1992	504	0.5	15
1995	532	0.7	15
1998	882	2.2	68
2000	998	2.8	83
2002	924	2.1	70
2003	501	1.4	68
2004	714	2.1	71

Sources: Oil output, OPEC (2006): 56. Per capita GDP and value-added estimates, calculated from United Nations, National Accounts Main Aggregates Database, and United Nations (1979): 448.

Yet the government was powerless to insulate the public from the collapse of incomes in the 1990s. The Gulf war in 1991 destroyed much of the economy's infrastructure, while economic sanctions prevented its reconstruction. The economic sanctions prohibited the export of oil, which paid for imports of food, medicine and capital equipment, and which financed most of the state's recurrent expenditures and almost all of its capital expenditures. Consequently, the state withdrew from providing many of the benefits to which Iraqis had become accustomed during the 1970s and early 1980s, concentrating only on those that it deemed essential for survival, such as the food rations programme.

The elevated estimates of per capita GDP in the late 1990s probably overstate the extent of economic recovery. Increased volumes of exported oil under the Oil for Food Program were registered to reflect expanded GDP, but this recovery did not signal a notably enhanced capacity to rebuild or expanded domestic expenditure. Under the programme, revenues generated from the sale of oil could not be spent domestically, while the UN Sanctions Committee tightly controlled imports. Fearing their use for military purposes, the Committee regularly interrupted imports of machinery. Thus, from the start of the programme until October 2000, 15 per cent or $2.4 billion of the requested imports were placed on hold (Cortright, Millar and Lopez, 2002: 205). As imports were often used in combination with each other, the effect of this delay was more serious than the numbers suggest. If the GDP estimates for the late 1990s are accurate, they nonetheless indicate that average living standards in 2000 had not recovered to the levels of 1990.

Even if correct, these estimates give an indication of average per capita income but may conceal deterioration in income distribution. That is, even if average incomes remain the same, the income of the average Iraqi may have declined if income distribution became more unequal. Income distribution improved until the 1970s but almost surely deteriorated thereafter, especially during the 1990s. Among the factors that account for the improvement in income equality before 1980 are: land reform, enacted shortly after the 1958 revolution that overthrew the monarchy, which redistributed land to the rural poor; and the expansion of the public sector, where wage and salary differentials were deliberately curtailed.

As a result, in 1971, the Gini coefficient of income inequality, reported in Table 8.2, was 0.36 for households (0.26 for individuals), when the data are adjusted to include in kind income. This level of income inequality compared favourably with those in many developing and some developed countries.[8] However, although the data are unavailable to support this contention, income distribution likely deteriorated in the 1990s. The incomes of the majority of the population, including those of Iraq's once large urban middle and working classes, were effectively destroyed by hyperinflation, which wiped out their savings. Skilled professionals were, for the most part, either reduced to penury or emigrated. Meanwhile, an emerging class of *nouveaux riches* – composed of Sunnis and Shi'a, Arabs as well as Kurds, with ties to the regime – benefited greatly from business activities that were legal and often illicit, particularly oil smuggling (Marr, 2000; Davis, 2007).

The picture of Iraqi development that emerges is one of improving levels

Table 8.2 Indicators of income inequality

Year		Ratio: bottom 40% to top 20%			Gini coefficient		
		Country	Urban	Rural	Country	Urban	Rural
1971	Households						
	Cash	15.9 : 47.1					
	Adjusted	18.3 : 44.1	17.7 : 44.6	19.4 : 42.2	0.36	0.37	0.34
	Individuals						
	Cash	20.8 : 40.7					
	Adjusted	23.9 : 37.3			0.26		
1975	Households						
	Adjusted				0.37	0.34	0.40

Sources: Issa (1979): 123–134; Hummadi (1978): 169.

and distribution of income until 1980 and, thereafter, deterioration. Incomes collapsed in the 1990s, ruining Iraq's once vibrant middle and professional classes, although incomes recovered somewhat later in the decade. Because income distributions deteriorated during the 1990s and GDP estimates likely overstate the level of income later in the decade, the average Iraqi's standard of living in 2000 is unlikely to have recovered to its 1970 level.

4. Trends in human development

The limited utility of per capita income as the main yardstick with which to measure development has been extensively discussed in the development literature.[9] Iraq presents yet another illustration of the lack of correspondence between the trends in per capita income and human development outcomes. These outcomes continued to expand despite the decline in per capita incomes during the 1980s, but were unable to withstand the economic collapse under sanctions. As shown in Table 8.3, child and infant mortality decreased rapidly from 1960 to 1990, as nutrition levels, expressed in caloric consumption, increased markedly. It may be that improvements in health outcomes would have been even more rapid were it not for the urban bias and emphasis on curative, rather than preventive medicine, which was historically prevalent (not only in Iraq but in most developing countries). It is notable that the advance during the 1980s occurred in the context of declining real expenditures by the government on health, necessitated by war austerity and facilitated by greater reliance on relatively cheap preventative techniques. For example, immunization rates for tuberculosis, diphtheria, polio and measles increased sharply during the 1980s.[10]

In the education sector, adult literacy rates rose gradually from 18 per cent in 1957 to 47 per cent in 1977, reaching 73 per cent in 1987. The latter jump was mostly the result of the state's adult literacy programme of the late 1970s (Yousif, 2001:129). Meanwhile, primary enrolment increased from 48 per cent in 1960, reaching near universal levels in the 1980s, and enrolment in secondary and higher education likewise increased (Yousif, 2001: 132–7). This was achieved largely

Table 8.3 Select human development indicators

Year	Daily caloric consumption in Kcal (provided by ration)	Registered births under 2.5 Kg (%)	Child mortality rates, per '000	
			Under five	Under one
1960	2012*	n.a.	171	117
1970	2256	n.a.	127	90
1980	2677	n.a.	83	63
1990	3150	4.5	50	40
1991	2310 (1300)	10.8		
1992	2270 (1770)	17.6		
1995	2268 (1093)	22.1	117	98
1996	2277 (1295)	22.6	126	97
1997	2463 (2030)	23.0		
1998			125	103
1999	(2150)		126	102
2002	(2215)		125	102

Sources: Garfield and Waldman (2003): 9, 17; Garfield (1999); Pellet (2000): 161; UNICEF; Yousif (2001): 179.

Note
* 1961–3 average.

through heavy state expenditure on education, which reflected the commitment of successive republican administrations to social justice and welfare. In real terms, state expenditures on education more than doubled between 1955 and 1959/60. Similarly, expenditures on education increased sharply during the 1970s and, much like other social expenditure, declined somewhat during the austerity of the 1980s.

The destruction of the nation's infrastructure and economic sanctions that were imposed after the 1990 invasion of Kuwait, in effect, until the beginning of the US occupation in 2003, reversed the trajectory of these achievements. The prohibition on oil exports generated a severe shortage of foreign exchange, which resulted in a sharp rise in the prices of imported commodities, including imported food and medicine, relative to domestic assets (Gazdar and Hussain, 2002). The state's rations programme probably averted a famine, but provided only a portion of caloric requirements. With much of the electricity generation capacity destroyed, water treatment and sanitation capabilities were degraded, resulting in the proliferation of water-borne diseases, to which children, especially malnourished infants, were vulnerable. As Table 8.3 shows, infant mortality more than doubled during the 1990s. According to an authoritative estimate, sanctions resulted in 227,000 extra deaths among children – that is, deaths which would not have occurred without sanctions – from August 1991 to March 1998.[11] This caused two UN humanitarian coordinators for Iraq to resign in protest at the continuance of this lethal regime of sanctions.[12]

While the Oil for Food Program, implemented in 1998, partly alleviated malnourishment – chronic malnutrition rates increased from 18.7 per cent in children under 5 years of age in 1991 to 32 per cent in 1996, but declined to 30 per cent in 2000 and to 20.1 per cent in 2002 – (Garfield and Waldman, 2003: 9–10), it was unable to reduce infant or child mortality. The Oil for Food Program was too small to allow meaningful rebuilding of the health and sanitation infrastructure, which had collapsed by the late 1990s. The Aga Khan's UN-commissioned report on Iraq's humanitarian needs in 1991 estimated that $6.8 billion per year was required to provide for a 'greatly reduced level of services' (Gazdar and Hussain, 2002). The Oil for Food Program provided for only a fraction of this requirement. Iraq's inability to import medical equipment and supplies, combined with the failure to retain vital staff such as physicians and nurses, many of whom emigrated, severely compromised the public health and sanitation systems. Diseases brought on by the consumption of contaminated food and water, and amplified by malnutrition, could neither be prevented nor cured.

5. Democratization, human rights and conflict

According to the modernization hypothesis the growth in income and enhanced human capabilities experienced in Iraq before 1980 would be expected to encourage democratization and the growth of civil society. In this section, we study whether this prediction materialized, as we evaluate the evolution of democratization and human rights in Iraq. In assessing democratization in the Arab world, Elbadawi, Makdisi and Milante (EMM) compare the actual polity score, an indicator of political democratization, for each Arab country with the country's polity score in the previous year, and the polity score that would be expected given the country's income and human development levels (i.e. modernization as described in EMM). Also, EMM compute a 'predicted polity without oil effects', which assumes oil exports to be zero, and a 'predicted polity without Arab war', which assumes there were no wars in the region (Elbadawi *et al.*, 2006). The results

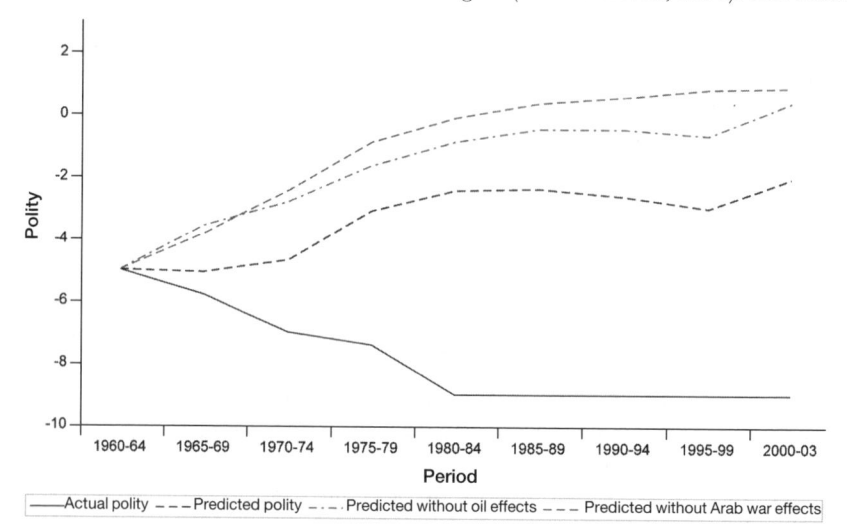

Figure 8.1 Actual and predicted levels of democratization in Iraq.

Source: Elbadawi, Makdisi and Milante, 2006.

for Iraq are shown in Figure 8.1 and indicate that, as with other Arab countries, Iraq's polity score is below what one would expect given the country's levels of income and human development. According the model, in a world without oil or regional wars, Iraq's polity scores would be higher still.

EMM do not discuss in detail the theoretical mechanism(s) through which oil and war stifle democratization. There is, however, a large body of literature on the rentier state to support their conclusions. According to Beblawi, the rentier state is characterized by a small minority of the population generating wealth, while the majority is engaged in its distribution, and where economic rents accrue largely to the state (Beblawi, 1987: 85–98). As these rents substitute for taxation in government finance, governments are released from accountability, so much so that the state may become independent of society (Anderson, 1987). Similarly, Luciani argues that the lack of taxation hinders the development of solidarities along economic lines (Luciani, 1990). Economic rents also augment the state's capacity to co-opt and/or repress political opponents (Wiktorowicz, 1999). Thus, whichever version of rentierism one finds convincing, the consensus is that natural resource rents have a negative influence on democratization.

6. The Humana Index

This discussion of rentierism raises questions on how democratization, freedoms and rights have evolved in Iraq and what insights the study of these factors reveals about the impact of oil and wars. In this regard, we are interested in assessing the process of democratization through a study of the expansion of freedoms and rights, rather than through a focus on political parties and regular elections. To track the evolution of these rights and freedoms, we apply the Humana Index (Humana, 1986), an index of human rights, political freedom and governance, to three points in Iraq's history: the monarchy, from 1947 to 1948; the 'Abd al-Karim Qasim government between 1958 and 1960; and the Ba'athist regime during the first part of the 1980s. This choice of periods is not arbitrary, but represents difficult periods for the regimes in question, thus facilitating a comparison across time. The period 1947–8 was a time of domestic agitation against the proposed Portsmouth treaty with Britain, and in 1958–63 the Qasim regime was under attack from its Arab nationalist and conservative opponents. In the early to mid-1980s, the Ba'ath regime was engaged in a costly and unpopular war with Iran, which forced it to implement cutbacks in its capital and social spending.

Another advantage of choosing these three periods is that information about rights and freedoms is relatively abundant. The index is calculated from responses to 40 questions related to freedoms, rights and governance, with the scores for each period.[13] The first six questions are rights or freedoms pertaining to freedom of movement and the flow of information. The next 12 questions are concerned with the extent of the state's use of various forms of coercion. Ten questions attempt to capture the rights or freedoms of political opposition as well as the extent to which various rights are available to women and minorities. Seven questions address the extent to which basic juridical rights are respected. The last five questions examine the extent to which one may exercise personal freedoms that may run counter to the values of society as a whole. Some of these questions are not utilized in the application of this index to Iraq. Eight rights[14] are excluded because there is too little information for a comparison through time. Rights concerning the position of women[15] are excluded from this index, because a discussion of these rights warrants a separate, detailed study. However, a correction to the possible distortion that this exclusion creates is made below. In total, 11 rights or freedoms are excluded from the calculation of the Humana Index as it applies to Iraq.

Arguably, not all the freedoms or rights in the Humana Index are equally important. For this reason, the Humana Index gives greater weight to certain rights, corresponding to questions 7 to 13 in the index. 'Freedom from': serfdom, slavery or child labour; extra-judicial killings or disappearances; torture or coercion by the state; compulsory work or conscription of labour; capital punishment by the state; indefinite detention without charge; and court sentences of corporal punishment are given three times the weight.[16] Four possible scores are possible for each question, with a maximum of 3 and minimum of 0. The scores for questions 7 to 13 in the index are multiplied by three to reflect the greater weight attached to the rights that correspond to these questions, therefore the maximum score that a single one of these weighted questions is able to receive is 9 (3 × 3). Since there are six weighted questions (one weighted question is excluded from the index because of lack of information), the maximum number of points possible from the weighted questions is 54 (9 × 6). The 23 remaining questions each receive a maximum of three points. Thus, the maximum number of points possible from these non-weighted questions is 69 (3 × 23), and the maximum attainable score is 123.

The results of the Humana Index, computed by dividing the total score received by the maximum possible score, are presented in Table 8.4. This table indicates that rights and freedoms were upheld most under the Qasim regime between 1958 and 1960, less so under the monarchy in 1947–8, and least under the Ba'athist regime in the early 1980s. The overall scores of this index, which excludes the questions concerning the rights of women and those questions for

Table 8.4 Results of the application to Iraq of the Humana Index (score, %)

Category	1947–1948	1958–1960	Early to mid-1980s
All included questions	45	53	14
Weighted rights (Questions 7 to 13)	33	44	17
Rights of movement and information (Questions 1 to 6)	67	73	20
Freedom from coercion (Questions 7 to 18)	38	46	20
Freedom of opposition (Questions 19 to 28	42	54	0
Juridical rights (Questions 29 to 35)	33	33	0
Personal rights (Questions 36 to 40)	50	50	50

which information is lacking, were found to be 45 per cent, 53 per cent and 14 per cent for the periods 1947–8, 1958–60 and the early to mid-1980s, respectively.

With one exception the pattern of the scores given above is the same in each category. For example, for the weighted questions, the results are 33 per cent, 44 per cent and 17 per cent for the noted periods, and for the questions about the freedom of opposition, the results are 42 per cent, 54 per cent and 0 per cent respectively. Only the results of the questions concerning personal rights deviate from this pattern, at 50 per cent for each of the periods. In this category only two rights were examined, as other rights were excluded for lack of information. The results may be biased, as they exclude the rights or freedoms of women and those rights about which not enough is known. Further, one might argue that the low overall score for the early 1980s can be explained by the ongoing Iran–Iraq war, because governments are often forced to restrict liberties or violate rights in time of conflict. If so, the score for this period will be biased downward compared to the periods 1947–8 and 1958–60, when the country was at peace.

We attempt to correct for these possible biases. First, the exclusion of rights, about which not enough is known, is unlikely to bias downward the overall score for 1982. Table 8.5 shows the questions omitted for lack of information, along with the score received for each period. Six of the eight questions omitted for this reason receive a score of 0 for the early 1980s; no information at all is available regarding the last question. It is therefore unlikely that these omitted questions introduced a downward bias to the score for the last period. Only on one omitted question (namely the freedom to use contraceptive pills or devices) does the early 1980s score the maximum three points. This may cause a slight downward bias in the overall score for this period, but is corrected in the table.

Second, to correct for bias, the three questions regarding the status of women and the question concerning the freedom to use contraceptive pills and devices will each be given the maximum score of three for the last period and the minimum score of 0 for the two other periods of 1947–8 and 1958–60. Of course, these freedoms and rights existed to some extent in the earlier periods but we assume nonetheless that they were absent. We do this to remove the possibility of

Table 8.5 Score for questions omitted for lack of information

Question	1947–1948	1958–1960	Early to mid-1980s
5. Monitor human rights violations	n.a.	n.a.	0
13. Court sentences of corporal punishment	n.a.	n.a.	0
26. Independent radio and television networks	n.a.	n.a.	0
31. Free legal aid and counsel of own choice	n.a.	n.a.	0
34. Freedom from police searches of home without warrant	n.a.	n.a.	0
35. Freedom from arbitrary seizure of personal property	n.a.	n.a.	0
39. Freedom to use contraceptive pills or devices	n.a.	n.a.	3
40. Freedom to practise homosexuality	n.a.	n.a.	n.a.

a bias against the score for the last period, although this modification will likely create a bias in the other direction, against the scores for the earlier periods.

Third, modifications that correct for the Iran–Iraq war during the early to middle 1980s period are also made. The modification envisioned here is to examine the 29 rights in August 1980, one month before the outbreak of war with Iran. Only three rights are affected: the rights to travel inside one's own country, the right to travel outside the country and freedom from compulsory work or conscription of labour. Only a few rights are affected because the policies that are typically enforced under war conditions, such as press censorship, were already in practice in Iraq by 1980.

Although travel inside Iraq in 1980 was generally unrestricted, travel outside the country, while restricted, was not banned until 1982. Travel abroad was generally restricted to two trips per year, except for some persons in the armed forces and security services for whom travel was prohibited. Exit visas were required for those who travelled outside the country. Further, while there was no compulsory conscription of labour in 1980 as there was later, it was difficult for government employees (who formed a large part of the labour force) to leave their jobs, because the required official approval was not easily obtained. Therefore the questions regarding these rights, namely the right to travel in one's own country, to travel outside one's country and freedom from compulsory work or conscription of labour will receive scores of 3, 2 and 2, respectively, for 1980 instead of the scores corresponding to the early to middle 1980s.

Finally, there are rights that the Humana Index does not consider, at least two of which are relevant to Iraq. These include the freedom from collective punishment, and the intensity of the use of the death penalty – not merely if it exists or not. In general, freedom from collective punishment was respected under the monarchy and the Qasim government, but was violated under the Ba'athist regime. Moreover if, as the Humana Index assumes, capital punishment is a violation of rights (namely the right to life), then the more frequent its application, the greater the violation of rights. The death penalty was in existence in all periods under question, but both the number of capital offences and the intensity of their application increased dramatically beginning in the late 1970s (Yousif, 2001). Accordingly, freedom from collective punishment will receive scores of 3, 3 and 0 for the periods 1947-8, 1958-60 and the early to mid-1980s respectively, while the intensity of use of the death penalty will receive scores of 2, 2 and 0 respectively. These rights will receive the normal weight, and will be evaluated in addition to the existing 29 rights, not replacing any existing questions in the index. There will thus be a weighted question regarding the existence of the death penalty and another non-weighted question regarding the frequency of its application. The modifications are summarized in Table 8.6.

These modifications have a limited impact on the results, as shown in Table 8.7. Modification 1, concerning the rights of women, yields the following results: 41, 48 and 21 per cent for the periods 1947–8, 1958–60 and the early to mid-1980s. The second modification to the index, regarding the conditions of war, yields the following overall results: 45, 53 and 20 per cent, respectively. When

Table 8.6 Proposed modifications to the Humana Index

Question	1947–1948	1958–1960	Early to mid-1980s	1980
Modification 1				
21. Political and legal equality for women	0	0	3	
22. Social and economic equality for women	0	0	3	
37. Equality of sexes during marriage and in divorce	0	0	3	
39. Use of contraceptives	0	0	3	
Modification 2				
1. Travel in own country	2	3	1	3
2. Travel outside the country	3	3	0	2
10. Compulsory work or conscription of labour	2	3	1	2
Modification 3				
Freedom from collective punishment	3	3	0	
The intensity of use of death penalty	2	2	0	

Table 8.7 Results of the modifications made to the Humana Index (overall score, %)

Modification	1947–1948	1958–1960	Early to mid-1980s	1980
Modification 1 only	41	48	21	
Modification 2 only	45	53		20
Modification 1 and 2	41	48		27
Modification 3	47	54	13	
Upper limit range	47	54		27
Lower limit range	41	48	13	

both of these modifications are taken together, the results are as follows: 41, 48 and 27 per cent, respectively. The two modifications together provide an upper estimate for the last period, early to mid-1980s, and a lower estimate for the periods 1947–8 and 1958–60. The third modification, regarding freedom from collective punishment and the intensity of use of the death penalty, yields: 47, 54 and 13 per cent, respectively. The results of this modification provide the upper limit for the periods 1947–8 and 1959–60 and the lower limit for the period early to mid-1980s.

These results are robust in relation to the three introduced modifications. Whichever modifications or combination of modifications are performed, the results indicate that political freedom and rights were best under the Qasim regime, less so during the monarchy and worst under the Ba'ath. The application of these modifications to the index yields an upper limit score of 27 per cent and lower limit score of 13 per cent for the last period under examination. This is consistent with the Humana Index's overall score of 19 per cent for Iraq in 1986 (Humana, 1986: 132). These results are thus plausible.

Before proceeding to explore the implications of these findings on the effects of oil and regional wars, two points are worth mentioning. First, as noted earlier, economic growth between 1950 and 1980, and markedly improved human capabilities (evident until 1990), are associated with lower rather than higher levels of democratization. This failure to conform to the Lipset hypothesis is not unique to Iraq and is found in other Arab countries as well (EMM, 2006).

Second, the highest Humana Index was achieved during the Qasim period, when the country was under military dictatorship. National elections were not held and political parties were banned under Qasim. However, the regime promoted a form of social democracy where the state pursued policies designed to better meet the needs of the populace, especially the poor, and promoted anti-sectarianism, both of which are critical to building a foundation for democracy. The experience of the Qasim government illustrates how, even under autocratic governments, policies may be implemented that establish at least the necessary conditions for a transition to democracy. In short, formal democracy is neither necessary nor sufficient to promote the process of democratization, that is, the expansion of liberal freedoms and rights. According to Sami Zubaida (2005), the expansion of these rights and freedoms is arguably an essential ingredient for the growth of civil society, itself necessary for the establishment of democracy. Indeed, Zubaida's claim that civil society in Iraq was most vibrant under Qasim supports our findings.

7. Oil effects

We now explore the question of whether oil accounts for the deteriorating levels of democratization and political rights in Iraq. As noted, one variant of rentierism suggests that the state's financial independence shields it from accountability, while another emphasizes the enhanced ability to bribe or repress opponents. This consideration raises the question of whether either of these aspects account for the low level of democratization in Iraq.

As a proportion of total revenue, oil revenue rose sharply after 1950. As Table 8.1 indicates, there was a sharp rise in oil output in the early 1950s. This was accompanied by a series of negotiations between the oil companies and the Iraqi government, culminating in a more favourable agreement in 1952, whereby the state received 50 per cent of the oil companies' profits annually, as well as other advantages (Alnasrawi, 1994).[17] As a result, oil revenues exploded, and the proportion of state revenue from oil increased from 11 per cent in the period 1946–50 to 54 per cent in 1951–5 (Batatu, 1978: 106–7), and remained high thereafter. Indeed, so large was the expansion in revenue that in 1950 an independent Development Board was established to invest the revenues derived from oil. When first established, the Board was empowered to invest the entire portion of oil revenues. This control over revenues was later reduced to 70 per cent in the mid-1950s and further still to 50 per cent in the late 1950s, the remaining funds being diverted to the government's recurrent expenditures. In time, oil came to pay for most of the current and almost all capital expenditures. At first glance, the general tendency for the period after the mid-1950s is one of elevated oil revenues as a proportion of all revenues – and hence the increased financial independence and enhanced ability to bribe or repress – which appears to be correlated with reduced democratization outcomes. Within the period, one can point to the oil price rise of the 1970s to claim a relationship vis-à-vis the growing political monopoly of the Ba'ath.

However, the overall correlation of higher oil revenues and increased political repression hides significant anomalies. First, neither variant of rentierism is able to explain why democratization, as expressed in the Humana Index, was higher in the late 1950s under Qasim than under the monarchy in 1947–8, even though Qasim had access to significant oil revenues which the monarchy in the late 1940s did not. Second, if one instead suggests that the proper comparison is between Qasim and an oil-revenue rich monarchy that was arguably more repressive after 1954 than 1947, the puzzle remains: Qasim's government, which could use 50 per cent as opposed to only 30 per cent of oil revenues to avoid accountability and engage in repression, was significantly less repressive than the monarchy of, say, 1955. Third, it is also unclear why, when Iraq was unable to export oil in the early 1990s, its polity scores remained low and unchanged. The simplistic attribution of Ba'athist political monopoly to increased oil revenues has to be balanced against the many other instances when the theory of rentierism cannot explain impediments to trends in democratization. This inconsistency, of course, does not disprove the rentier state hypotheses, but does suggest that rentierism's ability to explain the lack of democratization with reference to oil is limited and highly contextual.

8. The effects of war and conflict

We next discuss the effects of war on trends in democratization. Since the Iran–Iraq war is by far the longest and costliest (both in human and monetary terms) war that Iraq has experienced, we should see evidence of its effects on democracy, if regional war is to have the explanatory impact as argued by the Elbadawi–Makdisi model. However, the results of the Humana Index do not support the existence of a relationship (in either direction) between the Iran–Iraq war and democratization outcomes. There is no significant change in freedoms, rights and governance between the period from the eve of the outbreak of the war and the early to mid-1980s. This lack of political change can be explained by the Ba'athist regime's absolute monopolization of power by 1980, suggesting again the need for a historical contextualization of the 'regional war' hypothesis. All political opposition had been violently eliminated by the late 1970s, and the regime had attained complete control of the mass media.

The findings of the Humana Index do not support Workman's (1994) thesis that the Ba'athist regime used the war with Iran to consolidate its power and widen its social base. Workman claimed that the war provided the regime with a 'blanket pretext to do whatever was necessary to contain its opponents', and thus strengthen its own political position (Workman, 1994: 157). In contrast, our results indicate that the regime had already accomplished what was necessary to strengthen its position in relation to opposition forces. Indeed, the last real challenge to the Ba'ath's authority had occurred in 1973 when the then director of intelligence, Nazim al-Kazzar, attempted a coup d'état (Davis, 2005a: 149, 177; 2005b: 229–44). Responses to only three questions in the index changed for 1980 as compared to the early to mid-1980s, none of which concerned the rights of opposition. On each of the questions concerning the rights of political opposition, the Ba'athist regime scored a zero in both periods. That is, the Ba'ath did not need to start a war to crush its opposition, as it had already done so before the onset of the Iran–Iraq war.

9. Modifying the rentier state thesis and regional war hypotheses

Returning to the issues raised at the beginning of this chapter, we now look at what questions remain once 'rentierism' and 'regional war' are invoked as key explanatory variables for the lack of democratization in Iraq. We argue that both rentierism and regional war need to be conceptually broadened to incorporate a more dynamic and historical approach. Otherwise, both variables assume a static quality that undermines their explanatory capacity. We also argue for the need to avoid an economistic understanding of rentierism, namely, limiting its explanatory impact to a narrow economic focus.[18]

First, if rentierism was key to the expansion of the Ba'athist power during the 1970s, why did rentierism fail to protect the Hashimite monarchy from being overthrown in 1958? Oil revenues increased substantially after the Iraqi Petroleum Company and the monarchy revised their royalty agreement in 1952. While standards of living in Iraq improved after the restructuring of the royalties received by the Iraqi government, the monarchy was unable to translate its increased wealth into political power and influence (Batatu, 1978: 352–3). The key variable here, we would argue, was not the impact of oil wealth, but the manner in which the Iraqi nationalist movement had been able to undermine the legitimacy of the Hashimite monarchy prior to 1952. Nationalist agitation had been so vigorous that, even with substantial additional revenues at its disposal, the monarchy was unable to maintain its hold on political power.

This analysis suggests that the notion of rentierism needs to be historically contextualized. By the 1950s, the Hashimites, especially the Regent and later Crown Prince, 'Abd al-Ilah, as well as the regime's strongman and perennial prime minister, Nuri al-Sa'id, had become so unpopular due to their being viewed as Great Britain's handmaidens in Iraq that no social or political forces could have reversed the monarchy's lack of legitimacy. Throughout the monarchical period, the Hashimites made little effort to institutionalize their rule. Even the most powerful state institution – the army – was humiliated by a reduction in its size by the British, with the complicity of the monarchy, following the abortive May 1941 uprising.

The constant manipulation of electoral results from the 1920s onwards meant that the Iraqi parliament was viewed by the populace as an institution designed to enhance the fortunes of rapacious elites, namely the 'merchants of politics' (*tujjar al-siyasa*). Only the judiciary, which could trace its origins to the Baghdad College of Law, founded in 1908, maintained any degree of institutional legitimacy (Davis, 2005a: 117). While Faysal I (1920–33) had attempted to implement some development measures, especially in the area of education, subsequent rulers, whether his son Ghazi I (1933–9) or the Regent and, after 1953, Crown Prince, 'Abd al-Ilah (1939–58), were not only ineffectual in implementing any significant development projects, but highly repressive towards nationalist demands for social and political reforms (Davis, 2005a: 100–5).

The Iraqi case demonstrates that economic variables considered in isolation cannot explain whether political power is used in an effective manner. This suggests a need to distinguish between the necessary and sufficient conditions for rentierism to 'immunize' the state from mass-based social and political pressures. These considerations on the impact of rentierism require an assessment of the impact of the Iraqi nationalist movement on political and economic developments in Iraq prior to the movement's suppression by the first Ba'athist regime, which seized power in February 1963. Such an assessment suggests the need for a more dialectical understanding of state–society relations, rather than a 'top–down' approach, when analysing rentierism's impact.

In our efforts to expand the rentier state thesis, we argue that it represents a second order level of causality. Put differently, there is a need to understand the conditions that allowed rentierism to become a salient component of the Iraqi political equation in the first place. Unless we return to the collapse of the Ottoman Empire in 1918, we cannot put rentierism in a larger social and political context. The key factor is the *path-dependent* quality of domination of the state by a minority of the Iraqi population – namely members of Iraq's Sunni Arab community – and the implications that this path dependence had for economic, social and political development in Iraq.

The Ottomans favoured their co-confessionalists among the Sunni Arab community throughout their rule of the three provinces, Mosul, Baghdad and Basra, that would form the modern Iraqi state in 1921. While Ottoman officials controlled the pinnacles of the state, the lower echelon positions in the bureaucracy, namely the military and police, were primarily distributed to Sunni Arabs. Although some Kurds entered the army, the majority Shi'i population was largely excluded from government employment. It is true that significant commercial interaction between the Sunni and Shi'i Arab communities and the Kurds can be traced back at least to the sixteenth century, but the political exclusion of Iraq's Shi'a and Kurdish populations undermined trust between the three dominant ethnic communities.[19] This lack of trust was underscored by the Shi'i clergy who cautioned young Shi'is against enrolling in state-sponsored schools, fearing their contact with Sunni doctrine (Batatu 1978: 17).

The nationalist movement's importance arises within the context of its efforts to forge a cross-ethnic alliance to bring about economic and political development, which had already begun prior to the First World War. The efforts of the Committee on Union and Progress (CUP), which seized power in Istanbul during the so-called Young Turk Revolt of 1908, to 'Turkify' the Ottoman Empire, fostered a negative reaction on the part of the Empire's Arab subjects. This was particularly true in Iraq, where the CUP tried to abort a fledgling Arabic-language education system and replace it with schools using Turkish-language instruction. One of the first significant activities of the nationalist movement prior to the First World War was the efforts of a committee of Sunni and Shi'i notables to establish an Arabic-language education system that would provide the necessary administrative personnel to facilitate Iraq's economic development.[20]

Efforts at cross-ethnic cooperation continued during the First World War, when Shi'i clerics issued religious decrees (*fatwa*; pl. *fatawa*) against the British invasion of Iraq in 1914. What was highly significant was that the clergy defended not just Iraq's Shi'a population, but all of Iraq's ethnic groups, irrespective of religion. The *fatawa* were likewise significant because the clerics viewed themselves as defending a modern nation-state, with defined geographical borders, rather than an abstract and territorially ambiguous Islamic community (*umma Islamiya*). The ecumenical tendency of the emerging Iraqi nationalist movement crystallized in the rising opposition to the British occupation administration, which had promised independence for Iraq when British forces first arrived in Baghdad in March 1917. Iraqi nationalists used peaceful methods as delegations of Iraqi notables tried to convince the British to live up to their promises.

Instead, Great Britain sought and obtained a mandate from the newly established League of Nations, legalizing its rule over Iraq until 1932. The Iraqi populace saw this development as a betrayal of British promises, leading to one of the seminal events of modern Iraqi history, the 1920 June–October Revolt. While some rural tribes tried to exploit the uprising for particular gains, urban nationalists emphasized social and political solidarity. Sunnis and Shi'is prayed in each other's mosques, celebrated their respective religious holidays and rituals, and urged Jews (the largest ethnic group in Baghdad in 1920) and Christians to join the revolt because they were fully equal Iraqi citizens (Davis, 2005c: 47; Batatu, 1978: 23). The 1920 Revolt laid the basis for the subsequent Iraqi nationalist movement that would be characterized by: anti-sectarianism; extensive associational behavior in the form of professional syndicates, labour unions, artists' groups and student and women's organizations; a vigorous and democratically oriented press; and innovative artistic expression that encouraged Iraqis to have pride in their multiple cultural heritages and to challenge political authority (Davis, 2005c: 55–7).

The 1920 Revolt was vigorously suppressed by the British. Great Britain's refusal to seriously consider Iraqi demands for an independent and democratic polity thwarted the possibility of establishing Iraq as a multi-ethnic polity. Instead, British colonial rule helped enshrine sectarian politics at the state level by forcing into exile many of the Shi'i clerics who had demanded independence from British colonial control. The creation of the Hashimite monarchy, through a rigged referendum in August 1921, placed the son of the Sharif of Mecca, Faysal bin Husayn, on the new Iraqi throne, and was buttressed by a Sunni political elite drawn from Faysal's army officers, known as the Sharifians, recruited during the Arab Revolt against the Ottomans. The Sharifians, who were epitomized by Nuri al-Sa'id Pasha, would control the state until the 14 July 1958 Revolution.

Space does not allow for a comprehensive discussion of the Iraqi national movement. Suffice it to say that the movement was dominated by a cross-ethnic alliance that sought to implement democratic and social reforms. The 'Iraqist' or local nationalist wing of the movement was opposed by a smaller pan-Arabist group that was largely limited to the officer corps and the small proto-fascist al-Muthanna organization and its armed wing, the al-Futuwwa, that developed during the 1930s and was largely limited to Baghdad.[21] The pan-Arabists lost much of their strength in the army after the abortive May 1941 uprising, which led to a brief month-long war between British and Iraqi forces. The size of the army was reduced by the Hashimites at the behest of the British, and many officers were forced into retirement. However, Iraqi strongman Nuri al-Sa'id's skilful manipulation of the Arab–Israeli crisis, following the United Nations partition resolution in November 1947, and the 1948 Arab–Israeli war, dealt a serious blow to the nationalist movement, which contained significant numbers of Iraqi Jews. The Iraqi government accused the nationalist movement of being sympathetic to Zionism and, because one of the major parties in the coalition was the Iraqi Communist Party, of representing a Soviet Fifth Column in Iraq.

Despite the influx of oil revenues, the nationalist movement continued to pressure the Iraqi government throughout the early and mid-1950s to make concessions that would result in freedom to organize political parties, publish newspapers without censorship, allow unfettered participation in free elections and guarantee Iraqi workers the right to organize and receive a minimum wage and proper working conditions.[22] As the influence of the officer corps had been reduced, the banner of pan-Arabism shifted to the Arab Socialist Ba'ath Party, which was founded in Iraq in 1952. Initially led between 1952 and 1961 by a cadre of Shi'i activists under Fu'ad al-Rikabi, the Ba'ath Party cooperated with Iraqist nationalists for a brief period between 1955 and 1958.

However, the July 1958 Revolution brought the sharp cleavage between the cross-ethnic majority wing of the Iraqi nationalist movement and the pan-Arabists to the forefront. General 'Abd al-Karim Qasim had been chosen to lead the revolution due to the respect he had earned during the Iraqi army's campaign in Palestine in 1948. Pan-Arabists were deeply angered when Qasim refused to opt for immediate unity (*al-wahda al-fawriya*) with the United Arab Republic formed by Egypt and Syria earlier in 1958. Qasim instead allied himself with the Iraqist wing of the nationalist movement, especially the powerful Iraqi Communist Party (ICP). When the ICP became too powerful in 1959, Qasim moved to create an alliance with the pan-Arabists. His effort to rule through balancing Iraqist and pan-Arabist nationalists satisfied no one and ultimately weakened his power base. His invasion of Iraqi Kurdistan in 1961 to suppress the forces of Mulla Mustafa Barzani undermined his support still further, as the Iraqi army became bogged down in a highly unpopular war it could not win. Allied with Barzani, and with purported help from the CIA, the Ba'ath Party was able to overthrow Qasim in February 1963.[23]

Between 1963 and the second Ba'athist coup of July 1968, Iraq experienced a series of weak governments and political instability. Anger at the Iraqi army's poor performance in the June 1967 Arab–Israeli war facilitated the bloodless seizure of power by an alliance of Ba'athists, led by General Ahmad Hasan al-Bakr and the young Vice-Secretary of the Ba'ath Party, Saddam Husayn al-Takriti, in coalition with Nasirist forces. The Takriti Ba'athist regime followed a path similar to previous republican regimes in that it was characterized by extensive infighting and instability until 1973. Clearly, the massive influx of oil wealth, and Saddam Husayn's shrewd policy of staffing the regime's extensive security apparatus with family and tribal loyalists, were key factors that allowed the regime to stabilize its rule by the mid-1970s.

What does rentierism tell us about the political power of the Takriti Ba'ath? In certain respects, it explains much about Iraq's lack of progress towards democratization, but from other vantage points it explains very little, unless situated in a broader context. First, the Qasim regime, like the Ba'ath, had the benefit of oil revenues, even if these declined somewhat during the early 1960s. Nevertheless, it was unable to translate oil wealth into sustained political power. Second, Qasim was undermined by his concerted effort to break with the path-dependent quality of Sunni Arab domination of the state. Indeed, Qasim is the only modern Iraqi leader to have eschewed sectarian criteria in the recruitment of officials to positions within the state apparatus. While the Takriti Ba'ath placed individual Shi'is in some high positions, for example, Nazim al-Kazzar, Sa'dun Hammadi and Na'im Haddad, these officials always remained outside the 'family-party state' that Saddam Husayn gradually established throughout the 1970s and then consolidated after he seized power from Ahmad Hasan al-Bakr in 1979. Following the 1991 Gulf war and subsequent intifada, Saddam's regime became avowedly sectarian.

Third, what we may call 'successful rentierism' only existed in Iraq for a relatively short period of time. The regime was only able to consolidate its power after the unsuccessful 1973 coup attempt by security chief, Nazim al-Kazzar. However, it subsequently undermined its power through the ill-fated invasion of Iran in September 1980. By 1982, the war had turned against Iraq, which saw its oil exports and revenues plummet, requiring it to turn to its erstwhile nemeses, Saudi Arabia and Kuwait, for loans to sustain the war effort. In other words, the Ba'athist regime was only able to use oil revenues to establish stable rule for a relatively short period of time, between 1973 and 1982. The assertion that rentierism helps explain the strength of authoritarianism under the Ba'ath simultaneously raises the question of why it failed to lead to a prolonged period of stable and institutionalized authoritarian rule in Iraq.

The ability of two of the world's major oil producers, Saudi Arabia and Kuwait, to sustain Iraq's war effort points to the *indirect* effects of rentierism on Iraqi politics. It was these two countries' own access to substantial oil revenues that enabled them to make the necessary loans that allowed Iraq to sustain its struggle with Iran. Nevertheless, the inability of Iraq to experience anything more than a short period of stable rule under the impact of a rentier economy points to the potentially corrosive impact of rentierism on authoritarian rule as well as its negative impact on democratization. A strong argument can be made that both the invasion of Iran in 1980 and the seizure of Kuwait in August 1990 were the result of decisions made by Saddam Husayn, who was acting under the illusion that Iraq was militarily much more powerful than it really was. In other words, rentierism is often only analysed from the economic perspective of the state's ability to ignore societal pressures due to the extraction of external rents (Mahdavy, 1970: 428–9). The social and political contradictions caused by this type of economy and political rule still have not been adequately theorized.

From the perspective of state power, the state's isolation from the populace at large that is produced by rentierism can lead to dysfunctional and corrosive political effects, particularly in the realm of elite decision-making. One of these effects is the tendency towards personalistic rule (whether in the form of Saddam Husayn, the former Shah of Iran, or the emirs of the Arab Gulf States), in which the authoritarian ruler avoids consulting others in making critical decisions affecting the nation-state. Another problem caused by rentierism is the creation of the illusion of the state's political and military strength. What can be argued, then, is that, while rentierism helps explain the success of the Ba'athist regime in consolidating power after 1973, it also points to the unstable quality of the authoritarian rule based on oil wealth that followed.

Iraq's experience with rentierism points to its relationship with regional war as well. Without access to the massive influx of oil revenues during the 1970s, Iraq would not have been able to acquire the military arsenal that allowed it to invade Iran in 1980. Nor would it have been able to create the pervasive security apparatus that allowed the regime to so effectively crush all dissent. The complete suppression of all dissent meant that few if any constraints existed on Saddam Husayn's decision-making power and that few alternative policy options were presented to the Iraqi leader from advisers outside his inner circle. On the other hand, had not Saddam Husayn's regime begun two destructive wars, a strong counterfactual argument can be made that the regime would have become one of the most powerful in the Middle East. If it had continued to implement the development policies of the 1970s, unfettered by war expenditures, Iraq would certainly have attained the status as one of the wealthiest and most developed countries in the Middle East. There is little evidence to suggest that oppositional forces would have been able to challenge the regime's power had it not destabilized itself through the two Gulf wars.

Finally, let us examine post-2003 Iraq. Oil revenues still constituted 93 per cent of Iraq's federal budget in 2006 (Lando, 2007). Despite the state's continued reliance on oil, the Iraqi government is ineffectual and unable to provide citizens with their most fundamental needs, indeed the most basic public good, namely physical security, or services such as energy and transportation. Unemployment estimates reach levels as high as 60 per cent and much of the national economy is controlled regionally by sectarian militias and crime syndicates, continuing a pattern of oil smuggling, corruption and criminal activity that flourished under the Ba'athist regime during the United Nations sanctions period of the 1990s and early 2000s. While the structurally dependent relationship of the state to oil wealth has not changed, post-2003 Iraq represents a caricature of the Weberian model of the state, that is, that institutional entity which controls a monopoly of the use of force within specified territorial boundaries. Clearly, the 'decentralized rentierism' that characterizes much of contemporary Iraq, where militias and criminal organizations control significant amounts of oil wealth in various regions throughout the country, presents still further conceptual and analytic challenges to the notion of rentierism and the rentier state.

In sum, we find that the EMM model bears great relevance for Iraq. There can be no question that oil wealth and regional war have remained two of the most persistent barriers to democratization and development. However, we have argued that these two variables only acquire explanatory power when situated in a historical and socio-political context. The danger of ignoring the historical specificity of a nation-state when studying its inability to democratize, especially if democratization is impeded by rentierism, is the potential fallacy of reducing a complex political dynamic to a unidimensional economic calculus, that is, oil wealth = authoritarian rule and state autonomy.

For rentierism to achieve its full theoretical potential, it needs to be situated within the complex and overlapping set of cleavages that continue to plague Iraqi politics. These cleavages are ethnic in origin, particularly the need to restructure the historical dominance of the state by the Sunni Arab community and create a new system in which all ethnic groups feel that they possess meaningful access to political power. As Shi'i political parties have controlled the state since the parliamentary elections of December 2005, Iraq now faces the problem of the Sunni Arab population becoming a dispossessed minority and, in effect, trading places with the formerly dispossessed Shi'a. Having been subject to poison gas attacks by the central government, Iraq's Kurdish population will require significant trust-building measures before becoming a partner in the nation-building process. The core issue here is the need to establish trust among the country's constituent ethnic groups and promote norms of tolerance and respect for cultural diversity, a role in which the Iraqi government must take the lead.

Iraq's cleavages are also centred on the tension between an authoritarian legacy and the desire for democracy as expressed by the populace in numerous public opinion polls since 2003.[24] Confronting this cleavage entails the need to establish a political system based on the norms of 'polyarchy'.[25] Despite largely successful national elections in January and December 2005, the Iraqi government is characterized by extensive corruption, limited transparency and the sporadic application of the rule of law. Unless government officials can be held accountable and subject to sanctions should they transgress the law, Iraq is still far from having implemented a transition to democracy.

Finally, Iraq's problems remain those first articulated by the mainstream of the Iraqi nationalist movement almost a century ago. One of the core themes of the nationalist movement was that there can be no true democracy in Iraq without social justice. As public opinion polls since 2003 have indicated, Iraqis place their personal security and that of their families first, employment second and democracy third.[26] That material well-being comes before political rights emphasizes once again that democracy cannot take root without development.

The challenges facing democratic forces in Iraq were exacerbated by the

United States occupation administration, especially between 2003 and 2007, that promoted counter-productive security and economic policies, such as decommissioning the 385,000-man Iraq army in May 2003, and the firing of hundreds of thousands of Iraqi workers from state-run factories in an ill-fated attempt to turn Iraq into a market economy through 'shock therapy'.[27] The United States occupation administration likewise undermined trust among Iraq's major ethnic groups by fostering sectarian identities in the political process that developed after the overthrow of the *ancien régime*. This policy began when the United States used ethnic quotas in establishing the Interim Governing Council in 2003. Although this idea has recently lost favour, the sectarian basis of American policy in Iraq even extended to the idea, which has gained currency in some government and policy-making circles in 2006 and 2007, of dividing Iraq into three loosely federated mini-states based along ethnic lines.

As the Special Inspector General for Iraq recently reported, few development projects sponsored by the United States, for example, electric power-generating plants, have been able to be sustained once completed.[28] Many projects are in disrepair or non-functioning. To take one of the most egregious examples, there is less electric power in Iraq at present than there was on the eve of the United States invasion in March 2003, despite billions of dollars of investment in the Iraqi electric power grid. Further, huge amounts of development assistance were never adequately supervised by the United States and remain unaccounted for, which has helped create the widespread corruption that now characterizes the Iraqi government. Unless a comprehensive development programme for Iraq can be established, one that involves not only the United States, but also the United Nations, the Arab League and the European Union, there is little hope that Iraq will be able to face the problems of democracy and development that we have explored in this chapter.

Notes

1 This spelling is a closer transliteration of the Arabic than the 'Hussein' commonly used in the West.
2 The original formulation of the rentier state hypothesis is attributed to Hossein Mahdavy. See Mahdavy, 1970: 428–67.
3 See e.g. De Haan and Siermann, 1996: 175–98; and Helliwell, 1992. For a brief but helpful review of the evidence, see Sen, 1999: ch. 6. Also, see Rodrik and Wacziarg (2004), who find that transitions to democracy, in general, do not affect growth negatively.
4 To be fair to Lipset, it should be noted that he hypothesizes that expanded economic prosperity is associated with a number of variables that reinforce its impact, e.g. a rise in levels of education, greater associational behaviour, expansion of the mass media and higher levels of urbanization. For an expansion of the Lipset model, see Deutsch, 1961: 493–514.
5 For purpose of comparison, the official exchange rate for one ID was US$2.8 from 1950 to 1970.
6 Because Iraq is an oil economy, per capita income may be a misleading measure of development, as any increase in the price or exported volume of oil – the chief export – will translate into expanded GDP, regardless of whether there is a corresponding

expansion in final consumption or human development outcomes: the very indices of modernization that are correlated with democratization. GDP estimates will thus be supplemented with other development indicators when available.

7   UN Statistics Division, National Accounts Main Aggregates.
8   See Yousif, 2001: 115–19.
9   See e.g. Sen, 1990; Griffin and Knight, 1990.
10 See Yousif, 2001: 171–207.
11 See Garfield, 1999.
12 For the views of one of these humanitarian coordinators, see von Sponeck, 2006, and Graham-Brown, 1999
13 For explanations of the individual scores that are given, see Yousif, 2001: ch. 7.
14 These are: freedom to monitor human rights violations; freedom from court sentences of corporal punishment; freedom for independent radio and television; legal rights to free legal aid and counsel; legal rights from police searches without a warrant and from arbitrary seizure; the personal right to practise homosexuality with consenting adults; and the freedom to use contraceptive pills or devices.
15 These are: rights of women to political and legal equality; to social and economic equality; and personal rights to equality of the sexes during marriage and in divorce proceedings. For numerical scores and corresponding explanations of the scores given see Yousif, 2001: ch. 7.
16 This weighting system of course reflects value judgements about which rights are more important than others.
17 For a detailed history of oil agreements see Longrigg, 1961.
18 Mahdavy is aware of the social and political distortions that may be caused by rentierism, particularly the state's ignoring the development needs of the populace at large (Mahdavy, 1970: 437).
19 For a history of the economic interaction of Sunni Arab, Shi'a Arab and Kurdish regions of Iraq, see al-Khafaji (forthcoming).
20 For the rise of the Iraqi nationalist movement, see Davis, 2005a: 29–108.
21 The two wings of the Iraq nationalist movement are discussed in Davis, 2005a: 13–15. Essentially, the Iraqists or 'local nationalists' argued that domestic social and political reforms took precedent over creating a pan-Arab state. For pan-Arabists, especially those from the Sunni Arab community, a unified Arab state was viewed as changing their status from a minority in Iraq to becoming part of a larger Sunni Arab majority.
22 For an analysis of the powerful working-class movement that emerged from the Iraqi Artisan Association (*Jam'iyat Ashab al-Sana'i*) during the late 1920s and early 1930s, see Davis, 1994: 271–303.
23 Qasim's policies are discussed in detail in Davis, 2005a: 109–47.
24 See e.g. Iraqi Prospect Organisation 2005.
25 The concept of polyarchy, which was developed by Robert Dahl, requires seven core principles if a political system is to be considered democratic. These are: (1) control over governmental decisions on policy is constitutionally vested in elected officials; (2) elected officials are chosen and peacefully removed in relatively frequent, fair and free elections in which coercion is quite limited; (3) practically all adults have the right to vote in these elections; (4) most adults also have the right to run for the public offices for which candidates run in these elections; (5) citizens have an effectively enforced right to freedom of expression, particularly political expression, including criticism of the officials, the conduct of the government, the prevailing political, economic, and social system, and the dominant ideology; (6) they also have access to alternative sources of information that are not monopolized by the government or any other single group; and (7) they have an effectively enforced right to form and join autonomous associations, including political associations, such as political parties and interest groups, that attempt to influence the government by competing in elections and by other peaceful means (Dahl, 1989: 233) See also Dahl 1956, 1972.

26 There have been numerous public opinion polls taken in Iraq since the fall of Saddam Husayn's regime in April 2003. See e.g. March and Aug. 2007 polls, conducted by ABC and BBC; http://news.bbc.co.uk/2/hi/middle_east/6451841.stm, and http://news.bbc.co.uk/2/hi/middle_east/6983027.stm

27 See Yousif 2007: 43–60.

28 Quarterly reports to Congress of the Special Inspector General for Iraq Reconstruction, available at www.sigir.mil/reports/quarterlyreports/default.aspx

References

Abd al-Jabbar, F. (1995) *The State, Civil Society and the Democratic Transition in Iraq* (in Arabic), Cairo: Ibn Khaldun Center.

Al-Khafaji, I. (forthcoming) 'Authentic Nations, Artificial Nations: Modern Iraq and the Sykes-Picot Myth', in H. Fattah and M. Bernhardsson (eds), *Identity, Nation and State in Modern Iraq*, New York: Palgrave.

Alnasrawi, A. (1994) *The Economy of Iraq*, London: Greenwood Press.

Anderson, L. (1987) 'The State in the Middle East and North Africa', *Comparative Politics* 20/1 (Oct.).

Batatu, H. (1978) *The Old Social Classes and Revolutionary Movements of Iraq*, Princeton, NJ: Princeton University Press.

Beblawi, H. (1987) 'The Rentier State in the Arab World', in H. Beblawi and G. Luciani, (eds), *The Rentier State*, London: Croom Helm.

Central Statistical Organization (1970) *National Income in Iraq: Selected Studies*, Baghdad: Shafik Press.

Cortright, D., Millar, A. and Lopez, G. A. (2002) 'Smart Sanctions in Iraq: Policy Options', in David Cortright and George A. Lopez (eds), *Smart Sanctions: Targeting Economic Statecraft*, New York: Rowman & Littlefield.

Dahl, R. (1956) *A Preface to Democratic Theory*, Chicago: University of Chicago Press.

—— (1972) *Polyarchy: Participation and Opposition*, New Haven, CT: Yale University Press.

—— (1989) *Democracy and its Critics*, New Haven, CT: Yale University Press.

Davis, E. (1991) 'Theorizing Statecraft and Social Change in Arab Oil-Producing Countries', in E. Davis and N. Gavrielides (eds), *Statecraft in the Middle East: Oil, Historical Memory and Popular Culture*, Gainesville, FL: University Presses of Florida.

—— (1994) 'History for the Many or History for the Few? A Historiography of the Iraqi Working Class', in Z. Lockman, *Middle Eastern Workers: History, Historiography and Struggles*, Albany, NY: State University of New York Press.

—— (2005a) *Memories of State: Politics, History and Collective Identity in Modern Iraq*, Berkeley: University of California Press.

—— (2005b) 'History Matters: Past as Prologue in Building Democracy in Iraq', *Orbis* 49/2 (Spring): 229–44.

—— (2005c) 'The New Iraq: The Uses of Memory', *Journal of Democracy* 16/3 (Summer): 54–68.

—— (2007) 'Rebuilding a Non-Sectarian Iraq', *Strategic Insights* 1/6. Online at: www.ccc.nps.navy.mil/si/2007/Dec/davisDec07.pdf.6

De Haan, J. and Siermann, C. (1996) 'New Evidence on the Relationship between Democracy and Economic Growth', *Public Choice* 86 (1–2): 175–98.

Deutsch, K. (1961) 'Social Mobilization and Political Development', *American Political Science Review* 55/3 (Sept.): 54–68.

Diamond, L. (2003) 'Universal Democracy?', *Policy Review*, June/July.

Elbadawi, I. and Makdisi, S. (2007) 'Explaining the Democracy Deficit in the Arab World', *Quarterly Review of Economics and Finance*, 46/5 (Feb.).

——, —— and Milante, G. (2006) 'Technical Note on Democracy and Development in the Arab World', unpublished manuscript.

Garfield, R. (1999) *Morbidity and Mortality among Iraqi Children from 1990 through 1998*, Fourth Freedom Forum. Online at: www.fourthfreedom.org/Applications/cms.php?page_id=7

Garfield, R. and Waldman, R. (2003) 'Review of Potential Interventions to Reduce Child Mortality in Iraq', USAID. Online at: www.basics.org/pdf/iraq-child-health-review_garfield&waldman_final.pdf

Gazdar, H. and Hussain, A. (2002) 'Crisis and Response: A Study of the Impact of Economic Sanctions in Iraq', in Kamil A. Mahdi (ed.), *Iraq's Economic Predicament*, Reading: Ithaca Press.

Graham-Brown, S. (1999) *Sanctioning Saddam: The Politics of Intervention in Iraq*, London: I. B. Tauris.

Griffin, K. and Knight, J. (1990) 'Human Development: The Case for Renewed Emphasis', in Keith Griffin and John Knight (eds), *Human Development and the International Development Strategy for the 1990s*, London: Macmillan.

Helliwell, J. F. (1992) *Empirical Linkages between Democracy and Economic Growth*, National Bureau of Economic Research, Working Paper, W4066, Boston.

Humana, C. (1986) *World Human Rights Guide*, New York: Facts on File Publications.

Hummadi, I. A., (1978) 'Economic Growth and Structural Changes in the Iraqi Economy with Emphasis on Agriculture: 1953–1975', unpublished doctoral dissertation, University of Colorado.

Iraqi Prospect Organisation (2005) *Iraqi Constitution: Attitudes Towards Democracy*, March. Online at: www.iprospect.org.uk/Attitudes%20Towards%20Democracy.pdf

Issa, S. M. (1979) 'The Distribution of Income in Iraq', in Abbas Kelidar (ed.), *The Integration of Modern Iraq, 1971*, London: Croom Helm.

Lando, B. (2007) 'Oil Large Part of Iraq Conundrum', *United Press International*, 27 July.

Lipset, S.M. (1959) 'Some Social Requisites of Democracy: Economic Development and Political Legitimacy', *American Political Science Review* 53. Reprinted in *Political Man: The Social Bases of Politics*, Garden City, NY: Doubleday Anchor Books, 1960.

Longrigg, S. M. (1961) *Oil in the Middle East*, Oxford: Royal Institute of International Affairs.

Luciani, G. (1990) 'Allocation vs. Production States: A Theoretical Framework', in G. Luciani (ed.), *The Arab State*, Berkeley: University of California Press, 65–84.

Mahdavy, H. (1970) 'The Patterns and Problems of Economic Development in Rentier States: the Case of Iran', in M. A. Cook (ed.), *Studies in the Economic History of the Middle East*, London: Oxford University Press.

Marr, P. (2000) 'Comment on I. al-Khafaji, "The Myth of Iraqi Exceptionalism"', *Middle East Policy* (Oct.).

OPEC (2006) *Annual Statistical Bulletin 2005*, Vienna: OPEC.

Pellet, P. (2000) 'Sanctions, Food, Nutrition and Health in Iraq', in A. Arnove (ed.), *Iraq under Siege: The Deadly Impact of Sanctions and War*, Cambridge, MA: South End Press.

Przeworski, A., Alvarez, M. E., Cheliub, J. A. and Limongi, F. (2000) *Democracy and Development: Political Institutions and Well-Being in the World, 1950–1990*, Cambridge: Cambridge University Press.

Rodrik, D. and Wacziarg, R. (2004) *Do Democratic Transitions Produce Bad Economic Outcomes?* Online at: www.aeaweb.org/annual_mtg_papers/2005/0108_1015_0403.pdf

Sen, A. (1990) 'Development as Capability Expansion', in K. Griffin and J. Knight (eds), *Human Development and the International Development Strategy for the 1990s*, London: Macmillan.
—— (1999) *Development as Freedom*, New York: Knopf.
United Nations (1979) *Yearbook of National Accounts Statistics 1978*, New York: United Nations.
United Nations Children's Fund (UNICEF): www.unicef.org/infobycountry/iraq_statistics.html#7
von Sponeck, H. C. (2006) *A Different Kind of War: The UN Sanctions Regime in Iraq*, New York: Berghahn Books.
Wiktorowicz, Q. (1999) 'The Limits of Democracy in the Middle East: The Case of Jordan', *Middle East Journal* 53/4.
Workman, T. (1994) *The Social Origins of the Iran–Iraq War*, London: Lynne Rienner.
Yousif, B. (2001) 'Development and Political Violence in Iraq, 1950–1990', unpublished doctoral dissertation, University of California, Riverside.
—— (2007) 'Economic Restructuring in Iraq: Intended and Unintended Consequences', *Journal of Economic Issues* 41/1 (March).
Zubaida, S. (2005) 'Democracy, Iraq and the Middle East'. Online at: www.opendemocracy.net

NILE VALLEY COUNTRIES

9 Egypt: development, liberalization and the persistence of autocracy

Gouda Abdel-Khalek and Mustapha K. Al Sayyid

1. Introduction

Using the global Polity IV measure, Elbadawi, Makdisi and Milante (EMM) compare the Arab world with such regional comparators as Sub-Saharan Africa, East Asian countries, and Latin American countries, as well as other non-high income states. They conclude that the Arab world has lagged behind the rest of the developing world, with little to no progress in political representation in the past 40 years (Elbadawi and Makdisi, 2007; EMM, 2006).

Although the Arab world initiated movement towards more democratic practices in the 1950s, this movement was reversed in the 1960s. In the 1970s, there was further limited movement in the direction of democracy (Al-Kawary, 2000; Mansour, 1992). However the Arab world failed to catch up with the rest of the world, particularly more recently since the fall of the Soviet Union. Elbadawi and Makdisi (2007) refer to the relative position of Arab polity as the 'Arab democracy deficit', perhaps echoing the Arab Human Development Report (AHDR, 2002, 2004). According to the Polity IV democratization measure, the average Arab country entered the 1960s with a polity score of −5.58. In the 1970s, relapses to autocracy brought this average down to a low of −7.85. Since that time the scores have improved, but the Arab world (with the exception of Lebanon) has remained autocratic.

In searching for an explanation for this Arab democracy deficit, EMM experiment with the Lipset, or modernization, hypothesis. According to the pure modernization hypothesis, the centrality of the level of development in the analysis of democracy is governed by a view of modernity that emphasizes the roles of income, education and enlarged middle class in a country's propensity for experiencing democracy (Lipset, 1959; Barro, 1997). As shown by the empirical analysis in a technical note (EMM, 2006), the pure modernization hypothesis does not account for the lack of democratic progress in the Arab world.

In their endeavour to explain the Arab democracy deficit EMM test an extended modernization model with four alternative hypotheses, most of which can be found in popular literature or other conventional wisdom. These four competing explanations for lagging democratic progress include: (1) historical effects of colonization; (2) type of religion as a foundation for political governance; (3) social cohesion (including the interaction of cohesion and polity); and (4) Arab-specific effects, including the presence of oil and regional war. The model involves a cross-region Tobit regression of polity on eleven variables, in addition to the three regional effects dummies (EMM, 2006: table 4: column F). Based on the extended model, they argue that oil and conflicts might be the missing link to account for the observed democracy deficit in the region.

Three simulations were generated for each individual Arab country: predicted polity, predicted polity without oil effects and predicted polity without Arab war effects. In Egypt's case, the simulations show that the predicted polity score is lower than the actual polity score throughout the period 1960–2003. Only when war effects are excluded is it found that the predicted polity score becomes higher than the actual score. However, it is curious to note that, in the latter case, the predicted simulation fails to pull Egypt's actual autocratic (negative) polity score into the positive region.

Building on these results, the purpose of this paper is to examine more closely the relationship between democracy and development in Egypt from 1960 to 2003. We begin by highlighting in section 2 the trajectory of the country's political change. In section 3 we test the applicability of the extended modernization model to the case of Egypt. Section 4 supplements the quantitative work with a qualitative analysis of the relation between democracy and development in Egypt during the period under study. Section 5 concludes.

2. Trajectory of political change in Egypt

2.1 An overview

In the study of political liberalization/democratization, a distinction is made between a process of transition from the typical pattern of an authoritarian regime initiated from above, and a transition that follows a popular mobilization in the name of democracy, described as transition from below. In the first case, ruling groups are in a position to determine both the pace and modality of the transition. In the second case, the old ruling group is either overthrown or is compelled to act under pressure from the masses, taking decisions that it would not otherwise have contemplated. The process of liberalization in Egypt is of the first type, economic and political liberalization from above (O'Donnell, 1993; Schmitter and O'Donnell, 1986).

In the case of Egypt, the pre-transition regime was a revolutionary one which came into being following what started as a military coup d'état in July 1952, but which evolved into a revolutionary regime that introduced radical measures transforming the socio-economic structures of the country. The transition regime reversed most policies of the revolutionary regime. It is not an exaggeration to describe the later regimes of both President Sadat and Mubarak as counter-revolutionary regimes, notwithstanding the fact that the two continued to claim that their legitimacy was derived from the 1952 revolution. Political scientists who prefer to use less value-laden terms would call them post-populist or demobilization regimes (Hinnebusch, 1985).

The revolutionary regime that ruled Egypt from July 1952 until the death of Gamal Abdel Nasser, the leader of the July revolution, in 1970, ended the liberal regime that had marked the early period of Egypt's formal independence.[1] On 16 January 1953 the revolutionary regime abolished the liberal constitution of 1923, which until then had provided the legal framework for political activities in the country, although it had not been strictly observed. The constitution had provided for an elected bicameral parliament, with two-fifths of members of the upper house appointed by the king, presumably on the advice of the cabinet formed by the party that had obtained the majority in the lower house. Both King Ahmed Fou'ad (1917–36) and his son, Farouq (1937–52), who succeeded him interpreted the constitution in such a way as to give the king power to dissolve the elected parliament, appoint the prime minister and two-fifths of the members of the senate, as well as senior civil and military officials, without consulting the prime minister. Hence the Wafd party, indisputably the majority party in the country, and claiming to represent the popular will, was unable to exercise power for more than seven and half years of the twenty-eight years of the liberal period (1924–52). None of its cabinets or dominated parliaments was allowed to complete their constitutional term.

In place of the multi-party system under the 1923 constitution, the revolutionary regime established a number of single mass organizations as the only authorized framework for political participation. Pre-revolutionary political parties were outlawed, and their members were not generally allowed to join the mass organizations, although both the Muslim Brotherhood (MB) and the Communists, who were harshly suppressed, nevertheless continued underground activities. None of the mass organizations established by the revolutionary regime succeeded in providing meaningful opportunities for political participation. Thus one organization succeeded another after a few years of failed experiments at political mobilization. The Liberation Rally established in 1953 was succeeded by the National Union in 1956. The latter was followed in 1962 by the Arab Socialist Union, which was relatively more successful until it was allowed, under Sadat, to wither away before its formal demise in 1980.

The lack of effectiveness of these mass organizations did not affect the stability of the revolutionary regime, which relied on its populist policies and the charisma of its leader, Gamal Abdel Nasser, as foundations for its legitimacy. The regime succeeded in getting the British troops out of the country twice in 1956; nationalizing foreign properties as well as nationally owned large- and medium-sized enterprises; introducing agrarian reform; and adopting educational, health, housing, wage and employment policies in favour of the poor. But it maintained a tight grip on political activities in the country, with a massive security apparatus that curbed any attempt at political organization not authorized by the regime. It was therefore easy for the successors of Abdel Nasser to build their legitimacy on the claim that they were allowing a considerable measure of political liberalization without any basic change in the character of the political system, which continued to be dominated by the head of the state (for details, see Al-Sayyid Marsot, 1994; Waterbury, 1982; Mabro, 1974; Zaki, 1995).

In order to assess the scope of political liberalization in Egypt, it is important to compare the situation before and after. We examine the trajectory of political change in Egypt during the period 1960 to 2006. The period may be divided into seven subperiods, based on major events that shaped political change in the country throughout the last 47 years – a long enough span of time to assess whether any genuine political change took place.

1960–1967: This subperiod ended with the 1967 Arab–Israeli war.

1967–1971: This period witnessed the effective defeat of Nasserism, not only with the death of Nasser on 28 September 1970 but, more importantly, with the removal from the political scene of the ruling elite, which had been determined to maintain its radical domestic and foreign policies.

1971–1977: During this period was the onset of a process of economic and political liberalization in Egypt that ended in January 1977 with a popular uprising in protest against sudden price increases of basic consumer goods. It marked a retreat from policies of both economic and political liberalization (Hilal, 1978).

1977–1981: Tensions caused by the shrinking of political space in the aftermath of the popular uprising of January 1977 culminated in the assassination of President Sadat on 6 October 1981 (Haykal, 1983).

1981–1991: This subperiod was marked by a return to political liberalization with the release of politicians imprisoned during the last month of President Sadat's reign and expansion of political liberalization under President Mubarak. It ended with Iraq's invasion of Kuwait, which had important repercussions for the Egyptian economy.

1991–2000: The end of the Gulf war of 1991 opened the way for further economic liberalization in Egypt, but was associated with further shrinking of the political space (Kassem, 1999; Kienle, 2001).

2001–2006: This period witnessed an expansion of some political freedoms, with the famous decision of the Supreme Constitutional Court in 2000 that interpreted Article 88 of the Constitution to mean direct supervision of national elections by the judiciary, and an amendment to the constitution in 2005 to allow competitive presidential elections.

Table 9.1 summarizes the economic and political linearization measures in Egypt over the period 1960 to 2005.

The table tells a story of sustained economic liberalization from 1968. While initially slow, economic liberalization accelerated under the officially declared Open Door policy (*infitah*). It further expanded under the Economic Reform and Structural Adjustment Program (ERSAP) from the beginning of the 1990s (Abdel-Khalek, 1992, 2001; Ikram, 2006; El-Issawy, 2007). Even before ERSAP, Egypt had eclectically applied certain neo-liberal economic measures.

Political liberalization, on the other hand, has varied, exhibiting both ups and

Table 9.1 Periods of economic and political liberalization

Period	Economic liberalization	Political liberalization
1960–1967	=	↓
1968–1976	↑	↑
1977–1980	↑	↓
1981–1990	↑	↑
1991–2000	↑	↓
2001–2005	↑	↑

Source: Based on event count and authors.

downs, exhibiting a rising, albeit modest, trend of political liberalization. But according to the Freedom House score (based on the Political Rights Index), the gains in political rights achieved from 1975 to 1985 seem to have dissipated during the period 1985 to 1995 and continued at this lower level through 2005.

2.2 Polity simulations

Figure 9.1 shows the simulations generated for Egypt using the pooled Tobit model. These simulations indicate that throughout the 1960–2003 period the predicted polity score is lower than the actual polity score. In other words, Egypt's polity seems to be 'more democratic' than may be warranted by the country's level of socio-economic development. However, controlling for oil and regional conflict produces higher predicted scores. Excluding the oil effects, predicted polity becomes higher, starting with the mid-1970s, and exceeding the actual score for 2000–2003. Excluding regional wars would produce even higher predicted polity

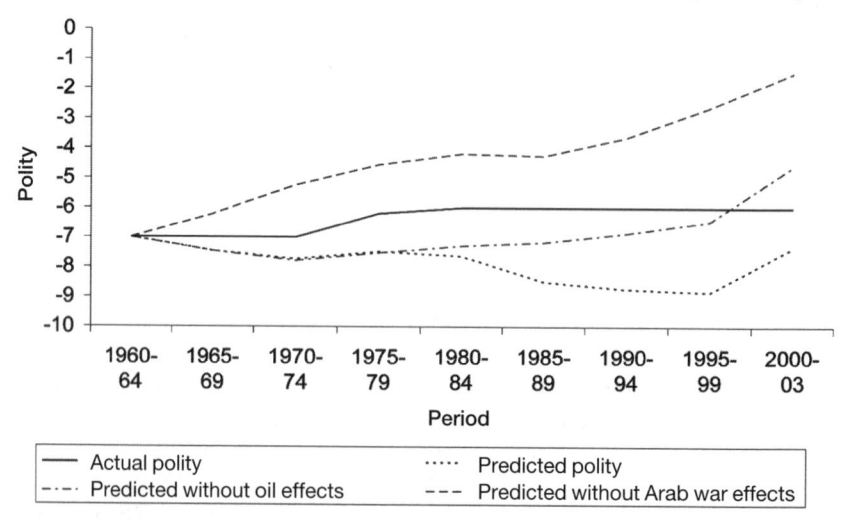

Figure 9.1 Democratization in Egypt.

Source: Elbadawi, Makdisi and Milante, 2006.

scores, rising above the actual polity scores throughout the period under study, but remaining in the negative zone. These simulations reveal the importance of regional conflict and, to a lesser extent, oil, as factors constraining the development of Egypt's polity. However, they do not tell the whole story of the continuing Egyptian democracy deficit. In this regard it should be noted that the modernization theory appears to ignore the fact that Egypt is a hydraulic society, where, historically, a strong autocracy has persisted based on the central development and control of the irrigation network – so vital for sheer existence in Egypt's arid environment.

Building on these results, we investigate supplementary factors that may shed further light on the lagging democratic development of Egypt, and indeed help to explain the noted circular pattern of Egypt's political development. For this purpose we first test whether the EMM model can be further enhanced by adding variables that we deem relevant to the Egyptian case, and then supplement our empirical work with a qualitative analysis of factors not captured by the model that may have had a direct bearing on the country's political development.

3. Testing the extended modernization model

It should first be noted that the variation in Egyptian polity described in section 2 above is not reflected in the recorded Polity IV scores for Egypt. We have therefore attempted to modify these scores along the same range (i.e. for -10 to $+10$) in light of the foregoing discussion of the country's political trajectory. The result is a modified polity score, or 'modpolity'. We then derived a normalized score ('moddem') which we use as our dependent variable in the regression model presented below. In contrast with the step pattern of the actual polity scores, the modified and smoothed out polity scores indicate an overall rise up to the early 1980s, followed by an overall decline to the present. Furthermore, as another alternative indicator of democracy we used the more subjective Freedom House political rights index 'FHpolrights,' which is available only from 1972. 'FHpolrights' runs along an ordinal scale ranging from 7 (for worst situation/condition) to 1 (for best situation/condition). We used the linear transformation to convert it to a normalized scale comparable to 'moddem'. The Annex details the methodology adopted in deriving the modified polity scores and includes figures that contrast the scores before and after their transformation, along with a figure that indicates the growth of real per capita income over the period 1960–2003.

In testing the applicability of the extended modernization model to the Egyptian case, we then include, in addition to various explanatory variables included in the EMM model, three additional variables that a priori appear relevant to the Egyptian case, namely: labour migration, foreign aid and urbanization.

Altogether, the following five equations are used to estimate a Tobit model, since we are dealing with a limited dependent variable (i.e. the observations for polity represent censored data):

1.   polity = $\beta_0 + \beta_1$ lagged income + β_2 lagged polity + β_3 lagged education + u_1
2.   polity = $\beta_0 + \beta_1$ lagged income + β_2 lagged polity + β_3 lagged education + β_4 lagged fuel exports + β_5 lagged regional wars + β_6 lagged neighbourhood polity + u_2
3.   polity = $\beta_0 + \beta_1$ lagged income + β_2 lagged polity + β_3 lagged education + β_4 lagged fuel exports + β_5 lagged regional wars + β_6 lagged neighbourhood polity + β_7 labour migration + u_3
4.   polity = $\beta_0 + \beta_1$ lagged income + β_2 lagged polity + β_3 lagged education + β_4 lagged fuel exports + β_5 lagged regional wars + β_6 lagged neighbourhood polity + β_7 labour migration + β_8 foreign aid + u_4
5.   polity = $\beta_0 + \beta_1$ lagged income + β_2 lagged polity + β_3 lagged education + β_4 lagged fuel exports + β_5 lagged regional wars + β_6 lagged neighbourhood polity + β_7 labour migration + β_8 foreign aid + β_9 urbanization + u_5

The empirical results of testing the model are presented in Table 9.2. Note that due to lack of data on education, life expectancy was used. Logarithmic transformation was applied to the original data.

Based on such results, we may make the following observations. First, the basic modernization model (Equation 1) does not hold in the case of Egypt. Both the coefficient of income and life expectancy are not significant. Only the coefficient of lagged polity is significant, but this may be the result of autoregression. The lack of positive correlation between per capita growth and polity is demonstrated in the Annex, Figures 9.2 and 9.3: while per capita income rose continuously, polity oscillated over the period under study, rising but then falling.

Second, the extended modernization model (Equation 2) includes oil, regional wars and neighbourhood polity. It performs better, although the coefficients of income and life expectancy are still not significant. As expected, the coefficient of regional war variable has the right sign (negative) and is significant. It tallies with the EMM conclusion for the Arab world as a whole. This implies that regional conflict has been an inhibitor of democratic transformation in Egypt. Neighbourhood polity has a significant negative coefficient, apparently the wrong sign. Surprisingly, fuel exports do not seem to have had a direct effect on Egypt's polity. The reason could be the relatively limited role of oil in total exports and budget revenues of Egypt. However one should also consider the indirect effects of oil wealth in the region; the Gulf oil boom has provided work opportunities for millions of Egyptians who have remitted large savings back home.

Third, going beyond oil and regional conflicts, the three additional variables (labour migration, foreign aid and urbanization) are tested in Equations 3–5.

The rationale for introducing labour migration is to reflect the 'exit-vs-voice' thesis proposed by Hirschman (1970). On a priori grounds, the larger the labour migration the less the pressure on the political regime to democratize (pressure relief notion). For empirical analysis, remittances are used as proxy for labour migration since the latter is not available on a time-series basis. The coefficient for remittances is expected, a priori, to be negative. Foreign aid is an eminent example of strategic rent. The hypothesis here is that the larger the amount of aid, the less

Table 9.2 Econometric results

	Equation 5	Equation 4	Equation 3	Equation 2	Equation 1
Log income, lagged	0.657109* *0.130755*	0.61446* *0.133209*	0.686064* *0.149823*	-0.05737 *0.096251*	-0.01892 *0.05865*
Polity, lagged	0.173444 *0.1236585*	0.134655 *0.126237*	0.148985 *0.154518*	0.81872* *0.108594*	0.947704* *0.105774*
Life expectancy, lagged	-0.037321* *0.007687*	-0.032146* *0.007186*	-0.036582* *0.007755*	0.005307 *0.004558*	0.001405 *0.003123*
Fuel exports, lagged	-0.000367 *0.000363*	-0.000601 *0.000343*	-0.0007 *0.000409*	0.000248 *0.0000491*	
Regional war, lagged	-0.00252* *0.000676*	-0.002673* *0.000697*	-0.002799* *0.000859*	-0.002505** *0.00093*	
Neighbourhood polity	0.019754** *0.007588*	0.016666** *0.007625*	0.020716** *0.008758*	-020838* *0.006312*	
Remittances	0.0722237** *0.037102*	0.035687 *0.029428*	-50 E-10** *3.8 E-10*		
Foreign aid	-0.00000326 *0.000156*	-0.00000686 *0.000157*			
Urban population share	-0.032942 *0.021719*				
Constant	-0.673782 *1.049284*	-2.091806* *0.496953*	-2.295008* *0.579006*	0.049104 *0.408082*	0.055991 *0.220386*
Adjusted R²	0.7449	0.7396	0.7414	0.7567	0.7033

Source: Empirical results of applying models in Equations 1–5.

Notes
Numbers in italics are standard errors of corresponding coefficients.
* Significant at the 1% level.
** Significant at the 5% level.

the internal pressure on the political regime to democratize, as the regime's legitimacy may depend more on external support than on public consent and approval. But in the post-9/11 international context, foreign aid may be viewed as an instrument of external pressure on the regime to democratize – provided this serves the interest of the donor power.

The share of urban population may correlate positively with the move towards democracy for two reasons. First, this population may be more vocal in expressing demands for democracy. Second, the urban populace tends to engage in activities that require better education and skills, and to organize larger units compared to the rural population.

Fourth, according to the econometric results reported for Equation 3 in Table 9.2, the coefficient of labour migration is negative and significant. This evidence corroborates the exit-vs-voice thesis in Egypt's case. When opportunities for migration to work are easily available, this may encourage the exit reaction mode of economy–polity interaction; citizens who are disenchanted with conditions at home may prefer to go abroad to further their own self-interest instead of struggling to change the status quo (the voice reaction mode). Migration has apparently relieved the pressure for democratization in Egypt.

Fifth, the empirical results in Equations 4 and 5 reported in Table 9.2 do not show any significant relation between foreign aid and Egypt's polity, or urban population and polity. Surprisingly, such results do not seem consistent with a priori expectation. This may be due to the limited variability exhibited by the foreign aid data in our case. Furthermore, when foreign aid and then urban population share are successively introduced in equations 4 and 5, the coefficient of the migration variable turns non-significant in the former equation, but significant with the wrong (that is, positive) sign in the latter.

To recapitulate, the results for migration, aid and urbanization are not robust, especially in the more encompassing regressions, 4 and 5. Instead, income – the standard modernity correlate of democracy – was positively associated in all of the three encompassing models, while the surprisingly negative and significant results for life expectancy in the same regressions might be due to multi-collinearity between the two modernity variables. Briefly, it seems that the Egyptian data does not corroborate the three key Egypt-specific hypotheses postulated above: migration, aid and urbanization though it lends support to the income version of the modernity hypothesis. Hence, to fully understand Egypt's complex relation between democracy and development, we supplement the findings of the extended modernization model with a qualitative analysis of major factors that we believe help explain Egypt's failure to transit into a genuine democracy.

4. Supplementary explanations for Egypt's lagging democracy

We offer five explanations on why Egypt could not sustain and build on the measures of liberalization it undertook in the 1970s and 1980s, and instead reverted to intensified political control. These are given in sections 4.1 to 4.5 and are as follows: Egypt's deindustrialization and crisis of distribution; the role of the state; entrepreneurial groups' attitudes towards political liberalization; fear of Islamists; and complicity of foreign powers with an authoritarian regime. They shed light on whether Egypt is caught in an autocracy trap and clarify the dynamics underlying this pendulum-like pattern of the country's polity.

4.1 Economy–polity interaction in Egypt: deindustrialization and crisis of distribution

To understand the relationship between the trend towards political liberalization and democracy and the similar trend towards economic liberalization, the concepts of 'participation crisis' and 'crisis of distribution' as in Binder (1971) are useful categories of analysis. Economic liberalization measures espoused by the international financial institutions invariably trigger a 'distribution crisis'. Such a distribution crisis may accentuate a 'participation crisis' which, in turn, may lead to a 'legitimacy crisis'. This will have clear implications for democratization.

Democratization and political liberalization mean wider popular participation and greater public contestation. On the other hand, economic liberalization means enlarging the scope of private ownership and increasing the role of the market. In developing countries, this invariably involves more concentration of economic power and, hence, political power. Such redistribution of power in both the economic and political domains would leave out the economically disfranchised, creating a participation crisis. The experience of Latin American countries and the Arab world in the 1970s and 1980s shows that economic liberalization may not necessarily lead to political liberalization. Conflict between popular preferences and efficiency criteria emerges in the main areas of economic 'reform' (wage rate, interest rate, exchange rate, subsidies, and foreign direct investment). Repression may be necessary to implement economic reform (Abdel-Khalek, 1992; O'Donnell, 1993).

The first half of the 1960s and second half of the 1970s were more prosperous times for Egypt. From the 1980s, the country faced mounting economic difficulties. The per capita GDP growth rate actually fell from 7.4 per cent during 1975–80 to 1.2 per cent in 1990–5 (World Bank, 2006). Inflation soared and nominal wages stagnated – implying falling real wages for the majority. Available evidence indicates that real wages fell by 44 per cent between 1981/2 and 1994/5. Despite the rise of the overall real wage rate in the second half of the 1990s, in 1999/2000 it was still below the level it had reached in 1981/2 (El-Issawy, 2007: 523).

It is well documented that under ERSAP the Egyptian economy has experienced significant deindustrialization (Abdel-Khalek, 2001). The gap between economic growth and population growth under ERSAP resulted in rising unemployment; growth was largely jobless.[2] Despite official announcements of increased job creation, unemployment steadily rose. According to census results, the overall national unemployment rate rose from 9 per cent in 1996 to 9.3 per cent in 2006.[3] The incidence of unemployment fell disproportionately on the young segment of the population. In 2006, the rate of unemployment for youth (age 15–30) stood at

25 per cent. In 2000, youth unemployment accounted for 84 per cent of total unemployment (Ikram, 2006: 245). This socio-economic fact has clear political implications.

Distribution issues are much easier to deal with in a context of growth. In a largely zero-sum economic environment, Egypt has faced a real crisis of distribution, particularly after 1990/1. This was strong in the urban sector, as the Gini index increased from 34.0 in 1990/1 to 37.5 per cent in 2004/5 (El-Issawy, 2007: 535). In the rural sector, there is no evidence of rising inequality after 1990/1. But a strong symbol of a distribution crisis in rural Egypt is the 1992 Law 96, which signalled a reversal of previous laws passed from the 1950s that ensured stability of rent and security of tenancy. Available evidence shows that the ratio of landholders to total population decreased from 6.1 per cent in 1960 to 5.8 per cent in 2000 (IDSC, 2007: 5), implying an increased sellers' market for agricultural land.

Related to the distribution crisis are clear symptoms of a crisis of participation. Witness the popular uprising in 1977, the political crisis of the fall of 1981 (culminating in the assassination of President Sadat), the internal security forces' dissent in 1986, and the current (2007–8) wave of labour unrest (strikes, sit-ins, slowdowns, etc.). Add to that the heated dispute over the latest constitutional amendment, in March 2007. In light of the discussion in section 2 above, we may posit that the intensifying conflict over distribution in Egypt has so far resulted in a swinging political pendulum: oscillating between more open and a less open polity.

These observations suggest that in trying to understand the question of democratization in Egypt we also need to consider structural/institutional factors. We put forth the following hypothesis: despite the growth of GDP per capita, the non-industrial and service-oriented development strategy adopted by Egypt since the economic liberalization of the post-October war has contributed to less democratization. Deindustrialization of Egypt since the mid-1970s and the concomitant rise in the share of services in GDP appear to have arrested the country's democratic transformation, despite improving overall economic and educational standards. Egypt's case may be contrasted to such comparators as South Korea, where industrialization and structural change were conducive to more democratization.

As suggested by Acemoglu and Robinson (2006: 318): 'as an economy develops, factors of production accumulate, and per capita income rises, it is the change in the structure of the economy toward a more capital-intensive endowment of assets that leads to democracy and its consolidation'. Egypt's experience is at variance with this scenario. Evidence shows that the increase in income per capita was associated with less capital-intensive and more resource-intensive endowment of assets. There is also a tendency for employment to be concentrated in service sectors, where productivity is low and labour is largely unorganized. Further, such pattern of growth created a crisis of distribution, as noted above (Abdel-Khalek, 2003; El-Ghonemy, 2003; El-Issawy, 2007; Ikram, 2006; World Bank, 2006).

4.2 Role of the state

A clear change in the economic role of the state in Egypt is seen across the various subperiods. During 1960–7, the state role increased significantly, thanks to nationalization and the large-scale injection of public funds into new investment projects. The High Aswan Dam is a good example. During this period, public investment accounted for more than 80 per cent of total investment. Even when public investment began to decline after 1967, its share remained at 75 per cent during 1975–81/2, falling to 56 per cent during 2002–4 (El-Issawy, 2007: 272). Thus, throughout the period 1960–2003 the state played a dominant role in investment.

It is logical to correlate major public investment with greater government control in the areas of production, consumption, employment and foreign trade. This has clear implications for the nature of polity and the democratization process in the country. A strong government hold on the economy extends by necessity to the polity.

Another indicator of the economic role of the state is the size of the government's budget. Since 1980/1, the government has claimed an increasing proportion of GDP, in terms of public revenue and expenditure in the state budget. The proportion of revenue increased from 29.25 per cent in 1975 to 43 per cent in 1980/1, and the proportion of expenditure rose from 59.6 per cent in 1975 to 62.63 per cent in 1981/2 (El-Issawy, 2007: 780, 785). Parallel to this, the share of the public sector (both government and the business sector) in GDP continued rising until the mid-1980s, reaching 48 per cent in 1985/6.

Although there has been a clear decline in the economic role of the state in Egypt, particularly since the 1990s, the government has continued to play a strong role. Despite the declining importance of public-sector banks in the banking system, their share of total bank credit and deposits remained at high at about 50 per cent of the total at the end of 2007. Approximately five million people were employed in 2007 by the government at various levels (central and local). These employees are usually mobilized to ensure the election of those candidates favoured by the government (mainly National Democratic Party candidates).

4.3 Entrepreneurial groups' attitudes toward political liberalization

Studies of transition from authoritarianism in East Asia and in Latin America suggest that entrepreneurial groups were among the agents of democratization. In countries as far apart as South Korea and Brazil, they were among the social groups that took part in popular mobilizations that led to the transition from military-dominated regimes to civilian elected regimes in the 1980s. Along with other social groups, entrepreneurs played a similar role to that of the bourgeoisie in the history of more advanced countries.

By contrast, entrepreneurial groups in Egypt have not played such a role. Big business is perhaps the only social class supporting the authoritarian regime. Prominent entrepreneurs in the country are to be found in the leading bodies of the National Democratic Party (NDP). Six business owners occupy ministerial positions in the second cabinet of Dr Ahmed Nazif, formed in September 2005 after the election of President Hosni Mubarak to a fifth term.

Other indicators of the strong influence of entrepreneurs under Mubarak's regime include:

- number of new business associations;
- number of entrepreneurs in the main institutions of the ruling NDP;
- number of business people in the Parliament, particularly the more important People's Assembly; and,
- number of entrepreneurs owning media, particularly newspapers and television channels.

The number of business associations has increased under the regime of President Hosni Mubarak. Besides the two umbrella organizations, the Egyptian Federation of Industries and the General Federation of Chambers of Commerce, smaller, but more powerful organizations came into being, including the Investors' Societies, particularly those of Tenth of Ramadan, October, and Sadat industrial towns, chambers of commerce of foreign countries, and thinktanks including the Egyptian Center for Economic Studies and the Egypt International Economic Forum.

The General Secretariat of the ruling NDP includes a number of influential business owners. The policy committee of the party, headed by Gamal Mubarak, the president's son, who presumably is being groomed to succeed his father, was formed in 2002 to become the most powerful organ in the party, as it holds meetings in which ministers are called to account for their performance. As of mid-2008, this committee had no less than 25 entrepreneurs among its 125 members, amounting to one-fifth its total membership. Under President Mubarak the number of entrepreneurs in the People's Assembly increased from 37 in 1995 to 77 in 2000 and 83 in 2005. They lead a number of important committees including Planning and Budget, Economic Affairs, and Housing.

Finally, business owners are active in shaping public opinion through their ownership of media. Two independent newspapers that began publication in the last three years – *Nahdet Misr* and the very popular *Al-Masry Al-Youm* – are owned by entrepreneurs. Three of the current independent television channels (Al-Mehwar, Dream and OTV) are owned by Hassan Rateb, Ahmed Bahgat and Naguib Sawiris, all prominent and well-known business people.

It is not surprising, therefore, that big business in the country is a major pillar of support for the government of President Hosni Mubarak, and that generally business owners are not known to have taken a public position in favour of democratization of the Egyptian regime. Instead of being an agent for democratization, the nascent bourgeoisie in Egypt has become, in fact, a major foundation of support for an authoritarian regime.

Why would business owners support such an authoritarian regime? The answer may be found in the economic policies pursued by both President Sadat and

Mubarak, his successor. Their policies succeeded in expanding the role of the private sector in the national economy and opened the way for a gradual return to capitalism, replacing the public sector and centrally planned economy of the Nasser period. Besides, big business is concerned that genuine democratization would bring to power the MB, which could carry out policies that might destabilize the economy, for example, by prohibiting banks from paying or receiving interest[4] or by imposing harsh puritanical measures that could drive tourists away. Very few business owners join opposition political parties or movements. Those who do so are mostly adhering to family traditions. This is particularly the case in the Neo-Wafd party, a liberal party that retains leaders and ideas of the pre-revolution Wafd, which embodied at that time the multi-class nationalist movement (Zaki, 1995: 231–2).

4.4 Fear of Islamists

The concern felt by ruling groups in some Arab countries that Islamists might win a landslide victory in a free and fair election led them to introduce legislative and administrative measures to render such electoral victory a remote possibility. For example, in Algeria, an Islamist victory in municipal and provincial elections in 1990 and in the first round of legislative elections in December 1991 led to the overthrow of the Algerian government by the military. It subsequently outlawed the Front of Islamic Salvation. It remains banned in the country 16 years later despite efforts at national reconciliation by President Abdel-Aziz Bouteflika. The Tunisian government had earlier guarded against such possibility by banning the Nahda party, which came in second in the first legislative elections in 1989 under President Ben Ali, far distanced by the President's own Constitutionalist Rally. In Jordan, the government changed the multi-vote electoral system that had enabled the Islamic Action Front to win close to 40 per cent of parliamentary seats in 1991.

The argument used by the governments was that a free and fair election that would bring Islamists to power could be the last free election. They would claim that the Islamists were intent on using a democratic electoral process to win government power, but once in power would not allow such elections again lest they lose to secularist parties. The Islamists are viewed by these governments, as well as by many Western governments, as enemies of democracy who should not be allowed to put an end to a democratic process (Al-Sayyid, 2003: 5–7). However, the attempt to minimize the probability of an electoral victory by the Islamists has been accompanied by several restrictions on civil and political rights, as well as limitations on the freedom of other political parties.

Egypt is no exception to this pattern. Following President Sadat's assassination by militants of the Jihad Organization on 6 October 1981, martial law was reintroduced, having been lifted only months earlier. Thousands of young people were detained in the years that followed (1981–97), which witnessed confrontations between security forces and militant Islamist groups on suspicion that they might be sympathizers with the organization. The mainstream Islamist organization, the MB, was allowed to contest general elections as well as those of professional associations, as its rank and file was committed to peaceful methods of political action. At the same time, the official ban on the activities of the MB imposed by the military-dominated Revolutionary Command Council in 1954 was maintained. However MB candidates did well in the legislative elections of 1984 and 1987, taking advantage of their alliance with legally recognized parties to avoid the official ban of their organization.

With the assassination of the Speaker of the People's Assembly in the fall of 1990, renewed acts of armed resistance to the government offered a pretext to the government to to curb not only activities of the militant Islamist organizations, but of the MB as well. A law raising the quorum for validity of elections in professional associations was rushed through the People's Assembly in 1993 in an attempt to forestall their takeover by Islamist groups. A broader definition of terrorism was adopted and the penal code amended to stiffen penalties for actions that constitute instigation of terrorism. Elected councils of several professional associations were replaced by appointed councils in 1995 and 1996, and since then elections have been postponed in most professional associations believed to be 'vulnerable' to Islamist electoral victories. Several leading members of the Brotherhood were arrested and tried before military tribunals following the adoption of the penal code amendments. The government extended its harassment to one legally recognized political party, namely the Socialist Labor Party, which had entered into an electoral alliance with the Brotherhood in 1987 and adopted an Islamist political discourse. Taking advantage of an article in the party's paper calling on young people to protest publication by a government institution of a novel alleged to be blasphemous towards Islam, the government ordered closure of the paper and outlawed the party. Court rulings annulling the government decision to close the twice weekly *Al-Sha'b* newspaper and the banning of the Socialist Labor Party were not enforced by the government, on flimsy legal arguments.

Renewed electoral successes of the MB, which began to contest general legislative elections with independent candidates in 1995, prompted the government to escalate its harassment of their leaders and militants; despite this they increased their presence in the People's Assembly fivefold in 2005. Part of the explanation for MB's electoral success is due to direct judicial supervision of balloting in 2000 and 2005, in conformity with a Supreme Constitutional Court ruling that interpreted Article 88 of the Constitution to mean the presence of a judge in every voting post as a means of guaranteeing freedom of elections. The government, surprised by the impressive show of the MB in the first round of legislative elections, found no way to counter their increasing influence except by resorting to using security forces to prevent citizens from casting their votes in the second and third rounds of elections in those constituencies believed to be sympathetic to the MB. Finally, President Hosni Mubarak proposed amendments to the constitution in late 2006 which, among other things, aimed to weaken the ability of the MB to continue as a major political force. The amendments included banning any party or activity based on religion. The amendments also called for replacing direct judicial supervision by a so-called independent electoral commission, to be established by the two houses of parliament dominated by the NDP. These amendments entered into force following a referendum organized hastily in March 2007, were boycotted by most opposition parties and movements, and did not attract much support among the electorate.[5]

The worst fears of the MB concerning the aim behind these amendments were confirmed a few weeks after their ratification and entry into force, on the occasion of the partial elections of the Shura Council. Not only did the so-called Independent Electoral Commission not perform its supervisory role, but the MB was subjected to various forms of harassment including arrests. As a result they failed to win a single seat in the in the partial Shura Council election on 11 June 2007 (Kenney, 2006; Wickham, 2002; *Al-Ahram*, 2007)

Fear of the Islamists led the government to suspend elections in several professional syndicates since 1992 lest they be controlled by Islamist parties, to arrest over the years thousands of MB members and other Islamists, many of whom were put on trial, and to launch through the official media attacks on Islamist organizations (For details see Al-Sayyid, 2003; Abdel Aziz, 2007; Kamal, 2008)

Unfortunately, fearing the political domination of the Islamists, many of the secular intelligentsia, entrepreneurs and Copts tacitly approved the repressive measures. However we submit that no progress towards democracy in Egypt is possible without finding a legitimate place for the Islamists, who enjoy wide support, in an open political environment.

4.5 Complicity of foreign powers with an authoritarian regime

Certain studies of democratization point to the importance of external variables in the process of transition from authoritarianism, whether through diffusion, demonstration effects, or snowballing. According to these studies, democratization came in waves, as suggested by Samuel Huntington (Huntington, 1991: 85–105; Schwartzman, 1998). However, in the Arab world, the international environment seems to be more supportive of the continuation of authoritarian regimes, despite the rhetoric of the Western countries in support of democratic reform. As with the ruling classes, fear of Islamist electoral victories cast a dampening effect on their enthusiasm for democratic reform, particularly in the wake of the Islamists' impressive showing in elections in countries as far apart as Palestine, Morocco and Bahrain, to name only a few.

The USA, for example, oblivious to the Egyptian government's worsening record on human rights (Carothers and Ottaway, 2005), continued to provide both military and economic assistance to Egypt and to consult with its leadership over matters related to the Palestinian question and other crises of the Middle East (Carothers and Ottaway, 2005). The overriding concerns of the Western countries did not relate to issues of democracy in the region but rather to how their regional interests, which include both oil and Israel, could best be served.

There have been occasions when external environment might have helped push the process of democratization not only through pressures exerted on authoritarian governments, but through support to opposition groups struggling to end authoritarian regimes. Thus, opposition groups in Greece, Korea, the Philippines and several Latin American countries enjoyed sympathy and solidarity from public opinion in Western countries and international political groups when they were ruled by military juntas or authoritarian regimes. By contrast, opposition groups in the Arab countries have lacked this kind of support from Western non-governmental groups or international public opinion. For one thing, many of them, especially Nationalist, Marxist and Islamist parties, are suspicious of foreign support, which is viewed by them as not altruistic, masking imperialist designs over Arab countries. For another, Arab governments are ever ready to seize on any manifestation of foreign sympathy to claim that such groups have become agents of foreign powers. Thus in the case of Egypt political parties are banned not only from getting foreign funding but are not even allowed to affiliate with an international movement. Civil society organizations must seek government approval for any foreign funding.[6] Any negative comment on the human rights situation in Egypt by a foreign government or an international human rights organization is immediately condemned by official spokespersons of the Egyptian government as constituting flagrant interference in the internal affairs of the country and a violation of its sovereignty.

Outside criticism of violations of human rights or lack of substantive democratic development in Egypt (e.g. heavy-handed interventions in the elections process) has usually been mild in nature and the Egyptian government has been able to live with it. Such criticism has rarely affected formal relations between the Egyptian government and Western governments, and foreign economic and military assistance has continued to flow into Egypt from Western countries. Reduced foreign economic assistance to Egypt (e.g. Official Development Assistance) declined from an annual average of US$3.2 billion for 1990–9 to $926 million for 2005, while US economic aid dropped from $0.8 billion for 1998 to $348 million for 2005) was not due to any intended pressure on the Egyptian government to undertake serious democratization measures. Rather it reflects a new orientation in US foreign aid policy to move Egypt gradually towards reliance more on trade than aid as a way of supporting its economy, which has been improving in recent years.[7] More importantly, annual US military assistance, which is highly political in character as an indicator of close strategic relations between donor and recipient countries, has continued to flow to Egypt at the same pace ($1.3 million annually from 1998 to 2006), unaffected by worsening relations between the Egyptian government, opposition political parties and civil society organizations.

Finally, in the past several years the frequency of high-level official visits between the two countries might at times have been interrupted as result of specific political events in Egypt (e.g. the imprisonment in 2005 of Ayman Nour, head of the Ghad party and former presidential candidate) or of unwelcome pronouncements on the part of high-level US officials concerning political developments in the country. However, any strained political relationships between the two countries that may have been caused by such events were of marginal importance and temporary in nature, and in the end did not lead to any significant change in the political behaviour of the Egyptian government. High-level visits of officials of the two countries resumed in 2007.

5. Conclusions

Using the global Polity IV scores to measure progress in political representation in the past 40 years, EMM conclude that the Arab region has lagged behind the rest of the world in its democratic status. An Arab democracy deficit continues despite the notable growth in the region's level of per capita income and, on average, significant improvement in health and educational standards. Accordingly, they conclude that the pure modernization hypothesis does not account for the lack of significant democratic progress in the Arab world. Instead they propose an extended modernization model which includes historical, religious, social and Arab-specific factors to explain this phenomenon. Their model shows that oil wealth and regional conflicts are the major explanatory variables of the persisting Arab democracy deficit.

Building on these above results, we examined more closely the relationship between democracy and development in Egypt over the period 1960–2005. Examination of economic and political linearization measures in Egypt over this period reveals that economic liberalization has been sustained, particularly since 1968, while political liberalization has fluctuated in a rising, albeit modest, trend.

Our empirical analysis shows that the basic modernization model does not explain the persistence of a democracy deficit in the case of Egypt, whereas EMM's extended model (which includes oil, regional wars and neighbourhood polity) performs better. Regional conflict, according to this model, has been a real inhibitor of democratic transformation in Egypt. Surprisingly, fuel exports do not seem to have had a direct effect on Egypt's polity, though the region's oil wealth may have had an indirect negative influence. Going beyond oil and regional conflicts, we introduced three additional variables (labour migration, foreign aid and urbanization). While both foreign aid and urbanization were insignificant, labour migration (measured by remittances) proved significant. This provides support for the exit-vs-voice thesis as per Hirschman.

We also argue that the strong deindustrialization of Egypt since the late 1970s provides additional explanation of the retarded democratization in the country over the period of the study. This is in contradistinction to the case of South Korea, which had similar initial conditions as Egypt but which managed to undergo deep and extensive industrialization accompanied at a later stage by a process of democratization. While in South Korea the structure of the economy changed towards more capital-intensive assets, in Egypt's case the increase in income per capita was associated with a less capital-intensive and more resource-intensive endowment of assets. Further, deindustrialization in Egypt created a tendency for employment to be concentrated in service sectors, where productivity is low and labour is largely unorganized.

To what extent could the findings of this chapter be generalized? What does the case of Egypt tell the reader about conditions for democratic transition? Some of the findings are relevant for the literature on democratization in countries of the South and former Socialist countries, whereas others are relevant for the study of political change in the Arab countries.

As a test of the modernization hypothesis, the Egypt case demonstrates that higher per capita income levels and, more generally, standards of living do not necessarily go along with a process of democratization. However, if development is understood to mean structural transformation of the economy, then Egypt did not do well. From this perspective, the little political liberalization that took place in the country could be taken to support the argument that a high level of development often correlates with democracy. This is indeed the case of many of the newly developed countries: advances along the path of economic development preceded transition to more democratic regimes in countries of East Asia such as South Korea and Taiwan. As Egypt has not even become a newly industrialized country, it is perhaps not surprising that it did not move fast along the path of democratization. On the other hand, India, one of the world's largest countries, has been a democracy since independence, before it emerged as a major industrial power. And there are many poor developing countries in Africa, Asia and Latin America with liberal political systems. But it remains to be seen whether democracy can be consolidated in these countries before they reach higher levels of economic development.

The symbiotic relationship between entrepreneurial groups and state officials is quite relevant in understanding the causes of sluggish progress towards democracy in many Arab countries. In fact, maintaining close relations with state officials is very important as a way of accumulating and maintaining fortunes. Entrepreneurial groups are part of the political elite in several Arab countries. In some, for example Saudi Arabia, members of the ruling elite have strong business interests, with a few of them among the richest people in the world. In other countries, like Egypt, relatives of major figures of the ruling elite are active in business. Under these conditions, entrepreneurial groups are highly unlikely to press for democratization. Why should they seek to change a political regime of which they are not only the major beneficiaries, but also the leading actors?

There is no doubt that fear of the Islamists is invoked as a cause to refrain for pushing for political liberalization not only in Egypt but in other Arab countries as well. This is definitely the reason for limiting the political space to mostly secularist parties in Tunisia, continued harassment of Islamists in Morocco and the gerrymandering of the electoral law in Jordan. Islamists have emerged as the major opposition group in all these countries. Apprehension about the implications of their rising power is not confined to members of the ruling elite. Whether justified or not, it goes beyond this elite to members of non-Muslim minorities, and to large sections of the educated middle class and business groups.

Finally, fear of the Islamists serves also to demonstrate the hallowed commitment to democracy on the part of the G8 countries, who declared in 2004 at their Sea Island Summit in the US state of Georgia their support for political reform in the so-called 'Broader Middle East'. Electoral victories of Islamists in Egypt in 2005 and in Palestine in 2006 brought these governments solidly behind authoritarian leaders in Egypt, Tunisia and elsewhere in the Arab and Muslim world, despite the less than honourable record of respect for human rights by their leaders. With such tacit or implicit support for Arab authoritarian leaders, governments of the G8 have lost all credibility as democracy advocates. Their action in favour of such rulers emboldened those leaders and contributed to the shrinking prospects for genuine transition to more democratic regimes in the Arab world.

In the final analysis, for the foreseeable future, such prospects rest to large extent on the ability of the advocates of democracy to mobilize the mass support that would allow them, via constitutional measures, to pressure the ruling elite to move in the direction of a substantive democratic state.

Annex

Modified Democracy Indicators for Egypt

Polity indictors have been frequently used in time-series analyses of political behavior to provide a measure of a regime's democracy and/or autocracy. The global polity score measures the difference between two sub-indicators: DEMOC and AUTOC. Measured along an ordinal scale, its value ranges from –10 for absolute autocracy to +10 for perfect democracy (aside from the standardized authority codes –66, –77 and –88, which represent cases of interregnums).

It is important to note that the annual polity values describe the political regime in place on 31 December of the data year. As stressed in the Polity IV documentation, it is always important for users of the database to consider whether it is more appropriate to use the annual ordinal measures (i.e. variables DEMOC, AUTOC or POLITY) or to collapse those ordinal values into categorical values or regime states (e.g. autocracies, democracies or transitional polities).

In Egypt's case, we have the following Polity IV scores:

DEMOC = 0 throughout 1960–2003
AUTOC = 7 for 1960–1975, and
= 6 for 1976–2003
POLITY = –7 for 1960–1975, and
= –6 for 1976–2003

This gives a step function-shaped trajectory of polity score (see Figure 9.2).

Such a polity score trajectory raises two problems. The first is factual: judged against our survey of political liberalization in section 2 above, the polity score ignores changes in Egypt's polity/democratization within each of the two subperiods. The second problem is econometric; with only values of either –7 or –6 throughout the period of analysis, the variability of the dependent variable (as expressed by the Polity IV score) during 1960–2003 is extremely low. Econometric estimation of the modernization model in this case becomes very difficult, and may even be a futile exercise.

To address these two problems, we used enlightened judgement (based on our detailed discussion of the trajectory of political liberalization in section 2 and Events Count data for Egypt, 1960–2003) to modify the polity score along the same range (i.e. from –10 to +10). The result was a modified polity score,

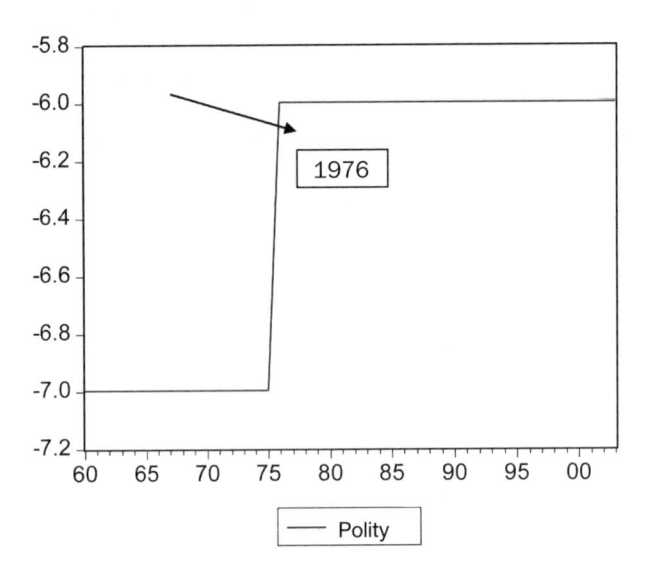

Figure 9.2 Polity score for Egypt, 1960–2003.
Source: Table 9.3.

'modpolity'. We then derived a normalized score, 'moddem', as our dependent variable for the regression, using the linear transformation

'moddem' = ('modpolity' +10)/20,

where 20 is the difference between the best and the worst polity score (= 10 − (−10)). As in the case of 'dem', it ranges from 0 for absolute autocracy to 1 for perfect democracy.

As another alternative indicator of democracy, we used the Freedom House political rights index, 'FHpolrights', which is available only starting 1972. But it should be noted that, as derived, 'polity' is an objective measure, while 'FHpolrights' is not. 'FHpolrights' runs along an ordinal scale ranging from 7 (for worst situation/condition) to 1 (for best situation/condition). To convert it to a normalized scale comparable to 'moddem' we used the linear transformation:

'fhplrtsdem' = ('FHpolrights' −7)/(−6),

where −6 is the difference between the best and the worst FHpolrights score (= 1 − 7). As in the case of 'dem' and 'moddem', 'fhplrtsdem' ranges from 0 (for worst situation) to 1 (for best situation).

Figure 9.3 shows the three alternative democracy indicators: 'dem', 'moddem', and 'fhplrtsdem'. It shows clearly that compared to the original democracy indicator, 'dem', both 'moddem' and 'fhplrtsdem' exhibit more variability – a feature which is desirable from an econometric standpoint.

Egypt: the persistence of autocracy 277

Furthermore, it is our judgement that they better reflect changes/developments in Egypt's polity over the period 1960–2003, as discussed in section 2. The dynamics of Egypt's polity revealed by the pattern in Figure 9.3 are rather interesting. For the period 1960–2003 as a whole, Egypt may have experienced a slight trend toward increasing democratization. But within this trend, there was a clear and strong cyclical pattern, very much like the movement of a pendulum. Not all the democracy gains in the 1970s and 1980s were sustained through the 1990s and the new millennium.

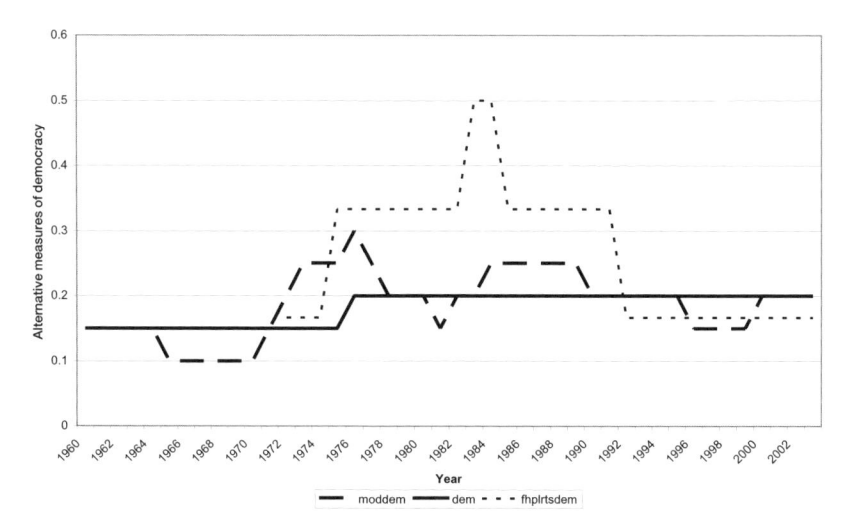

Figure 9.3 Alternative measures of democracy for Egypt, 1960–2003.

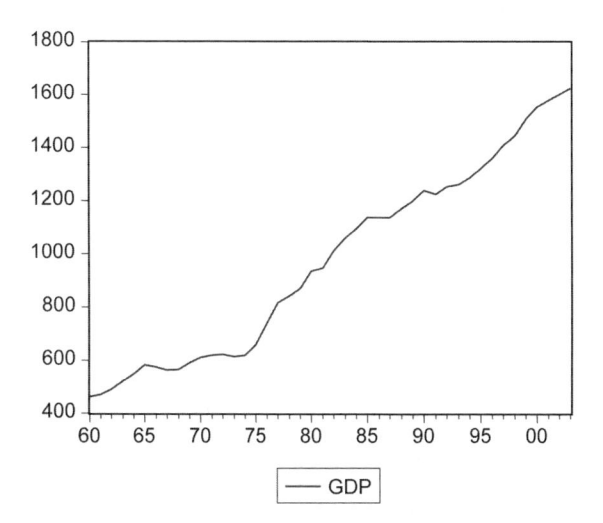

Figure 9.4 GDP per capita, 1960–2003.
Source: World Bank, 2005.

Table 9.3 Alternative democracy measures for Egypt

Polity year	FH year	FHpolrights	Polity	Modpolity	Moddem, based on events count	Dem	FHplrtsdem
1960			−7	−7	0.15	0.15	
1961			−7	−7	0.15	0.15	
1962			−7	−7	0.15	0.15	
1963			−7	−7	0.15	0.15	
1964			−7	−7	0.15	0.15	
1965			−7	−8	0.1	0.15	
1966			−7	−8	0.1	0.15	
1967			−7	−8	0.1	0.15	
1968			−7	−8	0.1	0.15	
1969			−7	−8	0.1	0.15	
1970			−7	−8	0.1	0.15	
1971			−7	−7	0.15	0.15	
1972	1972	6	−7	−6	0.2	0.15	0.166667
1973	1973	6	−7	−5	0.25	0.15	0.166667
1974	1974	6	−7	−5	0.25	0.15	0.166667
1975	1975	5	−7	−5	0.25	0.15	0.333333
1976	1976	5	−6	−4	0.3	0.2	0.333333
1977	1977	5	−6	−5	0.25	0.2	0.333333
1978	1978	5	−6	−6	0.2	0.2	0.333333
1979	1979	5	−6	−6	0.2	0.2	0.333333
1980	1980	5	−6	−6	0.2	0.2	0.333333
1981	1981–2	5	−6	−7	0.15	0.2	0.333333
1982	1982–3	5	−6	−6	0.2	0.2	0.333333
1983	1983–4	4	−6	−6	0.2	0.2	0.5
1984	1984–5	4	−6	−5	0.25	0.2	0.5
1985	1985–6	5	−6	−5	0.25	0.2	0.333333
1986	1986–7	5	−6	−5	0.25	0.2	0.333333
1987	1987–8	5	−6	−5	0.25	0.2	0.333333
1988	1988–9	5	−6	−5	0.25	0.2	0.333333
1989	1990	5	−6	−5	0.25	0.2	0.333333
1990	1991	5	−6	−6	0.2	0.2	0.333333
1991	1992	5	−6	−6	0.2	0.2	0.333333
1992	1993	6	−6	−6	0.2	0.2	0.166667
1993	1994	6	−6	−6	0.2	0.2	0.166667
1994	1995	6	−6	−6	0.2	0.2	0.166667
1995	1996	6	−6	−6	0.2	0.2	0.166667
1996	1997	6	−6	−7	0.15	0.2	0.166667
1997	1998	6	−6	−7	0.15	0.2	0.166667
1998	1999	6	−6	−7	0.15	0.2	0.166667
1999	2000	6	−6	−7	0.15	0.2	0.166667
2000	2001	6	−6	−6	0.2	0.2	0.166667
2001	2002	6	−6	−6	0.2	0.2	0.166667
2002	2003	6	−6	−6	0.2	0.2	0.166667
2003	2004	6	−6	−6	0.2	0.2	0.166667

Source: Freedom House and Polity IV data sets.

Notes

1 British military troops had occupied the country in Sept. 1882. The United Kingdom offered Egypt limited autonomy in 1922 and formal independence in 1936. British troops withdrew from Egypt in June 1956.
2 The elasticity of employment with respect to GDP (the ratio of the growth rate of employment to the growth rate of GDP) actually fell from 0.58 in 2004/05 to 0.42 in 2006/7 (Institute of National Planning, 2007: 17).
3 Many experts believe that official sources underestimate the rate of unemployment, which may be closer to 15–20 per cent.
4 According to certain interpretations of Islamic Shari'a law, interest payment by banks is a form of usury banned by Islam.
5 Official data indicate that 24 per cent of registered voters cast their votes, with 85 per cent of them approving the amendments. Human rights organizations estimated that the turnout rate probably did not exceed 2–3 per cent of registered voters (Brown *et al.*, 2007).
6 Sa'd el-Din Ibrahim, head of the Ibn Khaldoun private research centre, was tried in May 2001 on the charge that he received funding from the European Union without getting government approval to promote registration of women voters. The Egyptian Human Rights Organization was denounced in pro-government press for receiving a grant from the British parliament, allegedly for writing a report on the situation of Copts in Egypt. The grant had been meant for a project to help handicapped people. Most recently, the MB was also denounced in pro-government newspapers because their representatives in the People's Assembly met US congressmen in Cairo, together with other members of the Egyptian parliament, at the US Embassy in Cairo. The invitation had been passed on to them by the Speaker of the Peoples Assembly himself.
7 This reduction was also related to a congressional review of US foreign assistance, which reallocated US economic assistance away from countries in the Middle East such as Israel and Egypt in favour of countries mainly in Africa and the former USSR, which were seen by the US Congress to be in dire need of aid. The figures can be found in World Bank, 2007: 348, 352.

References

Abdel Aziz, Omar (2007) 'Niqabat Misr talga' ela al-omam al-muttaheda lehemayateha men al-hirasah' (Syndicates in Egypt Resort to the UN to Protect them Against Government Control), *Al Masry Al Youm* (26 May).

Abdel-Khalek, G. (1992) *Perestroika without Glasnost? Economic Liberalization and Democratization in the Middle East*, MERA Occasional Paper, 16.

—— (2001) *Stabilization and Adjustment in Egypt: Reform or De-Industrialization*, Cheltenham: Edward Elgar.

—— (2003) *Industry and Industrialization in Egypt* (in Arabic), Cairo: Academic Press.

Acemoglu, D. and. Robinson, J. A. (2006) *Economic Origins of Dictatorship and Democracy*, Cambridge: Cambridge University Press.

AHDR (2002) *Arab Human Development Report 2002: Creating Opportunities for Future Generations*, New York: UNDP.

—— (2004) *Arab Human Development Report 2004: Towards Freedom in the Arab World*, New York: UNDP.

Al-Ahram (2007) 'Al-Shura fi Misr wa al-'alam' (Consultative assemblies in Egypt and the World) (13 June).

Al-Kawary, A-K. (2000) *The Democratic Question in the Arab Homeland* (in Arabic), Beirut: Centre for Arab Unity Studies.

Al-Sayyid, M. K. (2003) *The Other Face of the Islamist Movement*, Working Paper, 33, Carnegie Endowment for International Peace: Washington, DC (Jan.).

Al-Sayyid Marsot, A. L. (1994) *A Short History of Modern Egypt*, Cambridge: Cambridge University Press.

Barro, R. J. (1997) *Determinants of Economic Growth: A Cross Country Empirical Study*, Cambridge, MA: MIT Press.

Binder, L. Leonard. (ed.) (1971) *Crises and Sequences in Political Development*, Princeton, NJ: Princeton University Press.

Brown, N, Dunne, M., and Hamzawy, A. (2007) *Egypt's Constitutional Amendments*, web commentary, March, Washington, DC: Carnegie Endowment for International Peace.

Carothers, T. and Ottaway, M. (2005) *Uncharted Journey: Promoting Democracy in the Middle East*, Washington, DC: Carnegie Endowment for International Peace.

Elbadawi, I., and Makdisi, S. (2007) 'Explaining the Arab Democracy Deficit', *Quarterly Review of Economics and Finance* 46/5 (Feb.).

Elbadawi, I., Makdisi, S. and Milante, G. (2006) 'Technical Note on Democracy and Development in the Arab World', unpublished manuscript.

El-Ghonemy, R. (ed.) (2003) *Egypt in the Twenty-First Century: Challenges for Development*, London: Routledge Curzon.

El-Issawy, I. (2007) *The Egyptian Economy in Thirty Years* (in Arabic), Cairo: Academic Press.

Haykal, M. H. (1983) *The Autumn of Fury: Assassination of Anwar Sadat*, London: Deutsch.

Hilal, A. al-Dīn (ed.) (1978) *Democracy in Egypt: Problems and Prospects*, Cairo Papers in Social Science, Cairo: American University in Cairo Press.

Hinnebusch, R. (1985) *Egyptian Politics under Sadat: The Post-Populist Development of an Authoritarian-Modernizing State*, Cambridge: Cambridge University Press.

—— (1990) *Authoritarian Power and State Formation in Ba'thist Syria: Army, Party and Peasant*, Boulder, CO: Westview Press.

—— (2006) 'Conclusion', in El-Ghonemy (ed.), 2003 *Egypt in the Twenty-First Century. Challenges for Development*, London: Routledge Curzon, ch. 10.

Hirschman, Albert O. (1970) *Exit, Voice and Loyalty: Responses to Declining Firms, Organizations and State*, Cambridge, MA: Harvard University Press.

Huntington, S. P. (1991) *The Third Wave: Democratization in the Late Twentieth Century*, Norman, OK: Oklahoma University Press.

Ikram, K. (2006) *The Egyptian Economy, 1952–2000*, London: Routledge.

Information and Decision Support Center (IDSC) (2007) 'Has the Pattern of Agricultural Holdings in Egypt Changed?', *Information Reports* 1/2 (Feb.).

Institute of National Planning (2007) *The Egyptian Economy 2006/07*, Cairo: Institute of National Planning.

Kamal, Abdallah (2008) 'A Forum for Investigating Anarchy: How could the Muslim Brotherhood be a Banned Organization while its Mission and Plans are Diffused Freely and Publicly?', *Rose El-Youssef* (30 April).

Kassem, M. (1999) *In the Guise of Democracy: Governance in Contemporary Egypt*, Reading: Ithaca Press.

Kenney, J. T. (2006) *Muslim Rebels: Kharijites and the Politics of Extremism in Egypt*, Oxford: Oxford University Press.

Kienle, E. (2001) *A Grand Delusion: Democracy and Economic Reform in Egypt*, London: I. B. Tauris.

Lipset, S. M. (1959) 'Some Social Requisites of Democracy: Economic Development and Political Legitimacy', *American Political Science Review* 53/2 (June).

Mabro, R. (1974) *The Egyptian Economy, 1952–1972*, Oxford: Oxford University Press.

Mansour, F. (1992) *The Arab World: Nation, State and Democracy*, London: Zed Books.
O'Donnell, G. (1993) 'On the State, Democratization and Some Conceptual Problems: A Latin American View with Glances at Some Postcommunist Countries', *World Development* 21/8: 1355–69.
Schmitter, P and O'Donnell, G. (1986) *Transitions from Authoritarian Rule, Tentative Conclusions about Uncertain Democracies*, Baltimore, MD: Johns Hopkins University Press, vol. 4.
Schwartzman, K. C. (1998) 'Globalization and Democracy', *Annual Review of Sociology* 24: 159–81.
Waterbury, J. (1982) *Egypt under Nasser and Sadat: The Political Economy of Two Regimes*, Princeton, NJ: Princeton University Press.
Wickham, C. R. (2002) *Mobilizing Islam: Religion, Activism, and Political Change in Egypt*, New York: Columbia University Press.
World Bank (2002) *World Development Report, 2002; Building Institutions for Markets*, New York: Oxford University Press.
—— (2005) *World Development Indicators*, CD ROM, Washington, DC: World Bank.
—— (2006) *World Development Indicators*, CD ROM, Washington, DC: World Bank.
—— (2007) *World Development Indicators*, CD ROM, Washington, DC: World Bank.
Zaki, M. (1995) *Civil Society and Democratization in Egypt, 1981–1994*, Cairo: Konrad Adenauer Stiftung, Ibn Khaldoun Center.
—— (1999) *Egyptian Business Elite: Their Visions and Investment Behavior*, Cairo: Konrad Adenauer Stiftung and the Arab Center for Development and Future Research.

10 Sudan: colonial heritage, social polarization and the democracy deficit

Ali Abdel Gadir Ali and Atta El-Battahani

> [W]ere the Sudan to become a kingdom he would be king; a republic he would be president; and in union with Egypt he would be Prime Minister.
>
> (*Manchester Guardian*, interview with Ismail Azhari, Sudan's first Prime Minister, 25 February 1947)

1. Background

In the study of democratic trends in the world, it is now generally agreed that a distinction needs to be made between 'mere' electoral democracy and a more substantial form of 'liberal democracy'. According to Diamond,

> [in] a liberal democracy, elected officials have power as well as authority, and the military and police are subordinate to them. The rule of law is upheld by an independent, and respected, judiciary. As a result, citizens have political and legal equality, state officials are themselves subject to the law, and individual and group liberties are respected. Newspapers and electronic media are free to report and comment, and to expose wrongdoing. Minority groups can practice their culture, their faith, and their beliefs without fear of victimization. Executive power is constrained by other governmental actors. Property rights are protected by law and by courts. Corruption is punished and deterred by autonomous, effective means of monitoring and enforcement.
>
> (Diamond, 2007: 2)

All of these aspects of 'liberal democracy' have been subjected to measurement by various specialized research teams and organizations. The measure of democracy chosen by Elbadawi and Makdisi (see Elbadawi and Makdisi, 2007; Elbadawi, Makdisi and Milante, 2006; and Chapter 2) is the Polity IV measure. The measure, which ranges from −10 (extreme autocracy) to 10 (advanced democracy), is used by Elbadawi, Makdisi and Milante (hereafter EMM) as the dependent variable in an econometric model designed to explain an observed democratic deficit in the Arab countries. Their complete model includes modernity, geographic, historic, religious, social cohesion and Arab-specific variables.

The Arab democracy deficit shows up as a large negative and statistically significant coefficient of the Arab dummy variable.[1]

The Lipset hypothesis, that increases in various measures of the standard of living tend to generate a gradual rise in democracy, as confirmed by Barro's (1998) cross-country study as having a strong empirical regularity, is believed to have failed to explain an Arab democratic deficit. In their companion technical note, EMM (2006) asserted that the only 'consistent exception to pervasive Arab autocracy has been Lebanon. Additionally, there was a short-lived democratic period experienced by the median poor Arab country during 1964–1965 accounted for by the two democracies in Sudan and Somalia.' It is conceded that the failure of these two relatively poor countries to sustain democracy appears to be consistent with the prediction of the Lipset hypothesis. According to Barro (1998: 52), 'democracies that arise without prior economic development – sometimes because they are imposed by foreign colonial powers or international organizations – tend not to last'.

This chapter is a case study on Sudan, the largest country in the Arab region with an area of approximately 2.5 million square kilometres. Sudan became independent on 1 January 1956. Prior to independence, over the period 1889–1955, it was a colony under a non-conventional Condominium Rule with Britain and Egypt as colonial powers, but with Britain as the effective colonial state. This rather late colonization experience was preceded by an earlier period when the country was under Turkish rule (1824–85). Turkish rule was ended in 1885 by a nationalist resistance movement that waged a war from 1881 to 1885. After defeating the Turkish occupying power, the resistance movement eventually established a nationalist regime until the reconquest in 1889. The resistance movement, better known as al-Mahdia, named after its leader Mohamed Ahmed al-Mahdi, ruled the country over the period 1885–98. In a very real sense the nature of the Condominium Rule shaped the post-independence democratic history of the country.

At independence the total population of the country was estimated as 10.3 million. The regional distribution of the population was such that the north and central region accounted for 50.8 per cent of the total; the southern region 27.1 per cent; the western region (mainly Darfur) 12.9 per cent; and the eastern region 9.2 per cent. Of the total population, 91.7 per cent lived in rural areas. The 10 largest cities, with populations in excess of 10,000, accounted for about 5.2 per cent of the total population of the country, with the capital, Khartoum, accounting for about 2.4 per cent of the total population and 48 per cent of total urban population.

Sudan at independence was a very poor country, with a per capita GDP of about US$78 (equivalent to about US$ 670 in 1985 purchasing power parity), placing it among the poorest countries in the world.[2] There was a pronounced disparity in the level of development among the regions: the Blue Nile region with a population share of about 20 per cent, accounting for about 30 per cent of GDP and a per capita GDP of about US$117; the northeast, with a population share of 22.6 per cent, a GDP share of 26.7 per cent and a per capita GDP of US$92; the northwest region, with a population and GDP share of 30 per cent, and a per capita GDP of about US$76; and the south, with a population share of 27 per cent, a GDP share of about 14 per cent, and a per capita GDP of about US$39.

In addition to the disparity in development achievement among regions, independent Sudan was born as a rather highly polarized society, on an ethno-cultural and religious basis. Ethnic, religious and linguistic polarization indexes of 0.625, 0.7496 and 0.764, respectively, are calculated and reported in Ali *et al.* (2005: 205–7).[3] Moreover, and perhaps not surprisingly, the country gained its independence with the majority of its people unable to read and write. In 1960, four years after independence, 87.5 per cent of the population was illiterate, 8.5 per cent had incomplete primary education, 2.4 per cent had complete primary education, and 1.2 per cent had incomplete secondary education. At higher levels of education, only 0.3 per cent had complete secondary education and 0.1 per cent had incomplete tertiary education. The percentage of those having complete tertiary education was too insignificant to be approximated to the relevant decimal points.[4]

Independent Sudan, though poor, highly polarized and largely illiterate, began as a British-styled democratic state with a transitional constitution, a number of parties and an independent judiciary. Had it not been for a security problem that broke out in the southern part of the country prior to independence, the country would have scored a relatively high mark on any democracy rating system. As it happened, however, the security problem in the south escalated into a civil war in 1962. The overall security problem in the south destabilized the country for about 38 years, 1956–72 as a low-intensity war, and in 1983–2005 as a relatively high intensity war. Needless to say, such long-duration civil conflict had obvious implications for the democratic development of the country. The motivation for the outbreak of these civil wars was, to be admitted 43 years later, political in nature.[5]

Having noted this background, the remainder of this chapter is organized as follows. Section 2 deals with the predictions of the EMM model for Sudan and discusses possible ways of understanding the Arab-specific effect of oil and regional wars in explaining the democracy deficit. This section also offers an alternative hypothesis that has to do with the persistence of the features of the colonial state into the post-colonial period. Section 3 gives evidence in support of the alternative hypothesis by tracing the colonial origins of the dominant political parties. Section 4 provides evidence of the carry-over of political practices and behaviour that began during the colonial period into the post-colonial era. The major characteristic of such behaviour was the personalization of politics and the neglect of national issues of development and conflict resolution. Section 5 provides evidence of the absence of relevant development programmes in political manifestos, as judged by the performance of the economy.

2. Model predictions and a supplementary hypothesis

2.1 Model predictions

This section discusses the results for Sudan of using the reference model estimated by EMM (2006). The estimated model is a pooled Tobit one with 879 country-year observations and with the Polity IV score as the dependent variable. For each country there are nine observations, but in view of the fact that for 'each country period the previous period polity score is employed as an independent variable', the average for the first period, 1960–4, is not used as a dependent variable. The empirical strategy used involved estimating the model to test for the modernity hypothesis (proxied by lagged values of the logarithm of per capita income, an education index, polity and neighbour polity) with four regional dummies for the Arab region, Sub-Saharan Africa (SSA), East Asia and Latin America. The results showed a large negative and highly significant Arab dummy, indicating that there exists an 'Arab democracy deficit'. Groups of explanatory variables were then added sequentially, with an eye on when the Arab dummy would cease to be significant. Among the groups of explanatory variables is one that deals with Arab-specific effects: net fuel exports and regional wars. The value of the coefficient of the Arab dummy dropped and became insignificant when these two specific Arab variables, in addition to interaction of the four regional dummies with the regional wars variables, were included in the regression. Following this, a selection process was implemented where all insignificant variables, starting with the Arab dummy, were dropped sequentially. The selection process gave rise to the most narrowly defined version of the estimated model in preparation for country simulations.

In the simulation, the coefficients for 10 explanatory variables were used. The values of these variables (period averages) for Sudan are shown in Table 10.1, where the estimated coefficients are given in figures between brackets. The constant of the EMM preferred estimated equation is −1.475, which is statistically insignificant and so is not used in the predictions. We do not report the coefficients of the SSA dummy and its interaction with regional war, as Sudan is being considered an Arab country.

The general rule used for identifying the Arab democratic deficit is that countries with actual polity higher than predicted polity are more democratic than would be expected, given the model. Countries with lower polity than predicted are less democratic than would be expected.[6] Based on the above estimated coefficients and the averages for the variables in question for the eight periods, the results for the predicted polity index compared to the actual index and the status of democracy are given in Table 10.2.[7] These estimates are based on excluding the constant and the SSA dummy and its interaction with the regional war variable.

Knowing that the lagged polity score is used as an explanatory variable, looking at the status designation in the last column, it seems reasonable to conclude that the estimated model is able to predict the democratic development of Sudan as an Arab country. It successfully identified the second (1965–9) and third (1985–9) democratic periods as 'more democratic' than would have been justified by the model. The remainder of the subperiods are identified as 'less democratic', as indeed they were.

EMM conclude that

> The Arab oil dependency has been a hindrance to the region's democracy . . . [and, that] while inter-state wars and other violent conflicts usually lead to

Table 10.1 Polity score, modernization and other variables for Sudan: averages 1960–2003

Variables	1965–1969	1970–1974	1975–1979	1980–1984	1985–1989	1990–1994	1995–1999	2000–2003
Average polity	6	−6	−7	−7	2.8	−7	−7	−6.5
Lagged log of income (0.453)	5.4241	5.3632	5.3220	5.5223	5.4538	5.4036	5.4881	5.6182
Lagged education index (0.47)	−2.0597	−2.0597	−1.7795	−1.6923	−1.4273	−1.3124	−1.1974	−1.0785
Lagged median polity of neighbour (0.087)	−5.1875	−7.5000	−7.7500	−7.1250	−5.0000	−7.1250	−3.1250	−1.5556
Colonial legacy (−6.151)	0.1111	0.0714	0.0526	0.0417	0.0345	0.0294	0.0256	0.0227
Lagged average polity (1.054)	−5.6	6.0	−6.0	−7.0	−7.0	2.8	−7.0	−7.0
Lagged social cohesion (−0.418)	−3.9150	−4.1947	−4.1947	−4.8938	−4.8938	1.9575	−4.8938	−4.8938
Lagged net fuel exports (−0.016)	−0.020	−0.030	−0.01	−0.13	−0.21	−22.52	−12.10	34.40
Arab *war interaction (−3.473)	0.3571	0.4000	0.2000	0.2381	0.3333	0.3810	0.4762	0.0952

Source: G. Milante by email communication; and authors' calculation for the net fuel exports.

democratic transformation, the Arab region has been a notable exception suggesting that the Arab world is different from comparator regions because of the peculiar influences of wars on democratization in the region.

(EMM, 2006: 33–4)

Given these conclusions, how could 'the Arab oil dependency' be understood as a hindrance to Sudan's democratization? As Sudan became an oil-exporting country only recently, in September 1999, a possible way to comprehend this is through the migration of Sudanese workers to the Gulf countries. In response to an emerging economic crisis in the mid-1970s, caused primarily by the first oil price increase, a large number of individuals migrated to the Gulf oil-producing countries. No exact numbers of Sudanese Nationals Working Abroad (SNWA) was ever reported in the relevant literature or official sources. However, a number of field survey studies were conducted at the time and fairly believable and consistent time-series data were constructed and used by, among others, Brown (1992: 227). According to these estimates the number of emigrants increased from about 185,000 in 1978 to about 350,000 in 1984, and stabilized thereafter. As would be expected, such an emigration process was highly selective in terms of educational levels, skill levels and age groups.

Thus, for example, in 1983 a comparison of SNWA skills to the labour force showed that: 0.4 per cent of SNWA were highly trained administrators, compared to 0.2 per cent for the labour force; 9 per cent were professionals, compared to 3 per cent for the labour force; 7 per cent were clerks, compared to 2.4 per cent, and 4.3 per cent were unskilled workers, compared to 11.9 per cent. In terms of educational levels only 16.6 per cent of SNWA were illiterate, compared to 68 per cent of the labour force; 32.4 per cent had primary education, compared to 6 per cent in the labour force; 17 per cent had an intermediate level education, compared to only 2.1 per cent; and, 26 per cent had secondary or higher qualifications, compared to 4.8 per cent in the labour force. Indeed, in 1983 it was officially reported that out of 5815 medical doctors, 2254 had left the country (a ratio of 39 per cent); out of 2640 engineers 950 had migrated (a ratio of 36 per cent); and, out of 1665 trained teachers, 965 had opted to migrate (a ratio of 58 per cent).[8] In one

Table 10.2 Democracy deficit in Sudan

Period	Average polity index (API)	Predicted polity index (PPI)	Difference (API minus PPI)	Democratic status
1965–1969	6	−5.2	11.2	More democratic
1970–1974	−6	7.1	−13.1	Less democratic
1975–1979	−7	−4.7	−2.3	Less democratic
1980–1984	−7	−5.3	−1.7	Less democratic
1985–1989	2.8	−5.3	8.1	More democratic
1990–1994	−7	2.2	−9.2	Less democratic
1995–1999	−7	−5.3	−1.7	Less democratic
2000–2003	−6.5	−4.5	−2.0	Less democratic

Source: Column 1 Milante; other columns authors' calculations and designation of status.

sense, then, emigration induced by the Arab oil effect served to depopulate the country of its most politically dynamic elements, thus hindering the democratic process.

In addition to the migration effect, it can also be argued that the seeds of the demise of the third democracy were sown through the Arab oil effect during the second phase of the Niemeri regime, from 1969 to 1985. Following a 1977 national reconciliation, the Muslim Brotherhood movement, under its charismatic leader Hassan al-Turabi, was brought into the ruling regime (along with its monolithic party, the Sudanese Socialist Union).[9] Apart from using the experience to learn the tricks of government, the Muslim Brotherhood started learning how to accumulate financial capital, a domain previously preserved for the urban followers of the unionist parties. The beginning of the drive towards commercial strength was the establishment of the Faisal Islamic Bank (FIB) in 1978.[10] The 'growth of Islamic banking in Sudan was a reflection of a process generated primarily by the rising power of the petrodollar economics and the corresponding politico-ideological leverage accorded to Saudi Arabia and the Gulf states' (Sidahmed, 1997: 207). There is evidence to suggest that the FIB was, for all intents and purposes, the strategic command centre of the Muslim Brotherhood (*Ikhwan*) movement.[11]

Moreover, though Sudan became an oil exporter only recently, as noted above, it can be argued that the Arab oil effect became operative on its own accord through lengthening the political life of the ruling autocracy. Oil revenues afforded the regime the opportunity to abandon a very unpopular policy of inflationary finance and to undertake a relatively successful stabilization policy, while spending lavishly on the military-security establishment – its core power base. Calculations based on information from the IMF (2000, 2007) show that total revenue available to the central government amounted to US$782 million in 1998 (i.e. one year before the export of oil, representing about 7.9 per cent of GDP); it increased to about US$ 4,315 million in 2004 (one year before the signing of the Comprehensive Peace Agreement, CPA, representing about 19.7 per cent of GDP). Thus, total resources at the disposal of the regime increased sixfold over the period, and prior to the CPA of 2005 the flow of oil revenue enabled the regime to successfully confront the rebel movement in the south (i.e. Sudanese People's Liberation Movement, SPLM, and Sudanese People's Liberation Army, SPLA) and bring the conflict to a stalemate that eventually facilitated the peace process.

Oil revenue also enabled the regime to expand its patronage networks and broaden its support base, by co-opting opposition groups drawn from northern political parties and rebels in western and eastern Sudan into its expanding governmental bureaucracy. In addition, the commercial exploitation of oil enabled the regime to forge a strategic alliance with China, a permanent member of the UN Security Council, that protected the regime in international circles (despite the many Security Council resolutions passed against the regime).

To appreciate the role of the second Arab-specific effect, itself an interaction between the Arab dummy and the regional wars variable, it is perhaps important to recall that the regional wars variable is a composite index. This index weights the three types of wars by the distance from the borders where the war was waged. For the case of Sudan, its civil war is given a weight of one, with smaller weights for the other wars. Thus, it seems reasonable to argue that the regional wars dummy reflects the role of the civil war in Sudan in its democracy deficit. We hasten to note, however, that the Sudanese civil war had a dual role as far as the history of democratic governance in the country is concerned. One role is that of catalysing the transitions to democracy from military regimes, as has happened in the transition from the first military regime to the second democracy, and in the transition from the second military regime to the third democracy. The other role is in precipitating military takeovers (i.e. coups d'état).

The catalysing role of the civil war in transitions to democracy is very well documented. For example, the October uprising of 1964 was a result of the police attacking a University of Khartoum student's public debate on the handling by the military regime of the civil war in the south, during which two students were killed.

> On 22 October a mass protestation against the regime was manifest in the funeral procession of the first student killed... Demonstrations continued until the beginning of strikes on 24 October and the declaration of a general political strike on 26 October.
>
> (Sidahmed, 1997: 76)

It is now known that by 26 October 1964 the military regime was overthrown; by 30 October a caretaker government was formed by a broad-based United Nationalist Front (composed of a trade union front and political parties); and by 15 November General Abboud had resigned and handed over his powers as head of state to the civilian cabinet. One of the crowning achievements of the October transitional government was the convening of a roundtable conference for all political parties to deliberate on the southern question, with the aim of reaching a democratic settlement. The conference was convened in Khartoum on 16 March 1965, with the very active participation of southern political parties. Despite its failure to achieve its stated objectives, it is now known that the recommendations of the conference formed the foundations of the Addis Ababa Accords (AAA) of 1972, which settled the first civil war and resulted in a period of peace that lasted for about 11 years. These accords, it will be recalled, were reached by the May regime with the southern rebel movement of the time, the so-called Anya Nya.

One of the motivations for the May 1969 coup d'état was the southern problem, as it was then known. As noted by Sidahmed,

> One of the first declarations of the regime was the one known as the June Declaration (made on 9 June 1969), which provided a new reading of the southern issue, recognizing that there existed historical and cultural differences between the North and the South and that the southern people were entitled to a kind of regional autonomy.
>
> (Sidahmed, 1997: 114)

As noted above, the June Declaration eventually gave rise to the AAA, which grouped the three southern provinces into a self-governing southern region with a Peoples' Regional Assembly (i.e. a parliament) and a High Executive Council (i.e. a regional cabinet).[12] At the end of the political day for the second military regime, and given the political dynamics in the country and the survival calculus of the then dictator, a new penal code based on Islamic Shari'a was announced on 8 September 1983. It suffices here to note that this move eventually led to the resumption of armed conflict in the south, culminating in the establishment of the SPLA, which was to wage the second civil war of the country, lasting about 22 years. In a sense, therefore, the first civil war caused the demise of the first military regime and helped the transition to the second democracy; but it also motivated the second military regime and prolonged its life, as an unintended consequence of the AAA.

In a similar fashion, it can easily be argued that the second civil war facilitated the transition to the third democracy on the one hand, and precipitated the Islamic coup d'état of 1989 on the other. In this respect it should be recalled that the second military regime was toppled by a popular uprising in April 1985, which eventually gave rise to the third democracy. At that time the civil war in the south had become a high-intensity conflict, with the SPLA recording an increasing number of military victories. Under democratic governance a number of initiatives to come to grips with the causes and nature of the conflict were proposed, involving political parties and civil society organizations. Towards the end of the third democratic period a broad agreement on approaches to resolving the conflict seem to have been reached by all political factions, save for the National Islamic Front (NIF), a metamorphosis of the Muslim Brotherhood movement of earlier days. This agreement was known as the Sudanese Peace Initiative (SPI), concluded between the SPLA/M and the Democratic Unionist Party (DUP) in the last quarter of 1988.[13] Under the SPI, a National Constitutional Conference was planned for 31 December 1988, but was never convened due to political wrangling regarding the agreement. Eventually, however, the government of the day adopted the SPI and started to implement some of its preconditions. Such peace dispensation on part of the government accelerated the NIF designs to abort the peace process. Eventually the NIF engineered its Islamic coup d'état of 30 June 1989. Once again, the dual role of the civil war in the democracy deficit in the country is too obvious to require further elaboration.

In addition to the dual role of the civil war in the democracy deficit of the country, the second Arab-specific effect can be understood as having been a hindrance to the democratic process in Sudan in an indirect way, working through the membership of Sudan in the League of Arab States (LAS). A careful review of the relevant Sudanese literature would show that the Arab Unity cause, save for admiration expressed for Nasser as a towering Arab leader, was never a compelling rallying point for any of the Sudanese political parties, including the so-called unionist parties. Ba'athist, Nasserite and Arab Unionist parties were, and remain to this day, embryonic and confined mainly to universities. Despite this, however, the Arab–Israeli conflict constituted one of the standard pillars of Sudan's foreign policy under all governing regimes.[14]

2.2 *A supplementary hypothesis*

Despite the observations noted above, it can easily be argued that Sudan is neither a typical Arab country nor a typical Sub-Saharan African country. In the World Bank's classification of countries for operational purposes Sudan is classified as an SSA country.[15] In the African context, an important historical influence on the long-term evolutionary process of institutions in general and governance institutions in particular has been the colonial encounter. There is evidence to show that where the colonial powers decided to settle they introduced democratic governance institutions, while where they decided not to settle they opted for 'despotic governance institutions'. Colonial institutions, it is argued, remained into the post-colonial period. It is these inherited institutions that have influenced the governance and development performance of African countries, including Sudan.[16]

Mamdani argues that the colonial state in Africa was

> a double-sided affair. Its one side, the state that governed a racially defined *citizenry*, was bounded by the rule of law and an associated regime of rights. Its other side, the state that ruled over *subjects*, was a regime of extra-economic coercion and administratively driven justice.
>
> (Mamdani, 1996: 19)

Late colonialism posed the question of how a tiny and foreign minority could rule over an indigenous majority. This is the famous 'native question'. The answer was indirect rule: 'a mode of domination over a free peasantry... For the subject population of natives, indirect rule signified a mediated–decentralized – despotism.' From experience, the colonial powers' answer to the native question was 'generalized decentralized despotism'. The colonial powers defined an all-embracing world of the 'customary', with the seat of the customary power in the rural areas being the local state. 'The functionary of the local state apparatus was everywhere called the chief. The authority of the chief thus fused in a single person all moments of power: judicial, legislative, executive, and administrative.' Thus, the 'African colonial experience came to be crystallized in the nature of the state forged through that encounter. Everywhere, the local apparatus of the colonial state was organized either on an ethnic or on a religious basis' (Mamdani, 1996: 16–24).

The colonial state created a civil society which was, first and foremost, a society of the colonists. 'The rights of free association and free publicity, and eventually of political representation, were the rights of citizens under direct rule, not of subjects indirectly ruled by customarily organized tribal authority' (Mamdani, 1996: 19). Between citizens (the few colonists) and subjects (the majority of the indigenous population) there was a third group of urban-based natives (mainly middle- and working-class individuals) who were exempt from customary law but who did not necessarily enjoy the rights bestowed by modern law. The colonial state was the protector of the civil society of the colonists.

In the context of the colonial encounter, the development of an indigenous civil society can be looked at as having proceeded in three phases. The first phase is that of the anti-colonial struggle. This phase can be seen as a struggle for entry into civil society by the middle and working classes. The second phase is that of independence. This phase is identified with the deracialization of the state, but not of civil society. During this phase the state–civil society antagonism diminished due to the shift of tensions within civil society. Important in this tension was the policy of Africanization (or Sudanization), which involved the dismantling of inherited privileges. Such dismantling had a unifying effect on the victims of the colonial state. It also had a divisive effect when it came to issues of redistribution. The same majority was divided 'along lines that reflected the actual process of redistribution: regional, religious, ethnic, and at times familial' (Mamdani, 1996: 20). The third phase is that of the collapse of the embryonic indigenous civil society, of trade unions and autonomous civil organizations, and their absorption into political society. This is the 'time when civil society-based social movements became demobilized and political movements statized' (Mamdani, 1996: 21). Sudan's experience, it can easily be argued, provides evidence in support of this phasing.

At independence, two major forms of states emerged: conservative and radical. Under the conservative African state the hierarchy of the local state apparatus was maintained. Thus, the decentralized despotism of the colonial state was reproduced. Under the radical African state, 'a constellation of tribally defined customary laws was discarded as a single customary law transcending tribal boundaries' (Mamdani, 1996: 25). The alternative was to 'develop a uniform, country wide customary law, applicable to all peasants regardless of ethnic affiliation, functioning alongside a modern law for urban dwellers'. Thus, a version of the bifurcated state remained. 'The antidote to decentralized despotism turned out to be a centralized despotism' (Mamdani, 1996: 25).

'In the back-and-forth movement between a decentralized and centralized despotism, each regime claimed to be reforming the negative features of its predecessor' (Mamdani, 1996: 25–6). The continuity of the form of the colonial state in post-colonial national regimes was underlined by the despotic nature of power:

1   intensification of the administratively driven nature of justice, customary or modern;
2   enforcement of administrative imperatives through extra-economic coercion in the name of development;
3   tightening and strengthening the power of the local state, despite changing functionaries' titles; and,
4   enforcement and deepening of the gulf between city and country.

The conservative states removed the sting of racism from a colonially fashioned stronghold but kept in place the native authority, which enforced the division between ethnicities. The radical states joined deracialization to detribalization, but put a premium on administrative decision-making. Thus the bifurcated post-colonial state was deracialized but it was not democratized.

On this basis we strongly believe that a creative adaptation of Mamdani's original thesis can offer a fruitful explanation of the democracy deficit in Sudan. Such an adaptation will help in understanding the observable schisms, factionalism and short-sightedness of the Sudanese political class. We argue that, perhaps due to its unique colonial experience, Sudan produced alternating periods of conservative and radical post-colonial regimes. Under either version of the post-colonial state, 'despotism' was interpreted as 'imposing discipline' on the political masses. Invariably, conservative states in Sudan were those guarded by democratically elected governments, while radical states were those guarded by military governments.[17] More importantly, the most enduring feature of its unique colonial experience is not only the continuity of the colonial institutions into post-colonial ones, but also the continuing nature of political practices and behaviour.[18]

3. The colonial roots of the democracy deficit

There is general agreement among political science analysts and historians that both before independence and in the post-independence period three major social groups came to hold great influence on the political, social and economic life of northern Sudan and the country as a whole: religious leaders, tribal leaders and merchants. This was due to historical factors relating to the domination of religious life in northern society by Muslim Sufi orders and to the policy of indirect rule of the colonial state. In the old days (sixteenth to eighteenth century), religious leaders consolidated their wealth and position through their ability to mobilize small savings from their followers, depending on a number of factors including the nature of the religious organization. The Mahdist revolution, despite scattered scepticism, was the culmination of such Muslim Sufi influence on northern political, social and economic life.

At independence, the most prominent, and politically involved, religious orders included: the Ansar, followers of Sayed (Mr) Abdel Rahman al-Mahdi; the Khatmiyyah, followers of Sayed Ali al-Mirghani; and the followers of Sharif (Honourable) Yusuf al-Hindi. Given their social status and influence, the colonial state followed a deliberate policy of enhancing the business interests of these families by preferential allocation of productive assets (mostly land), business contracts and bank loans (converted into grants), with the objective of minimizing the risk of resistance to the colonial regime.[19]

Tribal leaders were the cornerstone of the indirect rule policy, and as such their economic influence was deliberately increased by colonial policy (see e.g. Niblock, 1987: 53). Under the colonial state, the merchant class grew over the years. While export and import trade were dominated by British companies, with Egyptians, Syrians, Lebanese and Greeks sharing in the spoils, Sudanese merchants were allowed to trade in gum arabic, livestock and oilseeds. Some of these merchants had the foresight to invest their profits in related manufacturing ventures such as oilseed pressing and cotton ginning.

As early as 1918, the political life of the country started to revolve around the two most prominent religious leaders, al-Mahdi and al-Mirghani, with the other two social groups appropriately aligning themselves with one religious leader or the other. Thus, for example, the most influential 'civil society' organization of the time, Sudan School Graduates Club (SSGC), which started as an apolitical social organization, found itself engulfed in politics as a result of the Egyptian revolution of 1919. 'The club found itself split along the lines of the Co-Domini, with some supporting the Egyptians and others upholding the British' (Khalid, 1990: 76). The gradual evolution of a dual political system, with platforms articulated around the Co-Domini on the one hand and the sectarian leaders on the other, took shape following the 1924 revolt of the White Flag League, a pro-Egypt political organization. A Sudanese nationalist platform expressed pro-British sentiments with the ultimate aim of achieving a separate state for the country independent of Egypt. The political ideas of this platform reflected the posture of the leader of the Ansar sect, al-Mahdi. A unionist platform expressed pro-Egypt sentiments with the ultimate aim of achieving a union with Egypt. The political ideas of the platform reflected the posture of the leader of the Khatmiya sect, al-Mirghani. Signs of factional politics appeared as early as 1931, along these political alignments.

In 1938, the Graduates General Congress (GGC) was born as a civil society organization whose membership was open to former pupils of post-elementary schools, and whose aim was to promote the general welfare of the country and the graduates. The GGC governance structure featured a council of 60 members, to be elected annually by the general assembly, and responsible for the laying out the guidelines for overall policy; as well as a committee of 15, to be elected by the council of 60, responsible for the routine business of the Congress. Officers of the Congress, selected from the committee of 15, included a president (on a monthly basis), a general secretary, a treasurer and an assistant general secretary.

Over the period 1938–42 the GGC maintained a non-confrontational relationship with the colonial government, largely in view of the domination of its committee of 15 by an older and more senior group of graduates. Nonetheless, undercurrents of personal rivalries among its most active members could be detected at the time. 'Towards the end of 1941, it was becoming clear that individuals whose loyalties lay primarily with either Mahdist or Mirghanist coteries were beginning to squeeze out those who were committed to higher causes' (Khalid, 1990: 80). Over time, the GGC became increasingly split along sectarian lines.

It was in 1942 that these sectarian lines were clearly drawn in the wake of the famous GGC memorandum sent to the colonial government. The first of 12 demands required the issuance

> on the first possible opportunity, by the British and Egyptian governments, of a joint declaration granting the Sudan, in its geographical boundaries, the right of self-determination; this right to be safe-guarded by guarantees

assuring full liberty of expression in connection therewith; as well as guarantees assuring the Sudanese the right of determining their natural rights with Egypt in a special agreement between the Egyptian and Sudanese nations.

(Khalid, 1990: 443)[20]

In the context of the development of civil society under colonial states, the time of the memorandum could be considered as the historical moment of an attempt to 'enter the civil society' of the colonists. Under such an interpretation it is perhaps not surprising to find that the response of the colonial government was uncompromising. The colonial government rejected the GGC demands and warned the GGC to 'renounce any claim, real or implied, to be the mouthpiece of the whole country' (Khalid, 1990: 82).

In the face of the rejection of its demands, the GGC was faced with only two obvious choices: to continue to cooperate with the British authorities or to opt for confrontation. Cooperation was the choice of those moderate elements of the GGC who were aligned with the Mahdist sect; confrontation was the choice of those aligned with the Khatmiyya sect. At that moment, in addition to the two sectarian leaders, there appeared on the political scene as a major actor Ismail al-Azhari, who had long purported to lead a non-sectarian political party, the Ashiga party.[21] Eventually, al-Azhari opted for alliance with the Khatmiyya sect (i.e. that of al-Mirghani).[22]

The GGC ceased to be a national organization in November 1947, the time of the elections for its constitutional bodies.[23] The elections were contested by four major graduate groups: the unionists, the liberals, the Ashiga and the nationalists. Each group declared itself on the issue of the future of Sudan. The Ashiga group won the elections with a clear majority that enabled it to occupy all 15 seats of the GGC executive committee (for details see, among others, Taha, 2004).

In response to the results of the GGC elections, on 31 March 1945, the Umma party (UP) was established as a broad coalition of the Ansar sect, tribal leaders and a few nationalist intellectuals. A number of parties were established thereafter, including the Nile Valley Unity party on 4 October 1945, and the Republican party on 4 November 1945. The Sudanese Communist Party (SCP) was established in 1946, but operated under the name of the Sudanese Movement for National Liberation (SMNL).[24] The National Unionist Party (NUP) was established in November 1952.[25]

As noted by Brown (1992: 96), the two main religious leaders

> combined their existing popular support and growing economic power, with substantial political influence among the leadership of the country's educated elite. In turn, this meant that the main constituencies of the political parties lay within the social groups at the core of the economic elite, and not among the popular masses. In this way the values and objectives of the economic elite came to predominate and thus determine the political orientation of the main tendencies within the nationalist movement as the country approached its

independence. It also implied that Sudan's political leadership, during most of the post-independence era, remained the captive of its major clients among the economic elite.

One important consequence of these historical developments was that the policies pursued by the post-colonial state in Sudan were not designed to bring about radical changes to the existing socio-economic order, nor were they designed to attract popular support. 'Political parties maintained themselves in power by their ability to forge alliances with those elements among the economic elite whose religious, tribal or other bases of social prominence enabled them to command the support of the mass of the population' (Brown (1992: 97).

'Commanding the support of the mass of the population' is perhaps the most central element of liberal democracies with multi-party elections.[26] The very first parliamentary elections conducted in 1953, for a self-rule government, were contested by the two major parties, the NUP and the UP, in addition to a number of small parties including the Republican Socialist Party (RSP). In this respect it is interesting to note that the RSP was composed of tribal leaders and that its creation is credited to the British administration, which hoped that it would carry the political day of the country. In the light of the above it is perhaps not surprising that the results of the first parliamentary elections showed that 75 per cent of the 97 seats from geographic and graduate constituencies went to the two parties aligned with the two major religious sects: NUP with 50 seats and UP with 23. The total number of geographic constituencies was 92, with 22 allocated to the south and the remainder to the north. In addition to these geographic constituencies, five additional constituencies were reserved for 'graduates of secondary schools' in Sudan. These five graduate constituencies were open for competition at the country level. The details of the election results for the geographic constituencies are reported in Table 10.3.

Table 10.3 Regional basis of political parties in 1953: parliamentary seats from geographic constituencies

Province	National Unionist Party	Umma Party	Republican Socialist Party	Southern Party	Others	Total
Blue Nile	6	10	2	0	0	18
Kassala	6	1	0	0	1	8
Khartoum	9	0	0	0	0	9
Darfur	2	6	1	0	2	11
Kordofan	11	6	0	0	0	17
Northern	7	0	0	0	0	7
Bahr El Ghazal	1	0	0	2	4	7
Equatoria	0	0	0	5	2	7
Upper Nile	4	0	0	2	2	8
Total	46	23	3	9	11	92

Source: Compiled from Niblock (1987).

The table indicates that NUP's regional base was in the northeast of the country and Kordofan Province, while that of the Umma Party was in the Blue Nile and the northwest. As noted in the introduction, in terms of GDP the northeast contributed about 27 per cent while the Blue Nile and the northwest regions contributed 30 and 29 per cent respectively. The Blue Nile is the heart of the cotton-growing area, with both large-scale government and privately owned cotton enterprises. The northeast's GDP is dominated by transport and distribution activities; building and construction; the services sector, including banks and trade; and building ownership. While such information could be used as indicators for distinguishing between the economic bases of the political parties, it is perhaps safe to say that the two major parties had similar economic bases and hence represented similar economic interests, mainly those of agricultural 'capitalists'.[27] This was borne out in the results of the various democratic elections and the nature of policies pursued by the various governments.

Consistent with the observation on economic interests, and as noted earlier in the historical origins of modern politics in Sudan, were the social origins of the elected members of parliament (MPs). According to Niblock's (1987) classification, social origins can be looked at in terms of four major categories: tribal and religious leaders; ex-government employees and ex-army officers; merchants and farmers; and teachers and others. Table 10.4 summarizes the distribution of members of the first parliament according to social origins.

The political history that led to the capture of the post-independence Sudanese state by the economic elite (with their religious following) partly explains the involvement of the military in the politics of the country. The results of the 1953 self-rule elections indicated that the country was to be ruled by a coalition government, in view of the lack of a clear majority won by either of the two major parties. Indeed, the two major parties later split from within in various directions and for various reasons. The first split came in June 1956 when 'Khatmiyya loyalists among the tribal leaders, religious agents and factions of bourgeoisie with economic interests in rural areas of the northern and eastern Sudan, broke away from the NUP and formed the Peoples' Democratic Party (PDP)' (Ali, 1990: 117).[28]

Six months after the declaration of independence the NUP government fell. In its place, an unlikely coalition government of UP and PDP was formed.

Table 10.4 Social groups of the members of the first elected parliament

Social group	Northern constituencies	Southern constituencies	Graduate constituencies	Total
Tribal and religious leaders	31	3	0	34
Ex-employees and ex-officers	19	10	1	30
Merchants and farmers	14	1	0	15
Teachers and others	6	8	4	18
Total	70	22	5	97

Source: Authors' compilation from Niblock (1987).

> On virtually every policy issue the two parties were divided, the so-called radical elements of the PDP still paying lip service to causes similar to those taken on board by the current Egyptian government, whereas the Umma looked to the west for its political creed.
>
> (Khalid, 1990: 131)

Despite this, the coalition survived, mainly because of the threat posed by the NUP that started to gain a lot of popular support in urban areas. It is on the basis of this potential political threat that the UP–PDP coalition government turned to revising the electoral laws so as to guarantee the continuation of the coalition government following the elections to be held in 1958. The changes introduced affected, among other things, the number and distribution of geographical constituencies. The total number of constituencies was increased from 92 to 173, an increase of 88 per cent. Niblock (1987) provides evidence to show that the number of constituencies was increased in the various regions of the country where the coalition government had a large number of followers: by ratios from 94.4 per cent (Blue Nile) to 128 per cent (northern). The number of constituencies for Khartoum, the largest urban area and where the opposition parties had strong followings, was left unchanged.

As per the design of the UP–PDP coalition government, the 1958 election results came out in favour of the coalition parties (with UP winning in 63 constituencies and PDP 26), despite the surprising NUP gain of 44 constituencies out of a total of 173. The changing of the electoral laws resulted in a vote count anomaly of around 340,000 for the NUP compared to 310,000 for the UP. The unlikely coalition continued in power up to the time of the takeover by the military on 17 November 1958. The military was invited to take over the reigns of power by the UP Prime Minister.

Salih (2001: 87) quotes historians Holt and Daly as having noted that by 'mid-1958 the position of the government was fast becoming intolerable. Deteriorating economic conditions were underlined by obvious incapacity of the political parties to cope with them. Serious national issues were seen to be subordinate to increasingly hectic maneuvers necessitated by the unworkable' UP–PDP coalition. Salih (2001: 87–8) goes on to draw two lessons relevant to our alternative hypothesis: (1) that 'the Sudanese political elite continued their wrangling over office and prestige, often at the expense of pressing national issues'; and (2) 'political proliferation and the newly created offshoots of the conventional political parties and factions had barely transcended the sectarianism of the political parties they rejected'.

4. The persistence of political practices

It will be recalled that the main idea of our alternative hypothesis is that colonial institutions persisted into the post-colonial period.[29] We have already seen that, given the colonially induced sectarian roots of the political parties, the democratic practices of the country during the first period of democracy revolved around mostly unsustainable coalition governments. The evidence shows that, except for the very first pre-independence government, all other governments formed during the democratic periods of the country were coalitions. All in all there were 12 coalition governments over the 13 years of democratic rule:[30] NUP–UP and UP–PDP during 1956–8; UP–PDP in 1958; UP–PDP in 1965–6; NUP–SUP in 1966–7; IUP–NUP in 1967–8; IUP–DUP in 1968–9; UP–DUP in 1986–8 (two in number); UP–DUP–NIF in 1988; UP–NIF in 1988–9; and a broad coalition in 1989.

During the second democracy of 1965–9, party politics gave rise to the second significant split in a major party. This time around it was the Umma party that found itself split into two parties, one belonging to the religious leader of the Ansar (the Imam) and called the Imam Umma Party (IUP), and the other belonging to a young aspirant nephew of the Imam, Sadig al-Mahdi, called the Sadig Umma Party (SUP).[31] Prior to the split, the 1965 elections produced an UP–NUP coalition government. The NUP leader, al-Azhari, became the president of the Supreme Council (SC) following a mechanical amendment to the transitional constitution. The amendment gave al-Azhari the opportunity to become the permanent president of the SC, a position that was originally supposed to be filled on a rotating basis among five members. Mahjoub, a veteran UP politician supported by the Imam of Ansar, was elected as Prime Minister. At the time of the elections, Sadig al-Mahdi was below the statutory age of 30 years for parliamentary candidature, but he was the president of the UP. As soon as he became 30, a geographical constituency was vacated for him; and after winning the arranged by-election, on 27 July 1966 he became Prime Minister, presiding over yet another coalition government (this time NUP–SUP).

The sorry story of why and how the second democracy ended is very well documented in the relevant literature. Suffice it to note for our purposes that the elected parliament, in addition to amending the constitution to satisfy al-Azhari's thirst for overall leadership, also amended the constitution to ban a legal party, the Communist party, and oust its MPs. Moreover, when the Supreme Court ruled against the ban, the government ignored the court's ruling, forcing the chief justice to resign.[32] A major political crisis was thus created, precipitating the May 1969 military takeover. In the latter days of the second democracy, following the elections of 1968, the leading politicians had already 'exhausted their energies in the intra- and inter-party feuds, neglecting, in the process, an ailing economy, a divided country and an escalating civil war' (Khalid, 1990: 226).[33]

However, it is important to note that during the second democracy, political Islam appeared as an organized mass political party in the form of the Islamic Charter Front (ICF), under the leadership of Hassan al-Turabi. As subsequent events would show, the emergence of al-Turabi increased the number of political players in the country and diversified the portfolio of intrigues. The political platform of the ICF was the need to draft and implement a so-called Islamic constitution. The advocacy for an Islamic constitution embarrassed and intimidated the two major parties, given their religious constituencies. In a multicultural and multi-religious society, such advocacy proved to be increasingly divisive, but also broadened the field for political wrangling. As subsequent events proved, the ICF, modern in its organization and highly efficient in its operations, eventually emerged as a neo-sectarian party.

In addition, the second democracy saw a deepening of the sectarian structure of political parties that had been inherited from the colonial period. Though there is repeated reference in the literature to the aspirations of Sayed Abdel Rahman al-Mahdi to becoming the King of Sudan, in practice his involvement in politics was as a mentor of the UP, being the Imam of Ansar. Sayed Ali al-Mirghani was not known to have any political ambitions and was the mentor of the unionist parties. Thus, up to the beginning of the second democracy there was a separation between the spiritual and the political in the structure of the two dominant parties. However, the mentoring of political parties was sufficiently damaging to the democratic culture and practices of the country. As succinctly noted by Salih (2001: 103), the 'nature of the political culture expected to support democracy' was such that 'affiliation to a political party is secondary to religious belief in the divinity of the leadership'. From the days of colonialism, the followers of the political parties constituted

> a horde of disciples, who have never been in a position to challenge the divine leadership from whom they seek religious blessing more than political or economic rewards. The leaders of these parties bask in the homage bestowed upon them by their disciples, including an educated political elite.

Before the end of the second democracy, the separation between the spiritual and the political started to wane. The new Imam of Ansar, Sayed Elhadi al-Mahdi, supported an Islamic constitution and expressed an interest in becoming the president of the Islamic Republic whenever it was created. Sayed Sadig al-Mahdi, since that time the president of the UP, argued for and eventually succeeded in merging the leadership of the sect and the party. His original argument was couched in terms of modernizing the Ansar followers, but the political expediency of creating a captive party was clear. Similarly, Sayed Mohamed Osman al-Mirghani eventually became the president of the DUP. The inability to 'challenge the divine leadership' of the political parties became more entrenched in the political culture of the country despite the passage of time and changing circumstances. The persistence and the deepening of the political culture inherited from colonial times further weakened a number of the fundamental principles of democracy noted in the introduction.

The third democracy came in the wake of the toppling of the May military regime by a popular uprising (intifada) in April 1985. The political force behind the intifada was the Alliance for National Salvation (ANS), which was composed of most of the political parties as well as most of the trade unions and professional syndicates.[34] The army, under the influence of the middle-ranking officers, sided with the popular uprising. As usual with Sudan's popular uprisings there was a transitional period, up to April 1986. During this period a transitional government, with a military council as the head of state and legislature, was charged with preparing for democratic elections. The transitional government inherited a weak economy, an intensifying civil war in the south and a set of controversial Islamic laws (the so-called Shari'a, or September, laws). The laws were enacted and implemented by the Nimeiri regime in 1983, with the full backing of the Muslim Brotherhood movement, which at the time was part of the regime.[35] Both were acting on pure political expediency. Without getting involved in details that are well documented in the literature, it should be noted that there was a popular political demand to abrogate the laws.[36] The political forces of the intifada sought to expunge the legal deadweight inherited from the May regime. The followers of Turabi, now recreating their political organization as the NIF, who had supported the discredited laws and were part of the defunct regime, were indeed in a very embarrassing political position. Some analysts would argue that the conditions that prevailed at that political juncture could easily have marked an end to political Islam in the country, due to the NIF's active collaboration with the May regime. The irony for Sudan was that the reverse happened. Under the NIF, and with their accumulated financial capital, the Islamists were able to turn the tables on all involved, launching an offensive against the transitional government (and the political forces it represented), opposing a peaceful settlement of the civil war, and forcing the issue of upholding Shari'a into the political debate.

After 18 years of military rule, elections were held in April 1986 and in June Sadig al-Mahdi formed the first of five coalition governments.[37]

> The old curse of Sudanese multi-party democracy returned in full force including intrigue, nepotism and personalized state authority, leading to political instability and public discontent [and] in less than a year, Sadig al-Mahdi had dismissed the government and formed a new coalition with DUP and the Southern parties.
>
> (Salih, 2001)

From the perspective of the persistence of political practices we need to note that in dissolving the various coalition governments that he formed during the third democracy, Sadig elected not to step down as prime minister. Of course, such behaviour is rather unconventional in the context of parliamentary democracy, where governance responsibility is usually held to be collective. This is similar to the political behaviour of Azhari during the second democracy, as noted above.

Another famous incident demonstrating the persistence of political practices has to do with the handling of peace initiatives by the prime minister at the time. In brief, it should be noted that during the transitional period the ANS, giving priority to resolving the civil war, was able to sign the now famous Koka Dam Declaration (KDD) with the SPLM/SPLA in March 1986. Among the signatories were representatives of the UP; the DUP, however, was conspicuously absent. The declaration stipulated certain prerequisite steps towards convening a national constitutional conference, among them the repeal of the Shari'a laws. Despite being a signatory to the KDD, the UP-led coalition government formed after the elections failed to act on the agreed upon prerequisites.

Without discussing historical details, we need to note that on 16 November

1988 the DUP, following lengthy contacts with the SPLM/SPLA, reached a peace accord that was signed by the leaders of the two parties. It is known that the terms of the DUP/SPLM accord were similar to those of the KDD, including the freezing of the Shari'a laws. Thus, by this time only the NIF remained outside the peace process. 'Partly because of their own ideological commitment to some form of Islamic Law and presumably because they wanted to deny the DUP the political advantage of the agreement with the SPLM/SPLA, leaders of the Umma' party opposed the al-Mirghani peace accord, as it became known at the time (Deng, 1993: 206). The parliament, with a mechanical majority of the UP and the NIF, rejected the accord but authorized the prime minister to negotiate with the SPLM/SPLA, taking into account all previous peace initiatives. In the end, a peace initiative complementary to that already signed by the UP was rejected and the peace process was sacrificed at the altar of political rivalry.

5. Absence of development programmes

The previously noted features of the political process, and the nature of the dominant parties, had obvious implications for the choice and pursuit of economic and development policies. A fair observation would be that while democratic governments were inclined to maintain the status quo by pursuing the same policies, military regimes have been relatively more adventurous in trying new policies – whether planning-oriented or more market-oriented. Thus, the first 10-year plan was launched during the first military regime while two other plans were drafted during the second military regime. It was also the second military regime that decided to formulate and implement structural adjustment programmes with support from the IMF and the World Bank. The third military regime, after some delay, decided to formulate a home-grown version of an adjustment programme, not supported by the IMF and the World Bank. Moreover, it was the first military regime that decided to receive the highly politically charged US foreign aid, while the second military regime, during its early days, went ahead with the adventure of trying to formulate an Egyptian-style socialist policy programme inclusive of nationalization and confiscation, prior to seeing the light of the Washington-consensus style of economic development.

It could be conjectured that the economic policy choices made by the various democratic governments stem mainly from the dominant political parties' adherence to the old style, pre-independence haggling over power, without their having developed legitimacy in the sphere of economic performance. In this respect Salih observes that the

> Sudanese political elite of different political persuasions still use the discourse of independence, the events that had shaped it and the configuration of political life that ensued, to claim and justify their right to rule. As a result they have offered virtually no new visions of governance, or alternative institutional arrangements.[38]

(Salih, 2001: 78)

There is abundant evidence to suggest that the pattern of investment chosen by the governments of the first two democratic periods was dictated by the economic structure inherited from the colonial state. The political parties forming the various democratic governments did not have articulated economic programmes to structurally transform the economy. As such, they continued the set of economic policies implemented during the colonial period, with major investments in the agricultural sector and possibly some investment in the transport sector. The orientation of the economic policy was largely benign with respect to the private sector, seeking to encourage it to invest in the import-substitution industrial sector with the government taking initiatives in some of the factories with the intention of privatizing them in the future. The emerging private sector invested in real estate, cotton pump schemes and mechanized rain-fed agriculture for the obvious reason of high returns to investment in these sectors. There was little technological progress, little innovation and little learning in terms of production and institutional organization. During this period the macroeconomic environment was fairly stable, but due to weak institutions and highly polarized politics, the period saw the escalation of the conflict between the north and the south. The result was negative, and volatile, economic growth.

The third democracy inherited a highly distorted economy due to the failed attempts by the second military regime to change the structure of the economy during its first phase (1969–72), and the subsequent market reorientation of the economy under the auspices of the IMF and the World Bank. Perhaps the inherited political practices noted earlier in section 4 did not allow time for the political elite of the three major parties of the third democracy to articulate relevant policies to address the economic and development problems of the country. As the governments of the third democracy decided to follow inherited policies, the end result, once again, was negative and highly volatile growth.

A summary of the evidence for these conclusions is presented in Table 10.5, where average per capita GDP and its growth rate for the relevant time periods are indicated. Figures between brackets under the growth rates are coefficients of variation reflecting the volatility of the growth process.[39] The evidence is available for the second and third democracy periods. In 1960, the first year in the first five-year period of the model, per capita GDP was US$861 in 1985 purchasing power

Table 10.5 Economic growth under political regimes in Sudan, 1960–1989

Period	Per capita GDP (US$)	GDP per capita growth rate (%)	Ruling regime
1960–1964	850	−1.24 (3.42)	First military regime
1965–1969	810	−0.62 (5.74)	Second democracy
1970–1974	779	−1.84 (3.95)	Second military regime-I
1975–1979	893	4.09 (2.70)	Second military regime-II
1980–1984	865	−0.34 (9.41)	Second military regime-III
1985–1989	806	−0.45 (14.93)	Third democracy

Source: Ali (2006): 30: table 1.

parity. At the prevailing economic conditions of the 1960s, including a capital–output ratio of three, it was thought feasible to double per capita GDP in 10 years as reflected in the 10-year plan of 1961/2–1970/1.[40] Despite this feasibility, however, there is evidence to suggest that, up to 1989, the terminal date for the third democracy, the country was unable to regain its 1960 real GDP per capita.

A number of observations can be made on Table 10.5. First, contrary to commonly held beliefs, the first military regime, which had been inherited by the second democracy, did not record an exceptional economic performance. Over the period 1960–4, the economy recorded an overall negative average growth rate of 1.2 per cent per annum. The annual details show that it was only in 1962 that a positive, relatively high growth rate of about 4.9 per cent was recorded. The second democracy started in 1965 with a per capita GDP of US$854 and a relatively high growth rate of 5.4 per cent. The remaining years of the second democracy saw a continuous decline in per capita income, with negative rates of growth every year. By the end of the second democracy, per capita income declined to US$790, less than that inherited from the first military rule. Moreover, the data also show that the growth process during the second democracy was highly volatile, as reflected by a coefficient of variation of 5.7, higher than the volatility of the growth process under the first military rule.

The third democracy, following a fairly long duration of the second military rule, inherited a devastated economy with a per capita GDP of US$791, about 92 per cent of the per capita income of 1960. The average growth rate for the third democracy period was negative and highly volatile. Indeed, this period recorded the highest volatility of the growth process in the economic history of the country, as reflected in a coefficient of variation of 14.9. Except for 1986, where a relatively high rate of growth of 7.7 per cent was recorded, the remaining years recorded rates that were negative, and relatively high in absolute terms. The average per capita income for the third democracy was even lower than that of the second democracy. This rather dismal economic and development performance can be explained partly in terms of the unstable international economic environment, with the dominance of international financial institutions in development policy-making, and partly in terms of the intensifying civil war in the south of the country.

Be that as it may, to the continuation of inherited political practices in the post-colonial phase we may now add the inherited economic structure. No government – military or democratic – was able to change the economic structure inherited from the colonial period. It is well known that development in a dual economy like that of Sudan is usually achieved through a structural transformation from a low productivity sector (usually agricultural or traditional) to a high productivity sector (usually industrial or modern). The structural transformation process involves the migration of resources (mostly labour) from the low productivity sector to the high productivity sector. Over a long period of time, say 10 years or more, the transformation process will be reflected in a decline of the GDP share of the low productivity sector and as an increase in the share of the high productivity sector.

Such transformation can be studied in the context of the now famous

Chenery–Syrquin cross-country regressions. In such an analysis, a development transformation variable (such as the share of various sectors in GDP) is used as a dependent variable, to be explained by: per capita GDP, its squared value (reflecting the stage of development of the country) and the population size and its squared value (reflecting the size of the market). Predicted values of the transformation variables can then be compared with actual values to determine the achieved transformation.

The most recent estimate of a structural transformation equation is that of O'Connell and Ndulu (2000)[41] According to these estimates, the three stylized facts of structural transformation may be summarized as follows:

1. The share of agriculture in GDP tends to decrease to a minimum as the economy develops. Such a minimum share is to be attained at a per capita GDP of US$8,854 (in 1985 PPP).
2. The share of industry tends to increase towards a maximum as the economy develops. Such a maximum share is to be attained at a per capita GDP of US$20,465 (in 1985 PPP).
3. The share of the services sector tends to increase towards a maximum as the economy develops. Such a share is to be attained at a per capita GDP of US$1,492 (in 1985 PPP).[42]

Table 10.6 summarizes the evidence for Sudan for the relevant periods where the actual shares of sectors in GDP are compared to the predicted shares, and where the actual GDP per capita is provided for easy comparison with the turning points of the stylized facts.

The table clearly shows that over the period from 1960 up to the end of the third democracy no discernible structural transformation took place in the economy. By the end of the third democracy, the economy continued to be dominated by agriculture, contributing almost a third more GDP than is predicted by the estimated model. The share of industry stagnated at around 16 per cent of GDP over the whole period, always less than that predicted by the model. Only the services sector showed signs of transformation, where the share in GDP is greater than

Table 10.6 Structural transformation in Sudan, share of sectors (%)

Period	Agriculture Actual	Agriculture Predicted	Industry Actual	Industry Predicted	Services Actual	Services Predicted	Per capita GDP (US$)
1960–1964	52	32	14	26	34	42	850
1965–1969	40	32	16	25	45	43	810
1970–1974	44	31	14	24	42	44	779
1975–1979	39	31	13	24	48	45	893
1980–1984	34	29	15	25	51	46	865
1985–1989	34	29	16	24	49	47	806

Source: Ali (2002): 266; table 3.

that predicted. Given the turning point for this sector the increase in its share of GDP should be understood as a sign of distorted economic growth, given the behaviour of the other two sectors, rather than a genuine transformation.

6. Concluding remarks

In this chapter we have explored the extent to which the model estimated by EMM (2006) to explain the observed democracy deficit in Arab countries could apply to the case of Sudan. Using a recommended procedure of comparing actual polity scores with predicted ones, we concluded that the model does indeed predict the democratic periods of the country. Our detailed analysis has shown that the two specific Arab effects causing such a democratic deficit – oil dependency and regional wars – have in the case of Sudan operated both directly and indirectly. Given the fact that Sudan is an atypical Arab country, however, we proposed a supplementary hypothesis that helps shed light on its continuing democracy deficit.

The supplementary hypothesis is that the observed democracy deficit in Sudan could be further understood in terms of its unique colonial experience, which shaped the emergence of a civil society under a condominium rule of Britain and Egypt as competing, rather than collaborating, colonial powers. The political parties that emerged under the colonial rule, with a tradition of sectarian patronage and personalized politics, persisted in the post-colonial phase and continued to dominate the political life of the country. We provided evidence to support the supplementary hypothesis. On the basis of the evidence provided, it could be conjectured that the explanation of the democracy deficit in Sudan, a poor and highly fractionalized country, lies in the nature of the social order and political discourse inherited from the colonial period.

If indirect rule was the genius of the colonial powers in answering the 'native question' of how a foreign minority could rule an indigenous majority, it seems fair to conclude that the national political elites were unable to either formulate or answer a similar question. Under colonialism the majority of the people were the 'subjects' of the colonial state, and only a very small minority were 'citizens'. This suggests that following independence the relevant question should have been the 'national question': how could a tiny, educated elite rule an illiterate majority? This question, far from being answered, was never posed.

Notes

1. They were able to essentially replicate their results using the Freedom House political rights and civil liberties measures of democracy. Hence their results appear to be robust against choice of democracy indicators as well as against a battery of econometric tests.
2. Purchasing Power Parity in US$ measures the actual value of a currency in terms of its ability to purchase similar products costing US$1 in the base year used. This allows for a more accurate comparison of income levels across countries and over time. The base year for the comparison can obviously be changed and the GDP estimates appropriately adjusted.

3 A polarization index is defined as $PI = 1 - 4 \Sigma(0.5 - \pi_i)^2 \pi_i$, where π_i is the percentage share of the ith group in total population. This index ranges from 0 (for totally homogeneous society) to 1 (for when a society is divided into two groups of equal size).
4 This evidence is taken from Barro and Lee (2000).
5 The admission of the political nature of the conflict is to be found in the Comprehensive Peace Agreement signed on 9 Jan. 2005 in Nairobi, Kenya, by the Government of Sudan and the Sudan Peoples Liberation Movement, the political arm of the SPLA.
6 Overall, to identify the deficit, simulations were run for each country such that predictions for the polity index below −10 and +10 are censored to the relevant 10 score.
7 Note that the predicted results, and the status designation, are not sensitive to including all estimated coefficients (including SSA dummy and its interaction and the constant), or to excluding the constant but keeping the SSA dummy and its interaction, or the reverse.
8 For similar survey-based results see, among others, Gelaleldin (1985) and Choucri (1985).
9 The Muslim Brotherhood movement was at the time an active member of an opposition formation known as the National Front, which included the Unionist Party (UP) and the Democratic Unionist Party (DUP). The National Front attempted to overthrow the Niemeri regime by staging a military action from Libyan bases. Feeling the threat to the regime, national reconciliation was initiated. Both the UP and the Muslim Brotherhood accepted reconciliation, while DUP declined.
10 The bank is named after a Saudi Prince and financier, hence the indirect Arab oil effect.
11 For evidence, see e.g. Mekki (1999).
12 On 3 March 1972 the AAA became the Regional Self-Government Act for the Southern Provinces; and in May 1973 they were incorporated into the so-called permanent constitution as Article 8.
13 At the time, it should be noted, the DUP was a new convert to the peace camp.
14 It is possible to argue, however, that the dominant Arab-Muslim Sudanese ruling class manipulated the Arab–Israeli conflict to derail a sluggish democratic process. Thus e.g. the May 1996 coup d'état is known to have had Nasserite sentiments among its leading officers; the attempted coup d'état of April 1990 is known to have been staged by Ba'athist officers; and, LAS gave support for the ruling government in the 1990s in the civil war.
15 In its *Human Development Reports* UNDP classifies Sudan as an Arab country.
16 From an economic perspective the relevant institutions are called 'market supporting' (see e.g. Acemoglu *et al.* (2001), and Rodrik *et al.* (2004)).
17 Conventional analysis of alternating post-colonial regimes is summarized by Landes:

> [The] post colonial Africans had no experience of self-government, and their rulers enjoyed a legitimacy bounded by kinship networks and clientelist loyalties. Abruptly these nations were pressed into the corset of representative government, a form alien to their own traditions. . . . But the legacy was rule by a strong man. Stability depended on one man's vigor, and when he weakened or died, the anarchy of the short-lived military coup followed.
> (Landes, 1998: 504)

18 The most widely used definition of institutions is that of North (1990: 3–5): institutions 'are the rules of the game in a society or, more formally, are the humanly devised constraints that shape human interaction'. The constraints could be formal, as in modern laws, or informal such as conventions, codes and customs.
19 Note that the authority and economic power of the tribal leaders increased under the colonial state in view of the fact that they represented the core of the indirect rule policy. Moreover, a quasi-modern commercial class started to emerge. For details see e.g. Niblock (1987).

20 The remaining demands included: the formation of a representative body; increased spending on education; separation of powers; increased mobility within the country; definition and legalization of nationality; control of migration; regularization of cotton production; employment in government posts; increased opportunities in economic activities; employment in the private sector; and, unification of the education system.

21 According to Taha (2004: 182), the Ashiga party came to be known with that name in Nov. 1943 when it broke ranks with Sayed Abdel Rahman al-Mahdi. Prior to that it was known as the Fadli-Azhari group, whose origins date to a 1931 cultural society established by a famous unionist politician, Yahia Al-Fadli.

22 For fascinating details of how GGC politics were run, see Abu Hassabu (1985).

23 A number of observers would argue that the use of the adjective 'national' in the context of GGC is rather generous. The political class represented by GGC excluded and marginalized non-Arab educated elites who created a parallel organization (the Black Bloc) to counterbalance the then emerging 'nationalist' movement heavily tilted towards the Arab north. However, it needs to be noted that the membership of GGC was open to all school graduates irrespective of their ethnic origins.

24 It was only in 1964 that the party took its SCP name. 'Although at this stage the SMNL was but a small grouping, and relatively weak, it was still an important departure for Sudanese politics, because, for the first time, Sudan had a political party with an expressly secular, unitary and radical ideology' (Khalid, 1990: 86).

25 NUP came about due to efforts by Egyptians to unify unionist factions.

26 This is indeed the most emphasized technical aspect of the current democratization wave sweeping various regions in the world since the collapse of the Soviet Union in the late 1980s.

27 For more detailed analysis of the economic interests of the political parties see e.g. Ali (1990); Mahmoud (1986).

28 Relating the creation of the PDP and the eventual coalition with the Umma party to the evidence of the social origins of MPs, Ali (1990: 119) concluded that 'the regime of July 1956 represented an alliance of the agricultural capitalists and the religious aristocracy with the latter exercising effective, undisguised and unmitigated hegemony'.

29 For a similar formulation, but without adopting the Mamdani framework, see Ahmed and El-Nagar (2003). See also Salim (2008).

30 NUP became the Democratic Unionist Party (DUP) in Dec. 1967 when NUP and PDP merged.

31 The Imam was Sayed Elhadi al-Mahdi.

32 The Chief Justice in question was Babiker Awad Allah, who was the Speaker of the first Sudanese Parliament and later the first Prime Minister under Nimeiri's May regime.

33 See also Abdel Rahim (1969); Beshir (1974).

34 The Muslim Brotherhood movement, and the Farmers Union were not part of the ANS.

35 The movement was officially dissolved in 1977 as part of the national reconciliation process by Turabi, but maintained its organization in an official manner. This gave rise to a split in the Islamic movement.

36 See e.g. Sidahmed (1997); Khalid (2003).

37 For the record it should be noted that the election results were such that three major parties emerged: UP won 100 seats; DUP 60 seats; and NIF 51 seats (of which 23 were from graduate constituencies). The NIF's strong gains were due to huge financial resources accumulated during the reconciliation process under Nimeiri's regime, highly efficient political machinery, the multiplicity of DUP candidates in geographical constituencies and a distorted electoral law for graduate constituencies.

38 In this respect it may need to be noted that the Sudan Communist Party, established in 1948, posed a serious challenge to the traditional parties in terms of its advocacy of distributive policies. The Muslim Brotherhood movement, which was to gain political ascendance in the middle of the 1970s, was also involved in political haggling through

its advocacy of the so-called Islamic constitution rather than economic or development policies.
39 For year-to-year details see Ali (2006: 30, table 10.1).
40 For the economic and development details of this plan see Mirghani (1983).
41 The estimated equation, for a world sample of 85 countries over the period 1960–1998, is: $x_{it} = \beta_1 \ln y_{it-1} + \beta_2 (\ln y_{it-1})^2 + \gamma_1 \ln N_{it-1} + \gamma_2 (\ln N_{it-1})^2 + \gamma t + \mu_i + \varepsilon_{it}$; where x is the structural transformation variable, y is real per capita GDP, and N is population.
42 Additional stylized facts include: (4) the employment share of agriculture tends to decline as the economy develops; and (5) the ratio of labour productivity in the non-agricultural sector to that of agriculture tends to increase up to a maximum as the economy develops.

References

Abdel Rahim, M. (1969) *Imperialism and Nationalism in the Sudan, 1899–1956*, London: Ithaca Press.

Abu Hassabu, A. (1985) *Factional Conflicts in the Sudanese Nationalist Movement 1918–48*, Khartoum: University of Khartoum, Graduate College Publication.

Acemoglu, D., Johnson, S. and Robinson, J. (2001) 'The Colonial Origins of Comparative Development: An Empirical Investigation', *American Economic Review* 91/5.

Ahmed, A. G. M. and El-Nagar, S. (2003) 'When Political Parties Fail: Sudan's Democratic Conundrum', in M. A. M. Salih (ed.), *African Political Parties: Evolution, Institutionalization and Governance*, London: Pluto Press.

Ali, A. A. G. (2002) 'Diversification and Structural Transformation of an Agrarian Economy: The Case of Sudan', Proceedings of the Expert Group Meeting on Economic Diversification in the Arab World, ESCWA-API, UN, New York.

—— (2006) *The Challenges of Poverty Reduction in Post-Conflict Sudan*, Kuwait: Arab Planning Institute.

Ali, A. A. G., Elbadawi, I. and El-Battahani, A. (2005) 'Sudan's Civil War: Why has it Persisted for So Long?', in P. Collier and N. Sambanis (eds), *Understanding Civil War*, vol. 1, *Africa*, Washington, DC: World Bank.

Ali, T. M. A. (1990) *The Cultivation of Hunger: State and Agriculture in Sudan*, Khartoum: Khartoum University Press.

Barro, R. (1998) *Determinants of Economic Growth: A Cross-Country Empirical Study*, London: MIT Press.

Barro, R. and Lee, J. W. (2000) *International Data on Educational Attainment: Updates and Implications*, Cambridge, MA: Department of Economics, Harvard University. Online at: www.cid.harvard.edu/ciddata

Beshir, M.O. (1974) *Revolution and Nationalism in the Sudan*, London: Rex Collings.

Brown, R. (1992) *Public Debt and Private Wealth: Debt, Capital Flight and the IMF in Sudan*, London: Macmillan.

Choucri, N. (1985) *A Study on Sudanese Nationals Working Abroad*, Khartoum: Draft Report for MFEP/UNDP/World Bank.

Deng, F. (1993) 'Hidden Agenda in the Peace Process', in M. Daly and A. A. Sikianga (eds), *The Civil War in the Sudan*, London: British Academic Press.

Diamond, L. (2007) 'Developing Democracy in Africa: African and International Imperatives'. Online at: www.democracy.stanford.edu

Elbadawi, I. and Makdisi, S. (2007) 'Explaining the Democracy Deficit in the Arab World', *Quarterly Review of Economics and Finance* 46/5 (Feb.).

Elbadawi, I., Makdisi, S. and Milante, G. (2006) 'Technical Note on Democracy and Development in the Arab World', unpublished manuscript.

Gelaleldin, M. A. (1985) *Some Aspects of Sudanese Migration to the Oil-Producing Arab Countries*, DSRC Monograph Series, 24, Khartoum: University of Khartoum.

IMF (2000) 'Sudan: Staff Report for 2000 Article IV Consultation and Fourth Review of the First Annual Program under the Medium-Term Staff-Monitored Program'. Online at: www.imf.org

—— (2007) *Sudan: Article IV Consultation and Staff Monitored Program*, Report 07/343. Online at: www.imf.org

Khalid, M. (1990) *The Government they Deserve: The Role of the Elite in Sudan's Political Evolution*, London: Kegan Paul.

—— (2003) *War and Peace in Sudan: A Tale of Two Countries*, London: Kegan Paul.

Landes, D. (1998) *The Wealth and Poverty of Nations: Why Some are So Rich and Some So Poor*, London: Abacus.

Mahmoud, F. (1986) *The Sudanese Bourgeoisie: Vanguard of Development*, Khartoum: Khartoum University Press.

Mamdani, M. (1996) *Citizen and Subject: Contemporary Africa and the Legacy of Late Colonialism*, London: James Currey.

Mekki, H. (1999) *The Islamic Movement in Sudan: 1969–1985. History and Political Discourse* (in Arabic), Khartoum: al-Dar al-Sudania for Books.

Mirghani, A.R. (1983) *Development Planning in the Sudan in the Sixties*, Graduate College Publications, monograph 2, Khartoum: University of Khartoum.

Niblock, T. (1987) *Class and Power in Sudan: The Dynamics of Sudanese Politics, 1898–1985*, Albany, NY: State University of New York Press.

North, D. (1990) *Institutions, Institutional Change, and Economic Performance*, Cambridge: Cambridge University Press.

O'Connell, S. and Ndulu, B. (2000) *Explaining African Economic Growth: Focus on Sources of Growth*, Nairobi: African Economic Research Consortium.

Rodrik, D., Subramanian, A. and Trebbi, F. (2004) 'Institutions Rule: The Primacy of Institutions over Geography and Integration in Economic Development', *Journal of Economic Growth* 9/2.

Salih, M.A.M. (2001) *African Democracies and African Politics*, London: Pluto Press.

Salim, A.S. (2008) *There is a Need to Understand the Sudanese Problematic in the First Place* (in Arabic). Online at: www.sudanile.com

Sidahmed, A.S. (1997) *Politics and Islam in Contemporary Sudan*, London: Routledge Curzon.

Taha, F. A. R. (2004) *The Sudanese Political Movement and the Anglo-Egyptian Conflict over Sudan: 1936–1953*, Omdurman, Sudan: Abdel Karim Mirghani Cultural Center.

UNDP (2006) *Human Development Report, 2006*. Online at: www.undp.org

Part III
Summing up

11 The democracy deficit in the Arab world
An interpretive synthesis

Ibrahim Elbadawi and Samir Makdisi

In this concluding chapter we present an interpretive synthesis of the factors that explain the persistence of the democracy deficit in the Arab region, and of why autocratic regimes in the Arab world have so far been able to survive in the midst of global democratic trends.

We then offer brief observations on some of the conditions that might allow the deepening of the Arab democratization process, a subject we plan to research as a sequel to the present work. While a number of studies have been carried out on the transition from autocracy to democracy in the Arab world, we believe it remains a promising area of research especially along the lines we have conducted in the present volume.

1. The persistence of the democracy deficit in the Arab region

As indicated in Chapter 2, the mutual relationship between democracy and development is a complex, multi-dimensional issue. Modernization theorem points to the positive influence of development in stimulating the democratization process. On the other hand, certain scholars also note a reverse positive influence from democracy to development. Countries that succeeded in democratizing have had higher growth rates than those that failed for most years, and have had higher growth rates than the average in those countries that did not attempt democratization. Democracies perform better than autocracies in a number of respects, for example, they produce greater stability and better handle adverse shocks that negatively affect long-term growth (see Rodrik, 1997). At the same time, other writers point out that autocracies can also promote development, and indeed for certain countries mild forms of autocracy might even be desirable for this purpose. The experiences of South Korea, Taiwan and Indonesia are given as examples of how strict central authoritarian regimes could promote domestic development and only later embrace democratic forms of government. And once they democratized, higher levels of per capita income significantly reduce the probability of their relapse into autocracy (cf. Przeworski, 2005). Whether the experiences of these countries are necessarily replicable in other developing countries is an open question.

The causal direction between democracy or autocracy on the one hand and development on the other may not be a settled issue in the literature on this subject. Nonetheless, as Sen (2000) puts it, if there is no clear direction between growth and democracy or between growth and autocracy, it still remains that since democracy and political liberty have important value in themselves the case for them is strong.

However, in the context of the Arab world, we argue that due to the social diversity in many Arab societies, including deep polarization in a few, along sectarian, religious or ethno-cultural lines, benevolent authoritarianism is not likely to lead to stable, middle-class-driven democratic transitions, akin to the experiences of Korea and other East Asian countries, as suggested by Przeworski (2005). The historic narrative of the case studies makes clear that authoritarian regimes in the Arab world have tended to be captured by subnational groups or other 'functional' special interests, which have so far been able to blunt the convergence to democracy despite an expanding middle class. Indeed, the capture of the state by such groups has often been accompanied by growing corruption and nepotism, especially manifested when conducting the process of privatizing public firms and enterprises, with all their distorting effects on governance and the national economy. Moreover, we also argue in Chapter 2 that the growth failure of the Arab countries relative to the fast-growing countries of East Asia was, in large measure, due to their inadequate capacity as autocratic states to manage exogenous shocks resulting from oil price fluctuations and the frequency of conflicts. Thus, apart from its own intrinsic values in terms of freedom and human values, democratization in the Arab countries will contribute to their long-term growth and stability. The question that the Arab world has continued to face is not whether to democratize, but how to overcome the persisting democracy deficit; hence the need to identify first the underlying causes of this deficit.

The research in this volume has identified a number of major causes of the persisting autocracy in the Arab world, albeit to varying degrees and in varying forms in different countries. While some of these causes are more or less common to the region, others are specific to individual countries. We will sum up the factors that explain the persistence of the democracy deficit in the Arab region under two broad headings: (1) oil, conflicts and external interventions; and (2) historical, political and societal issues.

1.1 Oil, conflicts and external interventions

The oil and conflict thesis brings out three important conclusions. The first two concern oil wealth and the rentier state, while the third relates to the role of regional conflicts and external interventions. To begin with, the research here makes it abundantly clear that the influence of oil wealth in permitting a trade-off between economic welfare and political freedom, important as it is, cannot be considered in isolation from the specific socio-political history of the country concerned. Rentierism should be situated in a social/political/historical context and its impact on governance and development assessed accordingly. Thus, in

Iraq the effect of oil wealth was tempered by the ability of the cross-ethnic nationalist movement to undermine the legitimacy of the monarchy, and following the overthrow of the monarchy in 1958, and especially after 1973, oil wealth alone failed to maintain a stable and institutionalized authoritarian rule of the country. In Algeria, the influence of oil wealth should be considered in the context of the political alliance of the party that took over power after independence with the military and bureaucracy. In Kuwait, the important merchant class was able to extract certain political rights before and after the oil era began. In Saudi Arabia, fundamentalist religious groups have throughout exercised great influence over the nature of the state. In the other Gulf countries, the power structure (personalized rule) inherited from colonial times has remained in place, with oil wealth simply reinforcing the hold on power of the ruling emirs. In other words, in oil-rich countries the extent of a trade-off between economic welfare and political freedom emphasized by rentier theory is significantly influenced by how they evolved historically and politically. The forces that led to the emergence of autocracies in the pre-oil era did not disappear after the discovery of oil. No doubt oil wealth has been the cornerstone of the 'authoritarian bargain' that provided the ruling families and dictators supplementary support to maintain their autocratic rule, though such a bargain has been difficult to sustain in some, as in the case of Algeria, or eventually became unstable, as in the Iraqi case. Moreover, oil has also been associated with other negative externalities for the cause of democracy, in the form of oil-related foreign interventions and influences. Nonetheless, the above overview of country-specific experiences suggests that, on its own, oil does not fully explain the persistence of the democracy deficit in the region.

Secondly, it is necessary to recognize fully the important indirect influences oil wealth has had on non-oil Arab countries in the region that tended to reinforce their autocratic regimes. In some of these countries, for instance, oil wealth has been used to support particular religious/political groups. This support, irrespective of its charitable aspects, has tended to accentuate already existing social/religious divisions and render the leaders of these groups politically beholden to their benefactors. In other countries oil wealth has been used to help autocratic regimes spend lavishly on their security/military establishment, or support them in their regional wars. Furthermore, the rapid economic development of the Gulf countries has acted as a magnet to the workforce in non-oil Arab countries. Migration to the Gulf region, especially of the educated classes, including politically sophisticated elites, has acted to depoliticize the population of the sending countries. It has provided an exit mode that has reduced domestic political pressures to democratize. Some analysts hold the view that, by working and residing in the Gulf region, migrants tend to acquire a socio-political culture not conducive to democracy; they return home with a higher level of tolerance for the autocratic practices of their own governments.[1] Also, the relatively large remittances flowing back to the non-oil countries, as well as direct Gulf investments, gives the Gulf countries additional political leverage in the Arab political arena. This is especially true in the smaller non-oil countries.

Thirdly, the role of regional conflicts in fostering autocratic regimes is clearly related to the ongoing Arab–Israeli conflict, the unresolved Palestinian question. The country research papers here have generally tended to support this finding, though to varying degrees, with the negative impact on polity of the Arab–Israeli conflict being felt more in countries nearer to the stage of the conflict, such as Jordan, Lebanon, Syria, Egypt and Iraq than, say, in Algeria or some of the Gulf States. For countries that have gone through a civil war, such as Sudan and Lebanon, the negative impact on polity has been manifested in a number of ways. For example, in the former case it encouraged military coups, while in the latter it contributed to a deepening of sectarian divisions and, in consequence, hindered a potential move to a more advanced democracy. And for the case of Egypt and Algeria, the violent contestation of power between the ruling elites in these two countries and their Islamic fundamentalists' opposition has been used by the former to prop themselves up due to the fear of an impending fundamentalist takeover. This strategy proved to be a potent instrument for shoring up external support of these regimes as well as for dividing the internal democratic opposition.

The rise of fundamentalist Islamist groups has been a cause of serious concern for a number of Arab regimes (e.g. Egypt, Syria, Jordan, Algeria and Iraq since its invasion by the USA in 2003). This concern is not necessarily related to the political ideology of these groups but rather to the rulers' fear of losing their hold on power, with all the benefits that come with it. Hence, they have not hesitated to use the potential threat posed by fundamentalist groups to the existing political order as an added justification for their authoritarian rule, with its attendant violations of political and civil rights of citizens. Also, the rise of fundamentalism has provided further ground for the Arab regimes to collude with foreign powers, in particular the USA, with the objective of securing additional political and military support in return for extending the geopolitical and economic interests of the USA in the region. A number of the chapters in this volume have demonstrated how foreign interventions and/or collusion with foreign powers have acted as obstacles to the process of democratization in the countries concerned.

Finally, international wars in the region such as the US invasion of Iraq in 2003,[2] or the earlier Iraqi occupation of Kuwait and the Iraq–Iran war have at once destabilized the region and promoted the rise of religious fundamentalism. The negative impact on polity of the various types of conflict that have ravaged the Arab region may differ from one country to another. One way or another, however, they have generally strengthened resistance to democratization, while the potential threat posed by religious fundamentalism has been used as a pretext by the ruling parties/families to justify their autocratic grip on power.[3]

Therefore, the interlocking of oil wealth, the Arab–Israeli conflict, civil wars and foreign interventions related to the geopolitical and economic interests of foreign, mainly Western, powers has generally helped render the Arab region less attuned to the democratization process despite the notable socio-economic development it has achieved in the past five decades. Even if we accept that there is no direct causality between development and democracy, the role of the above factors in retarding the democratic process remains: their absence would have created better opportunities for democracy to take hold in the Arab region regardless of the level of economic development it might have achieved. In any case we need to go beyond oil and conflicts to discern specific factors that also contributed to the stalling of the democratization process.

1.2 Historical, political and societal issues

Going beyond oil and conflicts, the case studies in this volume point out that a number of the Arab countries share other common factors that provide supplementary explanations for the persistence of their autocracy. At the same time, country-specific factors have been identified that shed further light on this matter.

Of the common factors, two stand out: historical legacies and the more recent fear of fundamentalist Islamist groups. For a number of Arab countries (e.g. Sudan, the Gulf States) historical legacies have played a role in perpetuating the autocratic nature of the state. In the case of Sudan the dominant political parties of the post-independence era have continued with the tradition of sectarian patronage and personalized politics that emerged under colonial rule. Consequently, a sustainable democratic system has so far not been established. In the Trucial States, British support of loyal rulers permitted them to establish their autocratic power base, which subsequent oil wealth tended to reinforce. In Saudi Arabia, the rise of the Al Saud to power and their hold on it is in large measure due – even in the post-oil era – to their alliance with the traditional 'Wahabi' Ulama establishment;[4] during their cold war of the 1960s with the radical regimes led by Abdel Nasser, the Saudi rulers aligned themselves with contemporary Islamist movements. The impact of historical legacies may be less important in other Arab countries, but in general the post-independence Arab states have continued to arrogate to themselves the same privileges and powers that the colonial state had enjoyed, thus alienating themselves from their societies as much as the colonial powers had done before them.

However, the story of persisting autocracy would remain unfinished without reference to country-specific factors. To illustrate, in Egypt, a process of deindustrialization since the 1970s, whereby the economy has become less capital intensive, has contributed to the retardation of the country's democratization, as has the ability of the regime to co-opt the elite business/entrepreneurial class as well as some of the country's intellectuals. In Jordan, the regime's cooption of the business and intellectual elites (the middle class), and its political exploitation of the Jordanian/Palestine divide of the population, have affected the democratic process negatively. In Syria, the regime has been able to neutralize any role the business class might have played in fostering the pace of liberalization and democratization. Instead this class (some of whose members have close family ties with the power elite) accommodated the regime and defended its stability, which it regarded as necessary for its own business interests. In Sudan, the nature of the social order, a highly polarized society based on ethno-cultural and religious lines and the association of politics with religion, have all helped to delay the process of democratization while inviting external interventions in the internal affairs of the country. In Lebanon, religious divisions, interacting with destabilizing foreign interventions including direct Israeli interventions, have led to domestic conflicts, the consequences of which have so far prevented moves towards a more advanced democracy. In Algeria, the national liberation movement that took over after independence perpetuated itself in power by cementing a triangular alliance of the military, the ruling single party and the bureaucracy. Consequently, a system of power has been created, characterized by an authoritarian bargain (among the three groups) of benefits–patronage–repression, depending on the size of the oil rents to be distributed. Considerable oil windfalls have permitted the state to trade off social welfare of the population for less freedom. At the same time, given that Algeria is a rentier state with limited resources to be distributed, the above equilibrium bargain has been inherently unstable. As for the Gulf countries, the role of their historical/social traditions in retarding the spread of democratic practices was noted above.

To conclude, while oil and conflict are two general, but pivotal, explanatory variables of the democracy deficit in the Arab region as a whole, a full understanding of the persistence of this deficit in particular Arab countries can only be explained by supplementary historical, political and societal factors. What is noteworthy is that religion as such (Islam, of course, being the major religion of the Arab world) does not appear to play a significant role, if any.[5] Rather, the survival of Arab autocracies is attributable to their success in maintaining a strong coercive apparatus which is derived from the ample resources at their disposal, and is supplemented by foreign support. They have succeeded in suppressing an independent middle class as well as civil society and have not hesitated to exploit religion for political ends.

2. Deepening the process of democratization: brief observations

Accelerating and deepening the process of democratization in the Arab region is clearly a complex process. This is both a region-wide question as well as one that concerns each Arab country individually. The conditions for the success of a substantive (as opposed to a formalistic) democratization process and its duration, if attempts at democratizing do eventually succeed, could of course differ from one country to another. The country research papers have drawn attention to specific areas where action would be needed to overcome obstacles to democratic reform. If the process of democratization does successfully take root in one Arab country, its beneficial impact is likely to be felt in other, especially neighbouring, Arab countries.

As noted above, the transition from autocracy to democracy will be the subject of a follow-up study we plan to undertake. In what follows we offer brief preliminary observations on region-wide issues of relevance to this question. Based on the research included in this volume, there are at least four interrelated issues to consider: (1) the just resolution of regional conflicts, in particular the Palestinian question; (2) the impact of adverse external interventions; (3) institutional reform that brings with it new social contracts in both oil and non-oil countries and, not least, (4) the growth and empowerment of the middle class intertwined with a more active role for independent civil society organizations and the promotion of the culture of democracy, to ensure, among other things, protection of minority rights and promotion of gender equality. We should like to emphasize that we do not have in mind an order of priorities of the importance of these issues to the question of the region's transition to democracy. Rather, they should he viewed as being mutually interacting; resolving one issue will help resolve the others.

The significance of resolving regional conflicts to the question of democracy appears to be straightforward. Conflicts, and in particular the unsettled Palestinian question, have been inimical to the development of democracy in the Arab region: this is unlike the experience of other regions where conflicts have helped pave the way for democratic reform. Conflicts in the Arab region have at once provided an incentive for the growth of fundamentalist religious movements, attracted destabilizing foreign interventions, and diverted resources away from economic and social development toward military and security apparatuses that have helped support autocratic regimes. Resolving justly the Palestinian question[6] and also other conflicts in the region may not on their own fuel the process of democratization, but would certainly create an environment that is more favourable to this cause.[7] For one thing their resolution would most likely lead to less destabilizing foreign interventions. These have been both a cause and a consequence of at least some of the major regional conflicts, including civil wars – the US invasion of Iraq in 2003, and the Israeli attacks on Lebanon in July–August 2006 and on Gaza in December 2008–January 2009 are only the most recent cases in point. Furthermore, resolving these conflicts would remove one important pretext used by rulers to maintain autocratic practices (i.e. defending national security), and this in turn would increase pressure on the Arab governments to become more open and attuned to the requirements of civil and political rights. Finally, settling regional conflicts would permit a reflow of resources to economic and social development projects. The role of independent civil society organizations that advocate and work for political and economic reform would be strengthened in the process. In this context, it should be noted that all too often the Arab regimes have either subjected civil society organizations to their control or sponsored their creation in an effort to have them serve the interests of the state. Unless civil society organizations are effectively independent, their role in furthering the public good and advocating reform will be compromised.[8]

Admittedly, resolving regional conflicts, in particular the Arab–Israeli conflict, is an international matter. Neither foreign nor regional powers can be expected to play a constructive role in this regard until they become convinced that it is in their interests to do so. Because as yet no just settlement has been reached, those countries closer to the centre of the conflict over Palestine (not to mention the Palestinian territories occupied by Israel in 1967) have had to bear heavy human, political, military, social and economic costs over the years. It may be difficult to predict how soon the Palestinian question will be resolved, but it is not difficult to conclude that its just resolution will positively and significantly influence the prospects for democratization in the region.

Domestic political and institutional reform, that is, developing more open, accountable and representative institutions, is of course an essential component of the democratic process. There is a vast literature on institution-building and its beneficial impact on development and democracy.[9] For example, adopting electoral laws that guarantee fair representation, strengthening the independence of the judicial system, protecting property rights, promoting greater gender equality, establishing needed regulatory bodies to correct market failures, creating social insurance organizations and establishing mechanisms that manage social conflicts are all aspects of building the institutional infrastructure of a genuinely democratic state. Building and sustaining democratic institutions would not only help guarantee political and civil rights (intrinsic values in themselves) but, as noted earlier, they would impart greater stability to the process of growth and, many would argue, promote a more equitable socio-economic development.

In Chapter 2 we referred briefly to the beneficial impact of democratization on growth in the context of the Arab region, and some of the case studies in this volume have pointed out potential areas of institutional reform. There is more than one route to reform, and the chosen paths could differ from one country to another. Whatever the path, institution-building in the Arab world faces a major challenge, namely how to move away from autocratic rule toward democratic institutions given the politico-cultural and religious environment in place, and in the process how to address the question of foreign support for existing autocracies.

To begin with we should like to emphasize what a number of the country chapters have alluded to, directly or indirectly, namely that institution-building is a national task and not one that can be externally imposed. In laying out the path for democratization, identifying problems and finding solutions for them are the collective responsibility of all segments of society in the country concerned. While the experience of other countries can shed light on how to proceed, the process itself cannot be imported. No country can move towards a substantive democracy in isolation of its history, tradition and social structure. Here the collective role of civil society, universities, NGOs and secular political parties is crucial in pushing for reform. Admittedly, by coercion, the autocratic Arab regimes have so far been able to thwart significant democratic development. Even in Lebanon, with its consociational democracy, politico-religious parties and groups have succeeded in delaying potential moves to a more advanced level of democracy, despite the country's traditional openness and its relatively highly educated population. Continuous pressure from various segments of society (mass mobilization) is inevitable if the cause of democracy is to be served.

This is not the place to discuss how pressure may be brought to bear on the Arab regimes to force a change; we can only note here that this could very well entail (short of an outright revolution) the forging of workable coalitions among various sectors of society that believe in reform, or among different political parties that may advocate different ideologies but are nonetheless willing to abide by the rules of the democratic game (for an extended discussion of this question see Bichara, 2007: part 1).[10]

This will no doubt be a difficult undertaking, though as we note below there are growing prospects for democratic reform in the Arab world. In a number of Arab countries the challenges posed by existing social divisions, historic legacies and/or social traditions would have to be addressed. Institutional development intended to pave the way for democratic reform cannot ignore them. In Lebanon, Iraq and Sudan, for instance, certain forms of consociational democracy based on ethno-religious lines may be deemed necessary interim moves before a full-fledged democratic system free of all discriminatory practices can be achieved.[11] In the Gulf region, new social contracts could be worked out that would open the way for greater political freedom and wider participation of women in society, while accounting for prevailing tribal or social traditions – indeed there are increasing calls from within the region for political reforms along these lines.[12] In Syria, Egypt and Jordan significant reform could begin by allowing multiple political parties to function in a freer political environment, alongside a more liberal but well regulated national economy. The common objective of these moves would be to foster a more genuine representation and participation of various segments of society in polity that, in turn, should lead to greater accountability and generally better governance.

What are the prospects for moving towards greater democratization in the region? In our view there are three main potential drivers: a growing independent middle class; an expanding role for independent pro-reform civil society organizations, including political parties (in contrast to the intended role for organizations that are created by or are dependent on the state); and, greater openness and interactions with the outside world, including the regional neighbourhood. All these potential drivers for democratic reform would become more potent were we to posit a situation in which regional conflicts, in particular the Arab–Israeli conflict, had been justly settled. Concomitantly, the negative influence of oil wealth will recede to the extent intra-Arab rivalries diminish as a consequence of such settlements.

The growth of an independent middle class is correlated not only with rising per capita income and standards of living but also with the transition from state-controlled economies to private-sector-oriented, though still regulated, economies. When the economy is basically state-controlled, the middle class often becomes beholden to the rulers who dispense favours in return for loyalty. With the reduction in the direct economic role of the state, the middle class (including intellectuals, business people and civil society organizations) becomes more assertive in their demands for greater political reform.[13] Coalitions of pro-reform advocates, as already pointed out, are emerging in the Arab world to challenge authoritarian regimes. A major concern in this context is that the economic transformation from public to private may simply lead to what has been termed the 'privatization' of the state itself, that is, the state becomes the preserve of the ruling families and their allies in the ruling 'political' parties, a phenomenon that has come to exist in a number of Arab countries. In this context, the ascendancy of an independent middle class will create a more favourable environment for a germane democracy to take hold. But while the interest of the business class in democratization is to a large extent driven by economic self-interest (hence their advocacy of a privatized national economy), the role of Arab intellectuals, universities and pro-reform organizations is crucial in fostering the ultimate objective of democratization as good governance. This is intrinsically related to their success in promoting a marriage, at the institutional level, of the universal principles of democracy (the culture of democracy) with the region's particular social conditions.[14]

This is inevitably an ongoing process. What we should like to note here is that the impact of outside influences (the external dimension) on the process of democratization in the Arab world has two opposing influences at work. The first influence is positive, and concerns the opening up of the Arab countries to an increasingly globalized world. This brings with it economic and other benefits, including greater awareness of political trends and reforms elsewhere as well a higher level of cultural interaction with the outside world. To varying degrees, Arab autocratic rulers have attempted to insulate their regimes from external influences they deem threatening to their own rule. In the end, however, the beneficial demonstration effects of democratic processes in other regions of the world will act as an additional incentive for domestic reform in the Arab countries.

The second influence is negative. It creates a real external challenge to the Arab world and derives from the adverse regional environment that regional conflicts (oil and non-oil related) have produced. If we posit that because of their geopolitical and economic interests foreign powers choose to support the autocracies in place (as has been the case), then we would have to assume that the task of democratic reform will be further burdened and the process of democratization delayed. Eventually, however, the potential drivers for democracy noted earlier are likely to prevail.

There are three likely factors behind our 'guarded' optimism regarding the future of democracy in the region. First, the authoritarian regimes' failure to establish military and strategic balance with Israel, and their subsequent failure to force a just and lasting resolution to the Palestinian question, have all but diminished their legitimacy, which has been a potent argument for authoritarianism, especially in the so-called revolutionary pan-Arab nationalist regimes. Second, the changing face of major political Islamist movements in the region, including their declared willingness to accept democratic elections and to mend fences with their counterparts in the secular democratic opposition, threatens to prevent ruling elites in key Arab countries (e.g. Algeria, Egypt, Syria) from dividing their opposition, which has been a potent strategy at the disposal of these regimes. Some observers of the Arab political scene point out that to the extent Islamist and secular movements can agree on a common political platform, including equal political and civil rights for all citizens and the acceptance of political plurality, then the push for democratic reform would become stronger, and the experience of non-Arab Muslim countries that have embraced democratic forms of governance is instructive (see e.g. Al-Ghannoushi, 2008). Admittedly it will take intensive efforts on both sides to overcome the long legacy of distrust that, by and large, has been fanned by the machinations of autocratic Arab regimes. This matter is perhaps what makes some political analysts express concern that a prior binding understanding or political pact between the Islamist and secularist groups must be reached whereby the essential features of democratic governance would be preserved, irrespective of which group or coalition comes to assume power via the electoral process (see e.g. Haseeb, 2008; Waterbury, 1994).[15] On the other hand, it could very well be, as pointed out by others (see e.g. Ottoway and Hamzawy, 2008) that under normal conditions, should the Islamist groups win in fair and free elections, then the probability of their changing the rules of the democratic game may turn out to be low, i.e. that their political participation appears to favour moderation and to strengthen the commitment to the democratic process.[16] Whatever the case, the politics of inclusion is preferable to the politics of exclusion.

Third, the long-term prospects of the 'authoritarian bargain' are likely to be less certain, in part because these regimes are not likely to achieve meaningful economic transformation to absorb an ever increasing working age population, while 'pure' oil resources are not likely to keep pace with rising population pressures, especially in the more populous countries. The implication of this factor is already manifest in terms of the difficulty in sustaining the 'authoritarian bargain' in the three relatively populous oil-rich countries of Algeria, Iraq and to a lesser extent Saudi Arabia.

3. Concluding remarks and further reflections

This research project has established that, given the level of socio-economic development in the Arab world, the region has clearly suffered from a 'democracy deficit' (as per the polity measure) or a 'freedom or political rights deficits' (as per the Freedom House measure of political rights and civil liberties).[17] Moreover, the role of conflicts and oil was found to be critical in explaining this deficit relative to other comparator groups of countries at the same level of socio-economic development. Though these two factors have been robustly associated with lower standards of democracy in the context of global cross-country econometric analysis, the insight from country studies suggests that the precise impact of oil and conflicts is path dependent: conditioned by the dynamic of country-specific idiosyncratic socio-political characteristics and their underlying political institutions. Nonetheless, the fundamental conclusion of this research is that the vast oil wealth and the proneness of the Arab region to conflicts, especially the defining Arab–Israeli conflict, have been the bedrock of the resilient 'authoritarian bargain' that has, so far, ruled the Arab world. At the same time, for individual countries, this bargain is influenced to varying degrees by supplementary historical, political and societal factors specific to each of them.

Thinking ahead, we would like to argue that this project has made a contribution to the literature, especially with regard to the long-term determinants of the persistence of the Arab democracy deficit.[18] It has not, however, directly addressed the critical question of how to affect a 'transition to democracy' in this region. This should be a natural sequel to this study. In explaining the prospects of regime survival, a recent study by Przeworski emphasizes the distinction between initial income level when an autocracy or a democracy is established and subsequent economic development. He finds that 'dictatorships that emerge at higher income levels inherent more instability, which in turn makes them less stable. But if they generate development, they are more, not less, likely to survive. In poorer dictatorships, development appears to be simply irrelevant for their stability' (Przeworski, 2004: 15)

This rather careful empirical study, we would argue, should be a good starting point for a more in-depth analysis of the factors that might lead to an accelerated 'death of autocracy' or 'transition to democracy' in the Arab world. Since actually most Arab authoritarian regimes have presided over economies that could be characterized as upper–middle income levels, there appear to be two factors that might accelerate the death of these autocracies: the frequency and extent of potential political instability and the failure of these regimes to achieve broad-based economic diversification that, among other things, would address the mounting unemployment problem, especially youth unemployment. These two factors are inextricably linked to the three that we discussed at the closing of the above section as reasons for our 'guarded' optimism regarding the prospects of future democratic transitions in the region. Investigating these transitions is a promising area for future research.

Notes

1 This view was expressed by Adnan Abu Oudeh in a workshop on 'Democracy and Development in Jordan', organized by the Institute of Financial Economics and the Center for Public Policy Research and Dialogue (Amman), at the University of Jordan, Amman, 20 March 2008.
2 It has yet to be seen whether the overthrow of the autocratic regime of Saddam in 2003 will eventually lead to a genuine Iraqi democracy or to a *de facto* fragmented country ruled by autocratic quasi-religious and/or ethnic entities.
3 We should also recall that during the Cold War era the US–USSR rivalry led them to prop up autocratic regimes aligned with them, with negative consequences on the democratic process in the region.
4 The Wahabi or *salafi* tendency is a very conservative tendency that advocates a return to traditional governance where the 'Imam' or ruler has absolute power and oversees the implementation of Islamic law assisted by the Ulama. Thus, the *salafis* reject democracy because they believe it usurps the role of the Ulama in interpreting Islamic law (El-Affendi, 2006). In reality, the Ulama establishment is an adjunct to the Saudi state and not fully independent. They have been used by the state against advocates of democracy.
5 Other researchers have reached more or less similar conclusions. Tessler (2002) concludes that Islam is not an obstacle to democratization, as some Western scholars allege it to be. Stepan and Robertson (2003) point out that Islam is not a cause of the Arab electoral deficit and that explanation for it lies elsewhere. Plateau (2008) argues that historical evidence does not sustain the thesis that politics has been the handmaiden of Islam. In fact, political rulers in Muslim countries have instrumentalized religion for political ends, especially in times of crises, though this does not necessarily imply that religion may not hinder the modernization of a country. And Noland (2008) points out that the Muslim population is not a robust explanatory factor of democratic status.
6 This is not the place to elaborate on what a just settlement implies, other than to say

that it has to be acceptable to the majority of the Palestinian people as reflected in a general plebiscite.
7 Cf. Plateau (2008), who makes the point that, had the Western powers taken an enlightened route early on in dealing with the Palestinian question, perhaps the nascent Arab secular movements in the 1950s and 1960s would have had a better opportunity to take root.
8 Al Najjar (2008: 29–31) has pointed out that the nature of civil societies in the Arab countries, especially in the Gulf region, differs from those in the Western countries. In the latter countries the emergence of civil societies was associated with the growth of an independent middle class, an autonomous legal framework, as well as private property. In the case of the Arab Gulf societies, the concept of civil society should be extended to include tribal, familial and religious traditions that influence the nature and working of non-governmental organizations.
9 See more detailed discussion in Ch. 2 and the literature cited therein.
10 To effect a democratic change, the author argues for a nationalist/democratic agenda spearheaded by organized political action and led by an elite that believes in the principles of democracy. The transition to a democratic state cannot be gradual as was historically the case, in at least some of the Western countries. Rather, existing conditions in the Arab world and more generally the developing world require that it be effected all at once in accordance with a detailed national democratic agenda. He critiques modernization theory and other current theories of the transition to democracy as providing a historical perspective on what occurred in Western countries that became democratic (useful as this may be), but does not provide a recipe for transitions to democracy in the contemporary Arab world.
11 Admittedly, the Lebanese experience does not provide an encouraging example of moving from a consociational model (with unequal political rights among citizens) to a full-fledged democracy. But the reasons for this failure are attributable in large measure to external interventions or, more specifically, to Lebanon's politico-geographic position in a region that has experienced conflicts, principally the unsettled Arab–Israeli conflict, and the influences of oil wealth.
12 In addition to numerous calls by Arab intellectuals in the form of published work or conferences (see e.g. Centre for Arab Unity Studies, 2007), a number of pro-democracy groups have been active in this regard, including: the Arab NGO Summit (the Civil Forum), which includes over 50 NGOs from various Arab countries; and the Arab Federation for Democracy and Workers Education Association.
13 Easterly (2006: 124) notes: 'that cross country studies have indeed found the incidence of democracy to be higher in more societies with a higher share of income going to the middle class – even when addressing possible reverse causality from democracy to the size of the middle class'.
14 Many scholars have analysed various dimensions of this question, and in particular the congruence between Islam and democracy (see e.g. Abdelwahab, Ch. 1 above; Sadiki, 2004; Centre for Arab Unity Studies, 1999, 2000). It is to be noted also that a number of forums have been set up to bring together Arab intellectuals and activists of different persuasions to debate and work for democratization in the Arab world. These include the Oxford-based Project for Democracy Studies in the Arab Countries (set up in 1988), the Arab-Islamic Congress (set up in Beirut in 1991) and the Network of Democrats in the Arab World (set up in Doha in 2007, but operated from Washington, DC).
15 Haseeb (2008: 55–68) makes the point that, to succeed, the forging of a common platform between Arab nationalist and Islamist groups for the purpose of addressing the major challenges facing the Arab world today, including the transition to democratic forms of government, would require that the Islamists accept democracy with its implied political plurality and also that they operate solely within an Arab context. Waterbury (1994: 41) advocates a transition to democracy with negotiated guarantees

between Muslim and secularist parties whereby all parties will accept 'the logic if not the spirit of the rules'.
16 Writing on democracy, development and Muslim women in Bangladesh, Shehabuddin (2008: ch. 1 and coda) observes that competition between secularists and Islamists to effect change in the lives of poor rural women, in line with their respective views on development, has led the Islamists to pay greater attention to issues of women's rights (admittedly within the framework of their own interpretation of Islam) in an effort to win their electoral votes, though they have not been very successful in this endeavour. The author further notes that writers who attribute undemocratic practices in Muslim counties to the situation of Muslim women in these countries overlook the actual views of women about Islam. According to field surveys which the author carried out, Muslim women, at least in Bangladesh, do not see a conflict between Islam and democracy, i.e. between observance of religious practices and democratic values including women's rights. It may be added that these positive attributes are a consequence of the ability of ideologically different political groups to compete openly.
17 In any case, the record of non-democratic governance including violations of political and civil rights is documented in the reports of various Arab and international human rights organizations.
18 The empirical cross-country analysis in this volume mainly focuses on the long-term differences in the levels (or standards) of democracy across countries, which in turn set the stage for the subsequent longer term country-specific analysis. On the other hand, democratic transitions have only been marginally addressed by the cross-country and case study analyses.

References

Al-Ghannoushi, S. R. (2008) 'Islamist and Secular Intellectuals: Possibilities for Dialogue', paper presented at the conference on 'Islamism, Democratization and Arab Intellectuals' organized by the Center for the Study of Democracy, the University of Westminster, London, 4–5 Dec.

Al Najjar, B. S. (2008) *The Contrary Democracy in the Arab Gulf* (in Arabic), Beirut: Dar al Saqi.

Bichara, A. (2007) *On the Arab Question, Introduction to an Arab Democratic Manifesto* (in Arabic), Beirut: Centre for Arab Unity Studies.

Centre for Arab Unity Studies (1999) *The Islamic Movement and Democracy* (in Arabic), Beirut: Centre for Arab Unity Studies.

—— (2000) *The Democratic Question in the Arab Homeland* (in Arabic), Beirut: Centre for Arab Unity Studies.

—— (2007) *Nationalist/Religious Dialogue: Papers Presented at a Conference Organized by the CAUS in Alexandria, December 9–11, 2007* (in Arabic), Beirut: Centre for Arab Unity Studies.

Easterly, W. (2006) *The White Man's Burden*, New York: Penguin Press.

El-Affendi, A. (2006) 'Democracy and its (Muslim) Critics: An Islamic Alternative to Democracy?', in Muqtader Khan (ed.) *Islamic Democratic Discourse*, Lanham, MD: Lexington Books.

Haseeb, K. (2008) *On Arab Issues: A Perception* (in Arabic), Beirut: Centre for Arab Unity Studies.

Noland, M. (2008) 'Explaining Middle Eastern Political Authoritarianism I: The Level of Democracy', *Review of Middle East Economics and Finance* 4/1.

Plateau, J.-P. (2008) 'Religion, Politics and Development: Lessons from the Land of Islam', *Journal of Economic Behavior* 68/2 (Nov.).

Ottoway, M. and Hamzawy, A. (2008) *Islamists in Politics: The Dynamics of Participation*, Carnegie Papers, Middle East Program, 98, Washington, DC: Carnegie Endowment for International Peace, Nov.

Przeworski. A. (2004) 'Economic Development and Transitions to Democracy', unpublished mimeo, New York University.

—— (2005) 'Self-Enforcing Democracy', in D. Wittman and B. Weingast (eds), *Oxford Handbook of Political Economy*, New York: Oxford University Press.

Rodrik, D. (1997) 'Democracy and Economic Performance', paper presented at a conference on Democratization and Economic Performance in Capetown, South Africa.

Sadiki, L. (2004) *The Search for Arab Democracy, Discoveries and Counter-Discoveries*, New York: Columbia University Press.

Sen, A. (2000) *Development as Freedom*, New Delhi: Oxford University Press.

Shehabuddin, E. (2008) *Reshaping the Holy, Democracy, Development and Muslim Women in Bangladesh*, New York: Columbia University Press.

Stepan, A. and Robertson, G. B. (2003) 'An "Arab" More than "Muslim" Electoral Gap', *Journal of Democracy* 14.

Tessler, M. (2002) 'Islam and Democracy in the Middle East; The Impact of Religious Orientations on Attitudes Toward Democracy in Four Arab Countries', *Comparative Politics* 34 (April).

Waterbury, J. (1994) 'Democracy without Democrats: The Potential for Political Liberalization in the Middle East', in Ghassan Salame (ed.), *Democracy without Democrats, The Renewal of Politics in the Muslim World*, London: I. B. Tauris.

Index

Algeria
   authoritarianism 196, 198, 200–1, 207, 209, 220–1, 315, 318
   development 197, 199, 201, 202–3, 206, 209–10, 215, 216, 219
   Islamists 26, 203, 205, 269, 316
   and the West 21, 203
Arab intellectuals *see* intellectuals
Arab nationalism 42, 55, 92, 94, 189, 190, 235, 322
Arab–Israeli conflict 29, 45, 55, 65, 77, 316, 319, 321, 323
   and Algeria 213, 221
   and Iraq 245
   and Jordan 92, 97, 98, 100, 111
   and Lebanon 30, 115, 117, 124, 135
   and Sudan 291, 307n14
   and Syria 147, 151, 156, 161
   see also The 1967 War
authoritarian bargain 196, 201, 209, 214, 221, 315, 318, 323
authoritarianism 28, 29, 55, 123, 126, 322
   in the Arab world 1, 20, 27, 47–8, 61, 314, 317
   arguments for 55
   democratic transition from 29, 271–2, 324
   and economic development 323–4
   'liberal autocracy' 15, 19
   oil wealth and 169, 214, 228, 246, 315
   and war 126
   see also Algeria; Egypt; Gulf States; Iraq; Jordan; Sudan; Syria
autocracy *see* authoritarianism

Ba'ath Party 13, 35, 152
   in Iraq 229, 235, 236, 241–2, 245–6, 247
   in Sudan 290
   in Syria 148, 149, 161
Bahrain 5, 166, 188, 189, 190, 271
   and Britain 179, 180, 181, 182, 191, 193n9

civil liberties 1, 4–5, 45, 55, 117, 198
   in Algeria 207, 220
   in Jordan 106
   in Lebanon 117, 126–7, 129, 137
   see also Freedom House Index; human rights
colonialism 30, 31, 86, 168, 317
   British 87, 91–2, 93, 166, 244, 283, 294–5
   Egyptian 283, 294–5
   French 200, 201, 202
   and polity 53–4, 60, 62, 156, 177
   in Sudan 291, 292, 293, 294–5, 298, 304, 306, 317
consociational democracy *see* Lebanon

democracy 4, 13, 14, 21, 23, 28, 31, 240, 274, 313
   in Algeria 204, 205–7, 219, 221, 318
   and economic growth 41, 42, 68–76, 78, 79n5, 166, 227–8, 229, 316–17, 314
   in Algeria 197, 212, 220, 221
   in Egypt 266, 268, 274
   in the Gulf 166, 315
   in Iraq 227–8, 229
   in Jordan 107

in Sudan 303
in Syria 144
see also Lipset hypothesis
and colonialism 168, 185, 191, 244, 291, 293, 306
and conflict 3, 191, 213, 241–2, 290, 319
  Arab–Israeli War 77, 98, 117
and culture 15, 18, 77
defining 13, 26–7, 45–50
determinants of 2, 42, 57
and development 50, 152–3, 198–201, 216, 219
in Egypt 273–4, 275–8, 317
institutions' role 158–61, 209, 266
in Iraq 240, 248
and Islam 3, 18, 23–6, 269–71, 274, 316, 318, 324n4
in Jordan 94, 95, 98, 106, 111–12, 317
in Lebanon 115, 117, 137, 317
and liberalism 15, 19, 282, 296
measuring 1, 3, 5, 6, 29, 43–4, 45–68, 80n29
neighborhood effect 129, 133, 191
and oil wealth 76, 77, 78, 166, 191, 214, 221, 228–9, 240–1, 242, 246, 314–15
and regional war 78, 123, 242, 273, 315–16
religion's role 60, 293
in Sudan 283, 306
in Syria 150, 153–4, 317
transition to 16, 78, 204, 257, 314, 318–19
and the West 22, 34, 45, 151–2, 271–2, 275
and women 3, 5–6, 77
Dubai 32, 181

economic development and democracy *see* democracy, economic growth
educated elite 97, 109, 154, 203, 295, 300, 308n23, 315; *see also* Arab intellectuals
Egypt
  autocracy 261, 267–9, 272, 317
  de-industrialization 265, 266, 273, 317
  development 261, 267, 273, 274
  Islamists 26, 269–71, 274, 316

EMM model 86, 89, 107, 155, 169, 213–14, 248
entrepreneurs, and democratization 154, 267–9, 271, 274, 317
extended modernization model *see* modernization theory

Fraser Institute Economic freedom index 155, 206
Freedom House Index 6, 27, 45–6, 47, 67, 206, 261, 276, 323

Gastil Index 198, 207, 214, 223n23
Gulf States
  autocracy 167, 169, 173, 175, 191, 192, 247, 317
  development 166, 192, 315
  and Jordan 99, 105, 111
  migration to 104, 150, 262, 315
  and oil 55, 120, 166, 186–8, 191, 315
  outside interests in 31, 55, 167, 179–82, 191
  and Syria 145, 150
Gulf War 21, 55, 65, 104, 105, 191, 229, 231, 259

Hamas 24
Hizbollah 24, 116, 269
Human Development Index 27, 28, 198, 219
human rights 21, 27, 29, 45, 158, 274
  and the West 152, 159, 271–2, 279n5, n11
  see also Humana Index
Humana Index 235–6, 238–9

ikhwan see Saudi Arabia
intellectuals 1, 20–3, 36, 79n9, 150, 160, 188, 317, 321, 322
Iran 24, 99, 123, 189, 210, 247
Iran–Iraq War 99, 100, 228, 230, 235, 237, 238, 241–2, 246, 316
Iranian revolution 23, 188, 190, 229
Iraq
  authoritarianism 35, 109, 241–2, 246, 248–9, 315
  development 228, 229–32, 244, 247, 249
  invasion of Kuwait 30, 104, 259, 316
  US invasion 30, 111

US occupation 11, 13, 31, 35, 45, 65, 248
Iraq–Iran War *see* Iran–Iraq War
Islamic fundamentalism 36, 43, 110, 189, 316, 317
  and democracy 18, 168, 111, 325n14, n15
Islamists 19, 23–6, 28, 32–3, 36, 188, 269, 272, 274, 322, 323
  in Algeria 200–1, 203–4, 205, 212, 220, 269
  in Egypt 269–71, 272
  in Sudan 299–300, 301
Israel 12, 17, 24, 29–30, 31, 33, 35, 42, 54, 97, 322
  and Jordan 94, 97, 99, 106, 110, 318
  and war on Lebanon 21, 115, 119, 120, 122, 123
  Western support for 4, 34, 45, 99, 111, 132, 271
  see also Arab–Israeli conflict

jihadism 17–18, 19, 33–4, 183, 204, 269
Jordan
  autocracy 50, 90–1, 94, 95, 98, 99, 103, 106, 111–12, 317
  development 92–3, 96–7, 100–2, 103–5
  tribal loyalties 109, 110, 112, 179
  Western involvement in 92, 93, 94–6, 99, 109

Korea *see* South Korea
Kurds 30, 148, 231, 243, 245, 248
Kuwait
  merchants 167, 179, 182, 183–5, 190, 315
  oil and rentierism 186, 187–8
  political liberalization 166, 175, 177, 186, 189, 191

Lebanon
  Arab–Israeli conflict 115, 117, 122, 123, 124, 129, 135
  Civil War 115, 117, 119, 131, 134
  consociational democracy 115, 116, 122–3, 129–34, 135, 137, 320, 325n11
  development 117, 118–22, 136
  Israeli invasion *see* Israel
  sectarianism 115, 116, 122, 123, 129, 131, 133, 137
Lipset hypothesis 42, 50–1, 76, 79n5, 112, 152–3, 167–8, 198–9, 227–8, 256, 283

migration 119, 121, 184, 231, 234, 262, 264
  to the Gulf 287–8, 315
modernity hypothesis *see* modernization theory
modernization theory 56, 57, 68, 197, 199, 234, 261, 264, 274, 275, 285
  and democracy 28–9, 42, 76, 112, 122, 166, 167, 221, 256, 273, 313
  extended modernization model 1–2, 57, 147, 154, 196, 256–7, 261–4, 273
  variables 52–3, 60, 62, 86, 99, 111, 168, 213, 229
Morocco 27, 50, 109, 271, 274
Muslim Brotherhood 148, 258, 269–71, 288, 290, 301
Muslim–Christian Polarization Index 123, 124
mutawwa see Saudi Arabia

Nasserism 190, 259
Nasserists 2, 90, 94, 188

oil
  Algeria 212, 213, 214, 219
  and authoritarianism 42, 55, 61, 62, 169, 173, 188, 190, 288, 318, 323
  and conflict 2–3, 6, 76, 78, 167, 242, 314–17, 318, 322, 323
  and democratization 60, 166, 198, 201, 212–13, 287, 323
  dependency 77, 78, 285, 306
  Egypt 260, 261
  Gulf *see* Gulf States
  foreign interest 4, 99, 144, 186, 271
  influence on Arab economies 42, 120, 262
  Iraq 240–1, 242–3, 245, 246–8
  price fluctuation 41, 75, 201, 203, 211, 214, 221, 287, 314
  rents 33, 123, 126, 127, 186–8, 210, 214, 219, 221
oil and conflict 2–3, 6, 76, 78, 167, 242, 314–17, 318, 322, 323

and autocracy 161, 196, 213
and democracy 147, 235, 248
testing the variables 64–6, 107, 154, 262
Oman 27, 166, 175, 179, 181, 187, 189, 191
orientalism 18, 20, 21

Palestinian question 1, 4, 45, 55, 124, 135, 161, 271, 316, 319
Palestinian refugees 92, 93, 115, 135
political culture 4, 15, 16, 17–19, 300, 315
Polity IV
country scores *see individual country chapters*
index 5, 6, 27, 43, 49, 86, 117, 198, 256

Qatar 27, 32, 166, 175, 188, 191
and Britain 179, 180, 181, 189
pearl industry 184, 187

regional conflict
and autocratic regimes
Algeria 197, 214, 219, 241, 242, 247, 248
Egypt 260–1, 262
Gulf States 173, 177
Iraq 241, 242, 247, 248
Jordan 108
Sudan 288–9, 306
Syria 147, 161, 147, 161, 173, 177, 197, 214, 219, 260–2, 273
role in democracy deficit 2, 54, 55, 61, 67, 72, 78, 169, 173, 229, 235, 315–16, 319
regional polity 123, 126, 127, 137
regional war *see* regional conflict
remittances 315
to Egypt 262, 273
to the Gulf 120
to Jordan 96, 97, 100, 102, 111
to Lebanon 118
to Syria 143, 150
rentier states *see* oil, rents
rentierism *see* oil, rents

Saddam Syndrome 12, 29, 34, 35
Saudi Arabia
authoritarianism 179, 187, 188, 189, 323
oil revenues 188, 191, 214
political and religious groups
fundamentalists 166, 167, 189, 191, 315
ikhwan 179, 182, 183
mutawwa 167, 179, 182–3
and the USA 31, 42, 45
Shari'a 23, 24, 25, 183, 290, 301, 302
Somalia 50, 285
South Korea 159, 266, 267, 271–2, 273, 274, 313, 314
Sudan
autocracy 30, 292, 293, 301, 317
civil society 291, 292, 294–5, 306
civil war 43, 289–90, 301, 316
development 283, 284, 288, 291, 304
Syria
autocracy 147–50, 152, 153–5, 156, 158, 161
development 142, 143–6, 150–1, 158, 317
and the West 144, 151–2, 160, 161

The 1967 War *see* Arab–Israeli conflict
tribalism 18, 20, 33, 35, 36, 112, 291, 292
in the Gulf 183, 188
in Jordan 112
in Sudan 286, 293, 297
Tunisia 26, 50, 199, 269, 274

United Arab Emirates (UAE) 32, 166, 175, 179, 180, 191
US foreign aid 66, 249, 272, 302

Van Hannen democracy index 6

women, in labor force 2, 3, 52, 57, 61, 62, 64, 77, 215
women's rights 3, 5, 6, 95, 236, 237

Yemen 35, 50

eBooks – at www.eBookstore.tandf.co.uk

A library at your fingertips!

eBooks are electronic versions of printed books. You can store them on your PC/laptop or browse them online.

They have advantages for anyone needing rapid access to a wide variety of published, copyright information.

eBooks can help your research by enabling you to bookmark chapters, annotate text and use instant searches to find specific words or phrases. Several eBook files would fit on even a small laptop or PDA.

NEW: Save money by eSubscribing: cheap, online access to any eBook for as long as you need it.

Annual subscription packages

We now offer special low-cost bulk subscriptions to packages of eBooks in certain subject areas. These are available to libraries or to individuals.

For more information please contact webmaster.ebooks@tandf.co.uk

We're continually developing the eBook concept, so keep up to date by visiting the website.

www.eBookstore.tandf.co.uk